HERBAL AND AROMATIC PLANTS
Boswellia serrata
SALAI GUM

HERBAL AND AROMATIC PLANTS
Boswellia serrata
SALAI GUM

CULTIVATION, PROCESSING
UTILIZATIONS AND APPLICATIONS

By
Dr. HIMADRI PANDA

Ph.D., F.I.C., F.I.C.S.
Industrial Consultant
Technical Consultant, Afro-Asian Countries, G.I.D.C.
Fellow of the Essential Association of India
Fellow of Indian Pulp & Paper Technical Association
Fellow of Indian National Science Congress
Fellow of Oil & Colour Chemist's Association (U.K.)
Member of Chinese Academy of Forestry
Former Chemist (R&D), I.T.R. Co. Ltd., Bareilly
Former Chief Chemist (QC & R & D), Tarpina Private Ltd.
Ramnagar, Uttarakhand

DPH

DISCOVERY PUBLISHING HOUSE PVT. LTD.
INDIA

Published by:
Namit Wasan

DISCOVERY PUBLISHING HOUSE PVT. LTD.
4383/4B, Ansari Road, Darya Ganj
New Delhi-110 002 (India)
Phone : +91-11-23279245, 43596064-65
Fax : +91-11-23253475
E-mail: discoverypublishinghouse@gmail.com
namitwasan9@gmail.com
sales@discoverypublishinggroup.com
web : www.discoverypublishinggroup.com

First Edition: **2018**

ISBN: 978-93-86841-26-1 (*Boswellia serrata*)

© **Author**

All rights reserved. No part of this publication should be reproduced, stored in a retrieval system, or transmitted in any form or by any means: electronic, mechanical, photocopying, recording or otherwise, without the prior written permission of the author and the publisher.

This book has been published in good faith that the material provided by authors/editors is original. Every effort is made to ensure accuracy of material, but the publisher and printer will not be held responsible for any inadvertent error(s). In case of any dispute, all legal matters are to be settled under Delhi jurisdiction only.

Preface

The resin of Boswellia species has been used as incense in religious and cultural ceremonies and in medicines since time immemorial. *Boswellia serrata* (Salai/Salai guggul), is a moderate to large sized branching tree of family Burseraceae (Genus Boswellia), grows in dry mountainous regions of India, Northern Africa and Middle East. Oleo gum-resin is tapped from the incision made on the trunk of the tree and is then stored in specially made bamboo basket for removal of oil content and getting the resin solidified. After processing, the gum-resin is then graded according to its flavour, colour, shape and size. In India, the States of Andhra Pradesh, Gujarat, Madhya Pradesh, Jharkhand and Chhattisgarh are the main source of *Boswellia serrata*. Regionally, it is also known by different names. The oleo gum-resins contain 30-60% resin, 5-10% essential oils, which are soluble in the organic solvents, and the rest is made up of polysaccharides.

Boswellia is a genus of trees in the order Sapindales, known for their fragrant resin which has many pharmacological uses, particularly as anti-inflammatories. The Biblical incense frankincense was an extract from the resin of the tree Boswellia sacra, and is now produced also from B. frereana

There are four main species of Boswellia which produce true frankincense. B. sacra (synonyms B. carteri and B. bhaw-dajiana), B. frereana, B. papyrifera, and B. serrata, and each type of resin is available in various grades. The grades depend on the time of harvesting, and the resin is hand sorted for quality.

Indian Olibanum is a deciduous tree endemic to India and has been recorded on dry hills and slopes, on gravelly soils between an altitude range of 275-900 m. It is a medium sized tree, 3-5 m tall, with ash coloured papery bark. Alternately arranged leaves are pinnate, crowded at the end of branches, 20-40 cm long. There are 8-15 pairs of leaflets, 3-6 cm long, with an odd one at the tip. Leaflets are ovate, with toothed margin. Flowers are tiny, creamy, about 8 mm across, borne in 10-15 cm long racemes in leaf axils. There are 10 stamens with a short style and a 3-lobed stigma. Fruits are 2 cm long, 3-cornered. Indian Olibanum tree, on injury, exudates an oleo-gum-resin known as Salai, Guggal or Indian Frankincense. Flowering: January.

Medicinal Uses: Gum-resin extracts of Boswellia serrata have been traditionally used in folk medicine for centuries to treat various chronic inflammatory diseases. The resinous part of Boswellia serrata possesses monoterpenes, diterpenes, triterpenes, tetracyclic triterpenic acids and four major pentacyclic triterpenic acids i.e. β-boswellic acid, acetyl-β-boswellic acid, 11-keto-β-boswellic acid and acetyl-11-keto-β-boswellic acid, responsible for inhibition of pro-inflammatory enzymes. Out of these four boswellic acids, acetyl-11-keto-β-boswellic acid is the most potent inhibitor of 5-lipoxygenase, an enzyme responsible for inflammation.

Recently, the boswellic acids that are a component of the resin it produces have shown some promise as a treatment for asthma and various inflammatory conditions. In West Africa, the bark of Boswellia dalzielii is used to treat fever, rheumatism and gastrointestinal problems. Boswellia incense may even relieve depression.

Extracts of Indian Olibanum have been clinically studied for osteoarthritis and joint function, particularly for osteoarthritis of the knee. A Boswellia extract marketed under the name Wokvel has undergone human efficacy, comparative, pharmacokinetic studies. Indian Olibanum is used in the manufacture of the supposed anti-wrinkle agent "Boswelox", which has been criticised as being ineffective.

We for the first time analyse the different fractions of resin and oil and exploit its commercial uses. This manuscript has been divided in to several chapters to explain its importace. All the Scientists, Students, Research Scholars will be benefited from the valuable treasure.

Author

Contents

Preface

1. Introduction 1
2. Isolation of Compounds from *Boswellia* 5
3. The Chemical History of Olibanum 18
4. Essential Oil of Olibanum 22
5. Resin Secretory Structures of *Boswellia* 38
6. Effect of oleo-gum-resin of *Boswellia serrata* (*Kundur*) on Renal Functions 48
7. Phytochemical Investigation and Biological Activity of Leaves xtract of Plant *Boswellia serrata* 52
8. Phytochemical and Pharmacological Studies of *Boswellia serrata* 88
9. Immunomodulatory Triterpenoids from the Oleogum Resin of *Boswellia carterii* 100
10. Anti-inflammatory and Analgesic Activity of Different Fractions of *Boswellia serrata* 114
11. Antimicrobial Activity of Silver Nanoparticles 120
12. Antiglycation and Antioxidant Activities and HPTLC Analysis of *Boswellia sacra* Oleogum Resin : *The Sacred Frankincense* 128
13. Formulation and Evaluation of Zidovudine Loaded Olibanum Resin Microcapsules 137
14. Toxicological Assessments of the Aqueous Extract of *Bosewellia dalzielli* 148
15. Synergistic Anti-inflammatory Compositions Comprising *Boswellia serrata* Extract 160
16. Water Soluble Bioactive Fraction Isolated from Gum Resin Exudate of *Boswellia serrata* 183
17. *Boswellia* Oil, Its Fractions and Compositions for Enhancing Brain Function 189

18. Herbal Pain Killer Compositions 235
19. Preparation for Weight Loss Management 258
20. Natural Composition for Treating Bone or Joint Inflammation 272
21. Topical Formulations for the Symptomatic Treatment of
    Musculoskeletal Disorders 284
22. Amazing Benefits of Frankincense for Skin, Hair and Health 290
    References 295
    Index 297

1 Introduction

Botanically, the frankincense tree belongs to the family of the *Burseracea*. Its genus is denoted as *Boswellia*, whereas the myrrh trees, another similar commonly known plant, also belonging to the *Burseracea* family, are denoted as Commiphora (genus). Both are historical important resin providing plants. The genus of *Boswellia* (named after Johann Boswell, who wrote a paper on ambergris in 1735) contains hitherto 25 species, whereby it is not clearly verified if some of the species are doubly counted. It is mainly distributed in the dry areas of the Horn of Africa (Somalia, Sudan, Ethiopia, and Eritrea), the Arabian Peninsula (Oman and Yemen) and in India. There are rather differing indications in literature on the specific names and spreading of the single species. A few representative species are given in Table 1.1.

Table 1.1: A Few Representative *Boswellia* Species and their Geographical Distribution. The Trees of *Boswellia carterii* Birdw. and *Boswellia sacra* Flück. Can be Regarded as the Same Species, According to the Chemotaxonomic and Biological Evaluations. They are Just Differing Because of their Geographical Origin.

Species	Geographical Distribution
Boswellia carterii Birdw.	Somalia, Nubia
Boswellia sacra Fluck.	Oman, Yemen
Boswellia frereana Birdw.	Somalia
Boswellia papyrifera Hochst	Ethiopia. Eritre, Sudan
Boswellia serrata Roxb.	India
Boswellia neglecta S. Moore	Somalia
Boswellia odorata Hutch.	Tropical Africa
Boswellia dalzielii Hutch.	Tropical Africa
Boswellia ameero Balf. Fils	Socotra
Boswellia elongata Balf. Fils.	Socotra
Boswellia socotrana Balf. Fils.	Socotra

The term *Boswellia carterii* is adopted for the Somalian tree and the term *Boswellia sacra* for the South-Arabian (Oman, Yemen) plant, although both species can be regarded as the same, at least on a chemotaxonomic and a botanical point of view. The Indian tree is called *Boswellia serrata*. The quite common species *Boswellia papyrifera* is primarily growing in Sudan, Eritrea and Ethiopia, and is often mistaken with the species *Boswellia carterii* from Somalia. Interestingly, these four species seem to be the only ones thus far which definitely have been described to contain the boswellic acids in great quantities, the class of pentacyclic triterpene acids specific for the *Boswellia* trees. The *Boswellia* plants are deciduous trees and can reach a height of up to 5 m and even more, dependent on the species and the growing area. They have bald stems and branches with a peeling bark and appear bush or tree like. The branches have compound leaves and an odd number of leaflets. They bloom in spring, mostly in April.

The term *Burseracea* means that these plants produce balms and resins in special tissue canals. A resin is generally a mixture of several organic compounds (e.g. terpenes, terpenoids and polysaccharides) which has an amorphous shape. When cold, these resins appear often as a viscous and glassy solid. When heated they start to liquefy, and when cooled again, they once more become an amorphous solid without any crystallisation. Resins are quite robust materials, staying inert towards chemical and environmental influences.

Plant resins are products of the secondary metabolism, which basically means that neither energy nor material for the growth of the plant is generated thereby. On the contrary, the primary metabolism serves for the decomposition (catabolism, delivering mostly energy) and composition (anabolism, for the functional cell construction) of biologically important molecules. The biological benefit of the secondary metabolism is not completely understood hitherto. A sensible reason may be the protection against hazardous environmental influences (e.g. against microorganisms, if the bark gets injured etc.). Furthermore, certain volatile compounds may serve for communication interactions between specific plants and insects (e.g. linalool, a monoterpene, produced by flowers often attracts moth pollinators during the night, while other plant species, not producing linalool, attract other insects like bees and butterflies during daytime.

The harvesting of the *Boswellia* resins begins in spring with start of the yearly hot period. Therefore, the stem and the thicker branches are cut with a special knife. During this process the resin containing excretion vessels in the bark are injured. The gum resin exudates can thus emerge. Due to the air exposure the viscous material solidifies to a gum resin. Gum resins are resins which contain besides ethereal essential oils and further non-polar terpenoids a greater amount of polysaccharides (ca. 25-30%). The congealed resin is then harvested during the whole summer period. The first cut and drying process delivers a resin of inferior quality. The second cut, ca. three weeks later, delivers the yellow dyed and resinous material in greater quality and quantity, forming teardrop like solids when congealed. These are finally scraped off for the first time after one or two weeks. Dependent on the age, height and condition of the tree, its exploitation is executed for three consecutive years. Afterwards, a several year taking period of rest begins. The yield of one tree is about 3 - 10 kg, depending on the health and growth of the tapped tree.

Another point to be discussed may be the sustainability of the frankincense production in the present and even its future tendencies. Many frankincense accommodating countries are considered as politically unstable states with low educational levels and a poorly economical strength (e.g. Somalia, Sudan, Eritrea and Ethiopia), not to mention randomly happening existential crisis such as starvation or violent conflicts.

The situation in India may be more promising, since most of the clinical studies have been implemented with extracts of *Boswellia serrata*, the Indian frankincense tree. Therefore, especially the Sallaki-TABLETS® (formerly known as H15 Gufic) from the GUFIC BIOSCIENCES LIMITED in Karnataka, India, have been evaluated. Hence, there may be precautions met in India to preserve this highly valuable plant.

In Oman the situation may be different, since the frankincense trade does definitely not have the same importance as it had in its early history. The reason therefore may be the modern economical development, especially the oil export, which binds most of the workforce of the country. Furthermore, the harvest of frankincense is tedious under the harsh conditions such as heat and dry climate. In addition to that, the agricultural economy will also decrease more and more in the country of Oman, if frankincense is not considered as a highly valuable resource anymore.

For the country of Yemen, which also accommodates the *Boswellia sacra* tree, the same problems as reported for the Oman may be recognisable. Furthermore, Yemen, one of the poorest Arabian countries, accommodates forces of the terror network al-Qaeda, and another problem may be the addiction of the farmers to the production of the drug kath (*Catha edulis*), which is strongly consumed among the locals. Thus, the country has definitely a lot of other worries and problems to overcome. And if the value of its indigenous Olibanum trees is understood there, is also questionable. The situation at the Horn of Africa may be even worse than for the countries mentioned above. Particularly Somalia, a country without any real government since 1991 and thus characterised as a "failed state", suffers regularly from food crises and terrorism. Well known may be the regularly reported piracy in the Gulf of Aden. How the situation is going to develop in this region can not be really predicted. Hitherto, *Somalian Olibanum* is still available on the market.

The situation in Ethiopia, Eritrea and Djibouti may be not really much better, since several border conflicts are reported (e.g. violent conflict over the border region Badme between Ethiopia and Eritrea; between 1998 and 2002, 100.000 people died in a war there). Thus, there may exist still great resentments between these two countries. Additionally, the real value of frankincense, as a possible economical resource, is probably also not realised.

In 2006, Ogbazghi *et al.* published their results of a field study on the distribution of the frankincense tree *Boswellia papyrifera* in Eritrea depending on environmental influences and land use. They concluded that the distribution of this tree has decreased during the past decades, mainly due to an increasing human population, resulting in the conversion of woodlands into agricultural fields and increasing livestock pressure hindering natural regeneration.

The temporary most reliable predictions on the future of frankincense have been made for the species *Boswellia papyrifera* in Eritrea and Ethiopia. The authors studied twelve populations of *Boswellia papyrifera* in northern Ethiopia and compared tapped (for resin harvesting used) and untapped populations in order to develop a matrix based model to predict the population dynamics. The studies took place from 2007 to 2009. Their outcomes are quite serious. It is concluded that under "business as usual" conditions (e.g. exploitation of the trees for firewood, grazing material for livestock and other environmental influences like beetle attacks etc.) 90% of both populations, tapped and untapped, are going to decline within the next 50 years. Furthermore, a 50% decline in frankincense yield within the next 15 years has been stated. Model simulations for restoration scenarios conclude that populations and frankincense production could only be sustained with intensive efforts leading to full sapling recruitment and a 50-75% reduction in adult mortality. This is hitherto the first large-scale study on population dynamics of a frankincense-producing tree. The results also suggest that a lack of regeneration and high adult mortality (6-7% per year), independent from resin tapping, is causing strong declines in the *Boswellia papyrifera* population. These findings may also be projectable to the situation in the other frankincense producing countries of Africa and Arabia (e.g. Somalia, Yemen).

2 Isolation of Compounds from *Boswellia*

In the following chapters a few specific classes of terpenic compounds found in *Boswellia* resins are presented. Principally, the most common classes are described. Thus far, merely the species *Boswellia papyrifera* (Bpap), *Boswellia serrata* (Bser), *Boswellia sacra* (Bsac), respectively, *Boswellia carterii* (Bcar) seem to definitely contain the boswellic acids in high quantities. We analytically compared the species *B. ameero*, *B. frereana*, *B. papyrifera*, *B. sacra*, *B. carterii*, *B. serrata* and *B. socotrana* and only detected for the species Bpap, Bser, Bsac/Bcar the specific boswellic acids. *B. frereana* for example consisted mainly of neutral compounds, revealing almost no quantity of acids.. Consequently, the species Bpap, Bser and Bsac/Bcar may be the most important classes of *Boswellia* species, if the pharmacological activity, based on triterpenic acids, is regarded.

Boswellic Acids

The first comprehensive and reliable investigations on resins of frankincense were realised by Alexander Tschirch and Oscar Halbey during the years from 1892 to 1899. Their results are published in several writings and publications. Basically, they separated the alcoholic extract into its neutral and acidic fraction by solvent extraction with diethyl ether (Et$_2$O) and an alkaline soda solution, a method still used today. After several reprecipitation steps they isolated a mono-basic raw product, which they denominated as "Boswellin$S\delta ure$".

(Note: The expression *Sδure* means acid in German). For this raw product they suggested the chemical formula $C_{32}H_{52}O_4$. About the chemical structure was nothing exactly known then (Note: The compound most probably had been a mixture of 3-O-acetyl-β-boswellic acid and its α-isomer; compounds 2 and 4 in Figure 2.1.

During the research of Halbey and Tschirch, the terpene chemistry had become increasingly important by development of the so called *isoprene rule*. This rule was proposed by Otto Wallach who wrote more than 100 papers on the chemistry of terpenes, and who finally obtained the Chemistry Nobel Prize in 1910 therefore. His findings on terpenes and especially the *isoprene rule* led to a rise of the natural product and terpenoid chemistry.

In 1932 two other researchers on *Boswellia* resins, Winterstein and Stein, revealed that the raw product isolated by Tschirch and Halbey is a mixture of four specific boswellic acids, namely the α-and β-boswellic acids (compound

1 and 3) and their acetylated derivatives (compound 2 and 4) as shown in Figure 2.8. They achieved to isolate the four compounds as pure substances and finally suggested the correct chemical formula $C_{32}H_{50}O_4$. Though, they did not have any clue about the correct chemical structures.

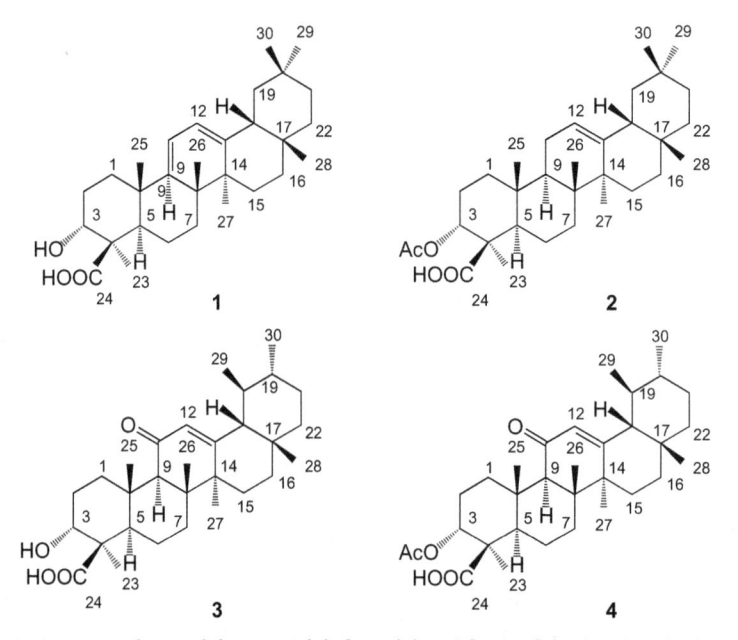

Fig. 1.1: The structures of α-BA (1), α-ABA (2), β-BA (3) and β-ABA (4). Thus far, the boswellic acid compounds are highly specific biomarkers for the species from *Boswellia*.

Simpson, in 1937, published his experiments about β-boswellic acid (3) and classified it as β-hydroxy-acid (Note that in this case only the position of the hydroxyl group at C-3, neighbouring to the carboxyl group, is meant, not the configuration; compare also with Figure 1.10 later in the text). He deduced this fact from reactions of chrom(VI)oxid (CrO_3) with the free acid giving a monoketone by decarboxylation, and with the methyl ester which instead delivered the stable keto-ester.

Ruzicka and Wirz published in 1939 and 1949 their own experiments, where they finally correlated a relationship between the boswellic acids and the triterpenes α- and β-amyrine. This was achieved by transformation of the α- and β-boswellic acids into their corresponding amyrines (see also Figure 2.2). By this relationship many attributes of the amyrine-derivates could be conveniently transferred to the boswellic acids. Ruzicka has been also the chemist who thoroughly developed the *isoprene rule* from 1921-1953, based on the proposal by Wallach. Furthermore, for his merits on the chemistry of terpenes he obtained together with Butenandt the Chemistry Nobel Prize in 1939. Thus, he had also a major impact on the structural elucidation of the boswellic acids found in incense resins.

In the 1950s of the last century Beton *et al.* elucidated finally the configuration of the OH– and COOH-group in β-boswellic acid. Their results were published in 1956, and as it is depicted in Figure 2.3 the configuration of the OH-group is α (meaning under the ring) and the configuration of the COOH-group is β (meaning above the ring).

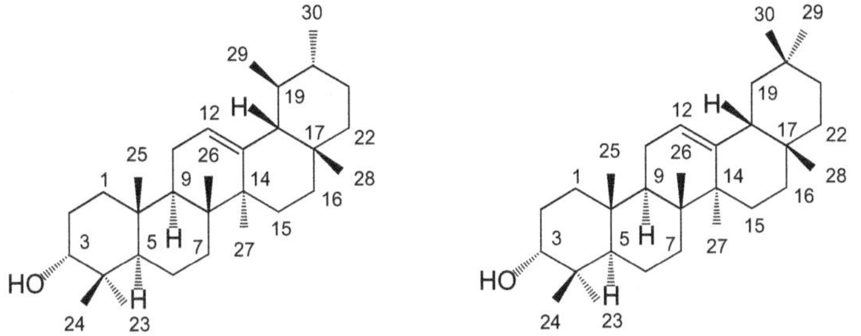

Fig. 2.2: The structures of α-amyrine (left, ursane-type skeleton) and β-amyrine (right, oleanane-type skeleton). Confusingly, the structures of β-BA (3) and β-ABA (4) refer to the α-amyrine, vice versa, for α-BA (1) and α-ABA (3), which refer to β-amyrine. This has unfortunately historical reasons.

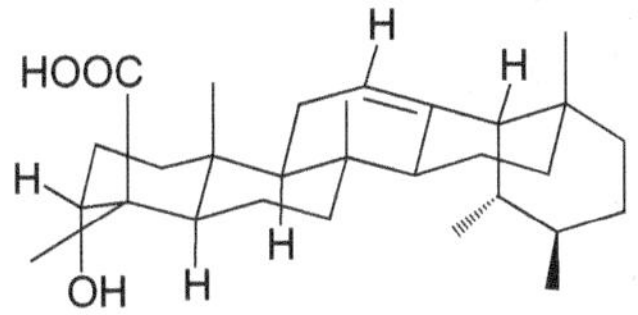

Fig. 2.3: The configuration of the OH- and COOH-function in β-BA. The OH-group is α-configured (under the plain) and the COOH-group is β-configured (above the plain).

The elucidation of organic molecules in the following two decades became increasingly easier. The reason therefore was the development and establishment of more precise techniques such as mass spectrometry (MS) and nuclear magnetic resonance spectroscopy (NMR). Both are instrumental measurement tools which made the work of organic chemists tremendously more convenient, especially concerning questions on unknown chemical structures.

Hence, in the year 1963 Budzikiewicz *et al.* published the first mass spectrometric data base on amyrine derivates. These data is even nowadays used for the characterisation of the molecular framework of unknown triterpenes. In 1978, Pardhy and Bhattacharyya, delivered first mass spectrometric and ^{1}H-NMR data for the β-boswellic acids (compound 3 and 4). Furthermore, they presented spectroscopic data for two other very specific incense resin compounds, 11-keto-β-boswellic acid (5, β-KBA) and 3-O-acetyl-11-keto-β-boswellic acid (6, β-AKBA) shown in Figure 2.4. The structure of compound 5 was firstly described by Snatzke and Vertesy in 1966. In the year 2000 the working group of Ammon published the crystal structure of β-AKBA (6), and in 2001 Gupta *et al.* published the crystal structure of β-ABA (4). However, it took over 20 years until Culioli *et al.* and Belsner *et al.* published in 2003 the first complete NMR data sets (^{1}H and ^{13}C) for α/β-BA (1 and 3), α/β-ABA (2 and 4), the β-BA-9,11-dehydro derivatives (9 and 10) and β-AKBA (6). Before, merely the chemical shifts of H-3 and H-12 were certainly assigned.

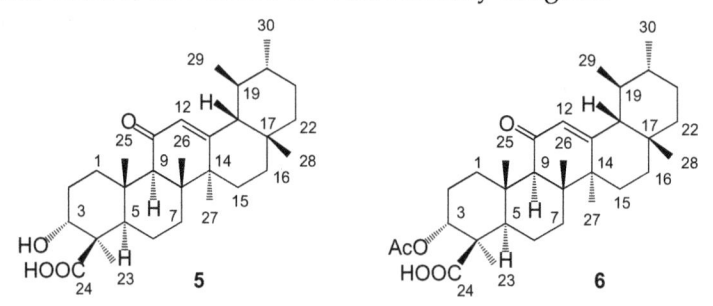

Fig. 2.4: The structures of β-KBA (5) and β-AKBA (6).

In 1964, Corsano and Iavarone isolated from the acid fraction of Olibanum the methyl ester of 3-O-acetyl-11-OH-β-boswellic acid (7, 11-OH-β-ABA). The compound, shown in Figure 2.5, is known to be rather unstable. The working group of Ammon was able to figure out in the 1990s the reaction pathway of compound 7, leading to 3-O-acetyl-9,11-dehydro-β-boswellic acid (10; 9,11-dehydro-β-ABA) via its methoxy derivate, 3-O-acetyl-11-OMe-β-boswellic acid (8; 11-OMe-β-ABA). The structures are altogether presented in Figure 2.5. Seitz firstly isolated compound 7 purely without any decomposition and defined the position of the 11-OH-group as α-configured. Furthermore, 3-OH-9,11-dehydro-β-boswellic acid (9; 9,11-dehydro-β-BA) was additionally described by Büchele *et al.* and quantified in the resin matrix by a RP-DAD-HPLC method (see also Figure 2.5).

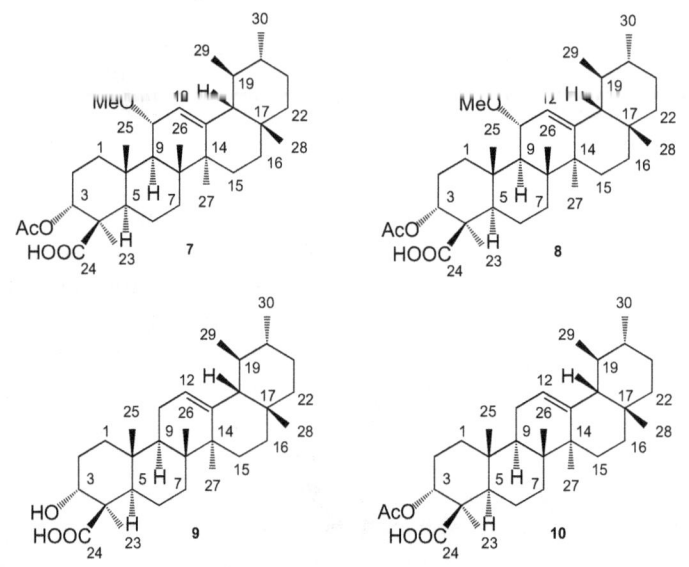

Fig. 2.5: The structures of 11-OH-β-ABA (7); 11-OMe-β-ABA (8); 9,11-dehydro-β-BA (9) and 9,11-dehydro-β-ABA (10).

Isolation of Compounds from Boswellia 9

Büchele *et al.* also isolated the corresponding 9,11-dehydro derivates of the α-boswellic acids (1 and 3) and quantified them by the HPLC method mentioned before. Their structures are shown in Figure 2.6.

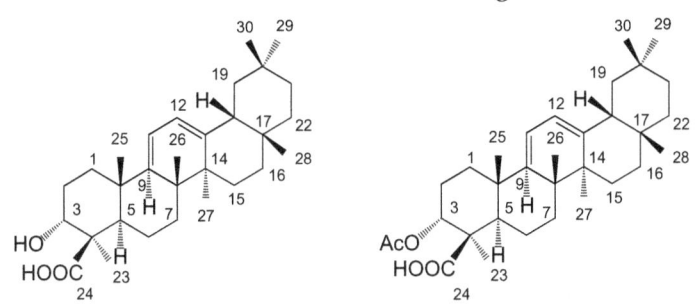

Fig. 2.6: The structures of 9,11-dehydro-α-BA (left) and 9,11-dehydro-α-ABA (right).

In accordance, Büchele *et al.* synthesised the 11-keto-derivative from α-ABA (3), α-AKBA (see Figure 2.7), and separated it from β-AKBA (6) by application of a fluorinated HPLC stationary phase. Thus, revealing also the difficulty of separating α-AKBA from β-AKBA (6) by application of conventional reversed phase stationary phases, normally, the separation system of choice for HPLC separations of boswellic acids. Additionally, α-KBA (see also Figure 2.7) and α-AKBA may occur naturally in minor amounts, but are just not easily resolvable. The hypothesis may be correct as shown in the HPLC publication of Paul *et al.* There, for each peak signal (β-KBA, 5, and β-AKBA, 6) at 250 nm detection wavelength, a minor fronting inhomogeneity is visible, which might refer to α-KBA and α-AKBA, respectively.

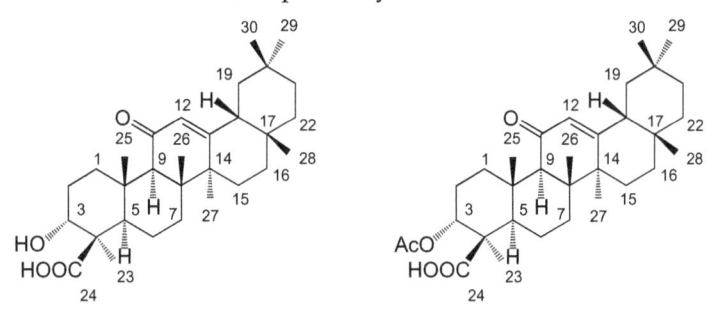

Fig. 2.7: The structures of 11-keto-α-BA (syn. α-KBA, left) and 11-keto-α-ABA (syn. α-AKBA, right). Both structures have yet not been isolated from a naturally source.

Moreover, the existence of several oleanane-type boswellic acids (e.g. α-BA/α-ABA), similar to already known ursane-type boswellic acids (e.g. β-BA/β-ABA), has been postulated by the working group of Simmet in Ulm, Germany. Their structures are shown in Figure 2.8. The molecules depicted there (11-OH-α-BA and 11-OH-α-ABA) seem to be the predecessors of 9,11-dehydro-α-BA and 9,11-dehydro-α-ABA shown in Figure 2.7, following basically the identical discussion about reaction pathways already given for Figure 2.6.

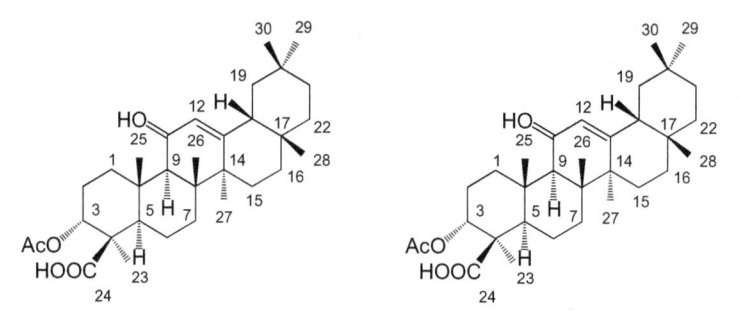

Fig. 2.8: The structures of 11-OH-α-BA (left) and 11-OH-α-ABA (right). Both structures have yet not been isolated from a naturally source. For further details see text.

Furthermore, Seitz firstly isolated another β-boswellic acid where the OH-function at position 3 is β-configured, namely 3-β-OH-β-boswellic acid. The structure, which was found in the species *Boswellia carterii*, is depicted in Figure 2.9.

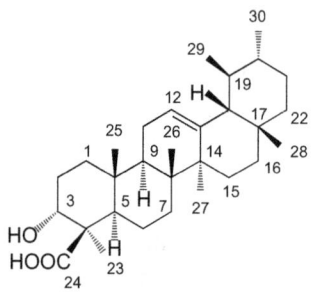

Fig. 2.9: The structure of 3-β-OH-β-boswellic acid.

Chemically, the boswellic acids refer to the class of pentacyclic triterpenic acids. There can be a vast amount of naturally occurring triterpenic acids found in several different plant species, with only a few single functional differences in their molecular framework. Hitherto, the boswellic acids have been merely isolated from resins of the genus *Boswellia*. Therefore, they can be regarded as genus specific thus far.

Lupeolic Acids

Another class of pentacyclic triterpenic acids found in the resins of *Boswellia* species are the lupeolic acids. These triterpenic acids are not specific for the genus of *Boswellia* and as well have been isolated from other plant material sources. Culioli *et al.* isolated in 2003 the lupeolic acid (11, LA) from an methanolic extract of a gum resin called "Erytrean-type". Shortly thereafter in 2003, the working group of Simmet published the isolation and structural elucidation of 3-α-O-acetyl-lupeolic acid (12, Ac-LA) from *Boswellia serrata*. The group of Choudray reported in 2005 on another lupeolic acid type derivative from the bark of *Boswellia papyrifera*. It revealed instead of a methyl group at C-27 a primary alcohol function and was denoted as 3-α-O-acetyl-27-

OH-lupeolic acid (12a). Furthermore, Seitz reported on the isolation of 3-α-O-acetyl-28β-OH-lupeolic acid (12b) from *Boswellia carterii*. The structures of all here discussed lupeolic acids are depicted in Figure 2.10.

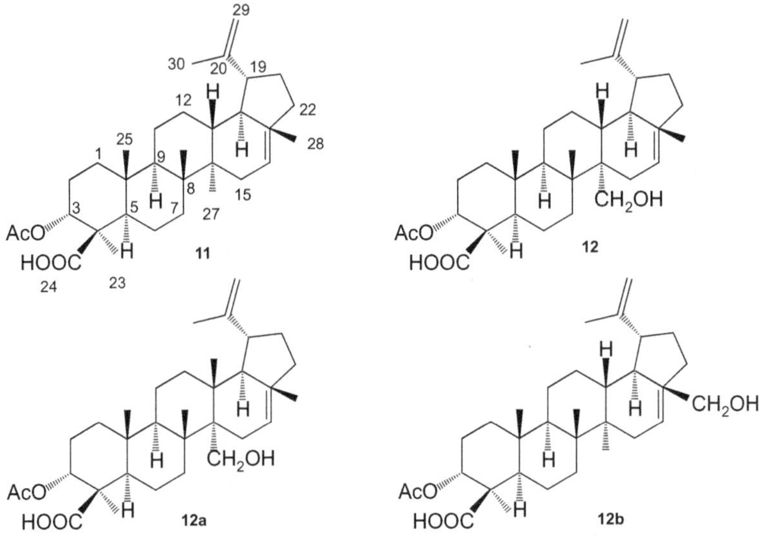

Fig. 2.10: The structures of compound 11 (LA), 12 (Ac-LA), 12a and 12b..

Tirucallic Acids

The tirucallic acids represent another class of tetracyclic triterpenic acids that have been isolated from *Boswellia* resins. They are not genus specific for the *Boswellia* species, since they were additionally found in other plants. In 1962, Corsano and Picconi isolated 3-Oxo-elema-8,24-dien-21-oic-acid from an incense extract. A synonym for this compound is also 3-oxo-8,24-dien-tirucallic-acid (13, 3-Oxo-TA), as the COOH-function can be normally always found at position C-21 for the class of tirucallic acids (see also Figure 11).

Similar compounds have been isolated from the resin of *Boswellia serrata* by Pardhy and Bhattacharyya in 1978. Beside the isolation of compound 13, they also reported on the isolation of 3-α-OH-8,24-dien-tirucallic acid (14, α-TA), 3-β-OH-8,24-dien-tirucallic acid (15, β-TA) and 3-α-O-acetyl-8,24-dien-tirucallic acid (16, α-Ac-TA). Additionally, Akihisa and Banno et al. reported on the isolation of 3-α-OH-7,24-dien-tirucallic acid (17, α-7,24-dien-TA) from *Boswellia carterii* in 2006, though the resin identity in their work had probably not been definitely verified. The crystal structure of compound 17 was published by Mora et al. in 2001. All tirucallic acids discussed hitherto (13-17) had been also isolated by Seitz from the resin of *Boswellia papyrifera*.

Two further tirucallic acid structures were reported by Estrada et al. in 2010, namely 3-α-O-acetyl-7,24-dien-tirucallic acid (18, α-Ac-7,24-dien-TA) and 3-β-O-acetyl-8,24-dien-tirucallic acid (19, β-Ac-8,24-dien-TA). Their chemical

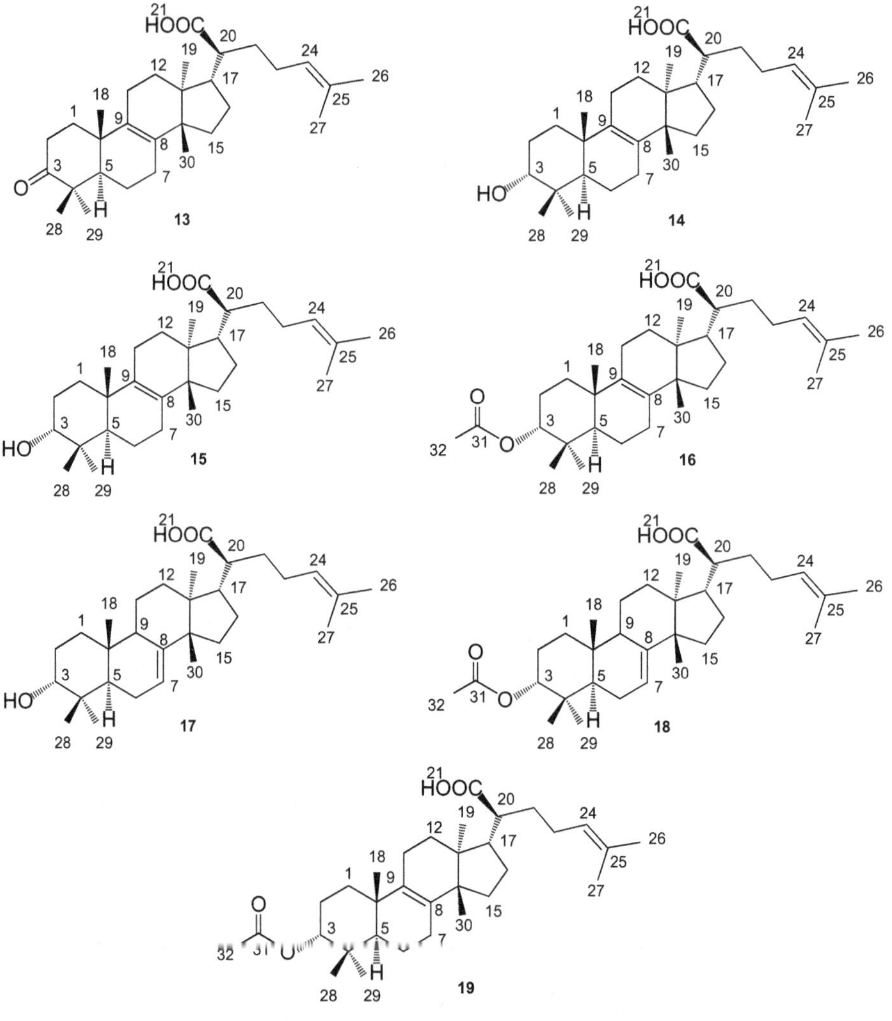

Fig. 2.11: The structures of the tirucallic acids (13-19). For further details see text.

structures are also presented in Figure 2.11. The authors claim that they isolated 18 and 19 from *Boswellia carterii*. However, about the isolation is nothing specific mentioned in their publication. Further on, the quoted reference, which should report on the isolation of 18 and 19, does not reveal anything about these two tirucallic acids in detail. As it will be later on concluded in this work, it was more likely the species *Boswellia papyrifera* instead, where these compounds (18 and 19) naturally originate from.

Roburic Acids

The roburic acids represent a class of tetracyclic triterpenic acids rarely found in natural sources. They are not considered to be specific for *Boswellia* resins, as they were also isolated from other plant sources (e.g. roburic acid from

Gentiana macrophylla by Jong et al. in 1994. Fattorusso et al., in 1983, have been the first research group who found a representative molecule of this class in the acid fraction of *Boswellia carterii*. The isolated compound was 4(23)-dihydro-roburic acid and was regarded by them as a probable degradation product, caused by geochemical processes. Seitz had also isolated the 4(23)-dihydro-roburic acid and additionally three more roburic acids from the acid fraction of the resin *Boswellia socotrana* (Note: Since this species did not reveal any boswellic acids, expectably typical for them, it may be doubtful if it really is a *Boswellia* resin, according to the comments given in the dissertation by Seitz). Thus, she elucidated the structures of roburic acid, 11-keto-roburic acid and 4(23)-dihydro-11-keto-roburic acid. The latter two keto-roburic acids have been firstly described by her. The structures are shown in Figure 2.12.

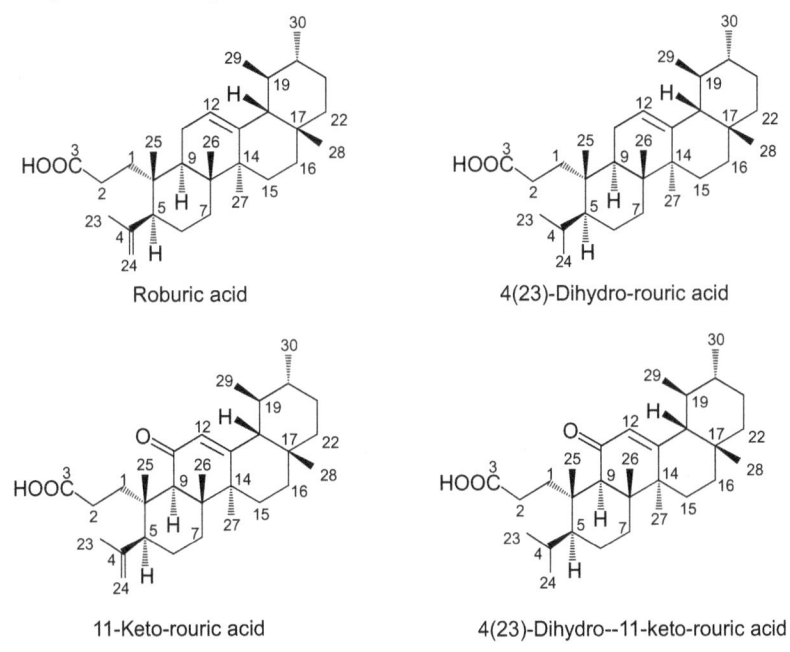

Fig. 2.12: The structures of the different roburic acids. For further details see text.

Neutral Terpenic Compounds

The neutral compounds from resins of frankincense have been evaluated thoroughly because of their significant odour intensities. Generally, these resins contain an innumerable amount of monoterpenes, sesquiterpenes, diterpenes and triterpenes. Many of them are ubiquitously occurring in nature. They can not be regarded as specific biomarkers for a certain species in general. However, in combination with other compounds they may be helpful for classification in some cases.

A good overview on the great volatile amounts of mono-, sesqui- and diterpenes, occurring in these resins, is given by Hamm et al., who published

14 *Salai Gum*

their results (GC-MS) in 2005. In the author's opinion, this paper can be regarded as highly important and reliable, since they used voucher specimens of these resins in order to evaluate the specific biomarker differences. Another paper by Mathe et al., published in 2004, gives a good overview on typical neutral triterpenic compounds, mainly amyrine and lupeol derivatives, occurring in these resins. Some exemplary terpenic compounds are shown in Figure 2.13.

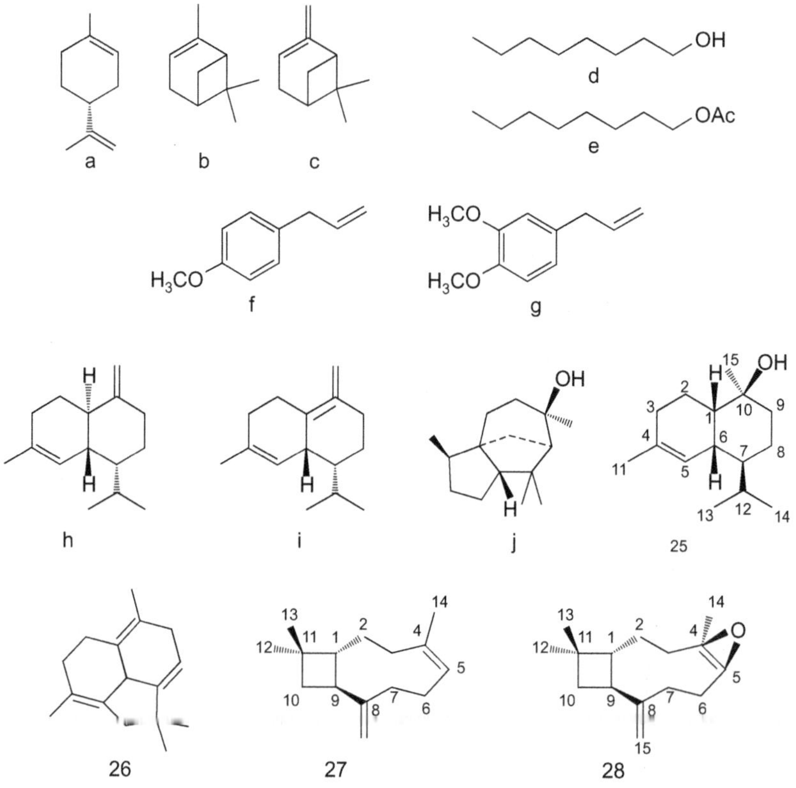

Fig. 2.13: A few examples of terpenes found in the essential oils of Olibanum resins. Monoterpenes: limonene (a), α-pinene (b), β-pinene (c). Sesquiterpenes: γ-cadinene (h), δ-cadinene (i), cedrol (j), τ-cadinol (25, τ-Cad-OH), α-humulene (26, α-Hum), β-caryophyllene (27, β-Car), β-caryophyllene-oxide (28, β-Car-Ox). Additionally, quite specific for some species are the following molecules (no real classical terpenic compounds): n-octanol (d) and n-octyl-acetate (e), which both are detectable in huge quantities in the species *Boswellia papyrifera*; and methyl chavicol (f) and methyl eugenol (g), which both seem to be specific for the species *Boswellia serrata*. See also the publications of Hamm et al. and Camarda et al..

A few specific neutral terpenes isolated from Olibanum are discussed here. In 1967 Corsano and Nicoletti described the structure of a new diterpene alcohol, isolated from frankincense, and denoted it as incensole (22, Inc). Furthermore, they described two different incensole derivatives, incensole-oxide (22a) and iso-incensole-oxide (22b), in the shortly following years. In Figure 2.14 their structures are depicted. The authors claimed that these molecules were isolated from the species *Boswellia carterii*.

22 **22** **22**

22 **23a**

R = H; Iso-incesole (23a), respectively, –oxide (22b)
R = Ac; Iso-Incensole-acetate(23a), repsectively, –oxide (22b)

3,7,11,13-cembratetraene (cembrene C)   3,7,11,15-cembratetraene (cembrene A)

Fig. 2.14: The structures of specific diterpenes found in incense: Incensole (22), incensole-oxide (22a), iso-incensole-oxide (22b, R = H) and its acetate (22b, R = Ac), incensole acetate (23) and iso-incensole (23a, R = H) and its acetate (23a, R = Ac). Iso-incensole and its acetate seem to be specific biomarkers for *Boswellia carterii*.

However, the research, concerning the oils from Olibanum, by Obermann and his co-workers at the DRAGOCO Company, Holzminden, Germany in the end of the 1970s gave differing results compared with the ones of Nicoletti and his team. Oberman analysed two different Olibanum oils, one was denoted as *"Aden"* and the other as *"Eritrea"*, by TLC and GC-MS and published his results in 1977. His final statement had been that the sort *"Aden"* mainly contains neutral triterpenes as it was already described by Snatzke and Vertesy in 1966. Incensole (22), the compound described by Corsano and Nicoletti in 1967 for *Boswellia carterii*, was merely found in traces by GC-MS in the *"Aden"*-type. On the contrary, for the sort *"Eritrea"* he could detect incensole (22) and additionally its acetate (23, Inc-Ac) in great quantities, comparable with the quantities given by Corsano and Nicoletti. Furthermore, Obermann realised that the commercial grades Somalia and Indian Frankincense were olfactorily similar to the commercial grade "Aden", whereas "Eritrea" had a significantly different odour. The same conclusions have been made by the author of this dissertation and are proved chemotaxonomically based on voucher specimens and reliable literature results. Thus, the sample "Aden" refers to the species *Boswellia carterii*, respectively, *Boswellia sacra*, since both species are chemotaxonomically identical. Moreover, the commercial brand "Aden" usually refers to the *Somalian Olibanum*, most likely to be *Boswellia carterii*, as it is transported from Somalia to the port of Aden, Yemen, and then internationally traded as "Aden"-type. The sort "Eritrea" had been the species *Boswellia papyrifera*, since the specific biomarkers were found for it. Therefore, the publications of Obermann, Hamm et al. and Camarda et al. may be comparably consulted for clarification. Additionally, Gacs-Baitz et al. published the first complete ^{13}C-NMR datasets on the fourteen-membered macrocyclic diterpene class of the incensole family. The chemical structures of all molecules discussed up to here are depicted in Figure 2.15. In the same year, 1978, Klein and Obermann in Germany, and, Pardhy and Bhattacharyya in India, reported on another new type of diterpenic alcohol of the cembrane type. Pardhy and Bhattacharyya, who isolated the compound from *Boswellia serrata*, denominated it as serratol (21, Ser-OH). Klein and Obermann isolated the compound from the species *Boswellia carterii* ("Aden") together with incensole (22). They also deduced already that serratol (21) is most probably the predecessor molecule of incensole. The structure is presented in Figure 2.15. In addition, Seitz isolated serratol (21) from the resin of *Boswellia carterii*,

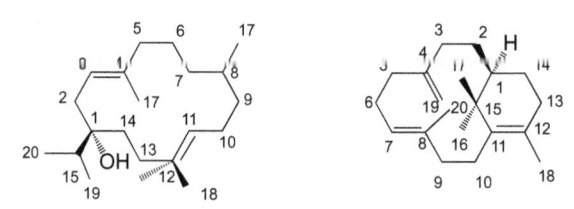

Fig. 2.15: The structure

and in 2001, Basar et al. reported on a new verticillane diterpene from the essential oil of *Boswellia carterii* (see also Figure 2.15). The compound was termed as verticilla-4(20),7,11-triene (24, Vert-4(20),7,11-triene). Interestingly, this compound has been merely found in the essential oils from *Boswellia papyrifera* by the groups of Hamm and Camarda. Thus, the sample of Basar was quite probably unfortunately mistaken as *Boswellia carterii*, while it had been indeed the species *Boswellia papyrifera* instead.

Three recent papers from Japan report on several new minorly occurring compounds, so called "Olibanumols", from the species *Boswellia carterii*. All these compounds are different terpenic alcohols (e.g. monoterpenes, tetra- and pentacyclic triterpenes with OH-functions at different positions). Additionally, the newly isolated compounds are only in quite minimal amounts present (e.g Olibanumol A = 0.037% to Olibanumol I = 0.00074% from) and though they show in some cases pharmacological activity, the concentrations are far too low to play a significant role for the major actions of anti-inflammatory Olibanum extract medications. However, particularly with regard to the finding of new bio-active compounds the research is definitely not unnecessary.

3 The Chemical History of Olibanum

Although the oil of olibanum had occupied the shelves of the 16th century pharmacies as "oleum thuris", the first investigation on its chemical composition was performed in 1788 by Johann Ernst Baer at the University of Erlangen. Following his work, the first elementary analysis was carried out by F.W. *Johnston* in 1839. The constituents of the essential oil were first investigated by J. Stenhouse in 1840, and he identified depending on the origin of the resin fourteen monoterpenoic constituents including pinene, dipentene, phellandrene and cadinene. In 1898, A. Tschirch and O. Halbey published for the first time that olibanum had acidic constituent, boswellic acid, with a molecular formula of $C_{32}H_{52}O_4$ but they could not suggest a structure at that time.

At the beginning of the 1930's, the olibanum resin was investigated in more detail. The study of A. Winterstein and G. Stein in 1932 drew the attention to the resin acids, the pentacyclic triterpenoic α- and β-amyrin like skeletons with different functional groups, which were attempted to be isolated and identified with the analytical methods possible for that time. Nevertheless, by the 1960's several of these acids such as α- and β-boswellic acids, 11α- hydroxy-β-boswellic acid and 3-O-acetyl-11-hydroxy-β-boswellic acid were identified by various derivatisation methods (Figure 3.1).

α-Boswellic acid

R_1 = OH, R_2, R_3 = H
R_1 = OH, R_2 = OH, R_3 = H
R_1 = Ac, R_2 = OH, R_3 = H
R_1 = Ac, R_2, R_3 = H
R_1 = OH, R_2, R_3 = O
R_1 = Ac, R_2, R_3 = O

β-Boswellic acid
11-Hydroxy-β-boswellic acid
3-O-Acetyl-11-hydroxy-β-boswellic acid
3-3-O-Acetyl-β-boswellic acid
11-Keto-β-boswellic acid
3-O-Acetyl-11-keto-β-boswellic acid

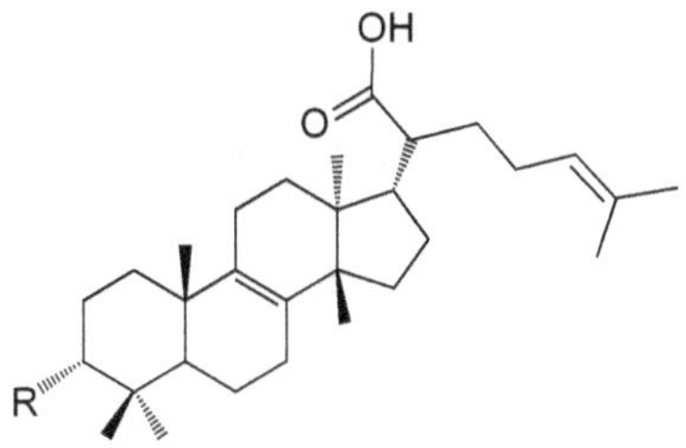

R = OH, 3-Hydroxy-8,9,24,25,-tetradehydrotirucallic Acid
R = Ac, 3-O-Acetyl-8,9,24,25,-tetradehydrotirucallic Acid
R = O, 3-Oxo-8,9,24,25-tetradehydrotirucallic acid

Fig. 3.1: Some of the triterpenoic acids that were identified from olibanum.

In 1967, G. Snatzke and L. Vértesy published the structures of acetyl-11-keto-β-boswellic acid as well as epi-α- and epi-β-amyrin and their acetates, α- and β-amyrenone and viridiflorol from the neutral fraction of olibanum, adding that it is composed of 5-9% essential oil, 15-16% resin acids, 25-30% of material insoluble in ether containing the polysaccharides and 45-55% ether soluble compounds.

In 1978 R.S. Pardhy and S.C. Bhattacharya identified tirucallic acids as well as β-boswellic acid, acetyl-β-boswellic acid, 11-keto-β-boswellic acid, acetyl-11-keto-β-boswellic acid from *B. serrata* Roxb. (Figure 3.1) and a diterpenoic cembrene derived alcohol, "serratol". Studies on the isolation and identification of the boswellic acids with modern analytical techniques and on their pharmacological effects are still going on. Therefore these topics will be further discussed in the following parts of this work.

The first important and comparative study on the essential oil of olibanum of different origins was performed by H. Obermann from Dragoco (Holzminden, Germany) in 1977. He investigated two different commercial brands of olibanum, *"Eritrea"* and *"Aden"* by GC-MS, which corresponded to *B. carterii* and *B. serrata* resins, respectively. As a result of this investigation it was reported that not only the fragrance of these two qualities but also the composition of the constituents in the oils were different.

The *"Eritrea"* oil was reported to have octylacetate as the major constituent (52%) as well as α-pinene, camphene, p-methoxytoluol, hexyl acetate, limonene, 1,8-cineole, octanol, linalool, bornyl acetate, cembrene A, incensole, incensyl acetate and an unknown diterpenoic constituent. In contrast, *"Aden"* oil was found to contain α-pinene as the major constituent (43%), camphene, β-pinene, sabinene, o-cymol, limonene, 1,8-cineole, p-cymol, campholenaldehyde, verbenone, octyl acetate and cembrenol, a diterpene alcohol with cembrene skeleton which was identified later by the same group, which was expected not be different than "serratol" described before (Figure 3.2, Figure 3.3 & 3.4).

20 *Salai Gum*

In 1985 a detailed review was published by P. Maupetit on the *"Aden"* brand of olibanum. He reported 47 new constituents identified in the resinoid and in the oil of olibanum in addition to 169 formerly identified substances including the pyrolysis products. Recent studies by Verghese on *B. serrata* oil and by A.M. Humprey *et al.* comparing *B. carterii* oil with cumin, ginger, rosemary oil, were reinvestigations of known facts. These studies pointed to the difficulties in the identification of the origin of olibanum resin as well as in the determination of standard olibanum oil. A complete list of major constituents of olibanum resin hitherto described are given in Figure 3.2, 3.3 and 3.4.

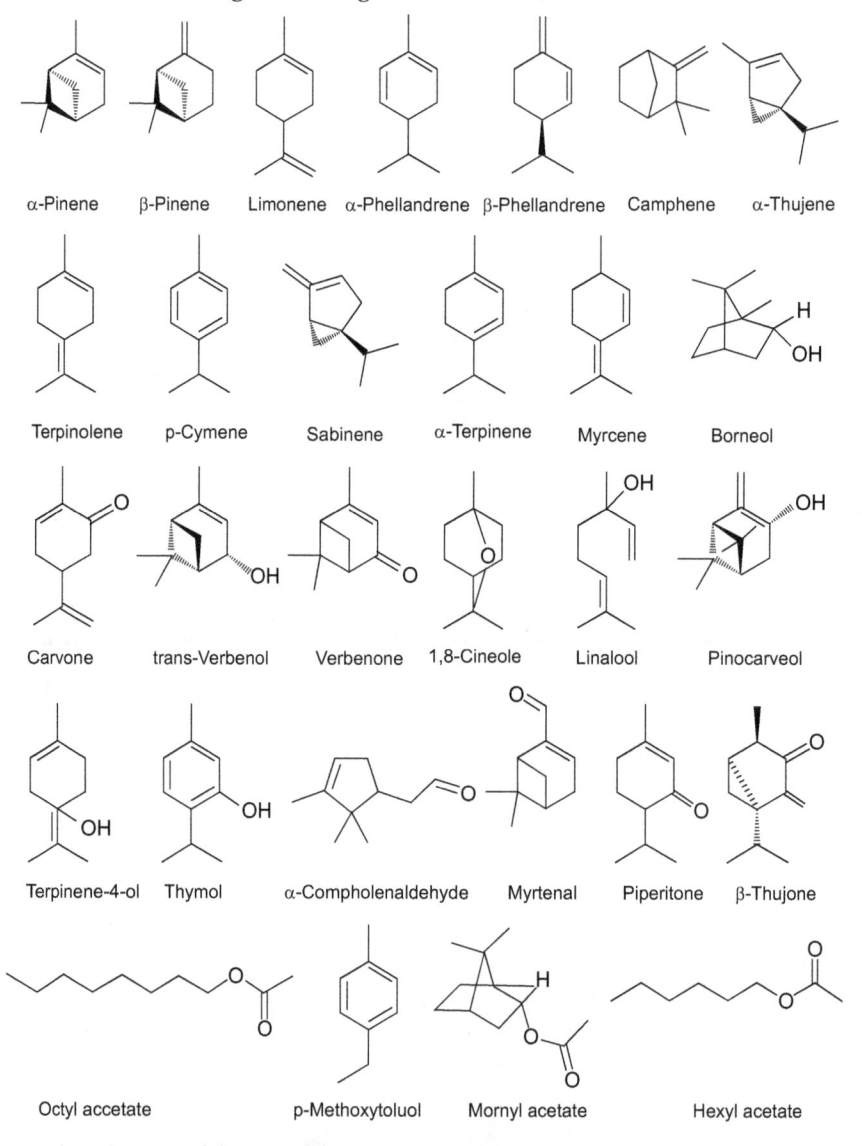

Fig. 3.2: Some of the monoterpenoic constituents identified in olibanum resin.

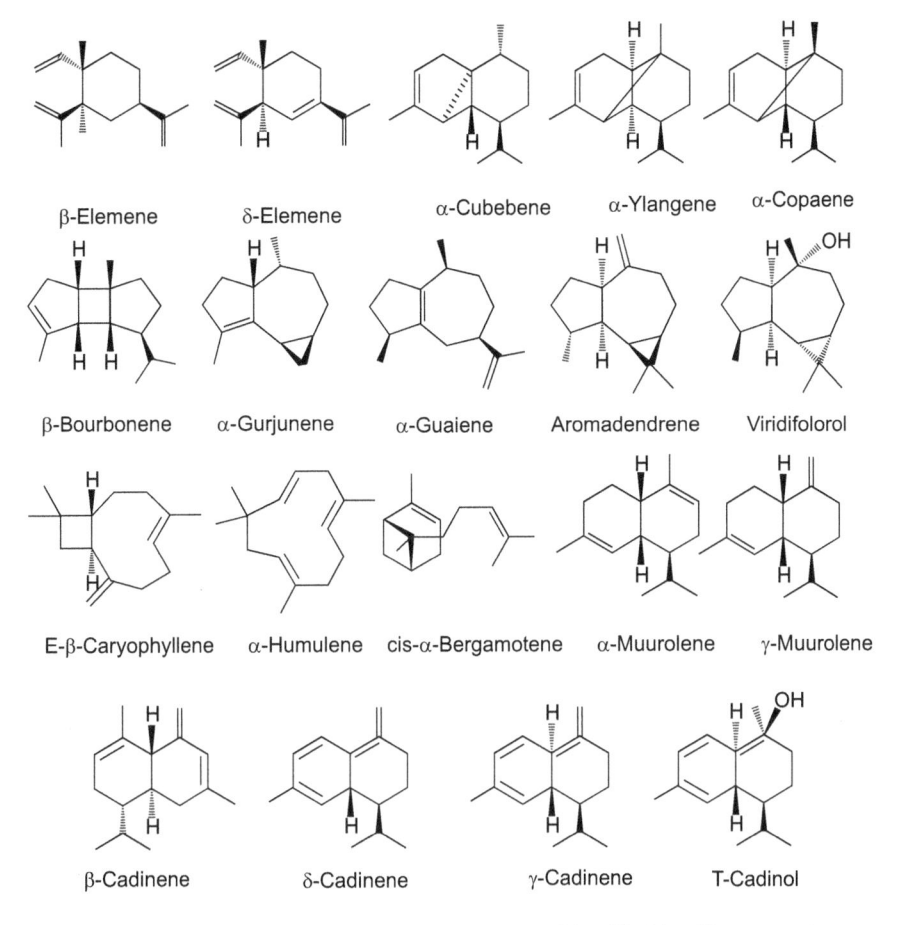

Fig. 3.3: Some of the sesquiterpenoic constituents identified in olibanum resin.

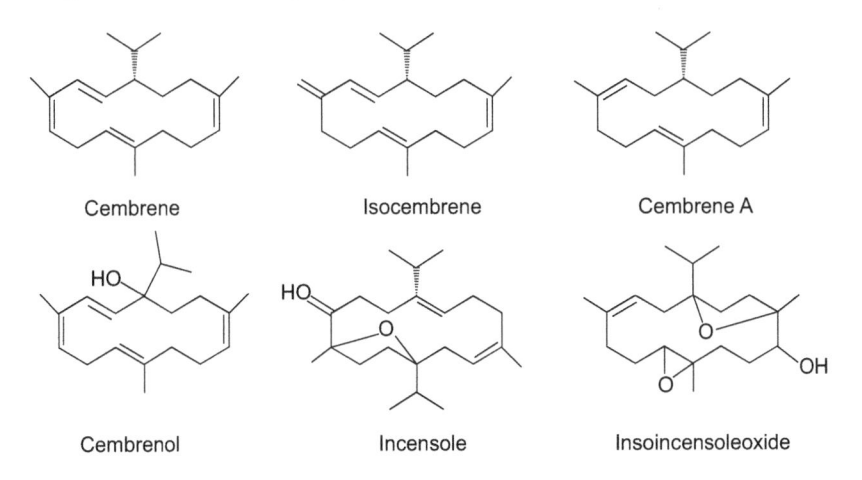

Fig. 3.4: Some diterpenoic constituents identified in olibanum resin.

4 Essential Oil of Olibanum

Essential Oil of *Boswellia serrata* Roxb

The essential oil of *Boswellia serrata* has also been well studied. It has been known as "*Indian olibanum*" or "*Aden*" type. The major component of the oil was reported to be α-pinene, representing approximately 45% of the oil.

The hydrodistillate of *B. serrata* is a colorless oil. The GC and GC-MS investigations indicated that the oil consists of α-thujene (12%), α-pinene (8%), sabinene (2.2%), β-pinene (0.7%), myrcene (38%), α-phellandrene (1%), p-cymene (1%), limonene (1.9%), linalool (0.9%), perillene (0.5%), methylchavicol (11.6%), methyleugenol (2.1%), germacrene D (2.0%), kessane (0.9%), cembrene A (0.5%) and cembrenol (6) (1.9%) as the major constituents. In addition to these, a monoterpene 5,5-dimethyl-1-vinylbicyclo-[2.1.1] hexane (3) (2%) and two diterpenoic components, m-camphorene (4) (0.7%) and p-camphorene (5) (0.3%) were isolated and identified from the essential oil of *B. serrata* for the first time (Figure 4.1, Figure 4.2).

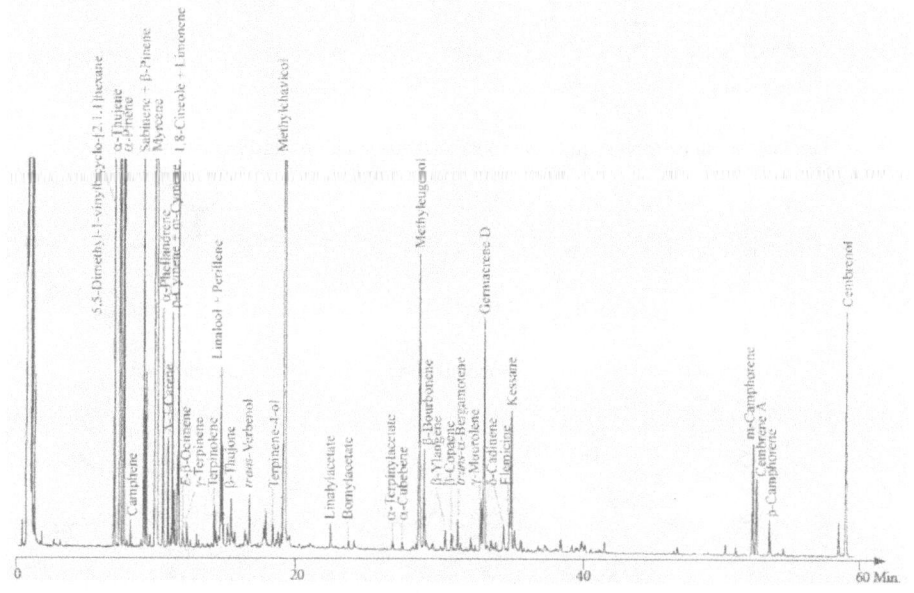

Fig. 4.1: Gas chromatogram of the essential oil of *Boswellia serrata* (25 m fused silica capillary column with CPSil 5CB, 50°C, 3 °C/min up to 230 °C, injector at 200 °C, detector at 250 °C, carrier gas 0.5 bars H$_2$).

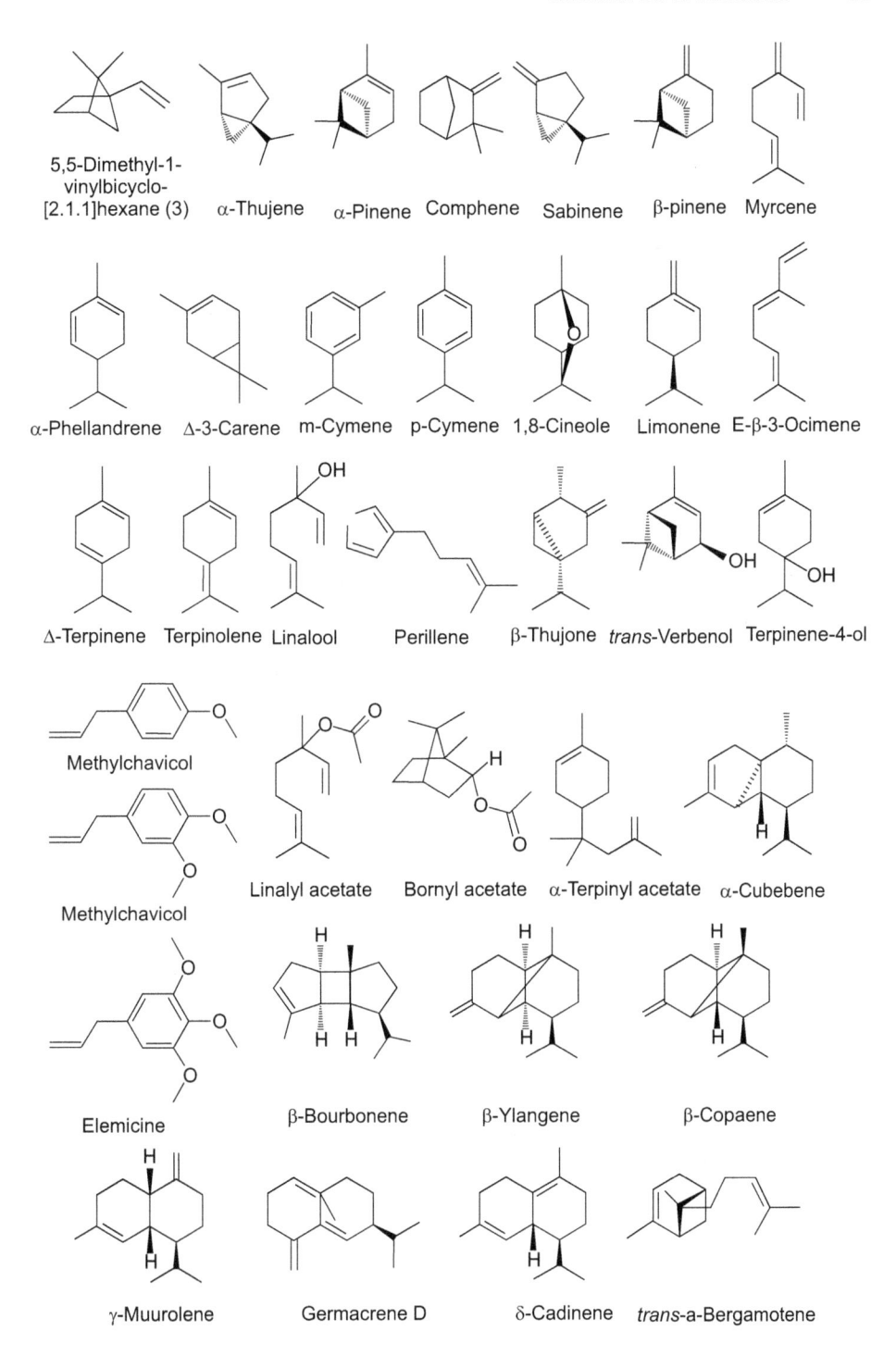

Essential Oil of Olibanum 23

5,5-Dimethyl-1-vinylbicyclo-[2.1.1]hexane (3)   α-Thujene   α-Pinene   Comphene   Sabinene   β-pinene   Myrcene

α-Phellandrene   Δ-3-Carene   m-Cymene   p-Cymene   1,8-Cineole   Limonene   E-β-3-Ocimene

Δ-Terpinene   Terpinolene   Linalool   Perillene   β-Thujone   trans-Verbenol   Terpinene-4-ol

Methylchavicol

Methylchavicol   Linalyl acetate   Bornyl acetate   α-Terpinyl acetate   α-Cubebene

Elemicine   β-Bourbonene   β-Ylangene   β-Copaene

γ-Muurolene   Germacrene D   δ-Cadinene   trans-a-Bergamotene

Kessane   **m-Camphorene (4)**   **p-Camphorene (5)**

Cembrene A   **Cembrenol (6)**

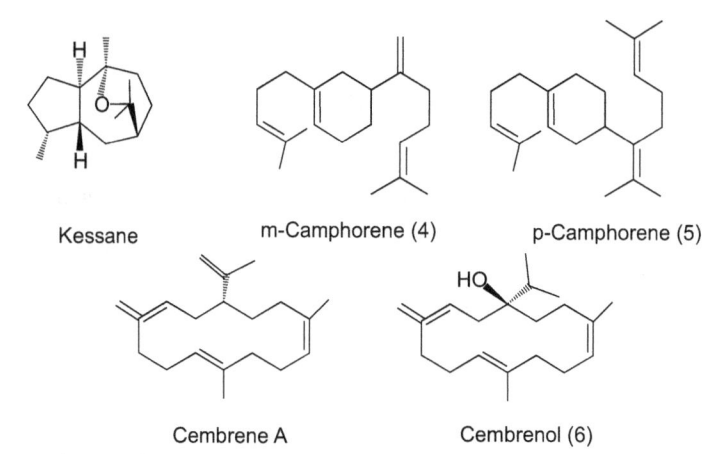

Fig. 4.2: The constituents of the essential oil of *Boswellia serrata*.

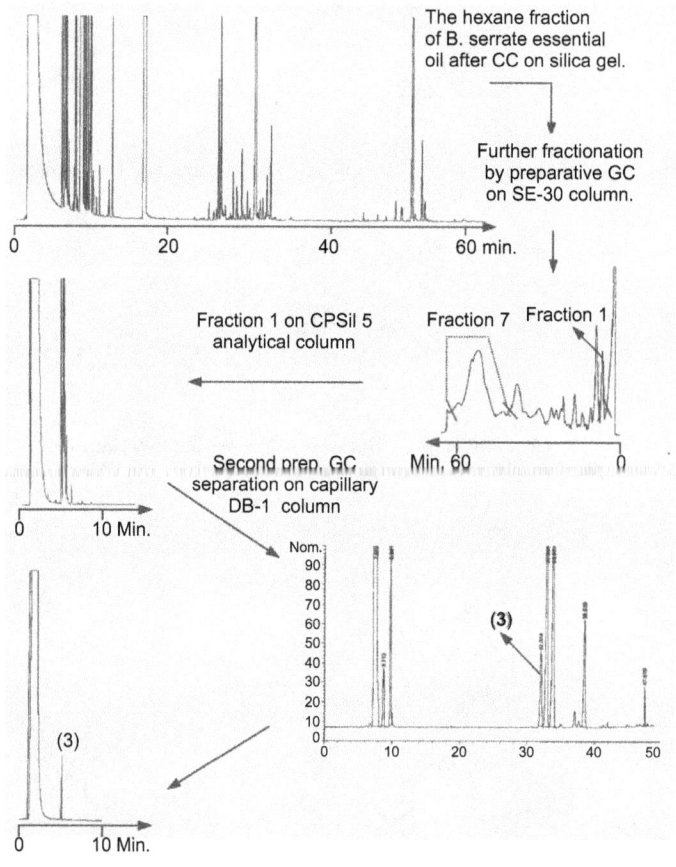

Fig. 4.3: Schematic expression of the isolation steps of compound 3. Left side: 25 m fused silica capillary column with CPSil 5CB, 50 °C, 3 °C/min up to 230 °C. Right side, above: 2 m packed SE-30 column, 75 °C, 2 °C/min up to 200 °C, below: 30 m capillary DB-1 column, 50 °C, 1.5°C/min up to 110 °C, 10 °C/min up to 200°C.

Isolation and Identification of 5,5-Dimethyl-1-vinylbicyclo-[2.1.1]hexane (3)

The hydrodistillate of *Boswellia serrata* was separated into its nonpolar and polar fractions by CC on silica gel with n-pentane and ethylacetate, respectively. The nonpolar part of the oil was further fractioned by preparative GC on SE-30 column. A further separation by preparative GC on a thick film capillary DB-1(Hewlett Packard) column was performed to obtain 3 as pure substance (Figure 4.3). The structure of the compound was elucidated by the interpretation of its mass-, 1- and 2-D NMR spectra.

The pure compound produced a molecular ion signal at m/z = 136 in its mass spectrum that corresponded to an elemental composition of $C_{10}H_{16}$ (Figure 4.4).

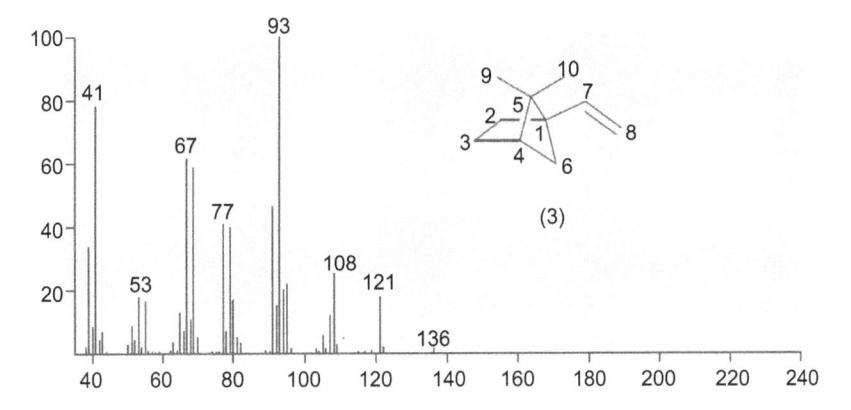

Fig. 4.4: Mass spectrum of 5,5-dimethyl-1-vinylbicyclo-[2.1.1]hexane (3).

Fig. 4.5: Possible fragmentation pattern of 3.

The 1H-NMR spectrum showed two singlets at δ 0.69 and 1.08 for two geminal methyl groups, a doublet at δ 0.89 (d, J = 7.25 Hz) for a single aliphatic proton and three olefinic protons at δ 5.02 (dd, Jtrans = 15.7, Jgem = 2.2 Hz), 5.08 (dd, J cis= 11.3, Jgem = 2.2) and 5.88 (dd, Jtrans = 17, Jcis = 10.7 Hz) (Figure 4.6).

26   *Salai Gum*

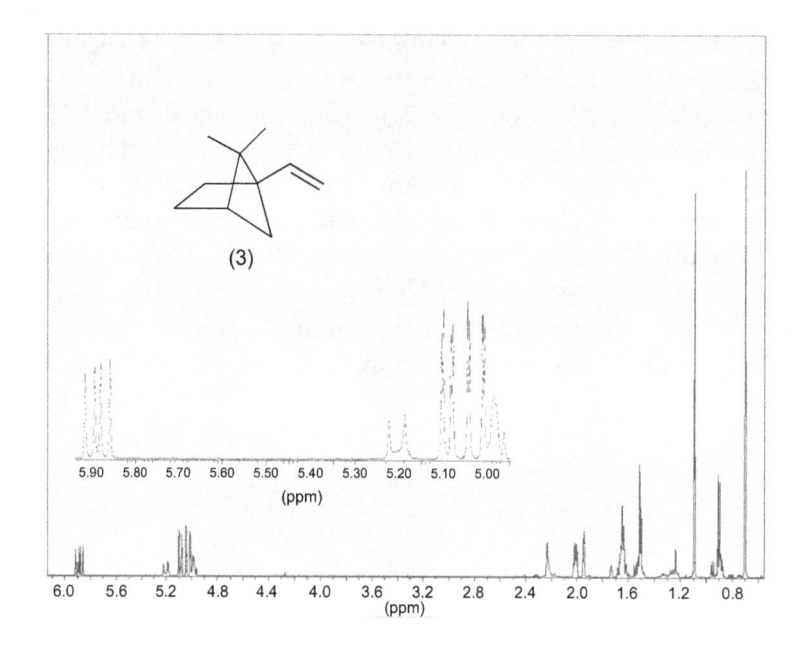

Fig. 4.6: 1H-NMR spectrum of 3.

The 13C-NMR and PENDANT spectra indicated eight carbon signals, two primary carbons at δ 19.83, 19.39, four secondary carbons at δ 26.55, 30.43, 39.12, 115.15, two tertiary carbons at δ 44.44 and 137.91. Two more quaternary carbons were identified from the HMBC spectrum at δ 56.2 and 47.0 (Figure 4.7). The carbon signals shifted to the low field at δ 115.15 and 137.91 indicated a double bond in the molecule.

The interpretation of the HMQC spectrum showed that C-8 (δ 115.15) correlated to the protons at δ 5.02 and 5.08 and C-7 was coupled with the third olefinic proton at δ 5.8. The broad singlet at δ 1.94 was found to correlate to the tertiary carbon C-4 (δ 44.44). The methyl groups were derived as CH3-9 (δ 19.83, 1.08) and CH3-10 (δ 19.39, 0.69).

The connectivity of the fragments was determined mainly from the HMBC spectrum. A double bond system was the first fragment formed from C-7 (δ 137.91) and C-8 (δ 115.15). The second fragment was established by the couplings of two geminal methyl groups to two quaternary C-1 (δ 56.2), C-5 (δ 47.0) and one tertiary carbon C-4 (δ 44.44). The coupling of olefinic protons, H-8 to C-1 confirmed the connection of these two fragments to each other. The positioning of the three secondary carbons, C-2 (δ 26.55), C-3 (δ 30.43) and C-6 (δ39.12) were deduced from the correlations observed in the 1H-1H COSY spectrum (Table 4.1, Figure 4.8).

This compound had already been isolated from Mentha cardiaca as a natural product 118 but it was identified for the first time in *Boswellia* species.

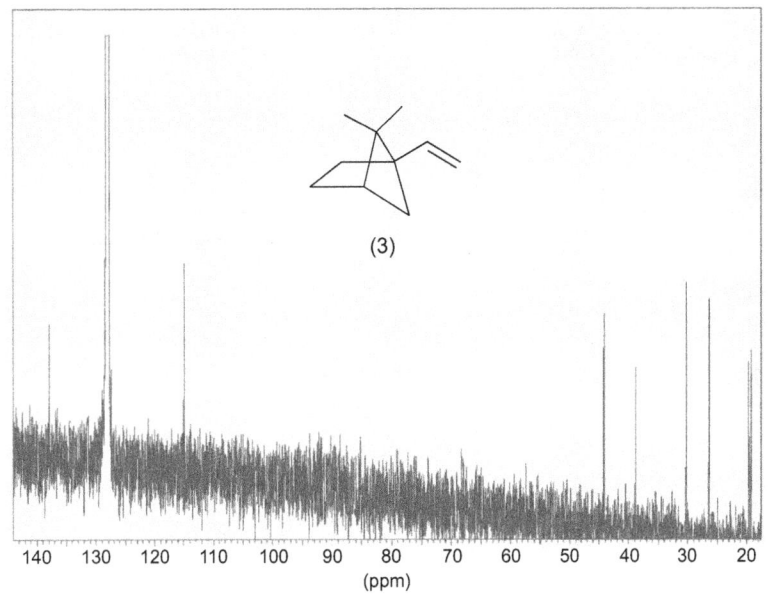

Fig. 4.7: 13C-NMR spectrum of 3.

Fig. 4.8: Numbered structure of 3.

No.	13 C (ppm)	1H (ppm)	No.	13 C(ppm)	1H (ppm)
1	56.20		6	39.12	0.89, 2.0
2	26.55	(1.49-1.54), (1.61-1.68)	7	137.91	5.88
3	30.43	(1.49-1.54), (1.61-1.68)	8	115.15	5.08, 5.02
4	44.44	1.94	9	19.30	0.69
5	47.00		10	19.80	1.08

Isolation of m-Camphorene (4) and p-Camphorene (5)

The non-polar part of the essential oil of B. serrata was fractionated by preparative GC on SE-30 column (Figure 4.3). Fraction 7 was found to contain the two diterpenoic compounds and cembrene A (Figure 4.9). The separation of these compounds was optimised on a modified cyclodextrin stationary phase (6T-2,3-methyl-β-CD) with a different order of elution. Pure compounds of m-camphorene (4) and p-camphorene (5) were obtained by performing the same separation on preparative scale.

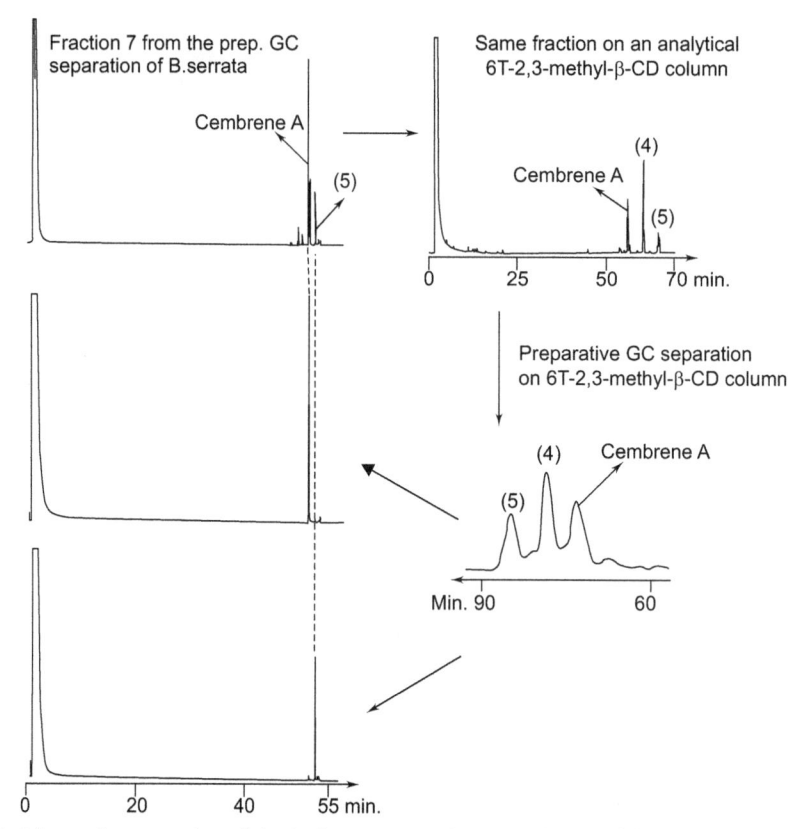

Fig. 4.9: Schematic expression of the isolation steps of m-camphorene (4) and p-camphorene (5). Left side: 25 m fused silica capillary column with CPSil 5CB, 50 °C, 3 °C/min up to 230 °C. Right side, above: 25 m capillary column with 6T-2,3-methyl-β-CD, 130 °C for 20 min, 1 °C/min up to 180 °C, below: 2 m packed column with 6T-2,3-methyl-β-CD, 130 °C for 20 min, 1 °C/min up to 150 °C, 0.5 °C/min up to 170 °C.

Identification of m-Camphorene (4)

The pure compound produced a molecular ion signal at m/z = 272 in its mass spectrum that corresponded to an elemental composition of $C_{20}H_{32}$ (Figure 4.10).

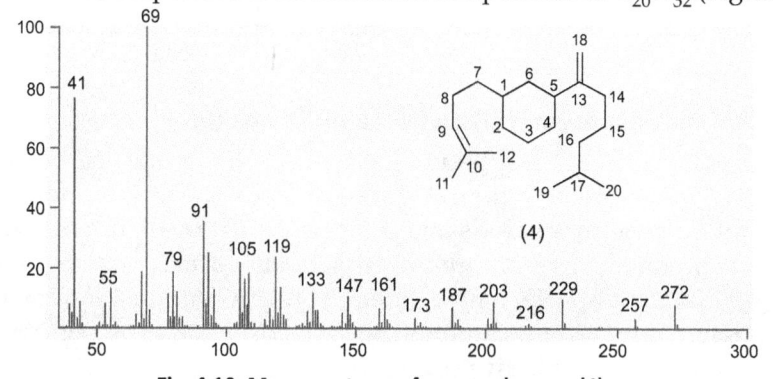

Fig. 4.10: Mass spectrum of m-camphorene (4).

Essential Oil of Olibanum   29

The fragmentation pattern of m-camphorene (4) showed primarily allyl cleavages or RDA reaction followed by allyl cleavages which explains the base peak at m/z = 69 (Figure 4.11).

Fig 4.11: Possible fragmentation of 4.

The 1H-NMR spectrum of 4 indicated four methyl groups two of which overlap at δ 1.68 and showed a singlet whereas the others absorbed at δ 1.61 and 1.60 as two singlets. Five olefinic hydrogens were recognized in the spectrum at δ 4.75, 4.76, 5.39 and at δ 5.10 (dd, J = 6.9, 6.6 Hz, 1H) and 5.12 (dd, J = 6.3, 6.3 Hz, 1H). The latter two appeared as overlapping doublets for two hydrogens (Figure 4.12).

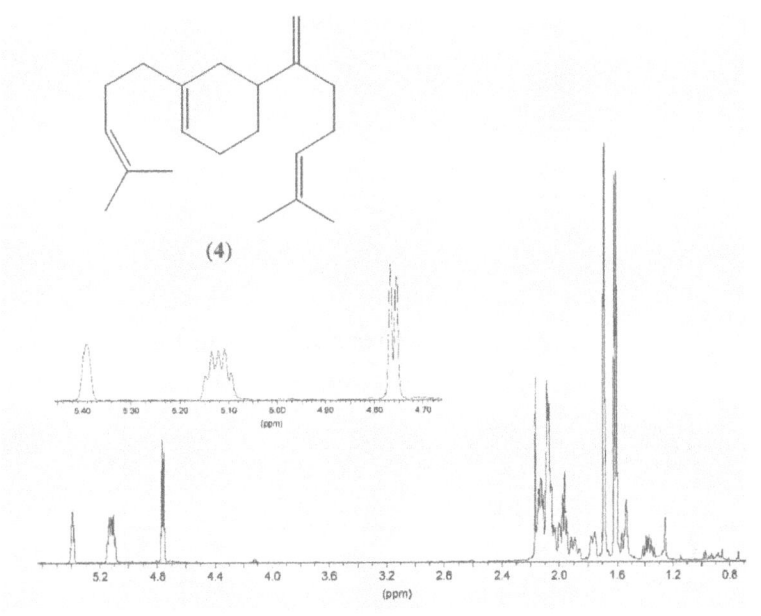

Fig. 4.12: 1H-NMR spectrum of 4.

The ^{13}C-NMR and PENDANT spectra of 4 showed three primary carbons at δ 17.70, 17.72, 25.70, eight secondary carbons at δ 25.87, 26.54, 26.87, 28.01, 34.62, 34.87, 37.87, 107.16, four tertiary carbons at δ 40.41, 120.29, 124.34, 124.43 and four quaternary carbons at δ 131.35, 131.51, 137.51, 154.45, a total of 19 signals. The integration of the carbon signals showed that two carbon signals were overlapping at δ 25.70. Additionally the low field carbon signals at δ 107.16, 120.29, 124.34, 124.43, 131.35, 131.51, 137.51, 154.45 indicated four double bonds in the molecule (Figure 4.13).

The HMQC spectrum of 4 indicated that the olefinic protons at δ 4.75 and 4.76 were correlating to a single carbon at δ 107.16. The other olefinic protons at δ 5.10, 5.12, 5.39 were found to couple to three tertiary carbons at δ 124.43, 124.34, 120.29, respectively. The two methyl singlets at δ 1.61, 1.60 were found to correlate with carbons at δ 17.70, 17.72, respectively. The methyl signals at δ 1.684 and 1.689 were overlapping with each other and showed a broad singlet. Both were correlated with the carbon signal at δ 25.70 which was already identified for two carbon atoms (Table 4.2, Figure 4.14).

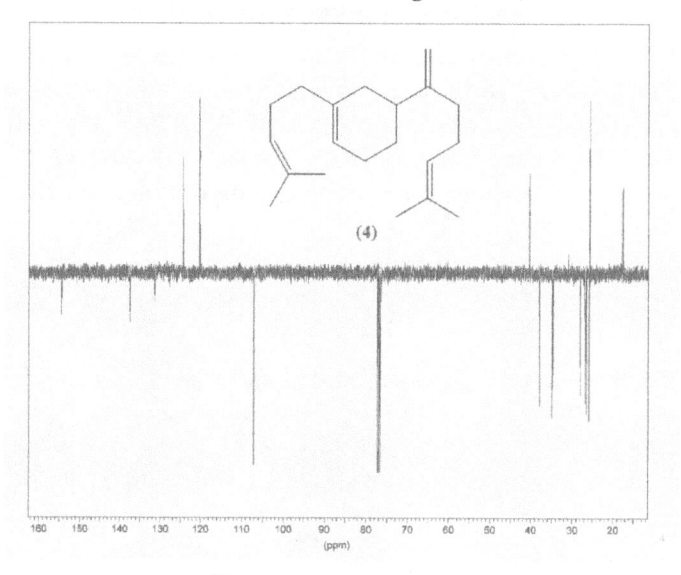

Fig. 4.13: ^{13}C-NMR (PENDANT) spectrum of 4

Table 4.2: HMQC correlations of 4.

No.	^{13}C (ppm)	^{1}H (ppm)	No.	^{13}C(ppm)	^{1}H (ppm)
1	137.51		11	25.70	1.684
2	120.29	5.39	12	17.72	1.60
3	26.54	(2.06-2.08), 2H	13	154.45	
4	34.62	(1.85-1.91), (1.99)	14	34.87	(2.02-2.05), (2.06-2.08)
5	40.41	(2.11-2.15)	15	26.87	(2.11-2.15).2H
6	28.01	(1.33-1.41), (1.75-1.77)	16	124.34	5.12
7	37.87	(1.94-1.97), 2H	17	131.51	
8	25.87	(2.06-2.08.2H)	18	107.16	4.75,4.76
9	124.43	5.10	19	25.70	1.689
10	131.35		20	17.70	1.61

Essential Oil of Olibanum 31

Fig. 4.14: Numbered structure of 4.

The connectivity of the carbons of compound 4 was derived from HMBC and 1H-1H-COSY spectra. First the double bonds in the molecule were determined. The coupling of H-9 (δ 5.10) to C-10 (δ 131.35) and the couplings of the methyl groups CH3-11 (δ 1.684, 25.70) and CH3- 12 (δ 1.60, 17.72) to C-10 and C-9 (δ 124.43) were assigned to the first double bond system. The second fragment was derived from the coupling of H-2 (δ 5.39), which correlated with C-2 (δ 120.29), to the quaternary carbon C-1 (δ 137.51).

The couplings of the C-18 protons (δ 4.75, 4.76) to a quaternary carbon C-13 (δ 154.45) indicated the third double bond.

The last fragment was deduced from the couplings of H-16 (δ 5.12) to C-17 (δ 131.51) as well as from the couplings of the methyl groups CH3-19 (δ 1.689, 25.70) and CH3-20 (δ 1.61, 17.70) to C-16 (δ 124.34).

The connectivity of the secondary carbons C-3 (δ 26.54) and C-4 (δ 34.62), C-7 (δ 37.87) and C-8 (δ 25.87), C-14 (δ 34.87) and C-15 (δ 26.87) were deduced from 1H-1H COSY spectrum through the correlations of the protons. Finally, the connectivity of these methylene bridges to the double bond fragments were derived from the HMBC spectrum (Figure 4.15).

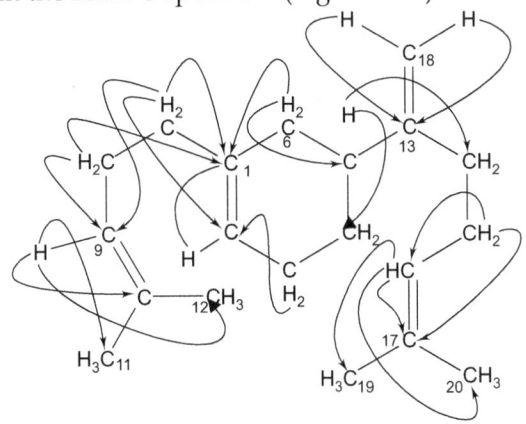

Fig. 4.15: HMBC correlations of m-camphorene (4).

The 3-D model of 4 provided to detect its NOESY correlations easily (Figure 4.16). The exocyclic double bond was found to be orthogonal to the

32 *Salai Gum*

plane of the molecule. This caused H-18 (δ 4.76) to correlate with the protons absorbing in β position. For this reason the correlations of H-18 (δ 4.76) to H-4β (δ 1.85-1.91), H-3β (δ 2.06-2.08), H-6β (δ 1.75-1.77), and to H-5 (δ 2.11-2.15) were observed in the NOESY spectrum. On the other hand H-18 (δ 4.75) was found to correlate to H-14α (δ 2.06-2.08) and H-15α (δ 2.11-2.15). The coupling of H-4β to H-14β (δ 2.02-2.05) confirmed these correlations. H-9 (δ 5.10) was observed to correlate to CH3-11 (δ 1.68, 25.70) as well as H-7β (δ 1.94-1.97) that was further coupled to H-2 (δ 5.39). CH3-12 (δ 1.60, 17.72) was found to correlate to H-8α (δ 2.06-2.08) and H-3β (δ 2.06-2.08) which was further coupled to H-6α (δ 1.33-1.41). On the other side chain of the molecule the correlations of H-16 (δ 5.12) to CH3-19 (δ 1.68, 25.70), CH3-20 (δ 1.61, 17.70) to H-15 (δ 2.11-2.15) were observed (Figure 4.17).

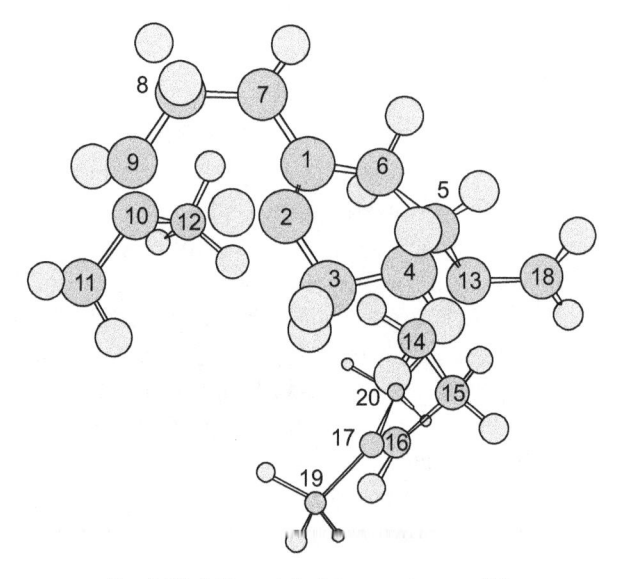

Fig. 4.16: 3-D model of m-camphorene (4).

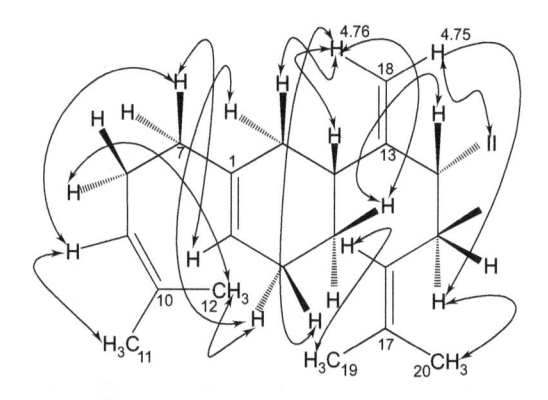

Fig. 4.17: NOESY correlations of 4.

Identification of p-Camphorene (5)

The pure compund produced a very similar mass spectrum as m-camphorene (4) with a molecular ion signal at m/z = 272 that corresponded to an elemental composition of $C_{20}H_{32}$ (Figure 4.18).

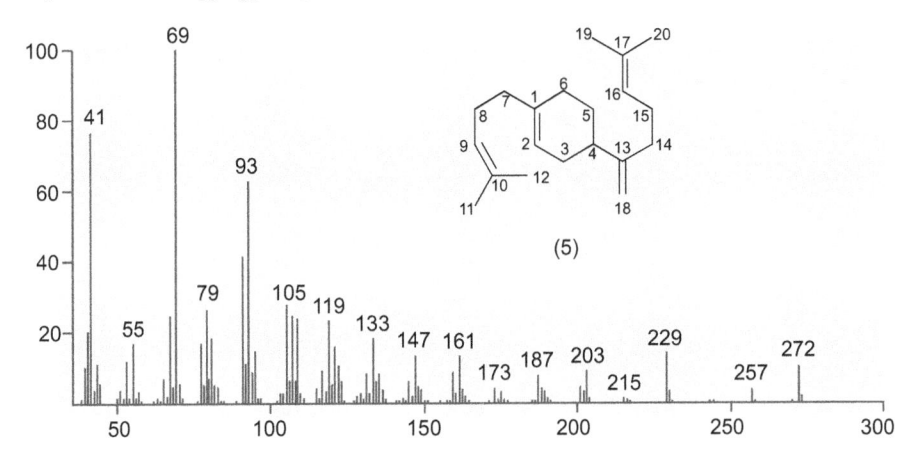

Fig. 4.18: Mass spectrum of p-camphorene (5).

The fragmentation of 5 was similar to m-camphorene (4). Allyl cleavages of the side chains and RDA reaction were the mainly observed splitting reactions of the molecule in its mass spectra (Figure 4.19).

Fig. 4.19: Possible fragmentation of p-camphorene (5).

Similar to m-camphorene (4), the 1H-NMR spectrum of p-camphorene (5) also showed four methyl group signals two of which overlap at δ 1.68 as a broad singlet whereas the others absorbed at δ 1.61 and 1.60 as two singlets. Five olefinic hydrogens were deduced from the spectrum at δ 4.74, 4.76, 5.41 as three singlets each were representing a proton and at δ 5.10 and 5.12 as two overlapping multiplets for two protons (Figure 4.20).

The 13C-NMR and PENDANT spectra of 5 showed three primary carbons at δ 17.70, 17.72, 25.69, eight secondary carbons at δ 26.53, 26.86, 28.37, 29.09, 31.44, 34.89, 37.61, 107.09, four tertiary carbons at δ 40.00, 120.40, 124.35, 124.43 and four quaternary carbons at δ 131.35, 131.50, 137.43, 154.34, a total of 19 signals. The integration of the carbon signals indicated that two carbon signals were overlapping at δ 25.69. Eight carbon signals found at low field of the spectrum between δ 107–154, indicated four double bonds in the molecule (Figure 4.21).

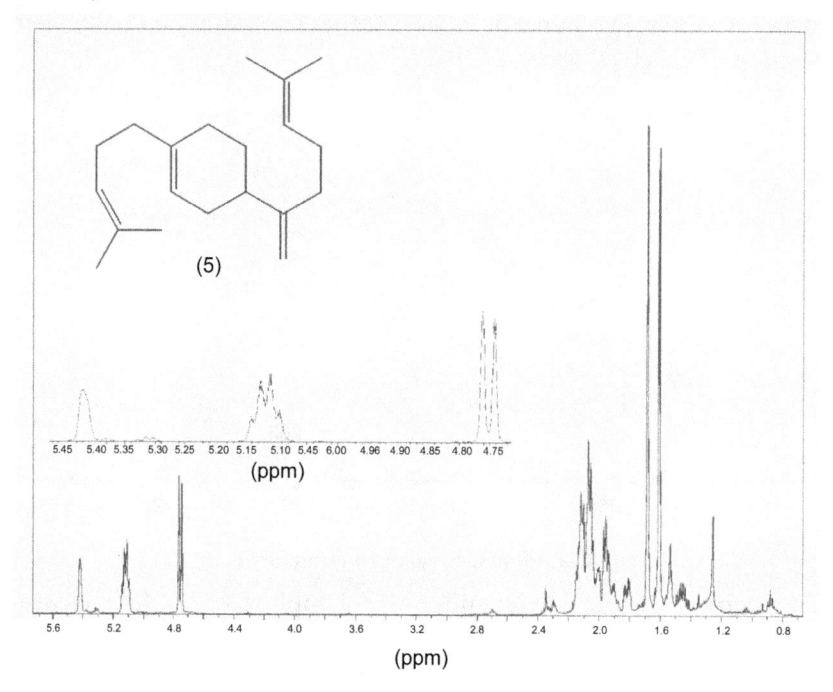

Fig. 4.20: 1H-NMR spectrum of 5.

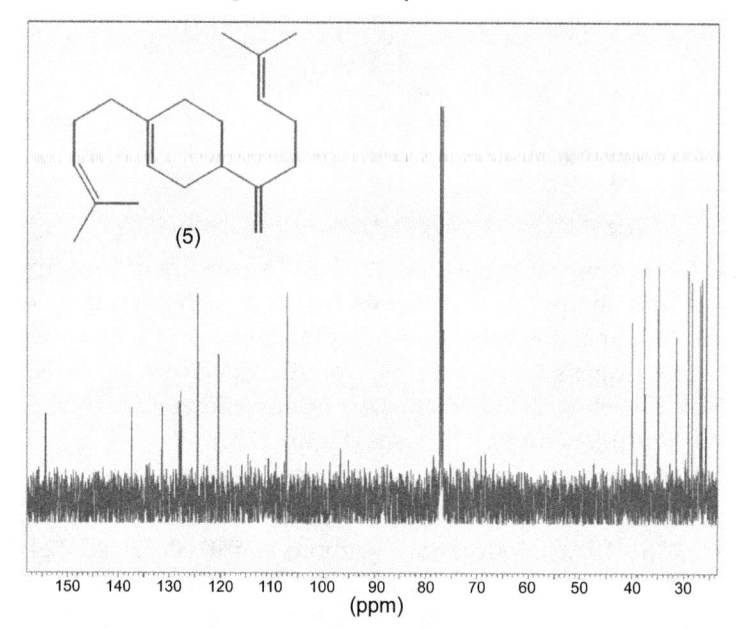

Fig. 4.21: 13C-NMR spectrum of 5.

Essential Oil of Olibanum   35

The HMQC spectrum of 5 indicated that the carbon at δ 107.09 correlated with both hydrogens at δ 4.74 and 4.76. The other olefinic protons at δ 5.10, 5.12 and 5.41 were found to couple to three tertiary carbons at δ 124.43, 124.35 and 120.40, respectively. The two singlets appeared for two metyhl group protons at δ 1.61 and 1.60 were found to correlate to the carbon signals at δ 17.70 and 17.72, respectively. Two overlapping methyl signals at δ 1.68 were found to be correlated to the carbon signal at δ 25.69. The chemical shifts of carbons and hydrogens in compound 5 were found to be very close to compound 4 and the connectivity of these signals showed that they were constitutional isomers (Table 4.3, Figure 4.22).

Table 4.3: HMQC Correlations of 5.

No.	^{13}C (ppm)	^{1}H (ppm)	No.	^{13}C (ppm)	^{1}H (ppm)
1	137.43	11	25.69	1.68	
2	120.40	5.41	12	17.70	1.61
3	31.44	(1.87-1.94), (2.10-2.14)	13	154.34	
4	40.00	(2.10-2.14)	14	34.89	(2.04-2.07), 2H
5	28.37	(1.41-1.49), (1.79-1.84)	15	26.86	(2.10-2.14), 2H
6	29.09	(2.00-2.02), (2.04-2.07)	16	124.35	5.12
7	37.61	(1.93-1.96), 2H	17	131.35	
8	26.53	(2.04-2.07), 2H	18	107.09	4.74, 4.76
9	124.43	5.10	19	25.69	1.68
10	131.50	20	17.72	1.60	

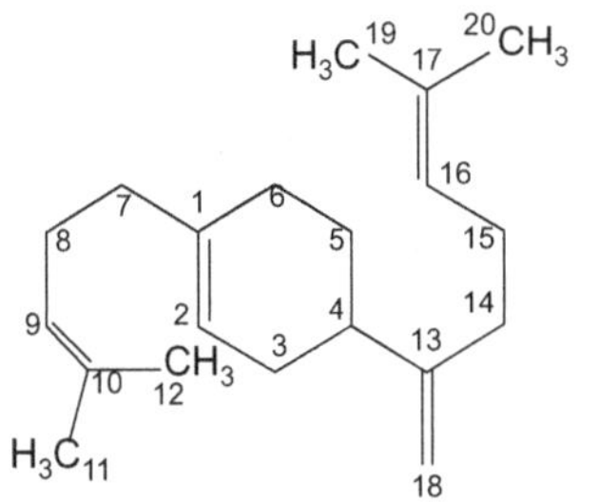

Fig. 4.22: Numbered structure of p-camphorene (5).

Four double bond systems were derived from the couplings detected in the HMBC spectrum of 5. The correlations of H-9 (δ 5.10) to C-10 (δ 131.50) and the couplings of the methyl groups CH3-11 (δ 1.68, 25.69) and CH3-12 (δ 1.61, 17.70) to C-10 and C-9 (δ 124.43) were established as the first fragment.

The second fragment was deduced from the couplings between H-2 (δ 5.41) with the quaternary C-1 (δ 137.43).

Salai Gum

The couplings of the C-18 hydrogens (δ 107.09, 4.74, 4.76) to another quaternary carbon C-13 (δ 154.34) indicated the third double bond.

The last fragment detected from the correlations of H-16 (δ 5.12) to C-17 (δ 131.35) and from the couplings of the methyl groups CH3-19 (δ 1.68, 25.69) and CH3-20 (δ 1.60, 17.72) to C-16 (δ 124.35).

The connectivity of the secondary carbons C-5 (δ 28.37) and C-6 (δ 29.09), C-7 (δ 37.61) and C-8 (δ 26.53), C-14 (δ 34.89) and C-15 (δ 26.86) were derived from the correlations detected in the 1H-1H COSY spectrum.

Finally, in 5, the change in the position of the tertiary carbon to C-4 (δ 40.00) instead of C-5 in compound 4 and its coupling with H-2 (δ 5.41) resulted in para configuration of the two side chains in the molecule (Figure 4.23).

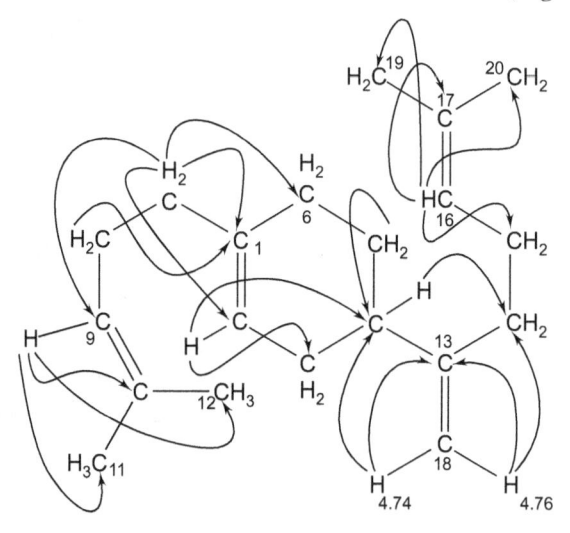

Fig. 4.23: HMBC correlations of p-camphorene (5).

Contrarily to m-camphorene (4) the 3-D model of 5 indicated that the H-18 protons were coplanar with the plane of the molecule (Figure 4.24). The NOESY correlations of 5 showed correlations of H-18 (δ 4.74) to H-5α (δ 1.41-1.49), H-7α (δ 1.93-1.96), H-6α (δ 2.00-2.02). The other H-18 proton (δ 4.76) was found to be correlated to H-15α (δ 2.04-2.07), H-14α (δ 2.10-2.14) and H-5α. H-5α was further correlated to H-3α (δ 2.10-2.14). H-10 (δ 5.10) was found in relation to CH3-11 (δ 1.68, 25.69) which was further coupled to H-7α (δ 1.93-1.96).

On the other hand H-2 (δ 5.41) was found to be coupling to H-7β (δ 1.93-196). The other side chain of the molecule showed correlations of H-16 (δ 5.12) to CH3-19 (δ 1.68, 25.69) and CH3-20 (δ 1.60, 17.72) to H-15 (Figure 4.25).

Both m-camphorene (4) and p-camphorene (5) were identified before as constituents of hop oil[119, 120]. Nevertheless, they were isolated and identified for the first time in *Boswellia*.

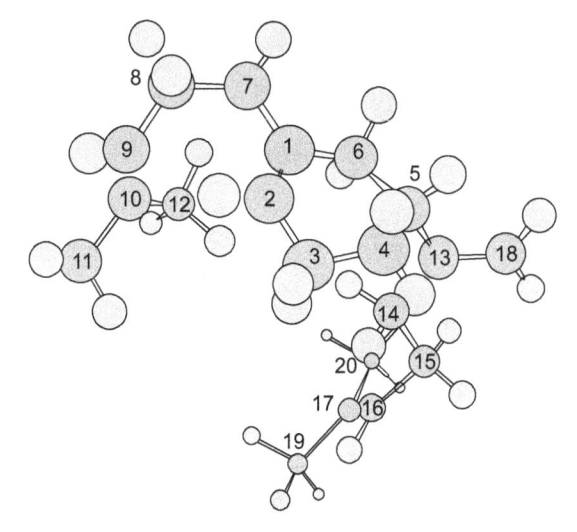

Fig. 4.24: 3-D model of p-camphorene (5).

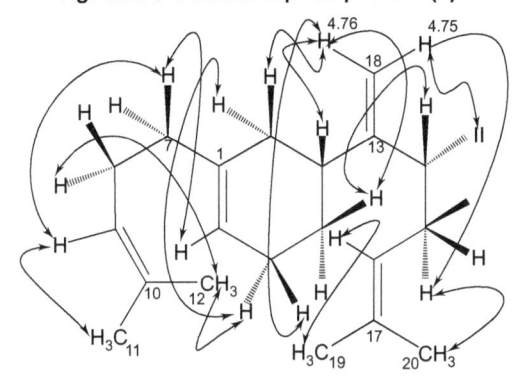

Fig. 4.25: NOESY correlations of p-camphorene (5).

The presence of a cembrene alcohol, serratol or cembrenol, from *B. serrata* was reported in earlier studies. However, both compounds were reported with different structures (Figure 4.26). The 1- and 2-NMR studies performed in this study was consistent with the cembrenol (6) structure.

Fig. 4.26: Two cembrene alcohols reported from *B. serrata*.

These diterpenoic constituents, m-camphorene (4), p-camphorene (5) as well as cembrenol (6) in *Boswellia serrata* essential oil turned out to be diagnostic markers for this species.

5 Resin Secretory Structures of *Boswellia*

Resin is considered to be the most versatile material in the preindustrial world. Resins from *Boswellia* and Commiphora species (respectively known as frankincense and myrrh) were traded as incenses from the southern coast of Arabia to the Mediterranean region and Mesopotamia for more than a millennium. Their historical value is illustrated by the gifts of the three kings (frankincense, myrrh and gold) to Jesus Christ (Matthew 2: 11). Currently, the main international trade is from *Boswellia papyrifera*, and Ethiopia is the main exporting country. The use of frankincense for ritual purpose in Ethiopia dates back to the Aksumite Empire, approx. 500 BC. The current commercial harvest of frankincense from this species provides an important export item and is a source of income for rural households in northern Ethiopia. In some areas collection of resin is economically a more attractive land use than crop production and accounts for the majority of income of rural households. Modern uses of frankincense include church ceremonies, perfume and medicine production.

Frankincense is produced by wounding the bark of *B. papyrifera* trees and collecting the resin that is subsequently released from the wound. This tapping practice is carried out at several spots along the stem, using a traditional type of axe. This procedure is repeated in 8–12 tapping rounds during the dry season which lasts about 8 months. The wound initially has a surface area of about 2.5 cm^2 and a depth of about 1 mm. At each tapping round, the hardened resin is removed and the tapping wound is re-opened and enlarged. The number of tapping spots on each tree depends on the diameter of the tree. In the past, trees were tapped with 6–12 tapping spots around the stem. Currently, due to the high demand for frankincense, up to 27 tapping spots are made per tree in some commercial sites. Frankincense yield per tree levels off after nine tapping spots. Frankincense yield per tree per season varies between 41 and 3000 g depending on tree size, site productivity and season, and the yield increases during the earlier tapping rounds after which it levels-off and ultimately decreases towards the end of the dry season.

Extraction of resin through tapping likely affects carbohydrate allocation in trees as it enhances the competition for assimilates. Resin extraction also induces mechanical damage to the trees found 80% reduction in radial growth in tapped trees compared with untapped trees in rubber wood (Hevea brasiliensis). Higher mortality of tapped adult trees was also reported for black dammar (Canarium strictum). For *B. papyrifera*, tapping reduced reproductive effort and seed size : tapped trees produced fewer flowers, fruits and seeds than non-tapped trees, and germination success of the seeds from non-tapped trees was much higher than from tapped trees. Tapping also reduced foliage production, annual carbon gain and carbon stock of *B. papyrifera* trees. Such negative effects could, at least partly, explain the recent lack of regeneration observed for *B. papyrifera* populations in northern Ethiopia.

Resin is produced by trees to protect against potential damage from abiotic or biotic stress. Depending on the type of species, resin may be accumulated in resin canals or resin pockets (blisters) in the wood and/or the bark. In some species, tangential rows of traumatic resin canals are induced after wounding. Resin canals (axial or radial) are elongated extracellular structures, which enable long-distance resin transport, while resin pockets are rounded intracellular isolated tissues with limited potential for resin transport. Resin secretory structures are formed by schizogeny or lysigeny. Lysigeny refers to the process of cell disintegration that occurs when new structures are differentiated with or without cell separation while schizogeny refers to formation of space by pulling apart of cells. In both cases, resin is produced by secretory cells known as 'epithelium' which surrounds resin canals or resin pockets. In some plants, the epithelial cells may become thick walled and lignified and become non-functional, while in others these cells remain thin walled, unlignified and functional for longer periods of tim.

Despite the intensive tapping and economic interest in frankincense production, information on the resin secretory structures of *B. papyrifera* is absent. This is the first study that both describes and quantifies the resin secretory structures in the bark of frankincense trees of *B. papyrifera*. After a bark incision a copious amount of white incense immediately oozes out. Hence we would expect the resin secretory structures of *B. papyrifera* to be abundant in the bark rather than in the xylem. We also hypothesized that density of axial resin canals show directional changes throughout the bark due to dilatation indicated high variations in frankincense yield among trees of the same size classes. Studies indicate that the most important resin canal trait that determines resin yield for Norway spruce and pine trees is the diameter of resin canals. This leads to the expectation that the diameter of resin canals in *B. papyrifera* varies among trees of the same size. This information is crucial to understand resin yield and will help to formulate recommendations for developing a more sustainable tapping regime.

MATERIALS AND METHODS

Study Species

Boswellia papyrifera produces the widely traded white incense and is distributed in Ethiopia, Eritrea, Nigeria, Cameroon, Central African Republic, Sudan, Chad and north-east Uganda. In Ethiopia, *B. papyrifera* grows in dry Combretum–Terminalia woodlands and wooded grasslands in the north. It is a deciduous tree that usually dominates on steep and rocky slopes, lava flows or sandy valleys and grows to a height of about 12 m.

Study Site

The samples were collected from trees growing in open woodland located at 870 m a.s.l. Based on data from National Meteorological Agency, for the period 1971–2009, annual rainfall in Shivpuri ranges from 665 to 1380 mm, with a mean annual rainfall of 960 mm. The major rainy season in the site is from June to September. The mean annual maximum and minimum temperatures are 36 8C and 19 8C, respectively. The study site is dominated by clay soil and its average soil depth is 27.7 cm.

Study Trees, Sampling and Sample Preparation

The field-data collection was done in February 2010, in the middle of the dry season. Twenty healthy looking, adult trees of about 10 m height with a straight stem and diameter at breast height between 20 and 25 cm were selected from the same site in Metema. Trees without traces of recent tapping were selected. Non-tapped trees were used since the objective of this study is to describe the basic structure of resin secretory structures of the species. One bark sample per tree was collected from the eastern side at breast height (1.3 m above the ground) using a Trephor 140 mm long and 5 mm in diameter.

All samples were stored and transported in plastic tubes filled with a 70% ethanol solution to avoid fungal infestation. In the laboratory, transversal, radial and tangential micro-thin sections (50 mm) were prepared with a sliding microtome (type G.S.L.1 light-weight microtome). The transversal sections were prepared from all 20 samples, while radial and tangential thin sections were prepared from a subset of five samples. The thin sections were stained with a mixture of Astra-blue and Safranin for 3–5 min to discriminate lignified (red) from unlignified (blue) tissues. The stained thin sections were rinsed with demineralized water and dehydrated with a graded series of ethanol (50%, 96% and 100%). Then, for permanent fixation, the sections were rinsed with xylol and embedded in Canada balsam and dried at 60 8C for 12 h in the oven.

Bark and Resin Secretory Structures

The micro-thin sections were inspected under a light microscope, with a magnification ranging from 12.5 to 400 times. Digital images of the secretory structures present in wood and bark of *B. papyrifera* were made from transversal, tangential and radial sections using a Leica camera (DFC 320) attached to the light microscope. The bark is described using the terminology of Trockenbrodt and Junikka. For the purpose of this study, we classified the inner bark into three zones (Figures 5.1B and 5.2). The first zone (called intact zone) represents part of the inner bark that is not affected by dilatation and it is found close to the vascular cambium (Figure 5.2A). The remaining part of the inner bark which is affected by dilatation is divided into partially dilatated and highly dilatated zones to account for the observed structural variation. The partially dilatated zone (Figure 5.2B) is an area adjacent to the intact zone and is less affected by dilatation and has a higher proportion of remnant sclerenchymatic tissues than the highly dilatated zone. The highly dilatated zone (Figure 5.2C) is largely dominated by parenchyma.

Data Analysis

For the 20 study trees, the diameter of all axial resin canals, as well as the density (number of resin canals per mm^2) of axial resin canals, was measured and calculated from digital images across the inner bark. Functional and non-functional resin canals were discriminated according to the presence or absence of lignification of the cell wall of epithelial cells, indicated by red (¼ lignified) or blue (¼ non-lignified) colour. All axial resin canals which did not lose their original shape during the cutting process of thin sections were measured for their internal lumen diameter. All measurements were conducted using the image analysis software ImageJ version 1.44p (http://rsbweb.nih.gov/ij/).

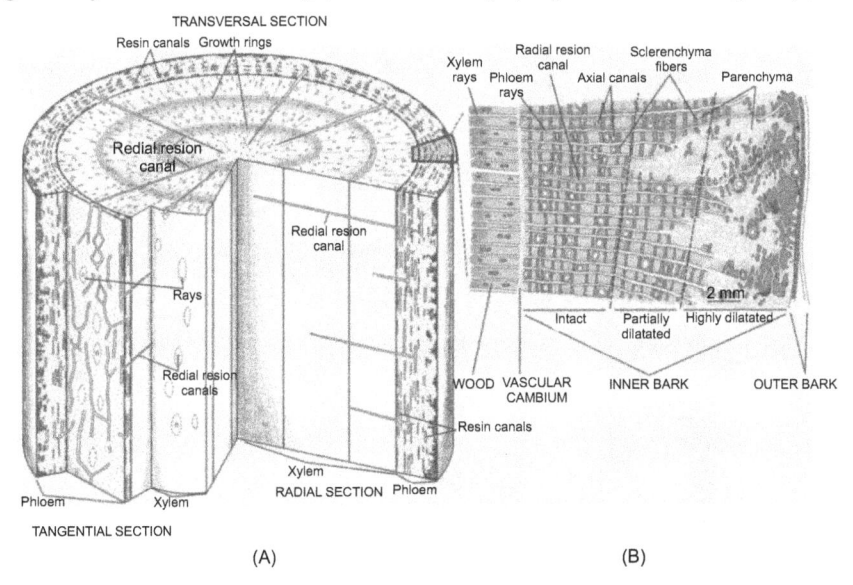

Fig. 5.1: Microscopic view of the bark and resin secretory structures of a *B. papyrifera* tree: (A) three-dimensional view of resin secretory structure in the xylem and bark ; (B) resin canals and other cell types observed in the bark (note: cell structures of the xylem part are not shown).

To test for differences in density of resin canals across the three zones of the inner bark, one-way ANOVA accompanied by Tukey post-hoc multiple comparison was used. Differences in density of lignified axial resin canals across the different zones of the inner bark were tested using Kruskal–Wallis accompanied with Scheffe's post-hoc test. To test for differences in average diameter of axial resin canals among the sample trees, one-way ANOVA was used and, to understand the relationship between density and average diameter of axial resin canals, correlation analysis was used.

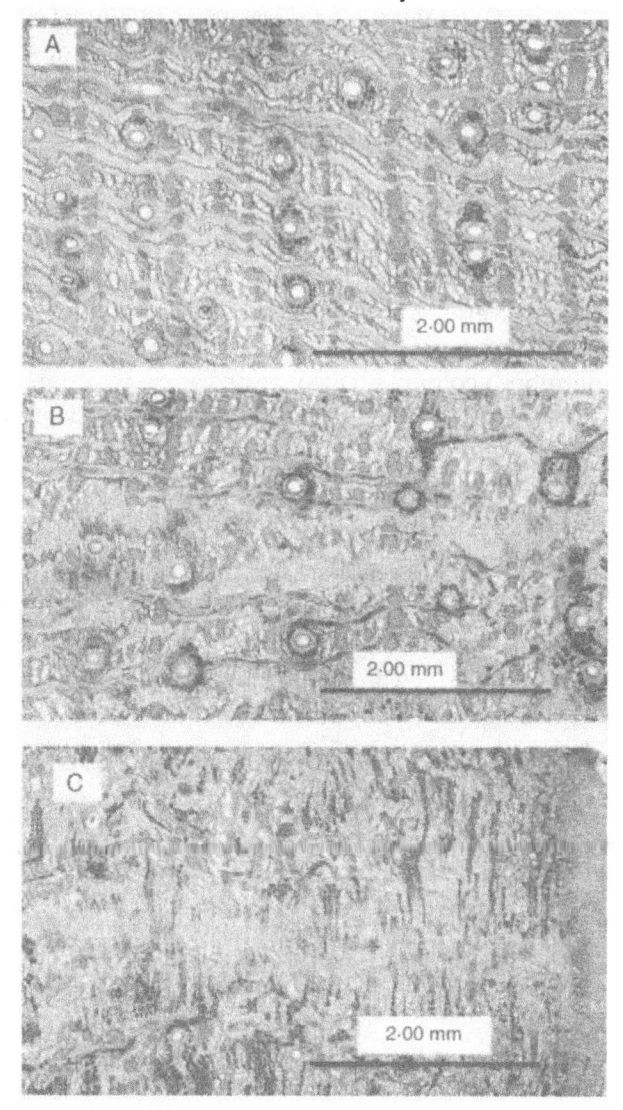

Fig. 5.2: The three zones of inner bark (transversal section) of *B. papyrifera*: (A) the intact zone, (B) the partially dilatated zone and (C) the highly dilatated zone.

RESULTS

Bark anatomical structure of *B. papyrifera* The bark of the studied *B. papyrifera* trees had an average thickness of 17.2 mm (s.d. ¼ 2.3; Table 5.1), which is about 15% of the stem radius. It consists of two main layers, the inner bark (17.0 + 2.3 mm), starting directly after the cambium and the much thinner outer bark (0.2 + 0.1 mm; Figure 5.1B). On the transversal section, the outer bark is seen as one to two layers of multiple cells with thin cell walls. These layers peel off in thin flakes. The inner bark is composed of multiple alternating tangential layers of thick-walled sclerenchyma fibers and thin-walled parenchyma layers (Figures 5.1B and 5.2). Sieve plates with companion cells were observed in the parenchyma layers. Phloem rays cut through sclerenchyma and parenchyma layers. Close to the cambium, these alternating layers are well-ordered and characterized as intact. However, the order gets disrupted with increasing distance from the cambium due to dilatation. Dilatation results in wedge-like structures, piercing into the inner bark. This leads to three distinct zones (Figure 5.2) in the inner bark: an intact, partially dilatated and highly dilatated zone. Phloem rays are abundant in the intact zone but decline in density towards the dilatation zones (Figure 5.2).

Table 5.1: Characteristics of Inner Bark of *B. papyrifera* Trees (n ¼ 20) from Metema, Ethiopia

Zones of the inner bark	Radial thickness (mm)				Density of axial resin canals (number mm^{-2})			
	Mean	s.d.	Min.	Max.	Mean	s.d.	Min.	Max.
Intact	6.6	1.8	3.8	10.5	1.0	0.3	0.4	1.5
Partially dilatated	4.7	1.5	2.5	8.3	0.8	0.2	0.4	1.2
Highly dilatated	5.7	2.5	1.2	9.8	0.6	0.2	0.3	1.1
Total inner bark	17.0	2.3	10.8	19.8	0.8	0.2	0.5	1.1

Distinction is made between intact, partially dilatated and highly dilatated parts, encountered in radial direction from vascular cambium to outer bark. All measurements are taken from transversal sections of the bark. s.d., Standard deviation; Min, Minimum; Max, Maximum.

Resin Secretory Structures of *B. papyrifera*

Resin secretory structures of *B. papyrifera* occur predominantly in the inner bark as axial and radial resin canals. The wood contains only a few radial resin canals, which are embedded in the rays (Figure 5.1A, B). These canals continue into the inner bark through phloem rays (Figure 5.3A) where they merge into a three-dimensional network of axial and radial resin canals. No other resin secretory structures such as resin pockets were observed on transversal, radial nor tangential sections of wood and bark samples. On the cross-section, axial resin canals are visible within the multi-layer sheets of axial parenchyma cells arranged in tangential rows (Figure 5.2A). Axial canals are much more abundant than radial canals. Both axial and radial resin canals are surrounded with epithelial cells. In the intact zone of the inner bark, epithelial cells around axial resin canals are exclusively non-lignified (Figure 5.3C), while epithelial cells around some of the axial resin canals in the dilatated areas are lignified (Figure 5.3D).

Tangential sections of the intact zone of the inner bark show that axial resin canals are mutually connected (Figure 5.1A). These canals split up and join neighbouring axial resin canals again (anastomosis), thereby forming tangential connections (Figure 5.3B). The elongated radial resin canals are connected to multiple axial resin canals (Figure 5.1A) completing the threedimensional network. In the dilatated parts of the inner bark this network gets increasingly disrupted.

Distribution, Density and Size of Axial Resin Canals in the Inner Bark

The intact, the partially dilatated and the highly dilatated zones, respectively, cover an average of 39%, 28% and 33% of the thickness of the inner bark (Table 5.1). On average, there are 0.8 axial resin canals per mm2 (s.d. ¼ 0.2) in the inner bark. However, the density of axial resin canals significantly decreases from the intact towards the highly dilatated zone (ANOVA, F2,57 ¼14.63, P, 0.001; Figure 5.4A and Table 5.1). Lignified axial resin canals which account for 4% of the average density of axial resin canals exclusively occur in the dilatated zones. The highly dilatated zone contains most lignified resin canals (Kruskal–Wallis, d.f. ¼ 2, × 2¼ 34.626, P, 0.001; Figure 5.4B).

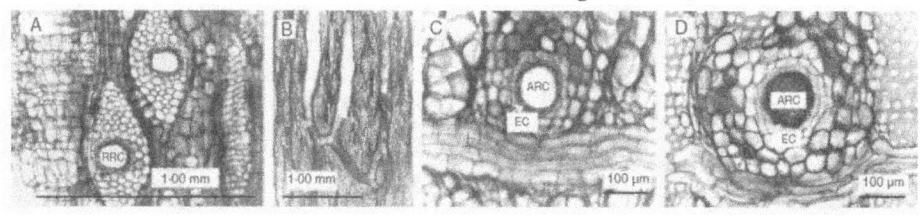

Fig. 5.3: Axial and radial resin canals in the bark of *B. papyrifera*: (A) radial resin canals (RRC) embedded in rays (tangential section); (B) anastomosis of axial resin canals in the inner bark (tangential section); (C) transversal view of axial resin canal (ARC) surrounded by non-lignified epithelial cells (EC, arrow) and other parenchyma cells (indicated by blue stain ¼ living) and (D) axial resin canal (ARC) surrounded by lignified (dead) epithelial cells (EC, arrow) and other parenchyma cells (stained red ¼ dead).

The average diameter of all individual axial resin canals measured from 20 trees ranges between 30 and 232 mm with an average of 113 mm (s.d. ¼ 30; n ¼ 1707 axial resin canals). The diameter of resin canals significantly differs between trees (ANOVA, F19,1687 ¼ 25.598, P, 0.001). Moreover, the studied trees showed a trade-off between density and average diameter of axial resin canals (Pearson correlation, n ¼ 20, r ¼ –0.625, P, 0.01; Figure 5.5).

DISCUSSION

Resin Secretory Structures of *B. papyrifera*

As expected, resin secretory structures of *B. papyrifera* are predominantly found in the bark. Axial and radial resin canals form a three-dimensional network in the intact zone. In this relatively small zone, which accounts for less than half of the thickness of the inner bark, the network of resin canals is mostly intact and so is most likely to be functional for short- and long-distance resin transport. Radial resin canals connect the canal network of the bark to the wood. This hints to the possibility of radial transport of resin between wood and bark. Previous studies showed similar results for *B. serrata* from India and interconnected canals are also reported for Pinaceae and Araliaceae. With increasing distance from the cambium, the density of axial resin canals decreases strongly. This decrease is caused by dilatation occurring due to increasing tangential strain as trees grow in circumference. The dilatation is realized by the production of new parenchyma cells that are formed by phloem parenchyma cells which regain meristematic status. Resin canals surrounded by lignified epithelium cells occur more frequently within the dilatated zones of the inner bark and can be taken as an indicator of nonfunctionality. Lignification of cells around resin canals is possibly related to the rupture of the secretory system as a consequence of dilatation. However, also without evidence from lignification, it can be assumed that disorder of cells, both in

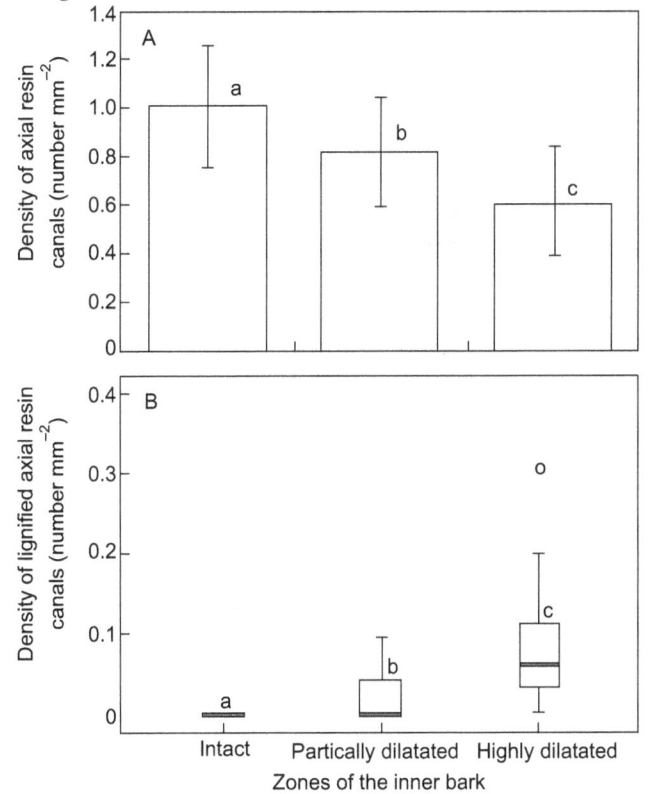

Fig. 5.4: Resin canal density in the three different zones of the inner bark of *B. papyrifera*. (A) Density of all lignified and unlignified axial resin canals (error bars ¼+ s.d.) and (B) a box plot of density of lignified axial resin canals. The circle above the 'Highly dilatated' box indicates an outlier value. Different letters indicate significant differences, using P, 0.05 [Tukey test (A) and Scheffe test (B), n ¼ 20]. Note difference in scales of y-axes.

partly and highly dilatated parts of the inner bark, will result in disruption of the network of resin secretory structures and disable – at least –long-distant transport of resin in these parts.

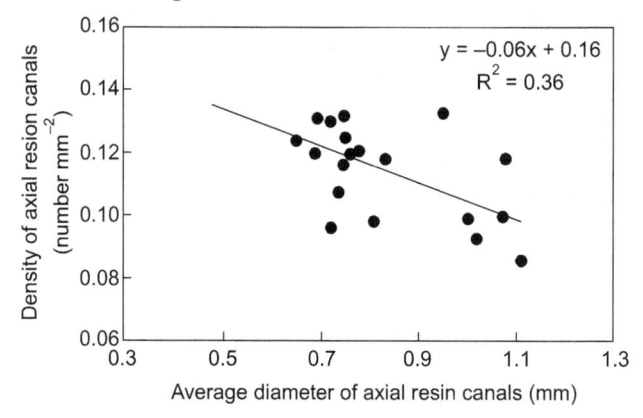

Fig. 5.5: Relationship between resin canal diameter and density in 20 *B. papyrifera* trees. Circles represent individual trees, and the scores represent density (number mm22) and average diameter (mm) of axial resin canals for each tree.

Implications for Tapping

This study showed that the diameter of resin canals varies among studied trees of the same diameter class. indicated that resin canal traits are strongly controlled by genetic variations. For spruce and pine, the diameter of resin canals is an important resin canal trait which is related to resin yield. Hence, differences in diameter of resin canals might partly contribute to observed differences in frankincense yield among trees of the same diameter class as described for *B. papyrifera* from our study area.

Previous studies showed that yield of frankincense per tree increases during the first five to seven tapping rounds and then declines when more tapping rounds are added later in the dry season.

In the context of the results of this study, this initial increase in resin yield can be related to the fact that in the case of successively deeper cuts into the bark, the tapping proceeds into the inner zones with a high density of resin canals and an intact three-dimensional network of functional resin canals.

The decline in yield after seven rounds of tapping suggests depletion of resin as it is drained through the well-structured network in the intact part of the inner bark. The strong reduction of resin yield towards the end of the tapping season most likely indicates depletion of the trees' carbon stock.

The anastomoses of resin canals facilitate long-distance resin transport and, presumably, work like a draining system in case of wounding, here specifically tapping. This may lead to a conclusion that larger wounds might not necessarily yield more resin while introducing more stress to the tree as it has to close the wound by production of wound tissue and wood to overgrow the wound. This is supported by results from who showed that enlarging the size of wounds for tapping *B. papyrifera* trees does not pay off in resin yield. Other results showing that resin yield per tree initially increases, then levels off and starts to decline with increasing number of tapping spots can also be explained by the findings of this study. The decline in resin yield beyond a certain number of tapping spots may occur because wounds drain resin from the same pool.

The presence of interconnected canals, coupled with our observation of immediate flow of resin from the bark when the tree is wounded, indicate that frankincense is present in the secretory system as a preformed resin. Therefore, it could be beneficial to drain all the preformed resin with a first deep cut into the intact part of the inner bark, i.e. to the depth that is usually reached during the tapping round that yields the maximum yield. Although the flow of resin will eventually be blocked by drying frankincense on the wound surface and the wound has to be re-opened to drain all preformed resin, the amount of labour required for production of frankincense could be reduced. This strategy would moreover be less harmful for the tree than initiation of multiple wounds to drain the same pool. The consequences of such one big deeper cut for frankincense yield as well as the related physiological processes require further research. We recommend additional specific experiments on different levels of cutting depths and on optimum distances between tapping wounds based on tree size.

From earlier studies, it is evident that tapping increases adult mortality, reduces reproductive effort, reduces growth of trees and exposes the trees to insect attack. The current decline in populations of *B. papyrifera* across large areas in Ethiopia and Eritrea can partly be attributed to over-tapping. This indicates that the current tapping strategies need to be improved. One of the strategies under discussion is reducing the number of tapping rounds per season and reducing the number of tapping spots per tree. Our findings on the bark anatomy and distribution and architecture of resin secretory structures of *B. papyrifera* will stimulate new experiments aimed at improving tapping techniques. This contributes to the development of a more sustainable frankincense production that enhances the contribution of frankincense to rural livelihoods and the national economy.

6. Effect of oleo-gum-resin of *Boswellia serrata* (*Kundur*) on Renal Functions

Kundur (Oleo-gum-resin of *Boswellia serrata*) is used for the treatment of various ailments such as dysentery, dyspepsia, lung diseases, haemorrhoids, rheumatism, urinary disorders and corneal ulcer in Unani System of Medicine and Ayurvedic System of Medicine for the last several years. It is also an ingredient of certain compound formulations viz. *Majoon Kundur, Majoon Murawwah-ul-Arwah, Dawa-ul-Kibrit* and *Habbe Suzak* used in Unani medicine for the treatment of different renal disorders. Various pharmacologically active chemical constituents were isolated from *Kundur*. *Kundur* is known to exhibit antifungal, anticomplementary, Juvenomimetic, anti inflammatory and anti-carcinogenic activities. Earlier investigations also revealed that *Kundur* topossess immunomodulatory properties, useful in bronchial asthma, Polyarthritis, Colitis, Crohn's disease and against Hepatitis C-virus.

Aminoglycosides including Gentamicin isolated from the *actinomycetes* were found effective against gram-negative bacteria, especially *Pseudomonas* species, and certain gram-positive bacteria. The major side effect of Gentamicin treatment is its nephrotoxic potential. Gentamicin was confirmed to cause acute renal failure and it induced dose-dependent cytotoxicity.

The proximal tubule was the most common site for Gentamicin induced nephrotoxicity and renal carcinogenesis as confirmed in different animal models. The Gentamicin induced nephrotoxicity was found to be mainly confined to the proximal convoluted tubules and parsrecta, where it produced tubular cell necrosis. However, the pathogenesis are yet to be elucidated. The effects of Gentamicin accumulation by crossing apical membrane, its action on lysosomes, mitrocondrial, and plasma membrane structure and function were studied by several researchers. Gentamicin treatment in rats was found to increase lipid peroxidation in renal cortex, which was decreased by selenium. These observations indicated a possible role of lipid peroxidation in aminoglycoside nephrotoxicity.

Usually for clinical studies, decline in glomerular filtration rate, serum creatinine and urea levels, N-acetyglucosaminidase, proteinuria, β_2–microglobulin, lysozymuria, and histopathological investigations are considered essential for patients to conclude possible nephrotoxicity. Based on the fact that reno-protective activity of *Kundur* has not been fully investigated, therefore, current study was design to explore the effect of *Kundur*-treatment on kidney function in order to justify its use in different systems of medicine.

MATERIALS AND METHODS

Kundur used in the current study, was obtained from Qadimi Unani Dawakhana Ballimaran, Delhi, India. The authenticity of *Kundur* was established as Oleo-gum-resin of *B. serrata* by Prof. S H Afaq and Dr Mohinul Haq Siddiqui, Dept of Ilmul Advia, Ajmal Khan Tibbiya College, Aligarh Muslim University, Aligarh. The voucher specimen MA-K-02-03 of this drug was preserved at the Department of Ilmul Advia, Faculty of Medicine, Hamdard University, New Delhi, India.

Albino wistar rats of either sex weighing 175-250 gm were used in the present study. The animals were obtained from Hamdard University, New Delhi and the Animal Ethical Committee of Hamdard University approved the study protocol. The animals were randomly assigned to five separate groups. Six animals were allotted to each group. Throughout the study all animals were kept under standard laboratory conditions: Temperature 28 + 1°C, and 12 hr light/dark cycle. The experiments were performed between 09:00 and 17:00 hours. The animals were fed with standard diet (supplied by the New Maharashtra Chakan oil Mills Ltd., Mumbai) and water *ad libitum*.

Kundur was dried over calcium chloride ($CaCl_2$) in a desiccator under reduced pressure. The dried oleo-gum-resin was crushed thoroughly and extracted with methanol by refluxing on boiling water bath for 10-15 minutes. It was filtered and the residue was further extracted with methanol two times. All the filtrates were combined together and the solvent was removed under reduced pressure. The extract obtained after removal of methanol was named as MS (Methanol soluble). The residue (Methanol Insoluble) left on the filter paper was named as MINS. The yields of MS and MINS were found to be 65% and 35%, respectively.

Carboxy methyl cellulose (CMC) and methanol were procured from Central Drug House, New Delhi, India, Gentamicin was obtained from Honday Pharmaceutical Pvt Ltd. India. The drugs were suspended in distilled water with 1% Carboxymethyl cellulose (CMC).

Experimental Procedure

The current study was designed for eight days. Group I: was given vehicle (1% CMC in D.W, 10 ml/kg/day, p.o.) and served as control. Distilled water was abbreviated as D.W. and body weight as b.w.

Group II: was given vehicle (1% CMC in D.W 10 ml/kg/d, p.o.) and Gentamicin (100 mg/kg) for 8 days. It was Gentamicin group.

Group III: The animals in group-III received *Kundur* (1 g/kg b.w/d) suspended in vehicle (10 ml/kg) and Gentamicin (100 mg/kg) for eight days.

Group IV: The animals received methanol soluble (MS) *Kundur* fraction (650 mg/kg/b.w/d) suspended in vehicle (10 ml/kg) with Gentamicin (100 mg/kg) for eight days.

Group-V: The animals received methanol insoluble (MINS) *Kundur* fraction (350 mg/kg b.w/d) suspended in vehicle (10 ml/kg) with Gentamicin (100 mg/kg) for eight days.

The animals in group II, III, IV and V were co-administered Gentamicin (100 mg/kg b.w.) dissolved in normal saline from the 1st day up to the end of the study (eight days). The dose of Gentamicin was injected subcutaneously in neck region in a volume of 1 ml/kg (10% concentration). Group I received normal saline instead of Gentamicin as suggested earlier. On the 9th day, blood samples from each animal were collected and analyzed for blood urea and serum creatinine levels following the standard procedure.

All the values were expressed as mean ± S.E.M. Student's t-test was used to analyze significance of the two means. Probability level of less than 5% was considered as statistically significant.

Table 6.1: Effect of Oleo-gum-resin of *Boswellia serrata*, (Kundur) and its Fractions (MS and MI) on BUN and Creatinine in Gentamicin Induced Nephrotoxicity

Groups	Dose Treatment (8 days)	N	BUN (mg/dl) Mean ± S.E.M.	Creatinine (mg/dl) Mean ± S.E.M.
I	CMC (1000 mg/kg)	6	5.93 ± 0.42	1.85 ± 0.07
II	CMC + Gentamicin (100 mg/kg)	6	23.34 ± 2.15***a	3.15 ± 0.12***a
III	kundur (1 gm/kg) + Gentamicin (100 mg/kg)	6	14.15 ± 0.39b	3.04 ± 0.10*b
IV	MS (650 mg/kg) + Gentammicin (100 mg/kg)	6	15.08 ± 0.80*b	2.74 ± 0.05*b
V	MINS (350 mg/kg) + Gentamicin (100 mg/kg)	6	22.34 ± 2.15*b	2.75 ± 0.08

***$p < 0.001$ statistically significant (a vs. control and b vs. a). NS (Statically more significant).
Student's t-test
N = Number of animlas in each group.
CMC (10 ml/kg), Gentamicin (100 mg/kg) kundur (1000 mg/kg), MS (650 mg/kg), and MI (350 mg/kg) doses were given to the above mentioned groups.

RESULTS

The effect of Oleo-gum-resin of *Boswellia serrata* Roxb. (*Kundur*) and its fractions MS and MINS on renal function was examined in Gentamicin nephrotoxicity model. The daily subcutaneous administration of Gentamicin at 100 mg/kg for 8 days caused renal dysfunction in the rats as evidenced by statistically significant increase in blood urea (373.59%) and serum creatinine (170%) as compared with control. Co-administration of *Kundur* with Gentamicin subcutaneously prevented the rise (P<0.001) in blood urea (49.93%) and serum creatinine (8.21%). About 44.27% inhibition in the rise of BUN (Blood urea nitrogen) and (30.90%) inhibition in the rise of serum creatinine with MS treatment was observed. MINS treatment on higher dose caused a statistically, while ($P > 0.05$) decrease in the studied parameters (Table 5.1).

Discussion

A relationship between oxidative stress and Gentamicin induced nephrotoxicity has been well documented in many experimental animal models. Administration of superoxide dismutase provides a marked protection against Gentamicin induced impairment of renal function Co-administration of antioxidant, vitamin E and selenium was found protective against Gentamicin induced nephrotoxicity. It has also been reported that the essential oils of *Kundur* (*B. serrata*) demonstrated antioxidant activity comparable with β-tocopherol (vitamin E) and butylated hydroxyl toluene (BHT). The renoprotective activity shown by *Kundur* and its MS (Methanol soluble) fraction against Gentamicininduced nephrotoxicity during current study, may be attributed to the chemical constituents of *Kundur* having antioxidative potential. It is worth mentioning that MINS (methanol insoluble) fraction also reduced serum creatinine level indicating its nephroprotective activity. During the current experiment it is fully justified that *Kundur* possesses renoprotective effect and further studies are warranted to explore its mechanism of action.

CONCLUSION

The results of our current study investigation revealed that essential oil of *Kundur* and the chemical constituents of its methanol soluble fraction are capable to reduce the nephrotoxicity caused by Gentamicin. However, to reach any conclusive decision before recommending *Kundur* in cases of renal disorders detailed phyto-pharmaco-toxicological studies are necessary to identify the active principle of *Kundur* and their exact mechanism of action.

7. Phytochemical Investigation and Biological Activity of Leaves Extract of Plant *Boswellia serrata*

Nature always stands as a golden mark to exemplify outstanding phenomenon of symbiosis. Nature has provided a complete store house of remedies to cure ailments of mankind. The knowledge of drug has accumulated over thousands of year as a result of man's inquisitive nature. The retrieval of knowledge on the use of medicinal plants has served as a valuable tool in the discovery of new drugs. Plants serve various purposes in the world. Their usefulness can be in the form of food, shelter, religious, medicines etc. Over 4,00,000 species of tropical flowering plants have medicinal properties.

In recent years, natural product especially those derived from plant sources is gaining much interest for therapeutic use than that of the conventional ones. This is due to development of resistance and unwanted side effects and other problems resulting from the use of synthetic drugs. But product from natural source exhibit minimal resistance and negligible side effects though they are well tolerated.

The history of herbal medicine is as old as human civilisation. Since old times before modern medicine, people became ill and suffered from various ailments. In absent of modern medicinal remedies people relieved on herbal remedies derived from herbs and spices. There are many medicinal herbs and spices, which find place in day-to-day uses, many of these, are used as herbal remedies. Many cooked foods contain spices. Some minor ailments like common cold, cough, etc. may be cured by herbal remedies with use of medicinal properties of spices. Herbal remedies can be taken in many forms. Infusions are steeping herbs or spices, with parts like leaves and flowers with boiling water for some time.

Filtered or unfiltered use this water extracts of spices as herbal remedies. Decoction from boiling roots, bark other parts of herbs and spices with water for a long time. Infusion and decoction both are known from herbal teas. Sometimes essential oil of herbs and spices are also used as herbal remedies.

The alternative system of medicine like ayurveda, siddha, unani and other tribal folklore medicines have significantly contributed to the health care of population of India. Today, these systems are not only complementary but also competitive in the treatment of various diseases. Initially the materials employed in these traditional medicines were almost botanical origin.

Ayurveda is a holistic health science, having diversity, flexibility, accessibility, affordability and have a potential to meet the new challenge to human life. As an alternative form of medicine, unani has found favour in Asia which is very close to ayurveda. Ayurveda (Davanagari: the 'science of life') is a system of traditional medicine native to the Indian subcontinent and practiced in the other parts of the world as a form of alternative medicine. According to the followers of Unani medicine, the five elements are present in different fluids and their balance leads to health and their imbalance leads to illness.

The universal role of medicinal plants in the treatment of disease is exemplified by their employment in all the major systems of medicine, irrespective of the underlying philosophical premises. The survey of literature of Indian system of medicine reveals that medicinal plants were in use as early as 4500 B.C. Nature has bestowed on us a very rich flora and fauna in addition to very diverse marine and microbial resources of natural product. Due to wide variation in climate, soil, altitude and latitude, India has medicinal flora and is largest procedure of medicinal herbs next to china. It has the reputation of being one of the world's leading Bio-diversity centers due to the presence of over 45,000 different plant species, India has 16 different agro climatic zones, 10 vegetation zones, 25 biotech provinces and 426 biomes, 1,800 species of flowering plants.

The use of medicinal plants for both primitive and curative therapies is not new as records of indigenous knowledge from various plant of the world illustrate an age long tradition of plant being a more bio resource base for health care. The documents many of which are of great antiquity revealed that the plants used for medicinal purposes were notified in India and other countries too. In the nineteenth century, the plant have played a major role as the basic source for the establishment of several pharmaceutical industries which are important for establishing and enhancing the economy of a developing country like India. Over 75% of the world population relies mainly on plants and plant extract for health care and more than 30% of the entire plant species, at one time or other, were used for medicinal purpose

The Word Health Organization (WHO) encourages the inclusion of herbal remedies that have been proven to be efficacious and safe, into primary health care. The long historical use of medicinal plants in many traditional medicinal practices, including experience passed from generation has demonstrated the safety and efficacy of traditional medicine. However, scientific evaluation is needed to provide evidences of their safety and efficacy. Several chemotherapeutic agents have been developed in the modern system of medicines as a result of screening of medicine of the medicinal plants in various parts of the world.

The isolation of biologically active phytoconstituents such as alkaloids, Quinine, serpentine, reserpine, norcotine, caffeine, nicotine, etc, are result the initial leads obtained from the traditional system of medicine. Explanation of chemical constituents of plants and pharmacological screening may provide us the basis for the developing the leads for the development of novel agents for curative purposes for treating various illness like diabetes, cancer, sexually transmitted diseases neurological and immunological disorders etc.

Plants contain number of metabolites. Among the estimated 250,000-500,000 plants species only a small percentage has been investigated phytochemically. Solvent fractions of them have been submitted for biological screening. The process of evaluation of plants for various pharmacological activities is a much time consuming/requiring large number of man hours. Natural products have proven to be the richest source of medicinal compounds. Although, many drugs are prepared by synthesis, most of the core structures of scaffolds for synthetic chemical are based up on natural products4. The key advantage of natural products over synthetic compounds is their chemical diversity. Almost one half of the chemical scaffolds from natural products cannot be reproduced by synthetic chemistry. Novel natural products and proprietary chemical scaffolds are in high demand by the pharmaceutical and agrochemical industries because compounds with novel chemical entities can be used to generate chemical libraries by parallel synthesis.

Phytochemistry is the art of resolving plants into chemically pure individual constituents. As a result of recent interest in the plant kingdom as a potential source of new drug strategies for the fraction of plant extracts based on biological activity rather than a particular class of compound developed. The chemical examination follows after the isolation and biological screening of the active fraction.

The structure determination and biological activity screening of natural products, especially those with a history of medicinal use taking clues from folklore medicines, ayurveda, tribal medicine etc., has been an important activity in medicinal chemistry. The plants often synthesise unexpected and novel structures by biosynthetic path to protect themselves from predator organisms. In spite of the fact, at present, we have at our command a formidable array of modern drugs andthe need to discover and invent new agent is genuine and primordial. It has been estimatedsatisfactory therapy is available only for about one third of all presently known human ailments, and several diseases such as cancer, AIDS, senile dementia, autoimmune diseases.

Approximately one third of the prescription drugs in the United States contain plants and more than 120 important prescription drugs derived from plants. Most of these drugs were developed because of their use in traditional medicine. Recently WHO studies indicate that over 30% of the world's plant species have at one time or another been used for medicinal purposes of the 2,50,000 higher plant species on earth, more than 80,000 species are medicinal.

Although traditional medicine is wide spread throughout the world, it is an integral part of each individual culture. Its practise is based mainly on traditional belief handed down from generation for hundred or even thousands of years.

The Chinese were the first to take full advantage of medicinal plants. Over 5000 years ago, the emperor ShenNung studied medicinal plant and verified the pharmaceutical properties. Over 11000 herbal remedies were developed and used in china for thousands of years. These include Ma Huang, also known as ephedra, the sources of the classic adrenergic drug ephedrine and artemisia. The source of artemisinin, a new antimalerial drug is currently under joint development by the WHO and the US for a long time, the only way to use plant medicine was either direct application or the use of crude plant extracts. Now, it is possible to rapidly build up extensively, libraries of certain classes of organic compounds by the method of combinatorial chemistry.

The structural determination and synthesis of natural products has received attention only during the early 19th century and extensive investigation of medicinally useful natural product is still in progress. A natural product lead structure is subjected to chemical modification to arrive at the therapeutically important molecular fragments, the pharmacophore only a few natural products are directly used as drug but in many cases the chemical modification of the lead structure gave a more potent synthetic and semi synthetic analogue.

A viable program of drug development, aimed at providing cheap drugs in this country, must take the following factors in to consideration. i) The prevailing socio-economic condition and the high cost of medical care. ii) Our vast and over increasing population, a majority of them live in rural areas often far away from means of communication.

Human beings are in the race of endemic and epidemic diseases since ages and have been a potential hunter in search of medicines from the nature. Illness has been a serious concern with the pain and suffering by the patients affected from various bacterial, viral, fungal, protozoa and parasitic diseases. Some of the diseases like typhoid, malaria, tuberculosis, ulcers, cancer, AIDS, syphilis, leprosy, diabetes etc are being treated with herbal therapies.

Ulcer is a serious gastrointestinal disorder that requires a well-targeted therapeutic strategy. A number of drugs including proton pump inhibitors and H2 receptors antagonists are available for the treatment of peptic ulcer, but clinical evaluation of these drugs has shown incidence of relapse, side effects, and drug interactions. This has been the rational for the development of new antiulcer drugs and the search for novel molecules has been extended to herbal drugs that offer better protection and decreased relapse.

Amongst the various diseases, the parasitic infection is one of the major challenges for the health care industries. Helminthes are recognized as a major problem to livestock production throughout the tropics. Parasitic helminthes affect human being and animals by causing considerable hardship and stunted growth. Most diseases caused by helminthes are of a chronic and debilitating in nature. The parasitic gastroenteritis is caused by mixed infection with several species of stomach and intestinal worms, which results weaknesses, loss of appetite, decreased feed efficiency, reduced weight gain and decreased productivity. Although some synthetic drugs are available to control such kind of infections but due to their high cost and untoward effects, the development of more effective and safe drugs from reasonably less expensive natural sources is our main consideration. This can rationally be approached through the study of indigenous traditional plant remedies.

Anthelmintics are therapeutic agents used to destroy parasitic worms or remove them from the infected host. The majority of helminth infections are acquired by contact with (*a*) Infected animals (*b*) Ground contaminated by human or animal excrement (*c*) Water infected with cereariae, and (*d*) Indestion of a infected meat. The filarial worms require arthopod vectors, such as blood sucking mosquitoes, which transmit the parasite from one host to another.

Surveys have shown that one-third of the human race suffers from helminth disease, of which a large number are multiple infections, though helmintic infections are usually associated with tropical regions. More than 40 million Americans are also victims of this infection.

Table 7.1: Drugs Obtained from Herbs and Plants, Source, Therapeutic Activity and their Synthetic or Semi-synthetic Analogs.

Sl. No.	Drugs from herbs and plants	Source	Therapeutic activity	Synthetic or synthetic analogs
1	Atropine	*Atropa belladonna*	Antimuscarinics	Dicyclomine HCl, Hyoscinebutylbromide
2	Benzyle penicillin	*Penicillin chrysogeum*	Antibiotic	Ampicillin, amoxicillin.
3	Codeine	*Papaver- somniferum*	Analgesic	Nolorphine, mepiridine.
4	Camptothecine	*Camptotheca- accumnata*	Anticancer	10-hydroxycaptothecine, animocamptothecine, topotecan, ironotecan.
5	Digoxin	*Digitails lanata*	Cardiovascular	—
6	Ephedrine	*Ephedra vulgaris*	Anti-asthma	Salbutamol, salmeterol.
7	Lovastatin	*Asparag- illusterrus*	hypercholesterolemia	Pravastatin.
8	Morphine	*Papaver- somniferum*	Analgesic	Heroine, naloxane, phthadine.
9	Podophyllotoxine	*Podoph- illumpettatum*	Anticancer	Etopside, tonipside.

10	Quinine	*Cinchona succirubra*	Antimalerial	Chloroquine, meploquinine, pamaquine, premquine.
11	Reserpine	*Rawolfia-serpentina*	Hypotension and anticholinergic	-
12	Tubacurarine	*Tuber curare*	Neuromuscular blocking agent	Decamethoxium, soxamethorium.
13	Taxol	*Taxusbaccata*	Anticancer	-
14	Teprotide	*Bathrops*	Antihypertensive	Captopril, enalapril, lisinopril.
15	Vinblastin, vincristine	*Cathran-thusroseus*	Anticancer	Vindesine.

Inaddition, these diseases present a serious economic problem to the animal is vulnerable to a large number of parasite worm infections. Next to schistosomiasis, hookworm disease and ascariasis are not most prevalent serious human infection in animals. The most serious helminthiasis is caused by flukes and round worm. Table 7.1. Presents some of the clinically very important natural product drugs, scaffold structures, synthetic or semisynthetic analogs.

Globally, there has been an unparalleled growth in the plant-derived medicinally useful formulations, drugs and health-care products. Its market covering more than 60% products derived from plant origin. India exhibits remarkable outlook in modern medicines that are based on natural product besides traditional system of Indian medicines. Almost, 70% modern medicines in India are derived from natural products. Medicinal plant plays a central role not only as traditional medicines but also as trade commodities, meeting the demand of distant markets. Ironically, india has a very small (1.6%) of this ever-growing global market. To compete with the growing market, there is urgency to expeditiously utilise and scientifically validate more medicinally useful plants while conserving these species, which seems a difficult task ahead.

Medicinal and Aromatic Plants

India has 2.4% of world's area with 8% of global bio-diversity. It is one of the 12 mega-diversity hot regions of the world. Other countries being Brazil, Colombia, China, South Africa, Mexico, Venezuela, Indonesia, Ecuador, Peru, USA and Bolivia. Across the country, the forest of India is estimated to harbour 90% of India's medicinal plants diversity in the wide range of forest type that occur. Only about 10% of the known medicinal plants of India are restricted to nonforest habitats. The estimated numbers of plant species and those used for medicinal purpose vary. According to one fifth of all the plants found in India are used for medicinal purpose. The world average stand at 12.5% while India has 20% plant species of medicinal value16 But according to Hamilton, India has about 44% of flora, which is used medicinally. Although it is difficult to estimate the number pf medicinal and aromatic plants present worldwide, the fact remains true that India with rich biodiversity ranks first in percent flora, contains active medicinal ingradient.

Table 7.2: (a) Number of Plants Used Medicinally Worldwide

Country	Plant species	Medicinal plant species	Percentage
China	26,0.92	4,942	18.9
India	15,000	3,000	20.0
Indonesia	22,500	1000	4.4
Malaysia	15,500	1,200	7.7
Nepal	6,973	700	10.0
Pakistan	4,950	300	6.1
Philippines	8,931	850	9.5
Srilanka	3,314	550	16.6
Thialand	11,625	1,800	15.5
USA	21,641	2,564	11.8
Vietnam	10,500	1,800	17.1
Average	13,366	1,700	12.5
World	422,000	52,885	—

Table 2: (b) Number and Percentage of Medicinal Plant Species Recorded for Different Countries and Regions

Country or region	Total no. of native species of flora	No. of species of medicinal plants	% of flora which is medicinal
China	27, 100	11,146	41
India	17,000	7,555	44
Mexico	30,000	2,237	7
North America	20,000	2,572	13
World	297,000-510,000	52,896	10-18

The existence of traditional depends on plant species diversity and the related knowledge of their use as herbal medicine. In addition both plant species and traditional knowledge are important to the herbal medicine trade the pharmaceutical industry whereby plants provide raw materials and the traditional knowledge prerequisite information.

India has the richest plant medical tradition in the world. It is a tradition that is of remarkable contemporary relevance for ensuring health security to the teeming millions. There are estimated to be around 25,000 effective plantbased formulations, used in folk medicine and known to rural communities in India.

There are over 1.5 million practitioners of traditional medicinal system using medicinal plants in preventive, promotional and curative applications. It is estimated that there are over 7800 medicinal drug-manufacturing units in India, which consume about 2000 tonnes of herbs annually. The market for ayurvedic medicine is estimate to be expanding at 20% annually.

Sales of medicinal plants have grown by nearly 25% in India in past ten years, the highest rate of growth in the world. Two of the largest users of medicinal plants are China and India (Figure 7.1). Traditional Chienies Medicine (TCM) use over 5000 plant species; India uses about 7000.

What is an Herbal Medicine?

Herbs has various meaning, but in the context of this article it refers to "crude drugs of vegetable origin utilized for the treatment of diseases states, often of a chronic nature, or to attain or maintain a condition of improved health". Herbal medicine sometimes referred to as Herbalism or Botonical medicine is the use of herbs for their therapeutic or medicinal value. An herb is plant or plan part valued for its medicinal, aromatic or savory qualities. Herb plants produce and contain a variety of chemical substance that act upon the body. Herbal preparations are called "Phytopharmaceuticals", "Phytomedicinal" or "Phytomedicine", are preparations made from different parts of herbs or plants. They come into different formulations and dosage forms including tablets, capsules, elixir, powder, extract, tincture, cream and parentral preparations. A single isolate or active principle derived from plants such as digoxin or reserpine tablets is not considered herbal medicine.

Why Herbal Remedies?

Their effectiveness, easy availability, low cost and comparatively being devoid of serum toxic effects popularised herbal remedies.

Popularity of Herbal Medicine

Theherbal medicine is largely gaining popularity over allopathic medicine because of the following reasons favorable to it.

1. Rising costs of medicinal care.
2. As these are from natural origin, so free from side effects in several cases.
3. Goes to root cause and removes it, so that the disease does not occur again.
4. Freedom from approaching various specialists.
5. Cure for many obstinate diseases.
6. Easy availability of drugs from natural sources.

Need and Scope of Herbal Therapy

The treatment of diseases with pure pharmaceutical agent is a relatively modern phenomenon. However, as European explores and merchants' spreads out to the Western and Eastern parts of the world, some of the benefits they would bring back were discovered pharmaceutical preparation of natural origin. One of the earliest success stories in developing a drug from a natural product was aspirin.

Today we are more concentrated with life-style disease like depression, cancer and heart troubles caused by faulty nutrition and stress. The need of alternatives therapy is to cover a good health for all. Herbal therapy is one of the best practices to overcome the illness.

Traditional Indian practice held that certain drugs should be formulated through the addition of chosen substance that enhances bioavailability enhancer property and point to the active component as the molecule piperine. An anti-TB drug Rimfampicin has to be given at higher dose that required in order to compensate for losses on the way to the target site. Formulation of Piperine with Rifampicin will have the counter effect.

Herbal Side Effects

Little is known about Phytomedicine safety. There has been increased in the number of side effects reported in the literatur. Many case however, could have gone unreported because herbal medicine usually self-prescribed and often times ignored by health practitioners during the patients care. Identifying adverse effect is further hindered because it is not always possible to assess the quality of certain herbal medicinal products.

Herbal Medicine Drug-interactions

The potential risk of an herbal medicine interacting with a prescribed drug is also a concern with the increased use of Phytomedicine. Recently, several interactions have drawn the attention of the medical community. Janetzky and Morrealc reported a probable interaction between ginseng one of the most popular herbs with multiple health claims and warfarin, drug with numerous well-recognised drug-drug interaction.

Understanding Drug-Herb Interactions

Drug interactions occur by 4 major mechanisms.

    1. Altered drug absorption

    2. Altered renal (kidney) elimination of drugs

    3. Additives effect or toxicities

       (Pharmacodynamic interaction).

    4. Altered hepatic (liver) metabolism of drugs.

The first three account for a relatively small number of problems, while the fourth is the major culprit in drug interactions. The potential seriousness of a drug interaction depends in part on which drugs are involved. Some drugs have what is called a "narrow therapeutic margin" which means that there is a relatively small difference between the amount of drug needed to achieve its beneficial effect and that causing adverse or unwanted effects. Classical examples of drug falling in this category are anticoagulant (blood thinners like warfarin), which can cause bleeding if the relative amount of drug is increased as a result of a drug interaction, anticonvulsants (anti-seizure medications such as phenytoin) and the heart drug digoxin.

1. *Absorption:* When drugs are given orally they are usually absorbed into the bloodstream through the stomach. Or by drug absorption may be due to alteration in pH, or acidity of the stomach, or by drugs binding together in the stomach to form complexes which cannot then be absorbed, for example because the molecule is too large to pass through the intestinal wall. Common examples include antacid, which increase stomach pH, and iron supplement, which can bind to some antibiotics, such as ciprofloxacin or tetracycline.

Another issue for absorption is the "motility of the gastrointestinal tract", in other words, how fast or slow your guts are moving. If you have diarrhea, the drugs or herbs are moving through your system quickly and may have less time to be absorbed. Laxative or bulk-forming agents speed up intestinal transit, and might interfere with intestinal absorbed drugs. Common stimulant laxative herbs are anthranoid-containing plants like senna, frangula, yellow dock and Chinese rhubarb, as well as Cascara sagrada and Aloevera leaf. Bulk-forming agents include guar gum and psyllium. The clinical significance of these interactions is not clear.

2. *Elimination:* Drug interaction due to alteration in elimination of drugs through the kidney can only occur if a drug is primarily eliminated from the body through the kidney. If a drug or herb causes decreased kidney function, levels of the drugs eliminated through the kidney may be increased as a result. Herbs containing diuretic properties, such as corn corn silk, dandelion, and juniper can increase the toxicity of lithium, a drug used to treat bipolar disorder.

3. *Pharmacodynamic interactions:* Some drugs (and herbs) that may be given together have similar beneficial effects, or similar toxic effects this is called a Pharmacodynamic interaction. For example, two antiretroviral drugs may both cause the side effects of peripheral neuropathy, increasing the likelihood of that side effect developing. Many drug-herb interactions fall in this category. For example herbs that have sedative properties, such as kava, nettle and sage may increase the sedative effect of some sleeping medications. Herbs that have antiplatelate activity, such as ginkgo biloba, ginger, ginseng and garlic may increase the risk of bleeding in patient taking traditional drugs with antiplatelet activity or blood thinners. Herbs that can increase blood pressure, such as blue cohosh, ginger, liquorice and bayberry can interfere with the effectiveness of drugs used to treat high blood pressure.

4. *Liver Metabolism:* The most complicated drug interactions, and those with greatest significance for antiretroviral medication, are those resulting

in altered liver metabolism of drugs. The activity of liver enzymes which are responsible for breaking down drugs can be increased (induced) or decreased (inhibited) by drugs or herbs. Many antiretroviral medications are enzyme inducers, enzyme inhibitors, or even both at the same time. The resulting drug interactions are complex, and not always predictable.

Ritonavir, a protease inhibitor, is a powerful inhibitor of liver metabolising enzymes, and can dramatically increase the blood level of the other drugs metabolized by the same enzymes. This interaction can be used to our benefit, so that lower doses of the drugs affected are required to achieve the same effect. If dose adjustments are not made however, toxic levels of the affected drug could result. Nevirapine, another antiretroviral is an enzyme inducer, and can decrease the blood levels of other drugs metabolized by the same enzyme. If we know how each drug is metabolised and how it affects metabolizing enzymes, we can predict the response and be prepared.

Many drugs in a wide variety of therapeutic categories are metabolized by liver enzymes and subject to this type of interaction. These include drugs used to treat anxiety and insomnia (diazepam and some of its relatives), drug used to treat depression, some anti-arrythymics (used to treat abnormal heart rhythms), oral contraceptives, painkillers and recreational drugs.

5. Common medicinal plants reported to interact with pharmaceuticals: A recently published comprehensive search of interactions between commonly used medicinal plants and pharmaceutical drugs published in clinical reports suggest potential interactions with the following herbals, betel nut, chilli pepper(capsicum), Danshen, Devils claw, dong quai, eleuthero or Siberian ginseng, garlic, gingkom guar gum, karela or bitter melon, liquorice, papaya, psyllium (St. John's wort, Saiboku-to Asian herbal mixture); Shankhapushpi (Ayurvedic mixed–herb syrup); Sho-saiko-to or xiao chai hu tang (Asian herbal mixture), tamarind, valerian and yohimbine.

Some specific cautions are that people with clotting disorders, those awaiting surgery, or those on anticoagulant therapy should be aware that ginkgo, Danshen, dong quai, papaya, garlic, feverfew, ephedra or ginseng may cause unexpected bleeding, increase bleeding times or inhibit blood clotting for about two week after you stop taking the herb. People taking protease inhibitors, serotonin is uptake inhibitors (newer antidepressants), cyclosporine, digoxin, phenprocoumon need to consider potential interactions with St. John's wort. Ginseng may interact with phenelzine, another antidepressant. People taking tricyclic antidepressant should avoid yohimbine. Liquorice, which has been shown to have antiviral properties and is a very common ingredients in Chinese herbal remedies, can have an additive synergistic effect with corticosteroids. Corticosteroids, like prednisone are commonly prescribed to ulcers in the throat and mouth that don't respond to topical preparations, or to treat rashes associated with some antiretroviral. These are only some of the herb-drug interactions for which clinical reports have been made. Many others are possible, and indeed likely. The complexity and potential gravity of drug herb interactions makes exercising caution and consulting a pharmacist or physician important.

6. *Toxicology and herbs:* In recent years there have been reports of death and poisonings attributed to the use of medicinal plants such as comfrey and chaparral. Herbalists have a responsibility to determine the inaccuracies in such reports. Literature concerning poisonous plant is replete with misinformation and erroneous reporting. These same mistakes continue to plague the reporting of poisoning by medicinal plants.

What is Toxicology?

The word toxicology is derived from toxicon-a poisonous substance into which arrow heads were dipped and toxikos-a bow. Toxicology is relative young biological science that involves a complex interrelationship among dose, absorption, distribution, metabolism and elimination.

What is a Poison?

A poison is substance which has a harmful effect on a living system. Paracelsus (1493-1541) was one of the first to distinguish between the therapeutic and toxic properties of substances. He thought the only difference between a medicine and a poison was the dose. Very few substances are actually classed as a "poison". Harmful chemicals are not necessarily poisons. We are exposed to potentially toxic substances every day without immediate harm. Our bodies can usually safely metabolize toxins if we are exposed to them in small amounts. It is only when we overwhelm our body and reach the toxic dose of a substance that life threatening results occur. That is all substances have a potential toxicity. All herbs can therefore be harmful, but most would have to be ingested in impossible amounts to cause harm. Herbs which have a high toxicity, such as Gelsemium and Aconitum, can be used safely and effective if taken in a small, therapeutic dose. Thus, the primarily determinate of the safety of a substance is the dose, not the herb, which makes the poison. A correct use of semantics and a correct understanding of these terms are crucial to avoid confusion and misinformation.

For example:
- Vitamin D has a very high acute toxicity. It would have to carry a poison label but it has been exempted from the federal Hazardous substances labelling act because it is classed as a food and a drug.
- Salt is not toxic in small doses. But a single large dose can be lethal. Just two tablespoon can kill a one-year-old child.
- Caffeine one of the many alkaloids found in coffee can kill-at a dose of 100 strong cups of coffee.

- A litre of scotch contains a lethal dose of ethanol.
- Water can be lethal if drink enough of it in a short period of time.

Toxicology sometimes refers to potentially poisonous substances as xenobiotics after the Greek xenos, strange, and bios, life. These are substances that are foreign to the body or exogenous as compared to substances produced by the body or endogenous. It is important to point out that endogenous substances can also cause poisoning and death.

Toxic substances fall into several classes in relation to how people are exposed to them. They can be classed as food additives, drugs, pesticides, industrial chemicals, environmental pollutants, household poisons and natural toxins, many natural products used in medicine are derived not only from plants, but also from marine organism like starfishes, sea urchins, sea cucumbers and fish. Chinese medicine makes use of chemicals produced from animal such as antelope horn, worms, scorpions and bee hives. Every substance has potential toxicity, from the most benign to the most obvious. Even so, the same dose will not affect every person in the same way. It is this fact which makes toxicology such a complex science. It is not enough to say a substance is toxic. There are a myriad of factors which may make the substance more or less toxic to particular individual.

Dose Response Relationship

Toxicity depends not only on the dose of the substance but also on the toxic properties of the substance. The relationship between these two factors is important in the assessment of therapeutic dosage in pharmacology and herbalism.

How Plant Substances Can Harm?

Toxicants can interrupt metabolism of carbohydrates, lipids and proteins and alter synthesis, release and harmones. Here are some examples of how substance from plant can harm; Oxalate crystals from Halogetonglomeratus can damage the tubules in the kidney because they insoluble precipitate and collect in the kidney tubules which then obstruct them. The alkaloid, aconitine in aconite, affects the sodium channels on the cell membrane which can lead to increased uptake in sodium and other ions. This can lead to cardiac arrhythmias and depression of respiration. Tubocurarine, the most potent constituent in curare denies access to neurotransmitters in nerve receptors. This results in paralysis of the muscles, including the respiratory muscles. The psychotropic plant alkaloids, harmine and harmaline resemble serotonin and are thought to block the serotonin receptors in the brain.

Morphine and other opiates bind to neurotransmitters receptors in the brain. In large amounts they can depress the respiratory centre in the brain. Glucosinolates are compound found commonly in plant of the mustard family. Some can be powerful irritant to eyes, skin and the respiratory tract.

Some alkaloids are distruptnerve tissue such as coniine from poison hemlock (conium) causing nervousness, trembling, bradycardia and fatal paralysis. Saponins can gastric upset because of its "soapy" properties which interfere with digestion.

India is a varietals emporium of medicinal plants. It is one of the richest countries in the world as regards genetic resources of medicinal plants. Even though the land mass of India occupies only 2% of the globe, it occupies 11% of the total known world flora and is one of the world's top 12 mega diversity nations. Two of the '18 hot spots' in the world are in India. The Indian system of medicine, ayurveda Siddha and unani uses over 2000 medicinal plants of which ayurvedic system of medicines uses about 700, sidda-600 and unani-700 medicinal plants in our country. Plants and other natural substances have been used as the rich source of medicine. All ancient civilizations have documented medicinal uses of plant in their own ethnobotanical texts. The list of drugs obtained from plant source is fairly extensive.

MATERIALS AND METHODS

Chemicals

Petroleum ether (400-600), benzene, chloroform, ethanol, methanol, silica gel-C (60-120 mesh) and silica gel-G (S.D. Fine Chem. Ltd. Mumbai), Tween-80, Piperazine citrate (Glaxo Smith line Ltd.), Lansoprazole (Lee Pharmaceuticals, Hyderabad)Aspirin (Shalg pharmaceuticals, Goregaon, Mumbai) and all other chemicals used were of the analytical grade.

Collection of Plant Material

*Boswellia serrata*were collected from the Western Ghat, Satara district, Maharashtra (India) in the flowering month of June-July 2010. The plant material was identified and authenticated by Dr. P.G. Diwakar, Botanical survey of India, Pune (KP/09/1203).

Helminth

Pheretimaposthuma(Indian adult earthworms) of 3-5 cm in length and 0.1-0.2 cm in width were procured from the Agriculture Research Centre, Gulbarga (Karnataka). All the earth worms were pre-treated with normal saline solution to remove the complete faecal matter.

Animals

Albino wistar rats of either sex weighing between 150 to 200 gm and Albino mice of either sex weighing between 20 to 25 gms. Were procured form registered breeders (149/1999/CPCSEA, Mahavir Enterprises, Hyderabad). The animals were housed under standard conditions of temperature (25 20C) and relative humidity (30-70%) with a 12:12 light-dark cycle. The animals were fed with standard pellet diet (VRK Nutrition, Pune) and water ad libitum. Approval at the Institutional Animal Ethics Committee (IAEC) of R.M.E.S's College of pharmacy, Gulbarga was taken for conducting antiulcer activity.

Extraction of Plant Material

The shade dried leaves of *Boswellia serrata* was powdered to 22 mesh size and then subjected to successive soxhlet extraction using highly nonpolar to polar solvent systems such as petroleum ether (40-600 C), chloroform, ethanol and distilled water until the solvent became colourless. The extracts obtained were further evaporated to dryness under vacuum and stored in the refrigerator for further use.

Preliminary Phytochemical Screening

Preliminary phytochemical screening is carriedout to determine the presence of various bioactive constituents in the crude extracts of petroleum ether (EE), chloroform (CE), ethanol (AE) and distilled water (AE).

Tests for Carbohydrates

1. *Molisch's test:* To 2-3 ml of extract, 1-2 drops of α-naphthol solution in alcohol is added, shaken and then concentrated H_2SO_4 is added along the walls of the test tube, a violet ring appears at the junction of two liquids.

2. *Iodine test:* To the test solution, 2-3 drops of iodine is added and then observed for blue colour occurrence.

3. *Fehling's test:* Equal volume of Fehling's A and Fehling's B reagents are mixed and few drops of test solution is added in a test tube and heated in boiling water bath for 5-10 min and observed for a yellow, then brick red precipitate appears.

4. *Benedict's test:* To 2-3 ml Benedict's reagent and few drops of the test solution is mixed thoroughly in a test tube and then heated in a boiling water bath for 10-15 min. Solution may appear green, yellow or red depending on amount of reducing sugar present in test solution.

5. *Barfoed's test:* Equal volume of Barfoed's reagent and test solution added in a test tube is heated for 1-2 min in boiling water bath and then cooled. Observe for red granular precipitate is observed at the bottom of the test tube.

6. *Selwinoff's test:* HCl reacts with ketoses to from derivatives of furfuraldehyde which gives red coloured compound when linked with resorcinol. Add compound solution to about 5 ml of reagent and boil. Fructose use red color within half minute. The test is sensitive to 5.5 mmole/lit, if glucose is absent but if glucose is present it is less sensitive and in addition large amount of glucose can give a similar colour.

Tests for Proteins

1. *Biuret test:* To 3 ml of the test sample, 4% NaOH and few drops of 1% $CUSO_4$ solution is add. Violet or pink colour is formed.
2. *Ninhydrin test:* Amino acid and proteins when boiled with 0.2% solution of ninhydrin (indane-1, 2, 3-trionehydrate) violet colour appears.
3. *Millon's test:* Mix 3 ml T.S. with 5 ml Million's reagent, white precipitate obtain. Precipited warm turns brick red or precipitate dissolves giving red colour.
4. *Xanthoprotein test:* 3 ml of test sample is mixed with 1 ml of concentrated H_2SO_4, white precipitate is formed.
5. *Test for protein containing sulphur:* Mix 5 ml T.S. with 2 ml 40% NaOH and 2 drops 10% lead acetate solution. Solution was boil, turns black or brownish due to $PbSO_4$ formation.
6. *Precipitation test:* The test solution was observed for white colloidal precipitate with following reagents:
   (i) Absolute alcohol
   (ii) 5% mercuric chloride solution
   (iii) 5% cupric sulphate solution
   (iv) 5% lead acetate
   (v) 5% ammonium sulphate

Tests for Steroids

1. *Salkowski reaction:* To 2 ml of extract, 2 ml chloroform and 2 ml concentrated H_2SO_4 was added. Shook well, whether chloroform layer appear red and acid layer show greenish yellow fluorescence is observe.
2. *Libermann-burchard reaction:* Mix 2 ml extract with chloroform. Add 1-2 ml acetic anhydride and 2 drops of concentrated H_2SO_4 from the side of test tube, observe for first red, then blue and finally green colour.
3. *Libermann reaction:* Mix 3 ml extract with 3 ml acetic anhydride. Heat and cool. Add few drops of concentrated H_2SO_4, observe for bluecolour.

Tests for Alkaloids

1. *Dragendroff's test:* To 2-3 ml of filtrate, few drop of Dragendroff's reagent is added. Observe for orange brown precipitate.
2. *Mayer's test:* To 2-3 ml of filtrate, few drops of Mayer's reagent are added. Observe for precipitate.
3. *Hager's test:* To 2-3 ml of filtrate, few drops of Hager's reagent added. Observe for yellow precipitate.
4. *Wagner's test:* To 2-3 ml of filtrate, few drops of Wagner's reagent is added. Observe for reddish brown precipitate.

Tests for Tannins and Phenolic Compounds

To 2-3 ml of the test solution, few drops of the following solutions is added and observed for the reaction formed.

1. *5% Ferric chloride solution:* Deep blueblack colour is formed.
2. *Lead acetate solution:* White precipitate occurs.
3. *Gelatin solution:* White precipitate occurs.
4. *Bromine water:* Decolourization of bromine water takes place.
5. *Acetic acid solution:* Red colour solution is formed.
6. *$KMnO_4$:* Decolourization of sample takes place.

Tests for Flavonoids

1. *Shinoda test:* To the dried powder or extract, add 5 ml 95% ethanol, few drops of concentrated HCl and 0.5 g of magnesium turnings. Pink colour appears.
2. To the small quantity of residue, lead acetate solution is added. Observe for yellow coloured precipitate.
3. Addition of increasing amount of sodium hydroxide to the residue, yellow colour occurs and latter it decolorize on addition of acid.
4. *Ferric chloride test:* To the test solution, add few drops of ferric chloride solution observe for intense green colour.

Tests for Glycosides

General test for Glycosides: Part A: To 2-3 ml of extract is mixed with dil. H_2SO_4 and heated on a water bath for 1-2 min. Neutralize with 10% NaOH, check with litmus paper and to resulting solution add Fehling's A & B. Increased red precipitate in this case shows glycosides are present. Part B:To 2-3 ml of extract is mixed with water and heated. After cooling, NaOH is added for neutralization along with equal quantity of water. To the resulting solution Fehling's A & B is add. Increased red precipitate in this case show glycosides are absent. Compare Part A and B.

Tests for Cardiac Glycosides

1. *Baljet's test:* The test solution on addition with sodium picrate forms yellow to orange colour.
2. *Legal's test:* To aqueous or alcoholic test solution, add 1 ml pyridine and 1 ml sodium nitroprusside, observed for pink to red colour.
3. *Keller Killiani test:* To 2 ml of extract, few drops of glacial acetic acid, one drop of 5% $FeCl_3$ and concentrated H_2SO_4 is added. Observe for reddish brown colour at the junction of two liquids and upper layers turns to be bluish green.

4. *Libermann's test:* 3 ml of extract is mixed with 3 ml of acetic anhydride. Heat the solution and then cool and add few drops of concentrated H_2SO_4. Observed for blue colour formation.

Tests for Saponins

1. *Foam test:* The extract or dry powder is shaken vigorously with water. Persistent foam is observed.
2. *Haemolytic test:* Add the test solution to one drop of blood placed on glass slide. Haemolytic zone is observed.
3. *Isolation and characterization of bioactives:* Based upon the preliminary phytochemical screening results, the ethanolic extract (EE) was subjected to column chromatography to isolate the various fractions of compounds. The elution was carriedout into the column containing activated silica gel-C (60-120 mesh), using non polar and polar solvents such as petroleum ether (PE), Benzene (BZ), Chloroform (CF), methanol (ME) and Double distilled water (H2O) with increase in their polarity and percentages like 100% PE, PE : BZ (95:05 - 05:95), 100% BZ, BZ : CF (95:05 - 05:95), 100% CF, CF : ME (95:05 - 05:95), 100% ME and ME: H2O (95:05 - 05:95). The various fractions obtained were collected separately into the beakers with the volume of 25 ml each eluent and immediately checked on TLC to identify the presence of single spot crystalline iodine was used for detecting the spot. The fractions which showed single spots on TLC plates were evaporated under reduced pressure and again repurified by eluting through the freshly prepared column using the respective solvent ratio. The purified compounds were subjected for IR, 1H NMR and GC-MS for spectral analysis for the characterization studies.

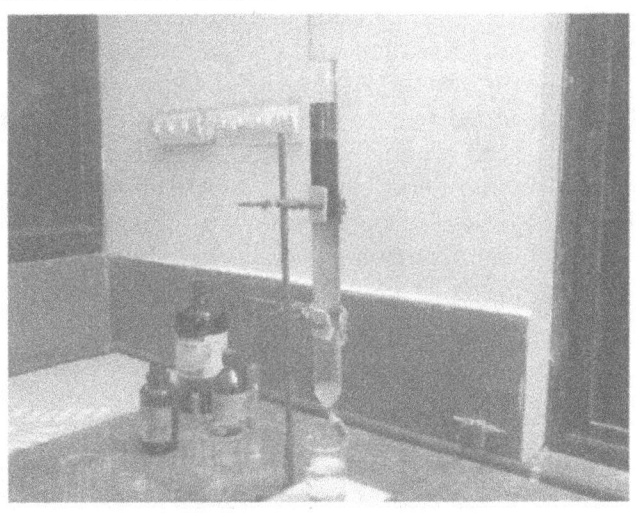

Fig: Column Chromatogram

Anthelmintic Activity

Ethanolic and aqueous extracts of the leaves of *Boswellia serrata* were investigated for their anthelmintic activity against Pheretimaposthuma. Various concentrations (25-10 mg/ml) of both extracts were tested in the bioassay, which involved determination of time of paralysis and time of death of the worms. Piperazine citrate was included as standard drug and normal saline as control, with minor modifications. The assay was performed on adult Indian earthworm, Pheretimaposthuma due to its anatomical and physiological resemblance with the intestinal roundworm parasite of human beings. Because of easy availability, earthworms have been used widely for the initial evaluation of anthelmintic compounds in vitro. Indian adult earthworms (Pheretimaposthuma) collected from moist soil and washed with normal saline to remove complete faecal matter were used for the anthelmintic study. The earthworms of 3 5 cm in length and 0.1 0.2 cm in width were used for all the experimental protocol. The earth worms were divided into ten groups (n = 6). Group I – control (0.9% normal saline), Group II – standard piperazine citrate (15 mg/ml), Group III – EE (25 mg/ml), Group IV - EE (50 mg/ml) Group VEE (75 mg/ml), Group VI - EE (100 mg/ml) and Group VII - AE (25 mg/ml), Group VIII – AE (50 mg/ml), Group IX - AE (75mg/ml) and Group X - AE (100mg/ml). Both the test samples and the standard drug are dissolved in 0.9% normal saline. Observations were made for the time taken to paralysis and death of individual worms. Time for paralysis was noted when no movement of any sort could be observed except when the worms were shaken vigorously. Death was concluded when the worms lost their motility followed with fading away of their body colours.

Acute (Oral) Toxicity Studies

Acute toxicity studies for aqueous, ethanolic extract and isolated compound of *Boswellia serrata* were conducted as per OECD guideline 420 (modified, adopted 23rd march 2006) using Albino Wister mice. Each animal was administered aqueous, ethanolic and isolated compound solution by oral route. The test procedure minimizes the number of animals required to estimate the oral acute toxicity of a chemical and in addition estimation of LD50, confidence intervals. The test also allows the observation of signs of toxicity and can also be used to identify chemicals that are likely to have low toxicity.

Antiulcer Activity by Pylorus Ligation Method

Albino wistar rats of either sex weighing between 150-200 gms) were divided into six groups of six animals in group.

Group-I – Control (2% gum acacia)
Group-II – Standard drug (Lansoprazole 8 mg/kg in 2% gum acacia).
Group-III – AE - Aqueous extract (250 mg/kg).
Group-IV – EE- Ethanolic extracts (250 mg/kg).

Group-V – IC- (Tetrahydro-2H-pyran-2, 3, 4, 5-tetrol) n (40 mg/kg)

In this method albino rats were fasted in individual cages for 24 hr. care was taken to avoid coprophagy. Extracts or isolated compound or standard drug or control vehicle was administered 30 min. prior to pyloric ligation. light ether anaesthesia, give an incision of 1 cm long in the abdomen just below the sternum. Expose the stomach pass a thread around the pyloric sphincter and apply a tight knot. While putting the knot care was taken so that no blood vessels are tied along the knot. The abdomen was sutured clean the skin from any blood spots and bleeding. Apply collodion over the wound. At the end of 4 hr. after ligation the animals were sacrificed with excess of anaesthetic ether. Open the abdomen and tie the oesophageal end (cardiac end) of the stomach. Cut and removed the entire stomach from the body of the animal. Gastric juice was collected into graduated centrifugation tube and was centrifuged at 1000 rpm for 10 min. and gastric volume was noted. The pH of the gastric juice was recorded by PH meter. Then the centrifuged supernatant contents were subjected to analysis for free and total acidity. Open the stomach along the greater curvature and washed running water to see for ulcers in glandular of the stomach.

The number of ulcers per stomach was noted and severity of the ulcers of the ulcers scored microscopically with the help of hand lens (10X) and scoring was done as following:

0 = normal stomach.
0.5 = red coloration.
1.0 = spot ulcers.
1.5 = hemorrhagic streaks.
2.0 = ulcer > 3 but < 5.
3.0 = ulcer > 5

Mean ulcer score for each animal is expressed as ulcer index. The percentage protection was calculated using the formula,

Percentage protection = $100 - U_t/U_c \times 100$

Where, U_t = ulcer index of treated group.

U_c = ulcer index of control group.

Determination of Free Acidity and Total Acidity

One ml of gastric juice was pipetted into 100 ml conical flask, added 2 to 3 drops of Topfer's reagent and titrated with 0.01N NaOH until all traces of red colour disappears and the colour of the solution turns to yellowish orange. The volume of the alkali added was noted. This volume corresponds to free acidity. Then 2 to 3 drops of phenolphthalein solution was added and titration was continued until define red tinge reappears. Again the total volume of alkali added was noted. The volume corresponds to total acidity.

Acidity was calculated by following formula:

$$\text{Acidity} = \frac{\text{Volume of NaOH} \times \text{Normality of NaOH} \times 100}{0.1} \text{ meq/L/100 gm}$$

In this method following parameters was studied-
1. PH of gastric juice.
2. Volume of gastric secretion.
3. Free acidity.
4. Total acidity
5. Ulcer index.
6. % protection.

Histopathological Evaluation

The stomachs were immersed in 10% formalin solution for Histopathological examination. These tissues were processed and embedded in paraffin wax. The central part of damaged or ulcerated tissue (if present) was cut on half along the long diameter. If the stomach was protected the damage then the section was taken from basal part using a rotary microtome, sections of thickness of about 5 μm were cut and stained with haematoxylin and eosin. These were examined under the microscope for histopathological changes such as congestion, haemorrhage, necrosis, inflammation, Infiltration, erosion and ulcer and photographs were taken.

Statistical Analysis

Results were expressed as mean ± SEM, (n = 5). Statistical analysis were performed with one way analysis of variance (ANOVA) followed by Dennett's 't' test P value less than <0.05 was considered to be statistically significant. *P<0.05, **<0.01 and ***<0.001, when compared with control and toxicant group as applicable.

RESULTS AND DISSCUSSION

The various extracts obtained from sequential extraction of *Boswellia serrata* leaves were assayed for the production of yield and detecting the presence of active constituents present in them. Further after preliminary screening, the bioactive were isolated, characterized and pharmacologically screened.

Table : Nature and Yield of *Boswellia serrata* Leaves Extracts

Sl. No	Extracts	Colour	Nature	% Yield (g)
1	PEE	Dark Greenish	Solid	6.5
2	CE	Brownish	Solid	3.5
3	EE	Brownish	Semi-solid	9.0
4	AE	Browinsh	Semi-solid	7.0

Key: PEE-Petroleum ether extract, CE-Chloroform extract, EE-Ethanol extract and AE

Aqueous Extract

Preliminary Phytochemical Analysis of *Boswellia serrata* Leaves Extracts

Tests	PEE	CE	EE	AE
Test for carbohydrates				
(a) Molish's test	−	+	+	−
(b) Iodine test	−	−	−	−
(c) Fehling's test	−	−	+	−
(d) Benedict's reagent	−	+	−	−
(e) Setwinoff's test	−	−	−	−
Test for proteins				
(a) Biuret test	−	+	+	−
(b) Ninhydrin reagent	−	+	+	−
(c) Biuret test	−	−	−	−
(d) Millon's test	−	−	−	−
(e) Xanthoprotein test	−	−	−	−
(f) precipitation test	−	−	+	−
Steroids				
(a) Salkowski reaction	+	−	−	−
(b) Libermann buchard's reagent	+	+	−	−
(c) Libermann reaction				
Test for Alkaloids				
(a) Dragendroff's test	−	+	−	−
(b) Hayer's test	+	+	+	−
(c) Mayer's test	−	+	−	−
(d) Wager's test	−	+	+	+
Test for Tannins				
(a) 5% $FeCl_3$	−	−	+	−
(b) Lead acetate	−	+	−	+
(c) Gelatine solution	−	−	+	+
(d) Bromine water	−	−	−	−
(e) Acetic acid	−	−	+	+

(f) KMnO$_4$	−	−	+	−
Test for Flavonoids				
(a) Shinoda test	−	−	+	+
(b) lead acetate test	−	−	+	+
(c) Sodium hydroxide test	−	−	+	+
(d) Ferric chloride test	−	−	+	−
Test for Glycosides				
(a) Legal test	−	+	+	+
(b) Baljet test	−	+	+	−
(c) keller-killiani	−	−	−	+
(d) Borntrager's test	+	+	+	+
Test for Saponins				
(a) Foam test	−	−	+	+

Key: PEE-Petroleum ether extract, CE-Chloroform extract, EE-Ethanol extract and AE-Aqueous extract.

Anthelmintic Activity

Based upon the preliminary phytochemical screening, both the AE and EE were subjected for antihelmintic activity compared with standard drug, Piperazine

In vitro Evaluation of Crude Extract of *Boswellia serrata* by Anthelmintic Activity

Group	% concentration (mg/ml)	Paralysis (min)	Death (min)
I (Control)	−	−	−
II (Piperazine citrate)	15	38 ± 0.31	56 ± 0.34
III (EE)	25	40 ± 0.36	58 ± 0.11
	50	29 ± 0.42	41 ± 0.35
	75	24 ± 0.57	32 ± 0.42
	100	20 ± 0.71	27 ± 0.20
IV (AE)	25	42 ± 0.62	67 ± 0.21
	50	30 ± .04	48 ± 0.53
	75	27 ± 0.65	36 ± 0.45
	100	21 ± 0.42	24 ± 0.33

Key: PEE-Petroleum ether extract, CE-Chloroform extract, EE-Ethanol extract and AE-Aqueous extract. All Values are expressed as Mean± SEM.

citrate. The result obtained in this study is based upon the observation made on helimentic paralysis and death at different time intervals. Table 7.6 shows the time taken for the paralysis and death of helminths by the action of both III (EE) and IV (AE). It can be seen that the highest activity was exhibited by the concentration greater than 50 mg/ml, but the high activity exhibited at 100 mg/ml within the time span of 30 min. These test samples were compared with group II (Piperazine Citrate), at the lowest concentration of 15 mg/ml depicts the paralytic condition and the death of the helminths at different concentration levels compared with the normal and standard drug.

Isolation and Characterization of Bioactive Constituent

Based upon the preliminary screening by the phytochemical and the anthelmintic studies, the ethanolic extract subjected through column chromatography for the isolation of pure compound was successfully carriedout. Various eluents collected at a flow rate of 5 ml/min, subjected for TLC separation to obtain a single spot made to analyze the compound obtained from the CH:Me (20:80) ratio for various spectral studies.

The IR spectrum of compound showed the broad and intense peak at 3386 cm-1 and a peak at 1701 cm^{-1} and 1652 cm^{-1} was also detected. Aromatic C-H absorption peak were not found, but peaks at 2926 cm^{-1} and 2854 cm^{-1} shows the presence of allyl C-H bond. The broad intense peak, 3686 cm^{-1} suggests that there may be number of secondary –OH group along with primary –OH. A peak at 1701 cm^{-1} may be due to the lactone rings. The H1 NMR spectrum exhibited absorption peaks at 1.25 W and 1.5 W and 2.2 W corresponding to CH-CH_2 protons present in the molecule. The sample gave number of fragment ions above 300 m/Z. These data suggest that the molecule under the investigation may be a polysaccharide containing number of primary and secondary hydroxyl groups and lactone ring systems. There is no aromatic ring systems in the molecule due to the absence of aromatic structure in H1 NMR system, but only absorption peaks corresponding to CH_2-CH protons has been observed at 1.3 W and 1.7 W and 2.2 W. In the mass spectral studies, the polysaccharide fragments gave rise to monomers corresponding to pentose sugars. This is for the substantiated by the presence of a base peak at 73 m /z, which is shown in the fragmentation of the molecule. It is possible to get the mass of the various fragments if recorded lesser electronic volt (eV).

Tetrahydro-2H-pyran-2, 3, 4, 5-tetrol Anthelmintic Effects of Ethanolic and Aqueous Extracts of *Boswellia serrata*

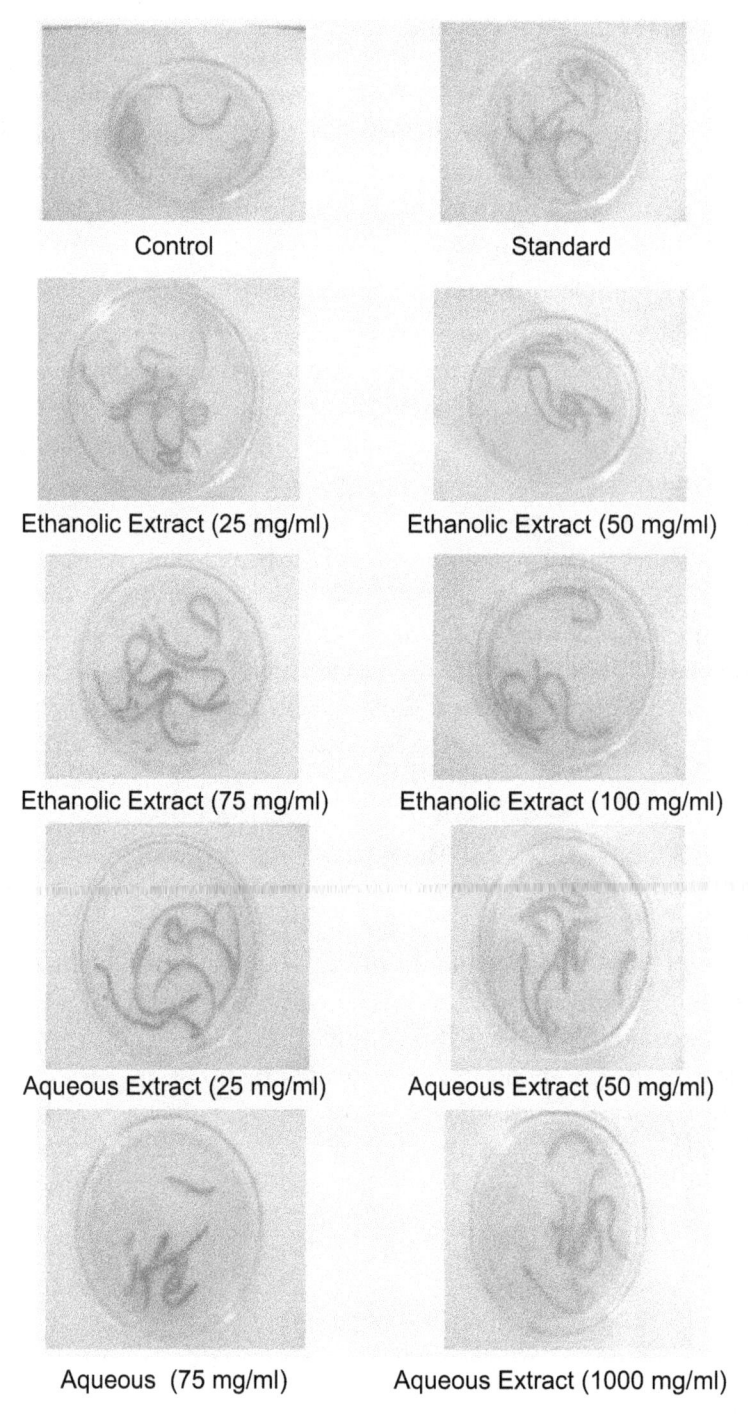

Control

Standard

Ethanolic Extract (25 mg/ml)

Ethanolic Extract (50 mg/ml)

Ethanolic Extract (75 mg/ml)

Ethanolic Extract (100 mg/ml)

Aqueous Extract (25 mg/ml)

Aqueous Extract (50 mg/ml)

Aqueous (75 mg/ml)

Aqueous Extract (1000 mg/ml)

Acute Toxicity (LD50) Studies

Acute toxicity studies based up on the continuous monitoring and observation for 72 hours as per the OECD guidelines 420, the oral acute toxicity studies revealed the non-toxic nature of the test samples of *Boswellia serrata*. During this study the effective dose (ED50) was notified as 250 mg/kg body weight with both crude aqueous and ethanolic extracts, and 40 mg/kg in case of (Tetrahydro-2H-pyran-2, 3, 4, 5-tetrol)n. No lethality of animals was found up to 2000mg/kg body weight. Hence the LD50 study was stopped at this dose.

Antiulcer Activity

Based upon the oral acute toxicity studies, an effective dose of 250 mg/kg of both the EE and AE, and 40 mg/kg in case of the isolated compound, (Tetrahydro-2H-pyran-2, 3, 4, 5-tetrol) n was administered orally. The test samples were compared with the standard, Lansoprazole (8 mg/kg).

Table 7.7 summarizes the effect of *Boswellia serrata* on the volume of gastric secretion, free acidity, total acidity and pH following pylorus ligation in rats. In case of volume of gastric secretion, a significant reduction in the Volume of gastric juice was exhibited in Group V with $P < 0.001$. While Group III and IV showed moderate reduction in the volume of gastric content with $P < 0.05$. In case of free acidity studies, a significant reduction in free acidity was exhibited in Group IV and V with $P < 0.001$. But lesser significance of $P < 0.05$ was found in Group III. In case of total acidity assay, a significant reduction in total acidity was seen in Group III and V with $P < 0.001$. Here the reduction in total acidity in Group V (IC) was greater than Group II (Lansoprazole). Group IV showed least significant, $P < 0.05$. The acidic and basic balance plays an important role

Table: Effect of *Boswellia serrata* on Gastric Secretion Following Pyloric Ligation in Rats

Group	Treatment	Vol. of Gastric Juice (M1)	Free Acidity (meq/L) 100 gm	Total Acidity (meq/L) 100gm	pH
I	Control	6.66 ± 0.084	76.78 ± 0.21	94.5 ± 3.56	2.56 ± 0.032
II	Lansoprazole (8 mg/kg)	2.89 ± 0.064***	27.99 ± 0.188***	34.00 ± 1.89***	5.71 ± 0.041***
III	EE (250 mg/kg)	4.79 ± 0.016**	45.2?0.107*	40.83 ± 1.35**	4.01 ± 0.014**
IV	AE (250 mg/kg)	5.27 ± 0.034*	38.25 ± 0.246**	64.33 ± 2.6*	3.02 ± 0.07*
V	IC (40 mg/kg)	3.01 ± 0.042***	35.85 ± 0.0611***	32.83 ± 2.02***	4.95 ± 0.11***

Key: EE-Ethanol extract, AE-Aqueous extract and IC- (Tetrahydro-2H-pyran-2, 3, 4, 5-tetrol) n
All Values are expressed as Mean± SEM; *$P < 0.05$, **$P < 0.01$ and ***$P < 0.001$ compared with Control.

in antiulcer effect. In case of ulceration there is increase in H⁺ ion concentration. The case of effect of PH studies, there was significant reduction of H⁺ ion concentration in Group III and V with $P < 0.001$. No significance was seen in case of Group IV. All the parameters studied in the gastric secretion produced due to the pylorus ligation in rats were compared with Group II, Lansoprazole.

Table 7.8 shows the effect of *Boswellia serrata* on pylorus ligation induced ulceration in rats. In this assay, the ulcer index and percentage of ulcer protection was found. It could be noted that Group V showed significant reduction in the ulcer index with $P < 0.001$ and $P < 0.01$ in case of Group III and IV compared to Group II, Lansoprazole.

Figure 7.10 – 7.13 shows the graphical illustration from the data represented in Table 7.7, showing the effect of *Boswellia serrata* on gastric secretion and fig 14 illustrated from Table 7.8 represents the effect of *Boswellia serrata* on ulcer index in pylorus ligation in rats.

Thus, the antiulcer activity exhibited by the all the three test samples that is EE, AE and IC when compared to Lansoprazole exhibited a significant reduction in the ulcers showing the potential healing property of *Boswellia serrata*.

Effect of *Boswellia serrata* on Volume of Gastric Juice Following Pyloric Ligation in Rats

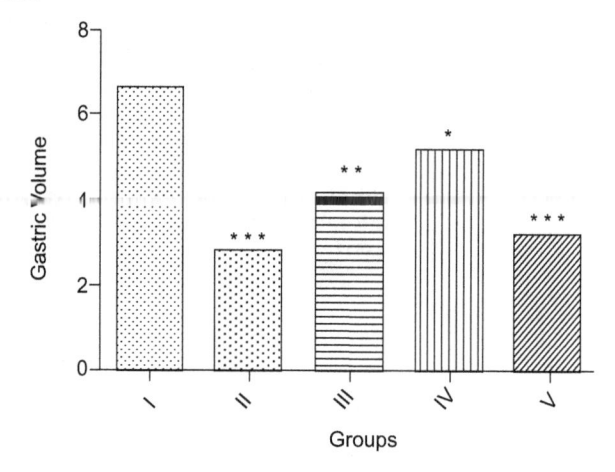

Key Groups:
- I– Control
- II– Standard
- III– Ethanolicextract (EE)
- IV– Aqueous extract (AE)
- V– (Tetrahydro-2H-pyran-2, 3, 4, 5-tetrol)

Effect of *Boswellia serrata* on Free Acidity Following Pyloric Ligation in Rats

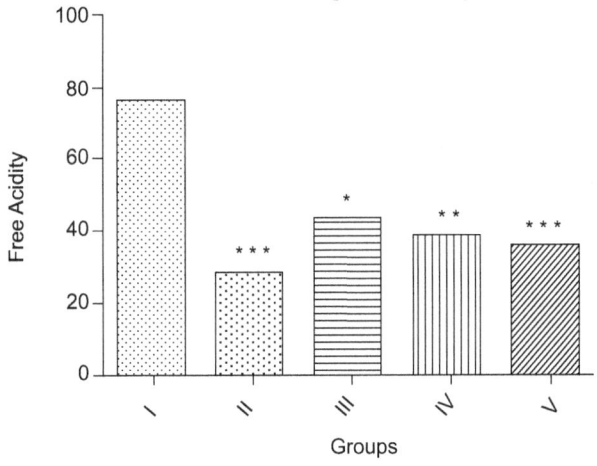

Key Groups:
I – Control
II – Standard
III – Ethanolicextract (EE)
IV – Aqueous extract (AE)
V – (Tetrahydro-2H-pyran-2, 3, 4, 5-tetrol) n

Effect of *Boswellia serrata* on Total Acidity Following Pyloric Ligation in Rats

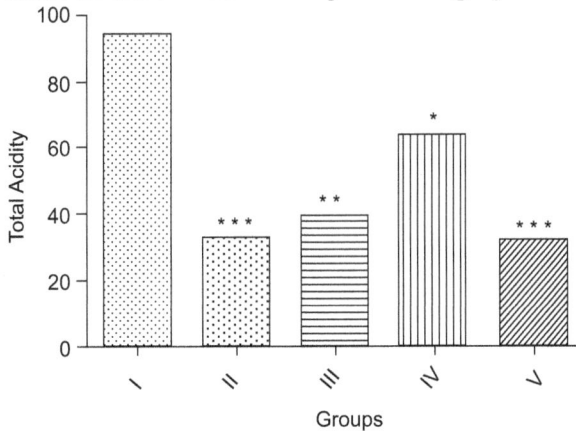

Key Groups:
I – Control
II – Standard
III – Ethanolicextract (EE)
IV – Aqueous extract (AE)
V – (Tetrahydro-2H-pyran-2, 3, 4, 5-tetrol) n

80 *Salai Gum*

Effect of *Boswellia serrata* on pH in Pyloric Ligation in Rats

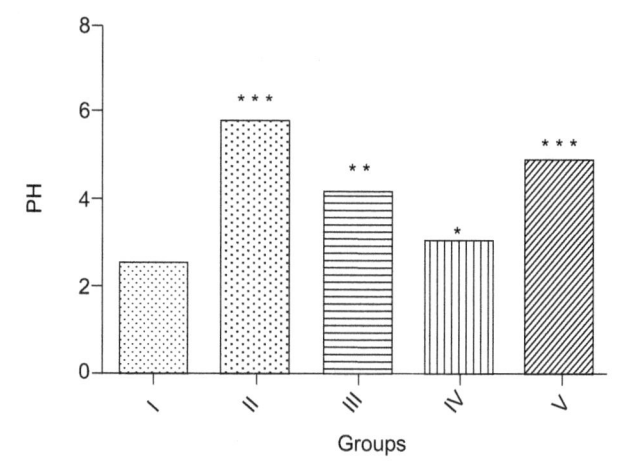

Key Groups:
I – Control
II – Standard
III – Ethanolicextract (EE)
IV – Aqueous extract (AE)
V – (Tetrahydro-2H-pyran-2, 3, 4, 5-tetrol) n

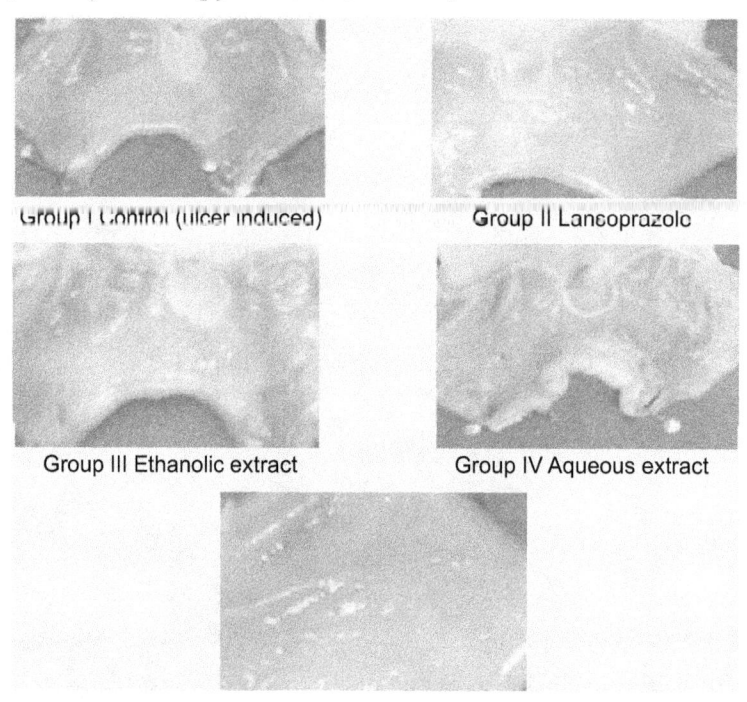

Group I Control (ulcer induced)

Group II Lansoprazole

Group III Ethanolic extract

Group IV Aqueous extract

Group V (Tetrahydro-2H-pyran-2,3,4,5-tetrol)

Effect of *Boswellia serrata* on Ulcer Index Pylorus Ligation Induced Ulcer in Rats

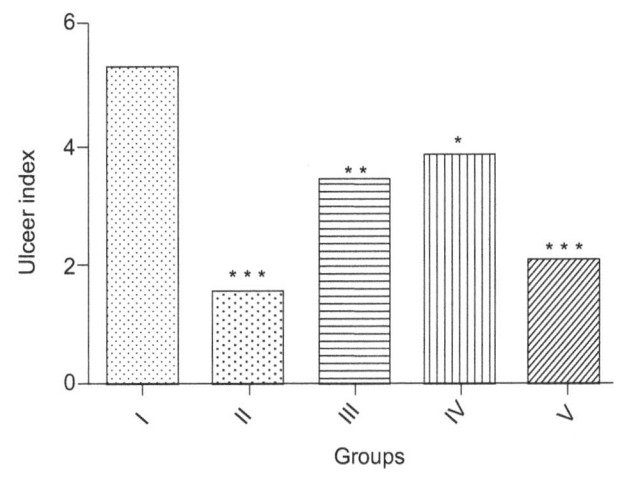

Key Groups:
I – Control
II – Standard
III – Ethanolicextract (EE)
IV – Aqueous extract (AE)
V – (Tetrahydro-2H-pyran-2, 3, 4, 5-tetrol) n

Histopathological Studies in Pylorus Ligation Induced Ulcer in Rat

The Histopathological studies in pylorus ligation induced ulcer in rat as shown in Figure 7.16a-7.16e exemplifies the comparative histopathological studies in various groups based upon the accessing the presence or absence of the redness, infiltration, congestion, hemorrhagic sticks, inflammation, necrosis and dilation of blood vessels. In case of Group I, the ulcer induced without treatment sample shows the presence of redness, infiltration, congestion, hemorrhagic sticks, inflammation, necrosis and dilation of blood vessels in the mucosa of the tissue. Group II, when treated with Lansoprazole shows the mild redness, no inflammation and dilation of blood vessels in the mucosa. Group III, when treated with ethanolic extract, the mucosa showed the mild inflammation and congested blood vessels. Group IV, treated with aqueous extract exhibited fibrosis and mild inflammation in mucosa.

No inflammation and no congestion of blood vessels was seen in Group V, treated with (Tetrahydro-2H-pyran-2, 3, 4, 5-tetrol) n. The yield production and the nature of the drug helps to study the safety and efficacy of the crude drug analysis and the formulations prescribed for the treatment of various illness. This helps in the analysis and standardization of natural products in the pharmaceutical care.

The Table 7.5 summarizes the Preliminary phytochemical constituents that are present in *Boswellia serrata* leaves extracts. Various primary and secondary metabolites such as carbohydrates, proteins, steroids, alkaloids, polyphenols like tannins, flavonoids, triterpenes and saponins has been detected in the preliminary phytochemical screening of the crude extracts of *Boswellia serrata*.

These bioactives synthesized during various metabolic pathways of the plant helps in curing the diseases without side effects or least effects. They resembles to various synthetic drugs as a structural analogues that are being used in pharmaceutical products. To assay these phytoconstituents a preliminary antihelmintic screening carried out showed the effective results from the two test samples i.e. ethanolic extract (EE) and aqueous extracts (AE) use for antihelmintic screening purpose.

The EE and AE used to evaluate anthelmintic activity, showed variable effective results at different concentrations with the mean time values. As in table 6 the significant result was exhibited in the concentration 50, 75 and 100 mg/ml of both extracts when compared with the standard drug Piperazine citrate. The activity was assayed by the observation of the helminthes with the paralysis and the death at different concentrations and varying time intervals in each case.

Table 7.1: Drugs Obtained from Herbs and Plants, Source, Therapeutic Activity and their Synthetic or Semi-synthetic Analogs.

Sl.No.	Drugs from herbs and plants	Source	Therapeutic activity	Synthetic or synthetic analogs
1	Atropine	*Atrobelladoma*	Antimuscarinics	Dicyclomine HCl, Hyoscinebuty 1bromide
2	Benzyle penicillin	*Penicillin chrysogenum*	Antibiotic	Ampicillin amoxicillin.
3	Codeine	*Papaversom- niferum*	Analgesic	Nolorphine mepiridine.
4	Camptothecine	*Campto thecaaccummata*	Anticancer	10-hydroxy- captothecine, aminocamptot hecine topotecan, ironotecan.
5	Digoxin	*Digitalis lanata*	Cardiovascular	—
6	Ephedrine	*Ephedra vulgaris*	Anti-asthma	Salbutamol, salmeterol.
7	Lovastatin	*Asparagillusterrus*	hypercho- lesterolemia	Pravastatin.
8	Morphine	*Papavesomniferum*	Analgesic	Heroine, naloxane, phthadine.

9	Podophyllotoxine	*Podophillum-petatum*	Anticancer	Etopside, toniposide.
10	Quinine	*Cinchona succirubra*	Antimalerial	Chloroquine, meploquinine, pamaquine, premquine.
11	Reserpine	*Rawolfiaserpentina*	Hypotension and anticholinergic	—
12	Tubacurarine	*Tube Neuromuscul curare*	Decamethoxiar blocking agent	um, soxamethorium.
13	Taxol	*Taxusb accata*	Anticancer	—
14	Teprotide	*Bathrops*	Antihypertensive	Captopril, enalapril, lisinopril.
15	Vinblastin. vincristine	*Cathramt-husroseus*	Anticancer	Vindesine.

However, when observed the response of worms in case of paralysis, there was significant variation among the results produced by both the extracts. The EE showed more significant effect on paralyzing the worms, in terms of paralysistime, at every concentration compared to that of AE. The effect of extracts on the paralysis (or) helminthiasis of the worm, as in Table 7.6 may be indicated. This may be due to the presence of active phytoconstituents and there potentiality for the antihelmintic activity. The polyphenols such as tannins in both the extracts may be one of the major causes for helminthiasis. These Tannins, the polyphenolic compounds, are shown interfere with energy generation in helminth parasites by uncoupling oxidative phosphorylation or, binds to the glycoprotein on the cuticle of parasite98, and cause death. Coming to the chemistry of nematode surface, it is a collagen rich extracellular matrix (ECM) providing protective cuticle that forms exoskeleton, and is critical for viability, the collagen is a class of proteins that are modified by a range co-and post-translational modification prior to assembly into higher order complexes (or) ECMS99. The mammalian skin also consists largely of collagen in the form of fibrous bundles. In leather making industry, vegetable tannins are commonly used in the tanning operation of leather processing that imparts stability to collagen of skin matrix through its reactivity and hence make the collagen molecule aggregate into fibres. This results in the loss of flexibility in the collagen matrix and gain of mechanical property with improved resistance to the thermal (or) microbial/enzymatic attack. Similar kind of reaction is expected to take place between the nematode cuticle (the earth worm) and the tannin of Enicostemmalittorale, possibly by linking through hydrogen bonding, as proposed in this study. This form of reactivity brings toughness in the skin and hence the worms become immobile and non-functional leading to paralysis followed by death.

84   *Salai Gum*

Group I Control (ulcer induced)

Group II Lansoprazole

Group III Ethanolic extract

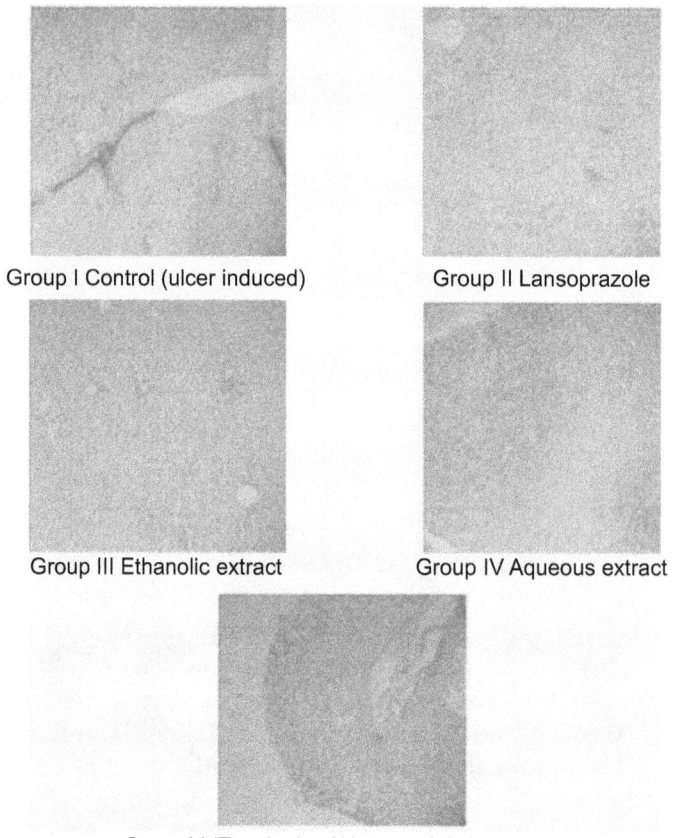

Group IV Aqueous extract

Group V (Tetrahydro-2H-pyran-2,3,4,5-tetrol)

With the confirmed preliminary screening by phytochemical analysis and antihelmintic activity carriedout, the ethanolic extract subjected for column chromatography has led with the successful isolation of various chemical constituents. Among them, the pure compound isolated from the elution of chloroform: methanol in the ratio 20:80, checked on TLC for the presence of single spot was further assayed through various spectral analysis such as IR, H1 NMR and GCMS. The interpretation of the data obtained by the IR studies reveals that peaks obtained at different wavelengths as described in results chapter, clearly signifies the presence of allyl C-H bond, the number of both the primary and secondary –OH groups, and the lactone ring system present in the molecule obtained. In case of H1NMR spectra, various absorption peaks obtained shows the presence of $CH-CH_2$ protons in the molecules with the number of fragment ion above 300 m/z. The spectral data do not contain aromatic ring system but the presence of polysaccharide with the primary and secondary –OH groups. The mass spectral studies signified the presence of various polysaccharide fragments giving rise to pentose monomer which has been substantiated at the ionic concentration with the base peak of 73 m/z.

Thus with spectral analysis of IR, H1 NMR and GCMS, has paved a tentative structural illustration of the pure compound (Tetrahydro- 2H-pyran-2, 3, 4, 5-tetrol) n and its monomer, a pentose called Tetrahydro-2H-pyran-2, 3, 4, 5- tetrol. Thus this pure compound has been successfully isolated and subjected for biological screening to check its antiulcer property as per the tribal practice is concerned with the administration of crude drug of *Boswellia serrata* without proper scientific investigation carriedout. It is generally accepted that gastric ulcers results from an imbalance between aggressive factors and the maintenance of the mucosal integrity through the endogenous defense mechanism100. Peptic ulcer results due to overproduction of gastric acid (or) decrease in gastric mucosal production. Further, the role of free radicals is also reported in the indication of ulcers. Prostate gland (PG) offer protection to duodenum through both increases in mucosal resistance as well as decrease in aggressive factors, mainly acid and Pepsin. Pylorus ligation induced ulcers are due to auto digestion at the gastric mucosa and breakdown of the gastric mucosal barrier. In case of pyloric ligation, ulcer formation is mainly due to the stasis at the gastric juice and stress. Prior to the biological activity, the effectiveness and the lethality of the drug has to be assayed to avoid unnecessary cruelty, trial and error methods carriedout on the experimental animals. Hence based upon the OECD 420, the oral acute toxicity studies carriedout has successfully fixed an effective dose of 250 mg/kg of both the EE and AE, and 40 mg/kg in case of the isolated compound, (Tetrahydro-2H-pyran-2, 3, 4, 5- tetrol) n.

Table 7.7 summarizes the effect of *Boswellia serrata* on the volume of gastric secretion, free acidity, total acidity and pH following pylorus ligation in rats. In case of volume of gastric secretion, a significant reduction in the Volume of gastric juice was exhibited in Group V ($P < 0.001$) and ($P < 0.05$) was seen in Group III and IV. In the free acidity parameter, a significant reduction in free acidity was exhibited in Group IV and V ($P < 0.001$) and ($P < 0.05$) in Group III. In case of total acidity assay, a significant reduction in total acidity was seen in Group III and V ($P < 0.001$) while Group IV showed least significant, $P < 0.05$. The acidic and basic balance plays an important role in antiulcer effect. In case of ulceration there is increase in H^+ ion concentration. The case of effect of PH studies, there was significant reduction of H^+ ion concentration in Group III and V ($P < 0.001$). No significant was found in Group IV. All the parameters studied in the gastric secretion produced due to the pylorus ligation in rats were compared with Group II, Lansoprazole.

Table 7.8 shows the effect of *Boswellia serrata* on pylorus ligation induced ulceration in rats. In this assay, the ulcer index and percentage of ulcer protection was found. The ulcer index in Group V ($P< 0.001$) and Group III and IV ($P < 0.01$) showed significant reduction compared to Group II, Lansoprazole.

The anti-secretory activity of the extracts noticed in pylorus ligation induced ulcer model, which decreased in the volume of gastric juice, reduction in free and total acidity and pH in the animals treated with the test samples may be due to the presence of potential and curative phytoconstituents present in *Boswellia serrata* and was found to be devoid of ulcerogenic potential. Literature review suggests that the majority of the antiulcer activity proposed in various models of antiulcer studies by pylorus ligation, aspirin and ethanol induced ulcer models has been attributed with antiulcer property due to the various active constituents like flavonoids, tannins, terpenes, steroids, Saponins, alkaloids and glycosides responsible as antiulcerogenic agents. Significant results without any toxicity has also been exhibited in the polyherbalformulation.

The Histopathological studies in pylorus ligation induced ulcer in rats as shown in Figure 7.16 exemplifies the comparative histopathological studies in various groups based upon the accessing the presence or absence of the redness, infiltration, congestion, hemorrhagic sticks, inflammation, necrosis and dilation of blood vessels. In Figyre 7.16a, Group I showed the ulcerogenic wounds with the presence of redness, infiltration, congestion, hemorrhagic sticks, inflammation, necrosis and dilation of blood vessels in the mucosa of the tissue. This is due to the interruption of the ulcerogenic agents on the parietal cells of gastric mucosal layer causing the disruption of the structural and functional aspects of gastric cells leading to the abnormal production of the gastric contents with decrease in pH and inhibited enzymatic activity and auto destruction of gastric cells. Group II, when treated with Lansoprazole shows the mild redness, no inflammation and dilation of blood vessels in the mucosa. Group III, when treated with ethanolic extract, the mucosa showed the mild inflammation and congested blood vessels. Group IV, treated with aqueous extract exhibited fibrosis and mild inflammation in mucosa. No inflammation and no congestion of blood vessels was seen in Group V, treated with (Tetrahydro- 2H-pyran-2, 3, 4, 5-tetrol) n. Changes in the histopathological view in various groups treated test samples may be attributed due to the dose dependence, mode of action, intensity and the potential efficacy of the drugs administered in the ulcerogenic animals as shown in Figure 7.16b – 7.16e.

Thus the *Boswellia serrata* has been successfully screened with antiulcer activity possessing various phytoconstituents exhibiting the curative property and can be further analyzed for various pharmacological screening and formulations to produce the scientific evidence abbot the usage of the plants used by the non-registered practitioners just based upon the collection and compilation of tribal and folklore knowledge.

CONCLUSSION

Herbs are an integral part of nature containing natural substances that can promote good health. Natural product especially those derived from plant sources is gaining much interest for therapeutic use than that of the conventional ones. This is due to development of resistance and unwanted side effects. But natural product exhibit minimal resistance and negligible side effects though they are well tolerated. The isolation of biologically active phytoconstituents such as alkaloids, Quinine, serpentine, reserpine, narcotine, caffeine, nicotine, etc is due to the result of initial leads obtained from the traditional system of medicine. Explanation of chemicalof plants and pharmacological screening may provide us the basis for the developing the leads for the development of novel agents for curative purposes for treating diseases like diabetes, cancer, sexually transmitted diseases neurological and immunological disorders etc.

The investigation carriedout on *Boswellia serrata*based upon the literature survey from the alternative system of medicine has made to establish the scientific basis of knowledge developed by the phytochemical and pharmacological screening. During this study various phytoconstituents were detected and screened successfully by the antihelminti. This has led to isolate the pure compounds and study their biological activity. isolated polysaccharide so called as Tetrahydro-2H-pyran-2, 3, 4, 5-tetrol) n screened for antiulcer activity along with other crude extract exhibited significant reduction in antiulcer activity.

Thus it could be concluded that the *Boswellia serrata* possess various bioactive compounds that can be used for the treatment of various diseases based upon the experimental evidences established in our studies. Furthermore, a detailed study needs to be carriedout to establish proper and complete scientific evidence to establish a novel drug formulation with least or no side effects. It is also mandatory to screen the isolated compounds with various pharmacological activities and the mechanisms of action of the drugs needs to be understood.

8. Phytochemical and Pharmacological Studies of *Boswellia serrata*

Boswellia serrata Roxb ex Colebr (*Kundur*) belonging to family *Burseraceae*, is commonly known as 'Salai' or 'Salia' in Orissa. The tree is commonly found in West Asia, Oman, Yemen, South Africa, Southern Arabia and many parts of India (Western Himalayas, Rajasthan, Gujarat, Maharashtra, Madhya Pradesh, Bihar, Orissa). A medium to large sized, deciduous tree; up to 18m in height and 2.4 m in the girth (normally 1.5m); The bark of this plant is thin, greenish grey, yellow or reddish and finally turning to ash colour, peeling off in smooth, exfoliating papery flakes; blaze pinkish and exuding small drops of resin. The leaves alternate, imparipinnate, 30-45 cm long, ex-stipulate and crowded at the end of the branches. The leaflets are 2.5-6.3 × 1.2-3.0cm, ovate or ovate-lanceolate, 8-15 in number, nearly sessile with short toothed, mostly pubescent. The flowers are bisexual, small, white in axillary racemes or panicles at the tip of the branches. The calyx is small cupular and 5-6 lobed. The petals are 0.5-0.8 cm oblong-ovate with basal disk.. The fruits are cotyledous, trifed, 1.25 cm long, trigonous, splitting into three valves. Seeds are heart-shaped and attached to the inner angle of the fruit, compressed, pendulous.

OLEO-GUM-RESIN

It is an exudate, which comes out from cortex after an injury or natural crack in the bark. It is fragrant, transparent and golden yellow. After solidification it turns into brownish yellow tears or drops and crusts. Its size varies from pea size to walnut size. The smell is agreeable. The oleo-gum-resin is tapped by shaving off a thin band of bark about 20 cm wide and 30 cm long, at a height of 15 cm from the base of the tree. This initial blaze should be made to a depth of about half the thickness of the bark, viz. up to 0.75 cm. Tapping should start from November and stopped before the monsoon. The number of blazes required depends upon the girth of the tree. For a tree of 90 cm girth, one blaze may be made, and for every increase of 50 cm girth one more blaze may be added. Blazes may be made horizontally leaving approximately equal space between them. The length or height of the blaze is to be increased by about 1.6 cm in fortnightly and 0.8 cm in weekly freshening every time on the upper edge. The surface already blazed or freshened may not be scraped. For continuous tapping on a 3-year cycle, the bole may be divided into three zones, each one being tapped for one year. For making another horizontal row of blazes in the subsequent year 7.5 cm space may be left above the blazed portions. The horizontal blazes of the subsequent years should be alternating or staggering with the preceding ones. Again alternating the blazes within the same zone, the blazed portions may be given complete rest for six years during which period the wounds heal up and are ready for fresh tapping. The oleo-gum-resin is scrapped off and collected in a circular tray suitably placed around the trunk. It is collected in a semi-solid state and the vegetable impurities are manually removed. It is then kept in baskets up to 30 days on a cemented and sloping floor, whence the fluid portion containing the volatile oil is collected and used in paints and varnishes. The remaining semi-solid to solid part is mainly gum-resin which is thoroughly dried and sometimes treated with soapstone powder to make it brittle. It is then broken into small pieces, cleaned and graded for marketing.

Following kinds of oleo-gum-resin (*Kundur*) have been described in Unani literature:

1. *Kundur*-unsa (Female), Deep pale tears 2. *Kundur*zakar (Male) Yellow tea 3. *Kundur* Mudahraj Artificial tears 4. Kishar *Kundur* (Karfa) (It contains bark or scurf tears) and 5. *Kundur* Dukak Dust of gum According to Unani philosophers '*Kundur* zakar' mentioned at serial number 2 above, is red in colour, considered the best in quality and can be stored up to 20 years. It is also mentioned that the *Kundur* unsa is white and mostly found in India. Usually the gum is white or yellow in colour but when old, it become ruby or blackish-red or some time golden colour. The smell of '*Kundur*-Zakar' is very similar to the smell of Mastagi (Pistacia trebinthus Linn.). The purity can be checked by the burning of the gum which gives the flames, while adulterated gum gives only smoke. *Kundur* is being used for various ailments such as dysentery, dyspepsia, lung diseases, haemorrhoids, rheumatism, urinary disorders and corneal ulcer in Unani system of medicine for the last several years. It is also an ingredient in certain compound formulations viz: *Majoon Kundur, Majoon Murawwah-ul-Arwah, Dawa-ul-Kibrit* and *Habbe Suzak* of Unani medicine used in renal disorders. Oleo-gum resin of *Boswellia serrata* Roxb (*Kundur*) possesses Anti-fungal, Anti-complementary, Juvenomimetic and Anti-carcinogenic properties. Investigations on *Kundur* revealed its beneficial effects in Immunomodulation, Bronchial asthma, Polyarthritis, Hepatitis C-virus, Colitis and Crohn's disease.

MIZAJ (TEMPERAMENT)

1. The temperament (mizaj) of *Kundur* (*Boswellia serrata*) is mentioned as Hot1 Dry2 temperament.

Action (Afal)

Kundur (Oleo-gum resin of *Boswellia serrata*) is recorded as Dafe humma (Antipyretic), Dafe khafqan (Palpitation), Dafe Tafun (Antiseptic), Mudire haiz (Emmenagogue), Muhallile auram (Anti-inflammatory), Muhallile reyah (Carminative), Muhallile Khoone Munjamid (Thrombolytic), Muharrike dam (Haemodynamic), Muhazil (Antiobesity), Muqavvie bah (Aphrodisiac), Muqavvie Qalb (Cardiotonic), Qatile kirm (Antihelmenthic), and Tiryaq (Antidote) in classical Unani texts.

Istemal (Therapeutic Uses)

Kundur (Oleo-gum resin of *Boswellia serrata*) is used for the treatment of Amraze jild (Skin diseases), Atshak (Syphilis), Nafe kasrate boul (Polyuria), Nafe suzak (Gonorrhoea), Nafe Ziabetes (Diabetes), Simane mufrat (Anti-obesity), and Wajaul mufasil (Arthritis).

PHYTOCHEMICAL STUDIES

The chemistry of *Kundur* (oleo gum resin) of *Boswellia serrata* is now thoroughly worked out. Sample of oleo gum resin analysed by Imperial Institute London showed following composition:-Moisture – 10 – 11%, volatile oil 8 – 9% resin 55 – 57%, Gum 20 – 23%, Insoluble matter 4 – 5%. (Try and find some recent reference for analysis of *Kundur*. The constituents can be grouped as under: A: Oil, B. Terpenoids and Gum.

A. Oil

The fixed oil is usually pale yellow in colour and has an agreeable odour. Essential oil is obtained in yield of up to 16% oleo-gum-resin by steam distillation. The specific gravity of essential oil is 0.8470; D 280, +240; nD 280, 1.4574; acid value, 0.76; ester value, 8.5; ester value after acetylation, 42.8; and iodine value, 182. ? and ?–pinenes were reported as the main constituents of oil. Simonson studied the low boiling fractions of the oil and found ?- thujene and major constituent ?–pinenes and ?–phellandrene in small quantities. High boiling fractions worked out in detail by the presence of terpenol, methyl chavicol and sesquiterpenes as the major components. On the basis of spectral data and interconversion isolation of acetyl-?-boswellic acid has also been reported. The methods for separation of essential oil, resin & gum, characteristics and uses of essential oil.

The physico-chemical characteristics of oil are quite variable because of the diversified sources. The constituents of the oil are ?-pinene dipentene, phellendrene, cadinene, camphene, p-cymene, d-borneol, verbenone and verbenol. Girgune *et al.*, have reported the presence of ?-thujene (50%), ?-pinene 6.2%, dlimonene (4.5%), p-cymene (14%), cadinene (4%), geraniol (0.8%) and elemol (1.3%) as the main constituents of the essential oil. The ? and ?-pinenes, and d-emonene as the major constituents. In the presence of terpinyl acetate 3.5%, methyl chavical 2%, linalool 1.5% and terpinol 1% is reported. Composition of essential oil prepared by steam distillation.

B. Terpenoids

Three triterpene acids, ???? and ?--boswellic acids by the use of barium hydroxide as precipitant. The constitution of ? & ? Boswellic acids have been described. Ruzicka *et al.*, 1940 converted ?-boswellic acid into ?-amyrin. They prepared surfactants from these acids. Bilhma *et al.*, have assigned the position of –COOH group in ?-boswellic acid. Ruzicka *et al.*, carried out various reactions in the ring A & B of the Boswellic acid and its derivatives. Beton *et al.*, have described the chemistry of triterpene and related compounds with special reference to isolation of ?-boswellic acid. A review with emphasis on Boswellic acid and abietic acids have been written by which describes the NMR and Mass spectrometry of triterpenes. ?-sitosterol from the bark of *B. serrata* has been isolated.

Critical examination of the non volatile fraction of the resin has been done by and has led to the isolation of terpene acids and several neutral products including methyl chavicol, ?- and 3-amyrins and a new diterpene alcohol serratol, four tetracyclic triterpene acids and four pentacyclic triterpene acids viz. 3-?-acetoxytirucall-8, 24-dien-2l-oic acid ($C_{32}H_{50}O_4$, m.p.2200), 3-ketotirucall-8, 24-dien-21-oic acid ($C_{30}H_{46}O_3$, m.p.2120), 3-?-hydroxytirucall-8, 24-dien-21-oic acid, 3-?- hydroxytirucall-8, 24-dien-21-oic acid ($C_{30}H_{48}O_3$, m.p.1980), ?-boswellic acid, acetyl-?-boswellic acid ($C_{32}H_{48}O_4$, m.p.2530), acetyl-11-keto-?-boswellic acid ($C_{32}H_{48}O_5$, m.p.2710) and 11-keto-?-boswellic acid ($C_{30}H_{46}O_4$, m.p.1950). Two new triterpenoids, 2?- 3?-dihydroxy-urs-12-ene-24-oic acid and urs-12-ene-3?, 24-diol, have been isolated from the gum resin of *Boswellia serrata*. Non aqueous titrimetric method was developed by for the estimation of total triterpene acids present in different forms of *B. serrata* on the basis of ?-boswellic acid which constitutes more than 30% of the total triterpene acids. Total triterpene acids include? ?-?boswellic, 11 ketoboswellic and acetyl 11-keto ?-boswellic acids. Estimation of triterpene acids alone or in combination of two was done using functional groups analysis. The functional groups analyzed were acetyl and hydroxyl groups at 3 position and keto group at the 11-position.

C. Gum

Analysis of Oleo-gum resin yielded: Moisture 10-11%, volatile oil 8-9% resin 55-57%, Gum 20-23%, insoluble matter 4-5%, have given methods of separation of the oleo gum resin into its various constituents and have also examined gum enzymes as diastase and oxidase. The gum contains 0.16% of nitrogen. Malandkar, 1925 has hydrolyzed the gum by heating it with 3% H_2SO_4 for 8 hours and identified sugars as arabinose, xylose and galactose. Sharma *et al.*, 1980 revealed that the emulsion prepared from *B. serrata* was slightly better than those prepared with acacia gum. Emulsifying properties of Na-Boswellata, which was found suitable for the preparation of emulsions for internal administration has been reported. Tablets prepared with 9% B.serrata mucilage were comparable to those prepared with 5% Acacia mucilage. Ashis *et al.*, isolated 4-O-methyl-glucuronoarabinogalactan from the water soluble protein of gum resin.

PHARMACOLOGICAL STUDIES

Analgesic and Psychopharmacological Effects

The *Boswellia serrata* (*Kundur*) exhibited marked analgesic activity in experimental animals in addition to its sedative effect. *Boswellia serrata* (*Kundur*) have found that it produces reduction in the spontaneous motor activity and causes ptosis in rats.

Anti-complementary Activity of Boswellic Acids (BA) –an Inhibitor of C3-Convertase

Boswellia serrata (*Kundur*) is found to possess anticomplementary activity. It inhibited in vitro immunohaemolysis of antibody-coated sheep erythrocytes by pooled guinea-pig serum. The reduced immunohaemolysis was found to be due to inhibition of C3-convertase of the classical complement pathway. The threshold concentration for inhibiting C3-convertase was found to be 100 micrograms. However, higher concentrations of BA showed constant inhibitory effects on immunohaemolysis. BA also exhibited weak inhibitory effects on individual components of the complement system. In vivo administration of BA also showed the inhibitory effect on guinea-pig serum.

Antifungal Activity of *B. serrata*

Boswellia serrata yield 0.6 percent of essential oil upon hydrodistillation. The oil has weak antifungal activity against human pathogens, and highly effective against plant pathogens, where it inhibited the tested organisms viz. Pytophothora parasifica.

Anti-hyperlipidmic Activity

Serum cholesterol and triglycerides levels, deposits of fat, in different organs and area of body of the rabbit, fed on high cholesterol and saturated fat containing diet, was noted and found the deposits in various organs including iris was significantly less marked in the Salai gum treated group. The protective effect was established, whereas, several effects was also confirmed in the other experiments. The effect was probably at the biosynthesis level. This mechanism of action was studied by incorporating the U-C14 acetate in cholesterol biosynthesis. They also suggested that Salai gum is mainly effective in checking the rats of biosynthesis and partly effective in enhancing the excretion of cholesterol. The alcoholic extract, tested at different dose level in 25-50 mg/kg. p.o. doses, shows anti-hyperlipidemic activity on hypercholesterolinic animals decrease the 30-50% in cholesterol level and 20-60% triglycerides level.

Anti-artherosclerotic Agent

The anti-artherosclerotic activity was taken up in rabbits fed on the diet containing cholesterol and saturated fat. Four groups of rabbits (five in each group) were employed and kept on high liquid diet for three months. DAESG treatment was started on day 50 in one group, day 90 in second and continued up to day 150. The other two served as controls. Serum cholesterol and triglycerides levels, deposits of fat in different organs and areas of the body including that in iris was significantly less marked in DAESG treated group as compared to control. Antiartherosclerotic studies made on rabbits fed on high lipid diet for three months showed that treatment with DAESG decreased serum cholesterol and triglyceride levels by 32-46% and 53-62% respectively, monitored at weekly intervals. DAESG treatment showed both prevention and reversal of artheroscelortic process as was evident from the start of high lipid diet.

Anti-inflammatory and Anti-arthritic Activities

Anti-inflammatory and anti-arthritic activities have been tested against carrageen in-induced paw oedema adjuvant arthritis in rats. DAESG treatment caused inhibition of the carrageen in induced rat hind paw oedema by 39.75% and 65-73%, administered orally (p.o) in dose ranges of 50-200 mg per kg-1 and interaperitoneal (i.p.) in dose range of 50-100 mg per kg respectively compared to 47% inhibition seen with phenylbutazone (50 mg/kg-1 p.o.). The anti-inflammatory effect was equally well marked in adrenalectomized rats. In the anti-arthritic study on the mycobacterial adjuvant-induced poly-arthritis in rats, salai guggal showed 34% and 49% inhibition of paw swelling with 50 and 100 mg per kg (p.o.) doses respectively as compared to controls. Phenyl butazone in doses of 50 and 100 mg per kg (p.o.) showed 26% and 60% inhibition respectively. The in vivo effect of a herbal based, non-steroidal anti-inflammatory product salai guggal, prepared from the gum resin exudates of *Boswellia serrata* active principle 'boswellic acids" on glycosaminoglycan metabolism has been studied in male albino rats. The biosynthesis of sulfated glycosaminoglycan evaluated by the uptake of [35S] sulfate, and the content of glycosaminoglycan were measured in specimens of skin, liver, kidney and spleen.

Statistical analysis of the data obtained with respect to the boswellic acids and salai guggal were compared with those of ketoprofen. A significant reduction in glycosaminoglycan biosynthesis was observed in rats treated with all of the drugs. Glycosaminoglycan content was found to be decreased in the ketoprofen-treated group, where as that of the boswellic acids or salai guggal treated groups remained unaltered. The catabolism of glycosaminoglycan was followed by estimating the activities of lysosomal glycohydrolases, namely be glucuronidase, beta-Nacetylglucosaminidase, cathepsin B1, cathpsin B2 at cathepsin D, in tissues and by estimating the urinary excretion and hexosami and uronic acid. The degradation of glycosaminoglycan was found to be reduced markedly in all drug-treated animals as compared to controls. The potential significance of boswellic acids and salai guggal was discussed in the light of changes in the metabolism of glycosaminoglycan.

Curcumine from Curcuma longa and the gum resin of *Boswellia serrata*, which was demonstrated to act as anti-inflammatory in in-vivo animal models, was studied in a set of in vitro experiments in order to elucidate the mechanism of their beneficial effects. Curcumine inhibited the 5-lipoxygenase activity in rat peritoneal neutrophils as well as the 12-lipoxygenase and the cyclooxygenase activities in human platelets. In a cell free peroxidation system curcumine exerted strong antioxidative activity. Thus, its effects on the dioxygenases is probably due to its reducing capacity. Boswellic acids was isolated from the gum resin of *Boswellia serrata* and identified as the active principles. Boswellic acids inhibited the leukotriene synthesis via 5- lipoxygenase, but did not affect the 12-lipoxygenase and the cyclooxygenase activities. Additionally, boswellic acids did not impair the peroxidation of arachidonic acid by iron and ascorbate. The data suggest that boswellic acids are specific, non-redox inhibitors of leukotriene synthesis either interacting directly with 5-lipoxygenase or blocking its translocation.

Anti-microbial and Anti-oxidant Effect

The essential oil of *Boswellia serrata* was analysed by GC and GC-MS, and their antimicrobial and anti-oxidant activity tested. The volatile oil exhibited considerable inhibitory effect against all tested organisms. The oil also demonstrated anti-oxidant activity comparable with alpha-tocopherol and butylated hydroxytoluene (BHT). Extracts of gum resins was found to be active against six text organisms-Staphylococcus aureus, Escherichia coli, Klebsiella species, *Pseudomonas* aeruginosa, Proteus mirabilis and Bacillus subtilis.

Anti-tumor and Anti-carcinogenic Activities

Boswellin (BE), a methanol extract of the gum resin exudates of *Boswellia serrata*, contains naturally occurring triterpenoids, beta boswellic acid and its structural related derivatives. Topical application of BE to the backs of mice markedly inhibited 12-O-tetradecanoylphorbol-13-acetate (TPA)-induced increase in skin inflammation, epidermal proliferation, the number of epidermal cell layers and tumor promotion in 7, 12-dimethylbenz[a]anthracene (DMBA)-initiated mice. Feeding 0.2% of BE in the diet to CF-1 mice for 10-24 weeks reduced the accumulation of parametrial fat pad weight under the abdomen, and inhibited azoxymethane (AOM)-induced formation of aberrant crypt foci (ACF) by 46%. Addition of pure beta boswellic acid, 3-O-acetyl-beta-boswellic acid, 11-keto-beta-boswellic acid or 3-Oacetyl-11-keto-beta-boswellic acid to human leukemia HL-60 cell culture inhibited DNA synthesis in HL-60 cells in a dose dependent manner with IC50 values ranging from 0.6 to 7.1 microM. These results indicate that beta-boswellic acid and its derivatives (the major constituents of Boswellin) have anticarcinogenic, anti-tumor and anti-hyperlipidemic activitie.

Effects of *Boswellia serrata* in Chronic Colitis

Patients studied were suffered from chronic colitis characterized by vague lower abdominal pain, bleeding per rectum with diarrhoea and palpable tender descending and sigmoid colon. The inflammatory process in colitis is associated with increased formation of leukotrienes causing chemotaxis, chemokinesis, synthesis of superoxide radicals and release of lysosomal enzymes by phagocytes. The key enzyme for leukotriene biosynthesis is 5- lipoxygenase. Boswellic acids were found to be non-redox, noncompetitive specific inhibitors of the enzyme 5-lipoxygenase. The gum resin of *Boswellia serrata* was studied for the treatment of this disease. Thirty patients, 17 males and 13 females in the age range of 18 to 48 years with chronic colitis were included in this study.

Twenty patients were given a preparation of the gum resin of *Boswellia serrata* (900 mg daily divided in three doses for 6 weeks) and ten patients were given sulfasalazine (3 gm daily divided in three doses for 6 weeks) and served as controls. Out of 20 patients treated with *Boswellia* gum resin 18 patients showed an improvement in one or more of the parameters; including stool properties, histopathology as well as scanning electron microscopy, besides haemoglobin, serum iron, calcium, phosphorus, proteins, total leukocytes and eosinophils. In the control group 6 out of 10 patients showed similar results with the same parameters. Out of 20 patients treated with *Boswellia* gum resin 14 went into remission while in case of sulfasalazine remission rate was 4 out of 10. In conclusion, this study shows that a gum resin preparation from *Boswellia serrata* could be effective in the treatment of chronic colitis with minimal side effects.

Effects of *Boswellia serrata* Gum Resin in Bronchial Asthma

The gum resin of *Boswellia serrata*, known in Ayurvedic system of medicine as Salai guggal, contains boswellic acids, which have been shown to inhibit leukotriene biosynthesis. In a double-blind, placebo-controlled study forty patients, 23 males and 17 females in the age range of 18-75 years having mean duration of illness, bronchial asthma, of 9.58 +/– 6.07 years were treated with a preparation of gum resin of 300 mg thrice daily for a period of 6 weeks. 70% of patients showed improvement of disease as evident by disappearance of physical symptoms and signs such as dysponea, rhonchi, number of attacks, increase in FEV subset l, FVC and PEFR as well as decrease in eosinophilic count and ESR. In the control group of 40 patients 16 males and 24 females in the age range of 14-58 years with mean of 32.95 +/– 12.68 were treated with lactose 300 mg thrice daily for 6 weeks. Only 27% of patients in the control group showed improvement. The data show a definite role of gum resin of *Boswellia serrata* in the treatment of bronchial asthma.

Effects of *Boswellic* Acids Extracted on Autoimmune Encephalomyelitis

Mixed acetyl boswellic acids, pentacyclic triterpenes extracted from the gum resin of *Boswellia serrata* Roxb., significantly inhibited the ionophore-stimulated release of the leukotrienes (LT) B4 and C4 from intact human polymorphonuclear neutrophil leukocytes (PMNLs), with IC50 values of 8.48 micrograms/ml and 8.43 micrograms/ml, respectively. Purified acetyl-11-keto-beta-boswellic acid was about three times more potent as inhibitor of the formation of both LTB4 (IC50 = 2.53 micrograms/ml) and LTC4 (IC50=2.26 micrograms/ml) from human PMNLs in the same assay. The comparative agent MK 886 (3-[1-(4-chlorobenzyl)-3-t-butyl-thio-5-isopropylindol-2-yl-]-2, 2-dimethylpropanoic acid, L-663, 536, CAS 118, 414-82-7) was about 10 to 100-fold more active than the boswellic acids in inhibiting. The formation of 5-lipoxygenase products in human PMNLs, with IC50 values of 0.0068 microgram/ml (LTB4) and 0.49 microgram/ml (LTC4). After daily intraperitoneal dosage the extract of mixed acetyl boswellic acids (20 mg/kg) significantly reduced the clinical symptoms in guinea pigs with experimental autoimmune encephalomyelitis (EAE)\ between days 11 and 21. However, the inflammatory infiltrates in the brain and the spinal cord were not significantly less extensive in the treated animals than in the respective control group. The multiple intraperitoneal application of boswellic acids did not inhibit the ionophore-challenged ex vivo release of leukotrienes B4 and C4 from PMNLs separated from the blood of guinea pigs with EAE. The boswellic acids have been characterized as selective, non-redox and potent inhibitors of the biosynthesis of leukotrienes in vitro.

Effects of *Boswellia serrata* Gum Resin in Ulcerative Colitis

Ulcerative colitis is a chronic inflammatory disease of the colon where leukotrienes are suggested to play an important role for keeping inflammation active. Boswellic acids, the biologically active ingredients of the gum resin of *Boswellia serrata* (Sallai guggal), have been shown to be specific, nonredox and noncompetitive inhibitors of 5-lipoxygenase, the key enzyme of leukotriene biosynthesis. In patients suffering from ulcerative colitis grade II and III the effect of *Boswellia serrata* gum resin preparation (350 mg thrice daily for 6 weeks) on stool properties, histopathology and scan microscopy of rectal biopsies, blood parameters including Hb, serum iron, calcium, phosphorus, proteins, total leukocytes and eosinophils was studied. Patients receiving sulfasalazine (1gm thrice daily) served as controls. All parameters tested improved after treatment with *Boswellia serrata* gum resin, the results being similar compared to controls: 82% out of treated patients went into remissions in case of sulfasalazine remission rate was 75%.

Effects of *Boswellia serrata* in Polyarthritis

Boswellia serrata are used in India for the treatment of chronic polyarthiritis. Employing the main constituents of both plants i.e. curcumine and bosellic acids, their effects on the pathways of arachidonic acid cascade in stimulated polymorphnuclear neutrophiles (PMNL) and platelets have been studied. Extracts from the resin of *Boswellia serrata* in a dose related manner inhibited formation of 5-lipoxygenase products in PMNL. A similar effect was observed employing boswellic acids EC50 being 2-7 micro M. Curcuma exhibited an antioxidative effect in Fe/ascorbate-induced peroxidation of arachiodonic acid. Moreover, curcumine inhibited the formation of cyclooxygenase and 5-lipoxygenase as well as 12-lipoxygenase products.

Effect of *Boswellia serrata* in Hepatitis C-virus (HCV)

The methanolic and water extract of *Boswellia* species used in traditional medicine were screened for their inhibitory effects on hepatitis C-virus (HCV) protease (PR) using in vitro assay methods. The methanolic extract showed significant inhibitory activities.

Effect of *Boswellia serrata* on Liver and Cardiac Function

Efficacy of six different gums Acacia ((A), Tragacanth (B), Butea monosperma (C), *Boswellia* glabera (D), Balsamoderon mukul (E), and Melia azadirachta (F),were investigated for various biochemical parameters : ALAT, ASAT, LDH, CK, bilirubin,and albumin in serum of rabbits. The serum level of transaminases showed a significant increase with all gums A, C, D, E and F while the effect of gum B was not significant. The serum level of LDH was reduced with gums A, B, C, D and F. the serum level of CK was decrease with gums A, B, C, and E. The serum albumin level was not affected significantly by the gums investigated. The bilirubin level was elevated with gums A, E and F while it was decreased with gums B and C.

Effect on the Gonads of Male Dysedercus of *Boswellia serrata* Oil

Topical application of the essential oil from B.serrata on the freshly moulted fifth insets nymphs resulted in production of super nymphus adult nymphs. In the resultant from both spermatogenesis were seriously affected. Thus the essential oil can act as a effective insect growth regulation.

Immunomodulatory Effect of *Boswellia serrata*

Boswellic acid, a mixture of pentacyclic triterpene acids (BA) from *Boswellia serrata*, was investigated for their effect on cell mediated and humoral components of the immune system and the immunotoxicological potential. A single oral administration of BA (50-200 mg/kg) inhibited the expression of the 24 hr delayed type hypersensitivity (DTH) reaction and primary humoral response to SRBC in mice. The secondary response was appreciably enhanced at lower doses. In a multiple oral dose schedule Ba (25, 50 and 100 mg/kg) reduced the development of the 24h DTH reaction and complement fixing antibody titres and slightly enhanced the humoral antibody synthesis. In concentrations greater than 3.9 micro g/mL BA produced almost similar and dose related inhibition of proliferative responsiveness of splenocytes to mitogens and alloantigen. Preincubation of macrophages with different concentrations of BA enhanced the phagocytic function of adherent macrophages. Prolonged oral administration of BA (25-100 mg/kg/dx 21 days) increased the body weight, total leukocyte counts and humoral antibody titers in rats. It is not found to be cytotoxic or to cause immunosuppression.

Inhibitory Activity of Human Leukemia HL-60 Cells in Culture

Four major tritperpene acids including beta-boswellic acid, 3-O-acetyl-beta-boswellic acid, 11-keto-beta-boswellic acid, and 3-O-acetyl-11-keto-boswellic acid were isolated from the gum resin of *Boswellia serrata* and examined for their in vitro antitumor activity. They inhibited the synthesis of DNA, RNA and protein in human leukemia HL-60 cells in a dose dependent manner with IC50-values ranging from 0.6 to 7.1 microM. Among them, 3-Oacetyl-11-keto-beta boswellic acid induced the most pronounced inhibitory effects on DNA, RNA and protein synthesis with IC50 values of 0.6, 0.5 and 4.1 microM, respectively. Its effect on DNA synthesis was found to be irreversible. This compound significantly inhibited the cellular growth of HL-60 cells, but did not affect cell viability. Acetyl-11-keto-betaboswellic acid (AKBA) is a pentacylic triterpene isolated from *Boswellia serrata*, AKBA treated cells showed morphological changes like membrane blebbing and subsequent flow cytometric analysis of propidium-iodide stained cells indicated that the cells underwent apoptosis. This was confirmed by flow cytometric detection of sub-G1-peaks in AKBA treated cells. As inhibitors of topoisomerases are known to be potent inducers of apoptosis. The effect of AKBA on topoisomerase 1 from calf thymus in vitro was examined. In a DNA-relaxation assay with OX174RF DNA, AKBA inhibited topoisomerase 1 and IC50 being 20 micro M. This suggests that induction of apoptosis in HL60 and CCRF-CEM by AKBA might be topoisomerase 1.

Inhibition of 5-LO by Boswellic Acids

Boswellic acids represent the active principle of *Boswellia serrata* gum resin with antiphlogistic and antirheumatic properties. Among the Bas, 11-keto-beta-BA was the most potent. The presence of a carboxylic function and an 11-keto function has been reported to be crucial for the 5-lipoxygenase inhibiting property of this unique pentacyclic triterpene derivative. Pentacyclic triterpenes from the 11-keto-boswellic acid series were identified as the active principal ingredients of *Boswellia* resin, inhibiting the key enzyme of leukotriene biosynthesis, 5-lipoxygenase (5-LO). Of the genuine boswellic acids hitherto characterized, 3-O-acetyl-11-keto-beta-boswellic acid, AKBA proved to be the most potent inhibitor of 5-LO. In the course of purification of further boswellic acid derivatives from *Boswellia* resin, degradation of the natural compound 3-O-acetyl- 11-hydroxy-beta-boswellic acid to the thermodynamically more stable product 3-O-acetyl-9, 11-dehydro-beta-boswellic acid was observed. The metastable intermediate of this conversion, under moderate conditions of workup in methanolic solutions, was identified as 3-O-acetyl-11-methoxy-beta-boswellic acid.

Juvenomimetic Activity of *Boswellia serrata*

The essential oil from the gumoleoresin of *Boswellia serrata* showed juvenomimetic activity when tested at 1:10-4:50 acetone dilution on Dysdercus similes V instar nymphs. Its terpene constituents were characterized by GLC and GC-MS analysis.

Table 8.1: Evidence Based Scientific Validation of (*Boswellia serrata*) Kundur.

Therapeutic Uses and Actions	Unani & other alternative medicine References
Antiseptic	Ibne Sina, 1912; Azam Khan, 1314; Anonymous, 1988; Varier's, 1994; Kirtikar & Basu, 1995;
Anti fungal, anti microbial	Ibne sina, 19812; Azam Khan, 1314; Anonymous, 1988; Varier's 1 Kirtikar & Basu, 1995
Anti-inflammatory	Ibne sina, 19812; Azam Khan, 1314; Ghani, N.; 1917; Kirtikar & Basu, 1 Varier's, 1994; Nadkarni, 1976; Asolkar, L.V., 1992; Anonymous, 1988
Arthritis	Azam Khan, 1314; Ghani, N., 1917; Asolkar, L.V., 1992; Varier's 1 Anonymous, 1988
Anti-obesity Asthma Cardiotonic	Ghani, N., 1917; Nadkarni, 1970 Kirtikar & Basu, 1995; Varier's 1994 Ibne Sina, 19152; Azam Khan, 1314; Ghani, N., 1917; Ibne Rushd, 1 Asolkar, L.V., 1992
Anticonvulsant (Gastropathy) Aphrodisiac	Kirtikar & Basu, 1995; Chopra, R.N., 1986; Varier's 1994; Ibne Sina, 1912; Azam Khan, 1314; Ghani, N., 1917; Ibne Rushd, 1980 Azam Khan, 1314; Ghani N., 1917; Ibnr Rushd, 1980 Azam Khan, 1314; Ghani, N., 1917

CONCLUSION

This review literature provides evidence based scientific validation (Table 8.1) to some of the therapeutic uses and actions described for *Kundur* in classical texts of Unani medicine. It clearly reveals that phyto-chemicals particularly secondary metabolites reported so far from Oleo-gum resin (*Kundur*) of *Boswellia serrata* and related pharmacological activities justify its recorded therapeutic actions in Unani literature. For example: antifungal and antimicrobial activities reported from essential oil provides clear cut evidence for its recorded use as Dafe Tafun (Antiseptic) in Unani system of medicine. Similarly there are clear evidences that *Kundur* is one of the potential antiinflammatory and anti arthritic drug popularly used for the treatment of arthritis in Unani system of medicine since long (Table 8.1). It is further suggested that phytochemical and pharmacological studies on some of the less known or controversial Unani drugs may be taken up on priority basis not only to scientifically validate therapeutic actions/uses recorded, but revive the faith and confidence of Unani practitioners in its actions to serve the large strata of the rural society.

9. Immunomodulatory Triterpenoids from the Oleogum Resin of *Boswellia carterii*

Frankincense oleogum resin is obtained by incision of the bark of several species of *Boswellia, Burseraceae*. It is known as Olibanum, Luban Dakar, Bakhor or Kendar (In Arabic), and Salai Guggal (In Ayurvedic medicine). The plant is native to India, Arabian Peninsula (Yemen, Sultanate of Oman), Red Sea region of North-East Africa (Somalia, Eritrea). *Boswellia* resin and its individual components has shown various biological activities; including anti-inflammatory activity ; leukotriene biosynthesis- inhibitory activity ; and anti-tumor activity. Frankincense oleo gum resin is a complex mixture containing a series of mono-, sesqui-, di-, and triterpenoids. Both the alcoholic extract of the oleogum resin and boswellic acids (a mixture of triterpenoids obtained from the oleogum resin *Boswellia serrata*), influenced both cellular and humoral immune responses in rats and mice. The defatted alcoholic extract of *Boswellia serrata* caused almost total inhibition of the classical complement pathway of the immune system while α-boswellic acid demonstrated a marked inhibitory effect on both classical and alternate complement systems. The extracts of *Boswellia serrata* gum resin and its constituents, the boswellic acids (BAs), activated the mitogen-activated protein kinase (MAPK) p42 and (MAPK) p38 in isolated human polymorphonuclear leukocytes (PMNLs). In view of such activities of the oleogum resin and its components, we initiated a bioassayguided fractionation to monitor the immunomodulatory activity of the frankincense resin obtained from *Boswellia carterii* Birdwood.

RESULTS AND DISCUSSION

The isolated compounds were separated adopting bioassay-guided fractionation from the oleogum resin of *Boswellia carterii* Birdwood. Lymphocyte proliferation (mitogenesis) assay involves the study of a specific immune response. The assay investigates the mitogenic effect of the crude drug on T-lymphocyte proliferation. Anti-proliferative activity on T-lymphocyte culture indicates immunosuppression while promotion of T-lymphocyte proliferative response means immunostimulation. The results of the assay expressed in terms of the% lymphocyte transformation are shown in Table 9.1. The total alcoholic extract of frankincense oleogum resin and the volatile oil have shown a significant immunostimulant action on T-lymphocytes (90% lymphocyte proliferation) that is comparable to the standard immunostimulants viz. Echinaceae purpurea extract and (S)-2,3,5,6-tetrahydro-6-phenylimidazo[

2,1-b]thiazole hydrochloride (levamisole). The individual components of the resin elicited mild to moderate immunostimulant activity. LTA proved that the total extract exhibited a better activity than that of any of the isolated pure compounds. This may be partly attributed to the synergistic effect among the different components of the total extract.

The spectral data of compound 1 indicated that it is palmitic acid, based on the EI/MS molecular ion peak at m/z 256 confirming the molecular formula of $C_{16}H_{32}O_2$. The IR spectrum showed absorption bands at 1701 cmD1 (C=O), and 3321 cmD1 (ODH). The 13C-NMR spectrum showed the presence of 16 signals, the multiplicities of which were determined using APT experiment, that revealed the presence of one methyl signal at δ 14.2 that could be assigned to a terminal methyl (C-16), and fourteen methylene signals, one quaternary carbon signal. The 13C-NMR signal at δ 22.7, 24.7, 31.9, and 34.0 could be assigned to methylene carbons (C-15), (C-3), (C-14), and (C-2), respectively. The remaining methylene carbon signals from 29.1 to 29.7 ppm could be assigned to carbons from (C-4) to (C-13). The remaining quaternary carbon signal at δ 179.6 could be assigned to the carboxylic acid function (C-1). 1H-NMR of compound 1 showed the following signals, one methyl triplet at δ 0.83

Table 9.1: Results of Lymphocyte Transformation (Proliferation) Assay.

Extract, or compound	Concentration	% Transformation	TC_{50}*
Total alcoholic extract	1.00 mg/ml	90	0.55 mg/ml
Gum	1.00 mg/ml	20	2.50 mg/ml
Volatile oil	1.00 mg/ml	90	0.55 mg/ml
1 (palmitic acid)	0.0039 µM	10	0.0195 µM
2 (lupeol)	0.0023 µM	40	0.0029 µM
3 (acetyl-β-boswellic acid)	0.0020 µM	20	0.0050 µM
4 (acetyl-α-boswellic acid)	0.0020 µM	35	0.0029 µM
5 (3-oxo-tirucallic acid)	0.0022 µM	10	0.0110 µM
6 (acetyl-11-keto-β-boswellic acid)	0.0019 µM	45	0.0022 µM
7 (β-boswellic acid)	0.0022 µM	50	0.0022 µM
8 (3-hydroxy-tirucallic acid)	0.0022 µM	20	0.0055 µM
9 (11-keto-µ-boswellic acid)	0.0021 µM	25	0.0043 µM

*Concentration showing 50% lymphocyte transformation.

(3H, t) which could be assigned to terminal methyl group (H-16). A multiplet at δ 1.23 ppm that could be assigned to protons (H-4) to (H-15). A multiplet at δ 1.6 ppm (2H, m) which could be assigned to methylene protons (H-3). A triplet at δ 2.3 ppm (2H, t) which could be assigned to methylene protons (H-2). The EI/MS mass spectrum confirmed the above assignments showing a base peak at m/z 60 that resulted from Mclafferty rearrangement. The rest of the EI/ MS spectrum consists of a homologous series of hydrocarbon clusters at intervals 14 mass units (DCH$_2$ group) due to gradual breakdown of the hydrocarbon side chain. Other characteristic fragments are those of [CH$_3$(CH$_2$)$_4$]$^+$ at m/z 71, and [(CH$_2$)$_2$COOH]$^+$ at m/z 73. The above mentioned data, co-chromatography with a series of fatty acids and previously reported literature data made us to figure out compound 1 to be the long-chain fatty acid, n-hexadecanoic acid (palmitic acid). To the best of our knowledge, this is the first report of isolation of palmitic acid from the genus *Boswellia*. The 13C-NMR spectrum of compound 2 (Table 9.2), showed the presence of 30 carbons, the multiplicities of which were determined using an APT experiment, that revealed the presence of seven methyl, six methine, eleven methylene, and six quaternary carbon signals. Compound 2 showed an EI/ MS molecular ion peak at m/z 426 suggesting a molecular formula of C$_{30}$H$_{50}$O. More evidences came from the 13C-NMR signals at δ 150.9 (C-20), and 109.5 (C-29), as well as 1HNMR signals for two vinylic protons at 4.57, and 4.68 ppm (1H, d, J = 2 each), the 13C-NMR signal for an oxygenated carbinylic carbon signal at 76.5 that was assigned to C-3. All the above evidences; suggested the presence of a lupane triterpene skeleton. The 3-hydroxyl group is _-configurated as reflected by the broad peak half-height width W1/2 (12 Hz) of axially oriented H-3 signal at 3.42 ppm (1H, dd, J = 19.5, 3.3). Such axial orientation of H-3 is corroborated by the presence of the relatively large coupling constant characteristic to H-2, H-3 axial-axial interaction. From the above data, and through comparison with literature data ; it was concluded that compound 2 is lup-20(29)-en- 3_-ol (lupeol), that has been previously isolated from the closely related species *Boswellia frereana* Birdwood.

Table 9.2: 13C-NMR Spectral Data of the Isolated Triterpenoids (2Ð9).

C #	Lupane derivative	Ursane derivatives		Oleanane derivative		Tirucallane derivatives	
	2	3	6	7	9	4	5	8
1	37.8	34.9	35.0	34.3	34.3	34.9	35.7	35.7
2	27.7	24.0	23.9	26.6	26.6	24.0	34.6	27.9
3	76.5	73.6	73.6	71.8	70.7	73.6	216.9	79.4
4	40.3	47.1	46.7	47.6	47.5	47.1	47.3	39.3
5	50.5	51.0	50.8	49.6	49.2	51.0	51.6	51.3
6	18.5	19.9	19.2	20.1	19.0	19.9	20.2	19.3
7	34.4	33.5	31.3	33.5	31.3	33.5	28.8	29.2
8	40.8	40.2	43.9	39.8	44.1	40.2	134.4	134.4
9	49.3	47.2	60.7	47.3	60.8	47.2	132.2	132.6
10	36.9	37.2	37.6	37.7	37.7	37.5	37.2	37.7
11	21.1	23.8	199.6	23.8	199.8	23.8	25.9	26.3
12	24.2	124.9	130.8	124.9	130.6	122.2	32.5	32.8

Immunomodulatory Triterpenoids from the Oleogum Resin of Boswellia carterii 103

13	38.3	139.9	165.3	139.8	165.4	145.5	43.9	44.3
14	42.5	40.4	45.3	39.9	45.3	42.3	49.7	50.0
15	25.9	28.5	33.2	38.5	33.3	26.5	2934	29.7
16	35.9	26.9	27.6	26.9	27.6	27.4	27.5	28.2
17	43.3	33.7	34.2	33.5	34.1	33.2	47.0	47.3
18	48.6	59.6	59.4	59.6	59.4	47.2	21.2	20.4
19	48.3	40.1	39.7	40.1	39.7	47.8	15.9	15.9
20	150.9	40.0	39.6	40.0	39.7	31.5	47.6	48.1
21	29.5	31.7	27.9	31.7	27.7	34.2	182.4	183.1
22	33.5	41.9	41.3	41.9	41.3	37.9	21.4	21.9
23	31.7	24.1	24.3	24.6	24.7	2.41	26.9	27.3
24	16.3	183.1	182.2	183.6	182.9	183.1	123.5	124.0
25	22.4	13.7	13.6	13.7	13.6	13.5	132.7	133.7
26	19.6	17.3	18.8	17.3	18.7	17.2	25.7	24.8
27	14.5	21.7	20.9	21.8	20.9	26.3	19.7	18.1
28	28.5	23.7	21.5	23.6	21.5	28.9	24.3	28.4
29	109.5	17.8	17.8	17.8	17.8	33.7	17.6	16.2
30	30.4	29.2	29.3	29.2	29.3	23.7	26.6	26.1
CH$_3$CO	-	-	21.7	21.7	-	-	21.8	-	-
CH$_3$CO	-	-	170.6	170.5	-	-	170.8	-	-

The 13C-NMR spectra of compound 3 (Table 9.2) showed the presence of 32 signals, the multiplicities of which were determined, by DEPT experiment, into seven methine, eight methyl, nine methylene, and eight quaternary carbons. The EI/MS molecular ion peak at m/z 498 suggests a molecular formula of $C_{32}H_{50}O_4$ thus giving a double bond equivalent of 8, five of which were assigned to the 5 rings of a pentacyclic triterpene skeleton. Two equivalents were assigned to an acetyl carbonyl (δ 170.5), and a carboxylic acid carbonyl (δ 183.1). The last equivalent was assigned to a double bond that was consistent with that of Δ12-ursane skeleton based on its 13C-NMR resonances, δ 124.9 (C-12), and 139.9 (C-13). The appearance of a vinylic proton at δ 5.30 (H-12) as a broad triplet, appearance of H-18 as a doublet at δ 1.31 (J = 13.6), in addition to the appearance of a two methyl groups signals, each as a doublet at δ 0.8, and 0.85 assigned for 29, and 30 positions, respectively, unambiguously confirmed the presence of Δ12-ursane skeleton. The location of the carboxylic acid group was found to be at 24-position based on the downfield shift of C-4 resonating at δ 47.6 ppm relative to similar compounds cited in literature. The 13C-NMR signal for an oxygenated methine carbon signal at 73.6 was assigned to C-3 on biosynthetic and analogy grounds, as well as HMQC correlations. The latter revealed crosspeaks between methyl protons (H-23) resonating at δ 1.24 (3H, s)

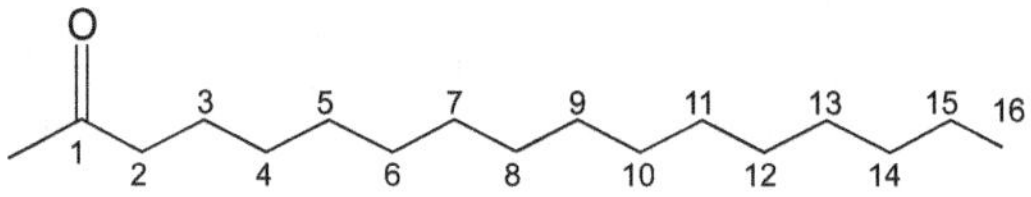

1 (Palamitic acid)

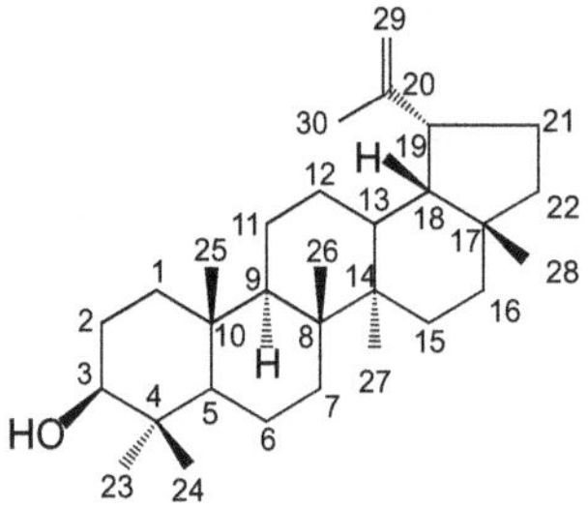

2 (lupeol)

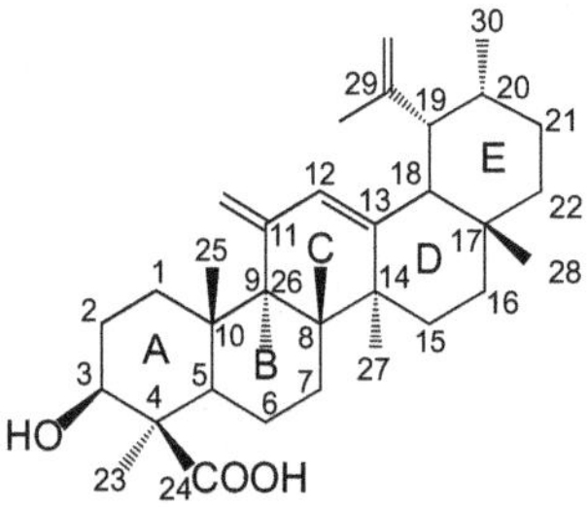

	R_1	R_2
3 (acetyl β-boswellic acid)	Ac	2 H
6 (acetyl 11-keto-β-boswellic acid)	Ac	O
7 (β-boswellic acid)	H	2 H
9 (11-keto-β-boswellic acid)	H	O

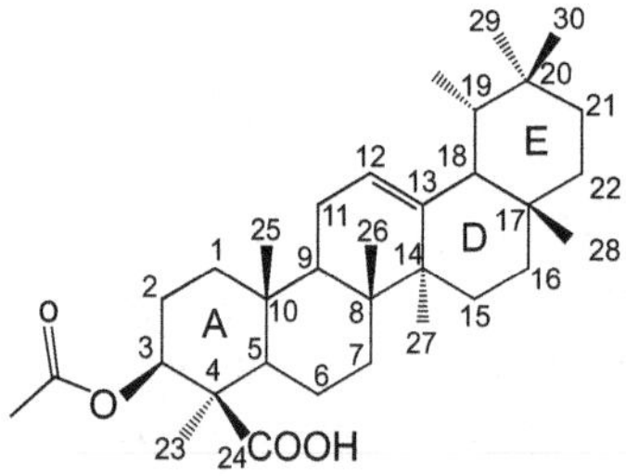

4 (acetyl-1-α-boswellic acid)

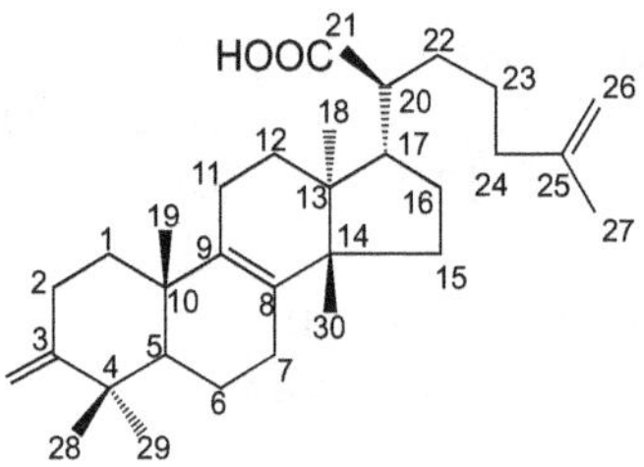

	R
5 (3-oxo-tirucallic acid)	O
8 (3-hydroxy-tirucallic acid)	β-OH, α-H

Fig. 9.1: The immunomodulatory triterpenoids isolated from the oleogum resin of *Boswellia carterii* Birdwood.

and the oxygenated carbinylic carbon (C-3) at δ 73.6, quaternary carbon (C-4) at δ 47.1, and methine carbon (C-5) at δ 51.0. In addition, HMBC showed strong contour between the carboxyl carbon (C-24) at δ 183.1 and methyl protons (H3-23) at δ 1.24. These established connectivities supported the substitution pattern of ring A. The interaction crosspeaks between the vinylic proton (H-12) at δ 5.15 (1H, t), and methine carbon (C-9) at δ 47.2, methyl carbon (C-27) at δ 21.7 (weak 4JCH interaction); between proton (H-9) at δ 1.61 (1H, m) and both the (C-11) at δ 23.8, and the methyl carbon (C-26) at δ 17.3 confirmed the substitution pattern of rings B, C. The interaction crosspeaks between the methyl protons (H3-27) at δ 0.90, and the quaternary carbons (C-8) at δ 40.2 ppm, as well as, (C-13) at δ 139.9, and (C-14) at δ 40.4 confirmed the substitution pattern of ring D. The presence of a 3-acetate group is evident from the downfield shift of ca. 2D3 ppm of (C-3), the upfield shift of ca. 3 ppm of (C-2), and the upfield shift of ca. 1 ppm of (C-4) relative to non-acetylated compounds viz. 7 and 9. The 3-acetoxyl group was found to be α-configurated, as reflected by the narrow peak half-height width W1/2 (5 Hz) of the equatorially-oriented H-3 signal at 5.3 ppm (1H, t). Such equatorial orientation of H-3 is corroborated by the absence of the relatively large coupling constant characteristic to H-2, H-3 axial-axial interaction, and this also was confirmed by the most recent X-ray crystallographic analysis. Assignment of other atoms was made by comparison with other separated compounds, referring to reported compilation data of a variety of similar compounds. The above evidences revealed that compound 3 is acetyl-_- boswellic acid.

EI/MS of compound 6 showed [M⁺] peak at m/z 512, suggesting the molecular formula; $C_{32}H_{48}O_5$. The analysis of all the spectral data for compound 6 indicated its similarity to compound 3, but it contains an additional α, _-unsaturated oxo function, an enone system, that was confirmed from IR spectrum where a carbonyl group absorption band was observed at 1658 cmD1, and by the appearance of a 13C-NMR carbonyl signal at 199.6 ppm. The location of this oxo group was concluded to be at 11-position, since H-12 proton signal was downfield shifted from δ 5.3 to 5.54, and appeared as singlet, rather than broad triplet. Furthermore, 13C-NMR signals of (C-9), (C-12), (C-13) were downfield shifted from δ 47.2, 124.9, and 139.9 to δ 60.7, 130.8, and 165.3, respectively. Further structure connectivities, and assignments by HMQC, HMBC, and COSY spectra confirmed that compound 6 is acetyl-11-keto-_-boswellic acid. The spectral data for compound 7 was found to be similar to that of compound 3, but lacking the 3-acetate group. This was proved through the absence of 13C-NMR signals at δ 21.7, and 170.5, as well as, 1H-NMR signal at δ 2.07, and the appearance of the 2 ppm upfield shifted hydroxylated carbinylic carbon (C-3) signal at δ 71.8, relative to that in compound 3. EI/MS spectrum of compound 7 showed a molecular ion peak [M]⁺ at m/z 456 suggesting a molecular formula of $C_{30}H_{48}O_3$, confirming the absence of a 3-acetate group.

Therefore, compound 7 was concluded to be _-boswellic acid.

EI/MS of compound 9 showed a [M⁺] peak at m/z 470 suggesting a molecular formula of $C_{30}H_{46}O_4$. It was found to be the 11-keto derivative of compound 7, as deduced from the appearance of carbonyl carbon signal at δ 199.8 (C-11), and based on a similar arguments as mentioned under compound 6. Therefore, it was confirmed that compound 9 is 11-keto-_-boswellic acid. The EI/MS of compound 4 showed a molecular ion peak at m/z 498 suggesting a molecular formula of $C_{32}H_{50}O_4$. The spectral data of 4 are more or less similar to that of compound 3, but with few differences. Firstly, the two 1H-NMR doublets for methyls at 29, and 30 positions are absent, and appeared as singlets at δ 0.87, and 1.11, respectively; referring to the possible presence of an oleanane skeleton. This was corroborated by the upfield shift of C-12 signals to δ 122.2, and down field shift of C-13 to δ 145.5. Accordingly, compound 4 has been identified as acetoxy-olean- 12-ene-24_-oic acid known as acetyl-α-boswellic acid.

The analysis of the spectral data of compound 5, concluded its structure as 3-keto-tirucall-8,24-diene-21-_-oic acid, known as 3-oxo-tirucallic acid. The 13C-NMR spectral data of 5 (Table 9.2) showed the presence of 30 carbon signals, the multiplicities of which were determined using an APT experiment, that revealed the presence of seven methyl, ten methylene, four methine, and nine quaternary carbon signals. The EI/MS molecular ion peak at m/z 454 suggests a molecular formula of $C_{30}H_{46}O_3$ thus giving a DBE of 8, four of which were assigned to the 4 rings of the tetracyclic tirucallane triterpene skeleton. Two of the remaining 4 double bond equivalents were assigned to 2 double bonds, C8DC9 double bond that is evident from the two quaternary 13C-NMR signals at δ 134.4 (C-8), and 132.2 (C-9), and C24DC25 double bond reflected by the 13C-NMR signals at δ 123.5 (C-24) and 132.7 (C-25), the two remaining DBEs were assigned to 2 carbonyl groups, the ketonic function (C-3) at δ 216.9, and the carboxyl carbonyl (C-21) at δ 182.4. The carboxylic group (C-21) is linked to (C-20) indicated by the 10D12 ppm downfield shift of that carbon relative to that closely related compounds lacking C-21 carboxyl. The ketonic function is definitely (C-3) as revealed by the 7 ppm downfield shift of (C-2) in comparison with similar compounds with hydroxyl group at (C-3) such as compound 7. Assignment of other atoms was made by comparison with literature data. EI/MS fragments corroborated the above assignments showing a molecular ion peak [M]⁺ at m/z 454 corresponding for the molecular formula $C_{30}H_{46}O_3$. The base peak at m/z 439 resulted from the loss of one methyl group. Subsequent loss of a water molecule resulted in the peak at m/z 421. Fragment at m/z 257 resulted from the retro-Diels Alder (RDA) fragmentation characteristic of several triterpenoids, followed by decarboxylation. The proposed EI/MS fragmentation pattern of compound 5 is depicted in Figure 9.2.

Compound 8 was analyzed for $C_{30}H_{48}O_3$ from EI/MS spectrum. It was found to be the 3-hydroxy analogue of compound 5. This was confirmed by appearance of 13C-NMR signal at δ 79.4 ppm that was assigned to an oxygenated methine carbo (C-3). The 3-hydroxyl group is _-configurated reflected by the wide peak half-height width W1/2 (16 Hz) of the axially oriented H-3 signal at 3.23 ppm (1H, dd, J = 11.5 and 4.4). Such axial orientation of H-3 is corroborated by the relatively large coupling constant characteristic to H-2, H-3 axial-axial interaction. The aforementioned data suggested that compound 8 is 3-hydroxy-tirucall-8,24-diene-21-_-oic acid known as 3-hydroxy-tirucallic acid. In conclusion, eight triterpenoids, in addition to a fatty acid isolated for the first time from the resin, were isolated from the oleogum resin of *Boswellia carterii* Birdwood. Compounds 3Ð9 have been previously isolated from the oleogum resin of *Boswellia carterii* Birdwood and *Boswellia serrata* Roxb.

All the isolated compounds exhibited immunostimulant activity as reflected by a lymphocyte transformation assay. Interestingly, it was found that the immunostimulant activity of the total extract (90% Lymphocyte transformation) is much greater than that of the individual components; accordingly it is advisable to use the total extract of the oleogum resin in herbal preparations intended for immunostimulation. These results suggested that frankincense could be a promising herbal immunostimulant that may be used in various immune disorders.

MATERIALS AND METHODS

Materials for Chromatographic Study

Silica gel G60F254 for TLC (E. Merck, Germany), silica gel for column chromatography (70Ð 230 mesh) (E. Merck, Germany), reversed phase silica (RP-C18) for column chromatography (E. Merck, Germany), precoated silica gel GF254 plates, aluminium and plastic sheets for TLC (E. Merck and Macherey-Nagel, Germany), precoated reversed phase silica plates for TLC (E. Merck, Germany).

Reagents for Lymphocyte Transformation Assay

Heparinized peripheral venous blood was obtained from healthy volunteers from the blood bank of Mansoura University Hospital; Ficoll/Hypaque obtained from Amersham Pharmacia, Uppsala, Sweden; phytohaemagglutinin (PHA) obtained from Difco, Detroit, MI, USA; Concanvalin A (ConA) obtained from Merck, Germany; Hank's balanced salt solution (HBSS); foetal calf serum (FCS); glutamine; HEPES (N-2-hydroxyethylpiperazine-N_-2-ethanesulfonic acid)-buffer and RPMI-1640 medium obtained from Gibco BRL, Life Technologies, Pailsey, Scotland; crystalline penicillin G and streptomycin obtained from El-Nile Pharmaceutical Co., Cairo, Egypt. Echinacea Purpurea extract (Immulone) obtained from Sekem Pharmaceutial Co., Cairo, Egypt. Levamisole (Ketrax) obtained from Elkahira Pharmaceutial Co., Cairo, Egypt (manufactured under

108   Salai Gum

license from AstraZeneca, Wilmington, Delaware, USA). Cyclophosphamide (Endoxan) obtained from ASTA Medica AG, Frankfurt, Germany. Cyclosporin (Sandimmune Neoral) obtained from Novartis Pharma, Switzerland.

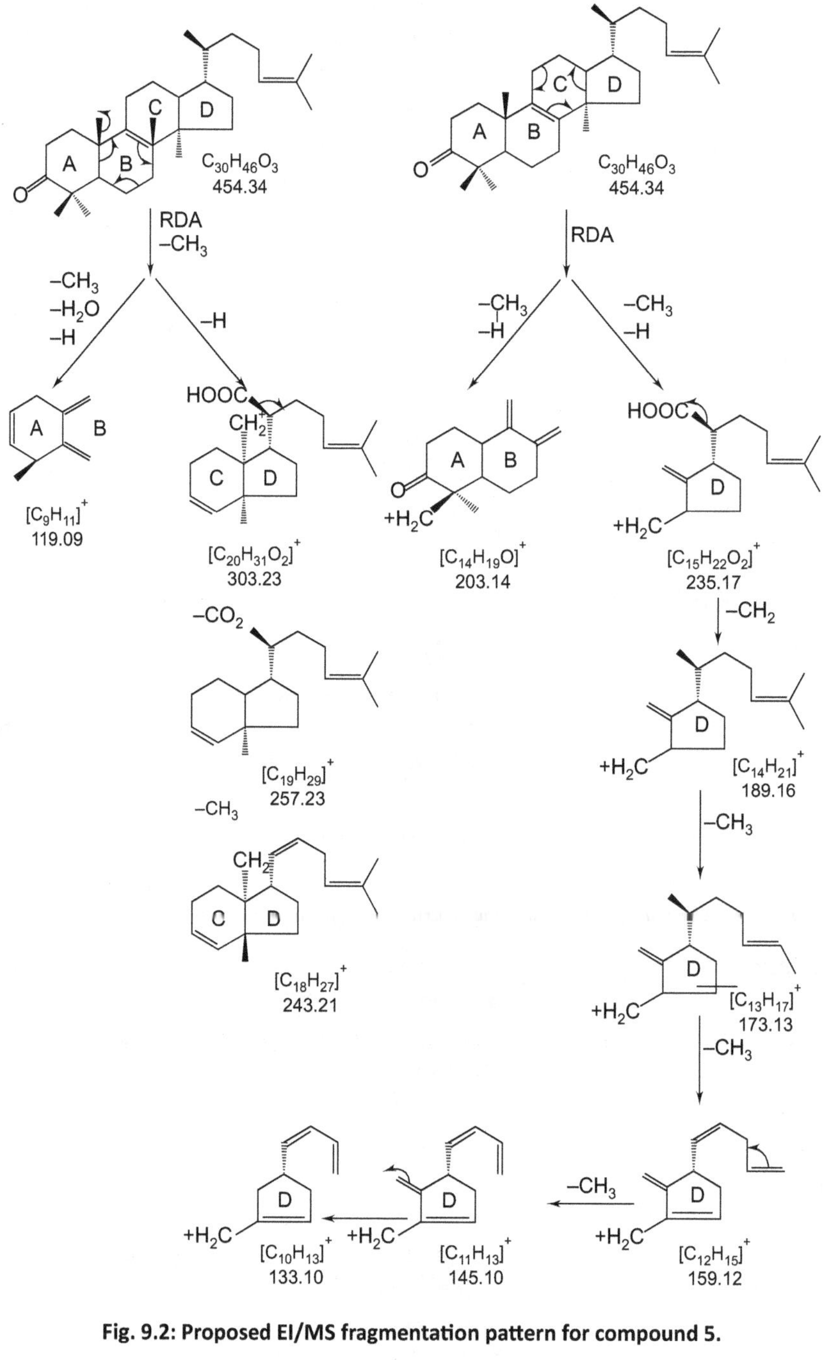

Fig. 9.2: Proposed EI/MS fragmentation pattern for compound 5.

General Instrumentation

UV spectra were recorded in MeOH using a Shimadzu 1601-PC UV/Visible spectrophotometer, IR spectra were recorded on Buck model 500 Infra red spectrophotometer, NMR spectra were recorded using Bruker AM-300 spectrometer, Drx-400, and Varian Mercury-300 spectrometer using CDCl3, and DMSO-d6 as solvents and TMS as internal standard. Chemical shifts (δ) are expressed in ppm. DEPT, APT, COSY, HMQC, and HMBC experiments were conducted under standard conditions. EI/MS were performed using a Finningan Mat SSQ 7000 mass spectrometer with a Digital DEC 3000 workstation.

Plant Material

The oleogum resin of *Boswellia carterii* Birdwood (Bursearceae) was purchased from the local herbal stores in Mansoura on March 1999. It was authenticated by comparison with a genuine sample kept in the Drug Museum of Pharmacognosy Department, Faculty of Pharmacy, Cairo University.

Extraction

The finely ground oleogum resin (500 grams) was extracted with methylene chloride (5 liters).

The extract was concentrated under reduced pressure to yield 330 grams of semisolid oleoresin.

Isolation and Identification

The total extract (15 grams) was applied onto the top of a glass column (120 \ 5 cm) previously packed with silica gel (300 g) in petroleum ether (b.p. 60D80 °C). The extract was gradiently eluted with petroleum ether containing increasing proportions of ethyl acetate. The effluent was collected in 250-ml fractions. Each fraction was concentrated, in vacuo. Fractions (51D70) gave white waxy crystals (400 mg) which were further purified by column chromatography (60 \ 1.5 cm) using (20 g) silica gel. Elution was adopted using petroleum ether (b.p. 60D80 °C) containing gradually increasing proportions of ethyl acetate. Sub-fractions (8D10) afforded 329 mg of 1. Fractions (71D 100) were subjected to reversed phase Rp-C18 flash column chromatography using isocratic elution with methanolDwater (8:2 v/v) to afford 2 (11.9 mg). Factions (101D130) were further purified by preparative TLC using petroleum etherD ethyl acetate (9:1 v/v) as solvent system affording 30 mg of 3. Fractions (131D160) were further purified by reversed phase Rp-C18 flash column chromatography using methanol Dwater (95:5 v/v) to afford 4 (86 mg). Upon crystallization, fractions (161D190) gave 5 (14 mg). Fractions (191D220), (221D250), and (251D280) were separately purified by reversed phase Rp-C18 flash column chromatography adopting isocratic elution with methanolDwater (9:1 v/v), to afford 6 (52 mg), 7 (130 mg), and 8 (12.1 mg), respectively. Fractions (311D340) were purified in the same manner butusing methanolDwater (80:20 v/v) as solvent system to afford 9 (28 mg).

Compound 1: Hexadecanoic Acid; Palmitic Acid

$C_{16}H_{32}O_2$; white waxy crystals; m.p. 57D62 °C; UV λmax (MeOH) nm, 202.5; IR (KBr) vmax cmD1: 723, 940, 1297, 1414, 1464, 1701 (C=O), 2851, 2955, and 3321 (ODH); EI/MS m/z (rel. int.): 256 (56.9) [M]$^+$, 228 (15.5), 213 (19.4), 185 (22.7), 157 (17.5), 129 (58.9), 97 (39.2), 83 (44.6), 73 (94.7), and 60 $[C_2H_4O_2]^+$ (100); 1H-NMR (300 MHz, CDCl3, δ in ppm, J = Hz): 0.83 (3 H, t, H-16), 1.23 (24 H, m, H-4D15), 1.58 (2 H, m, H-3), and 2.30 (2 H, t, H-2); 13C-NMR (75 MHz, CDCl3, δ in ppm): 14.2 (C-16), 22.7 (C-15), 24.7 (C-3), 29.1 (C-4), 29.3 (C-5), 29.4 (C-6), 29.6 (C-7), 29.7 (C-8 to C-11), 31.9 (C-14), 34.0 (C-2), and 179.6 (C-1).

Compound 2: lup-20(29)-en-3β-ol; lupeol

$C_{30}H_{50}O$; short fine colorless needles; m.p. 214D 217 °C; UV λmax nm (MeOH), 203.5; IR vmax cmD1: 1534, 1618 (C=C), 2366, 2970, and 3490 cmD1 (ODH); EI/MS m/z (rel. int.): 426 (61.7) [M]$^+$, 411 (32.1) [MDCH3]$^+$, 393 (15.7) [MDCH$_3$DH$_2$O]$^+$, 316 (13.0), 274 (12.1), 229 (10.6), 218 (100), 189 (90.6), 175 (29.4), 135 (54.1), 95 (61.6), and 69 (57.9); 1H-NMR (300 MHz, CDCl3, δ in ppm, J = Hz): 0.79 (3H, s, H-25), 0.94 (3H, s, H-27), 0.96 (3H, s, H-24), 1.04 (3H, s, H-26), 1.29 (3H, s, H-28), 1.33 (3H, s, H-23), 1.68 (3H, s, H-30), and 3.42 (1H, dd, 19.5, 3.3, H-3), 4.57, 4.68 (2H, d, 2, 2, H-29). The 13C-NMR data of compounds 2D9 are shown in Table 9.1.

Compound 3: 3α-acetoxy-urs-12-ene-24β-oic acid; acetyl-α-boswellic Acid

$C_{32}H_{50}O_4$; colorless needles; m.p. 250D252 °C; UV λmax (MeOH) nm, 206; IR (KBr) vmax cmD1: 1275, 1376, 1456, 1618 (C=C), 1702 (DCOOH), 1727 (CH$_3$COD), 2965, and 3400 (ODH); EI/MS m/z (rel. int.): 498 (4.5) [M]$^+$, 438 (0.7), 394 (0.42), 379 (0.17), 255 (3.0), 203 (17.3), 175 (5.1), and 119 (6.0); 1H-NMR (400 MHz, CDCl$_3$, δ in ppm, J = Hz): 0.80 (3H, d, 12.5, H-29), 0.85 (3H, d, 13, H-30), 0.90 (3H, s, H-25), 0.90 (3H, s, H-27),1.02 (2H, dd, 16.0, 2.0, H-16), 1.04 (3H, s, H-26), 1.12 (3H, s, H-28), 1.24 (3H, s, H-23), 1.28 (2H, dd, 10.2, 2.0, H 21), 1.31 (1H, d, 13.6, H 18), 1.49 (1H, dd, 13.0, 1.3, H-5), 2.09 (3H, s, H-3, Ac), 5.15 (1H, br t, H-3), and 5.30 (1H, br t, H-12).

Compound 4: 3α-acetoxy-olean-12-ene-24β-oic acid; acetyl-α-boswellic Acid

$C_{32}H_{50}O_4$; colorless needles; m.p. 247D250 °C; UV λmax (MeOH) nm, 204.5; IR (KBr) vmax cmD1: 1275, 1376, 1456, 1618 (C=C), 1708 (DCOOH), 1727 (CH$_3$COD), 2965, and 3450 (ODH); EI/MS m/z (rel. int.): 498 (0.55) [M]$^+$, 423 (0.59), 343 (0.03), 280 (0.16), 255 (2.57), 218 (100), 203 (22.5), 189 (8.9), 133 (6.4), and 43 (3.6); 1H-NMR (400 MHz, CDCl3, δ in ppm, J = Hz): 0.80 (3H, s, H-27), 0.80 (3H, s, H-28), 0.87 (3H, s, H-29), 0.90 (3H, s, H-25), 1.04 (3H, s, H-26), 1.11 (3H, s, H-30), 1.49 (1H, dd, 13.0, 1.3, H-5), 2.09 (3H, s, H-3 Ac), 5.14 (1H, br t, H-3), and 5.20 (1H, t, H-12).

Compound 5: 3-keto-tirucall-8, 24-diene-21-β-oic acid; 3-oxotirucallic Acid

$C_{30}H_{46}O_3$; colorless needles; m.p. 263D265 °C; UV λmax (MeOH) nm, 206; IR (KBr) vmax cmD1: 1193, 1347, 1420, 1448, 1620 (C=C), 1708 (C=O), 1710 (DCOOH), 2954, and 3450 (ODH); EI/MS m/z (rel. int.): 454 (64.1) [M]+, 439 (100) [MD CH₃]+, 421 (14.3), 393 (17.2), 311 (4.6), 297 (23.7), 243 (5.8), 173 (7.3), 159 (10.7), 119 (14.0), and 95 (12.6); 1H-NMR (300 MHz, CDCl₃, δ in ppm, J = Hz): 0.83 (3H, s, H-18), 0.91 (3H, s, H-19), 1.04 (3H, s, H-30), 1.05 (3H, s, H-28), 1.09 (3H, s, H-29), 1.29 (1H, dd, 9.0, 6.3, H-5), 1.54 (2H, dd, 9.0, 6.3, H-16), 1.59 (3H, s, H-27), 1.68 (3H, s, H-26), 2.3 (1H, dd, 12.5, 5.1, H-17), and 2.5 (2H, ddd, 15.5, 10.8, 4.0, H-2).

Compound 6: 3α-acetoxy-urs-12-ene-11-keto-24β- oic acid; acetyl-11-keto-β-boswellic acid (AKBA)

$C_{32}H_{48}O_5$; colorless needles; m.p. 274D276 °C; UV λmax (MeOH) nm, 250; IR (KBr) vmax cmD1: 1238, 1274, 1379, 1457, 1622 (C=C), 1658 (α,_- unsaturated C=O), 1706 (DCOOH), 1728 (CH₃COOD), 2864, 2970, and 3350 (ODH); EI/ MS m/z (rel. int.): 512 (0.01) [M]+, 408 (14.5), 393 (5.9), 353 (2.7), 273 (41.8), 232 (77.7), 189 (12.1), 175 (14.3), 161 (27.9), 119 (35.1), 105 (49.5), 91 (37.5), 55 (49.8), and 43 (100); 1H-NMR (400 MHz, CDCl3, δ in ppm, J = Hz): 0.78 (3H, d, 6.3, H-29), 0.80 (3H, d, 7.4, H-30), 0.93 (3H, s, H-28), 1.01 (2H, dd, 11.8, 3.0, H-21), 1.12 (3H, s, H-25), 1.17 (3H, s, H-26), 1.21 (3H, s, H-23), 1.33 (3H, s, H-27), 1.37 (1H, d, 12.3, H-18), 1.38 (1H, dd, 12.0, 2.0, H-5), 2.07 (3H, s, H-3 Ac), 2.39 (1H, s, H-9), 5.28 (1H, t, H-3), and 5.54 (1H, s, H-12).

Compound 7: 3α-hydroxy-urs-12-ene-24β-oic acid; β-boswellic acid

$C_{32}H_{48}O_5$; colorless needles; m.p. 226D228 °C; UV λmax nm (MeOH), 204; IR (KBr) vmax cmD1: 1367, 1456, 1629 (C=C), 1708 (DCOOH), 2918, and 3400 (ODH); EI/MS m/z (rel. int.): 456 (5.2) [M]+, 441 (1.6) [MDCH3]+, 379 (0.1), 326 (0.2), 293 (0.1), 238 (13.2), 218 (100), 203 (24.8), 159 (8.3), 133 (15.5), 119 (23.0), 95 (18.7), 69 (18.0), and 57 (15.9); 1H-NMR (400 MHz, CDCl3, δ in ppm, J = Hz): 0.78 (3H, d, 5.67, H-29), 0.79 (3H, d, 3.25, H-30), 0.81 (2H, d, 12.3, H-15), 0.89 (3H, s, H-25), 0.91 (3H, s, H-27), 1.02 (2H, dd, 16.0, 2.0, H-16), 1.03 (3H, s, H-26), 1.33, (1H, d, 8.9, H-18), 1.34 (3H, s, H-23), 1.48 (1H, dd, 11.8, 3.1, H-5), 1.68 (2H, dd, 14.1, 3.0, H-6), 2.22 (2H, dd, 14.0, 4.0, H-2), 4.08 (1H, t, H-3), and 5.14 (1H, t, H-12).

Compound 8: 3β-hydroxy-tirucall-8,24-diene-21-β- oic acid; 3β-hydroxytirucallic Acid

$C_{30}H_{48}O_3$; colorless long very fine needles; m.p. 258D260 °C; UV λmax nm (MeOH), 206; IR (KBr) vmax cmD1: 1466, 1622 (C=C), 1702 (DCOOH), 2942, and 3416 (ODH); EI/MS m/z (rel. int.): 456 (67.9) [M]+, 441 (85.6) [MDCH₃]+, 423 (93.3), 395 (10.9), 341 (7.4), 299 (12.9), 281 (32.9), 187 (70.9), 119 (65.2), and 82 (100); 1H-NMR (400 MHz, CDCl₃, δ in ppm, J = Hz): 0.74 (3H, s, H-19), 0.82 (3H, s, H-28), 0.87 (3H, s, H-30), 0.93 (3H, s, H-18), 0.99 (3H, s, H-29), 1.11 (1H, dd, 11.8, 2.0, H-5), 1.2 (2H, dd, 9.9, 3.1, H-1), 1.37 (2H, dd, 12.2, 6.8, H-16), 1.53 (2H, dd, 14.4, 7.3, H-7), 1.58 (3H,s, H-27), 1.67 (3H, s, H-26), 1.75 (2H, dd, 12.8, 3.0, H-12), 2.27 (1H, dd, 12.1, 3.5, H-17), and 3.23 (1H, dd, 11.5, 4.4, H-3).

Compound 9: 3α-hydroxy-urs-12-ene-11-keto-24β-oic acid; 11-keto-β-boswellic acid

$C_{32}H_{48}O_5$; colorless needles; m.p. 195D197 °C; UV λmax nm (MeOH), 249.5; IR νmax cmD1: 1235, 1457, 1625, 1669 (α-unsturated C=O), 1708 (DCOOH), 2921, and 3455 (ODH); EI/MS m/z (rel. int.): 470 (1.81) [M]$^+$, 425 (3.1), 408 (5.6), 287 (4.9), 273 (54.4), 232 (100), 189 (12.6), 175 (14.3), 148 (13.9), 135 (33.7), 119 (25.9), 105 (41.2), 69 (34.8), and 55 (74.9); 1H-NMR (400 MHz, CDCl3, δ in ppm, J = Hz): 0.78 (3H, d, 6.3, H-29), 0.79 (3H, d, 8.6, H-30), 0.93 (3H, s, H-28), 1.12 (3H, s, H-25), 1.17 (3H, s, H-26), 1.30 (3H, s, H-27), 1.33 (3H, s, H-23), 1.46 (1H, dd, 13.0, 3.0, H-5), 1.53 (1H, d, 11.2, H-18), 2.42 (1H, s, H-9), 2.49 (2H, dd, 13.0, 1.2, H-1), 4.07 (1H, t, H-3), and 5.54 (1H, s, H-12).

Assessment of the Immunomodulatory Activity: Lymphocyte Blast Transformation (mitogensis) Assay

The lymphocyte blast transformation (mitogensis) or proliferation assay was applied. The assay was adapted as a test for cell-mediated immunity. The cell-mediated immune response was determined in the peripheral blood lymphocytes (PBL) in response to mitogenic stimulation using either phytohaemagglutinin (PHA) or concanavalin A (Con A) as mitogens that stimulate human T and B cells but T-cells more vigorously.

(A) Separation of peripheral blood lymphocytes (PBL)

Lymphocytes were separated from peripheral human venous blood by Ficoll/Hypaque gradient technique. For each sample, 5 ml of heparinized blood was diluted with equal volume of Hank's balanced salt solution (HBSS) in a sterile plastic centrifuge tube. Diluted blood (6 ml) was carefully overlaid on 4 ml Ficoll/Hypaque solution gradient without allowing the solution to become mixed by keeping the pipette against the tube wall 5D10 mm above the fluid meniscus. The tube was centrifuged at 1200 rpm at room temperature. The lymphocytes were localized as a whitish layer on the upper meniscus of the gradient solution. Using a fine pasteur pipette, the zone containing lymphocytes was taken and washed twice in HBSS (10 min at 1200 rpm). The residue is a buffy coat of polymorphonuclear leucocytes (PMNLs).

(B) Lymphocyte transformation assay

The viable lymphocytes were adjusted to a concentration of 2 \ 106 cells/ml in RPMI-1640 medium supplemented with 600 µl penicillin, 0.1 ml streptomycin, 1% glutamine, 25% HEPES-buffer, and 20% foetal calf serum (FCS). The lymphocytes were plated into 96-well tissue culture plates (or Ependorff tubes). The test solution (100 µl) in DMF (100 µl/ml) and 20 µg of the mitogen (PHA) were added to each well. Cell cultures were incubated at 37 °C in 5% CO_2 atmosphere for 72 hrs, during which the mitogen produced its maximal effect on DNA synthesis. After culture, cell films were stained by Giemsa stain and the average count of percentage of transformed (proliferated) blasts was determined. Aqueous Echinaceae Purpurea extract (Immulone) and Levamisole (Ketrax) were used as positive control (standard immunostimulant) while Cyclophosphamide (Endoxan) and cyclosporin (Sandimmune Neoral) were used as negative control (standard immunosuppressant) 100 µg/ml of each drug in DMSO.

10. Anti-inflammatory and Analgesic Activity of Different Fractions of *Boswellia serrata*

Boswellia serrata (family *Burseraceae*) is an oleo-gum-resin found in dry hilly parts of India. It is a large branching medium size tree known as 'Dhup', Indian frankincense or *Indian olibanum*. *Boswellia serrata* (*B. serrata*) has been used for a variety of therapeutic purposes such as cancer, inflammation, arthritis, asthma, psoriasis, colitis and hyperlipidemia. The essential oil of *B. serrata* is a mixture of mono, di and sesquiterpenes whereas gum portion consists of pentose and hexose sugar with oxidizing and digestive enzymes.

Chemically resin is pentacyclic triterpenoid in nature in which boswellic acids (β-boswellic acid, acetyl-β-boswellic acid, keto-β-boswellic acid and acetyl-11-keto-β-boswellic acid) is the main moiety. BAs and its derivatives are novel, specific, non-redox inhibitor of 5-lipoxygenase (5-LOX), an enzyme in neutrophils responsible for the conversion of arachidonic acid to 5-HETE and leukotrienes which causes vasoconstriction, bronchoconstriction, increase vascular permeability and chemotaxis.

MATERIALS AND METHODS

Carrageenan, acetic acid, gum acacia, formalin, PVP were purchased from CDH, India. All chemicals used were of analytical reagent grade.

PLANT MATERIAL

Materials

The oleo-gum-rein was collected from the local market and was authenticated in Botany Department of Dr. H.S. Gour University, Sagar (M.P.) India.

Extraction and Isolation of Gum Essential Oil and Resin

About 100 g shade dried samples were extracted with petroleum ether (60-800C) in a soxhlet apparatus to get oleo-resin (70.6g). The marc, which contains gum was dried and extracted with hot water to get aqueous extract (29.0 gm). The petroleum ether extract (oleo-resin) was freed from the solvent and hydrodistilled using clavenger apparatus to isolate essential oil (11.0 ml). After the complete removal of essential oil the water layer from the flask was decanted off. The resin (59.6 g) was dried and weighed.

Animals

Albino rats (100-150 g) of either sex maintained in standard conditions for temperature, relative humidity light/day cycle and feed with food and water ad libitum.

Preparation of Suspension of Different Fractions

The different fraction of B. serrata suspended in 2% gum acacia for oral administration whilessential oil was given in the form of emulsion.

Anti-inflammatory Activity

Carrageenan induced paw edema in rats

Pedal inflammation in rats (100-150g) was described by Winter et al.. Oedema was induced by subcutaneous administration of 0.1ml of 1% aqueous solution of carrageenan into right hind paws. The test drug (oil, resin, oleo-resin and oleo-gum-resin) is suspended in 1% solution of PVP and diluted with saline. The control group received the vehicle (10 ml/kg body wt.). A test drug suspension (100 mg/kg or 10 ml/kg) was administered orally for 7 consecutive days prior to the infection of carrageenan paw volume were measured upto 5h after the carrageenan administration at an interval of 60 min and paw volume was measured with plethysmometer. Indomethacin and Ibuprofen were used as standard drug.

Analgesic Activity

Acetic acid induced writhing response

Whittle performed acetic acid induced writhing response (abdominal constriction) in rats. Vehicle, indomethacin (10 mg/kg) and test solution (100 mg/kg) were administered orally 30 min before the experiment and 0.1 ml per 10 g of 0.7% acetic acid saline was then injected i.p. 10 min after the injection. The number of writhing during the following 20 min period was counted. The per cent inhibition (% analgesic activity) was calculated by

$$\% \text{ inhibition} = 100 \times \frac{N - N_t}{N}$$

Where, N = Average number of stretching of control per group

N_t = Average number of stretching of test per group.

Formalin induced pain in rats

Pain was induced by injecting 0.05 ml of 2.5% formalin (40% formaldehyde) in distilled water in subplantar region of right hind paw. Rats (six per group) were given extract (100 mg/kg), indomethacin (10 mg/kg) and distill water (10 ml/kg) 30 min prior to injecting formalin. These rats were individually placed in transparent Plexiglas cage observation chamber. The amount of time spent licking and biting the injected paw was indicative of pain and was recovered in 0-5 min (first phase) and 15-30 min (second phase).

$$\% \text{ inhibition} = 100 \times \frac{N - N_t}{N}$$

Where, N = Average number of licking and biting in control per group

N_t = Average number of licking and biting in test per group.

Tail flick method

This method was described by Asongalem et al. Albino Rats (six per group) were used. This involve immersing extreme 3 cm of rats tail in water bath containing water at a temperature of 55 ± 0.5°C within a few minute, the rats reacted by with drawing the tail. The reaction time was recorded with a stop watch. Each animal served as its control at 0 and 10 min interval. The average of the two values was the initial reaction time. The test groups were given extract (100 mg/kg), ibuprofen (400 mg/kg) and distilled water (100 ml/kg). The reaction time for the test group was taken at interval 0.5-6 hr after a latency period of 30 min followed by the administration of the extract and drugs.

Hot plate method

The device consists of a water bath in which a metallic cylinder was placed. The temperature of the cylinder was set at 55 ± 0.5°C. Each rat (six per group) acted as its control before the treatment; the reaction time of each rat (licking of the fore paw or jumping response) was done at 0 and 10 min interval. The average of the two readings was obtained as the initial reaction time. The reaction time following the administration of the extract (100 mg/kg p.o.), indomethacin (10 mg/kg) and distill water (10 ml/kg) was measured at 0.5, 1-5 and 6 hr after a latency period of 30 min.

Statistical analysis

All values are expressed as mean ±S.E.M. Statistical significance was determined by using student's t-test values with $p < 0.05$ were considered significant.

RESULTS

Anti-inflammatory Activity

Carrageenan induced paw edema in rats

The essential oil (10 ml/kg), gum, resin, oleo-resin and oleo-gum-resin significantly (as compared to control) and dose dependently reduced carrageenan induced paw edema in rats. The standard drug Ibuprofen and Indomethacin shows better inhibitory activity than different fractions of B. serrata as shown in Table 10.1. The lower the paw volume the better the activity. The inhibitory activity of different fractions is very close to ibuprofen.

Table 10.1: Anti-inflammatory Action of B. serrata in Carrageenan Induced Paw Edema.

Group	Dose (mg/kg, p.o.)	1(h)	2(h)	3(h)	4(h)	5(h)
Control	10	1.65 ± 0.02	1.69 ± 0.01	1.80 ± 0.19	1.42 ± 0.007	1.15 ± 0.012
Essential oil	10	1.01 ± 0.05*	1.19 ± 0.04	1.36 ± 0.03*	1.12 ± 0.05*	1.10 ± 0.04

Gum	100	1.11 ± 0.11*	1.20 ± 0.14	1.34 ± 0.07*	1.15 ± 0.04*	1.13 ± 0.06
Resin	100	1.11 ± 0.03*	1.13 ± 0.31*	1.19 ± 0.03*	1.10 ± 0.09*	0.97 ± 0.05
Oleo-resin	100	1.13 ± 0.04*	1.14 ± 0.007*	0.98 ± 0.06*	0.90 ± 0.04*	0.85 ± 0.05*
Oleo-gum-resin	100	0.80 ± 0.03*	0.89 ± 0.06*	0.93 ± 0.03*	0.97 ± 0.02*	1.15 ± 0.03
Indomethacin	10	0.92 ± 0.04*	0.61 ± 0.10*	0.83 ± 0.03*	0.91 ± 0.03*	0.86 ± 0.03*
Ibuprofen	100	0.96 ± 0.01*	0.98 ± 0.01*	0.93 ± 0.03*	0.90 ± 0.02*	0.70 ± 0.003*

All values are expressed as mean ± S.E.M. $p^* < 0.05$ considered significant (n=6).

Analgesic Activity

Acetic acid induced writhing response

The different fractions of *B. serrata* reduce acetic acid induced writhing. The oleo-gum-resin fraction shows maximum inhibition (60.54) as compare to oil (20.70) and gum fraction (54.88). The results were shown in Table 10.2. The% inhibition is calculated by the following formula:

$$\% \text{ inhibition} = 100 \frac{N - N_t}{N} \times$$

Where, N = Average number of writhing of control per group

Nt = Average number of writhing of test per group.

Formalin Induced Pain

The different fractions of *B. serrata* reduce pain, induced by formalin, significantly and dose dependently (see Table 10.3). Between 0-5 min at a dose 100 mg/kg body wt. essential oil, gum, oleo-resin and oleo-gum-resin are move patent than indomethacin while resin is slightly less potent. The% inhibition is calculated by the following formula:

$$\% \text{ inhibition} = 100 \frac{N - N_t}{N} \times$$

Where, N = Average number of licking of control per group

Nt = Average number of licking of test per group

The first (0-5 min) and second (15-30 min) phase of formalin test corresponds to neurogenic and inflammatory pains, respectively. The different fractions of *B. serrata* had analgesic effect on both phase. The results were shown in Table 10.3.

Tail Flick Method

A significant reduction of painful sensation due to tail immersion in warm water was observed following oral administration of different fractions at a dose 100 (essential oil 10 ml/kg). The effect was noticed after a latency period of 1 hr and it was done dependent. The analgesic effect of oleo-gum-resin is more than other fractions and also standard drug. The results were shown in Table 10.4.

Hot Plate Method

To corroborate that the extract had no central analgesic actions, hot plate method were conducted. Significant results were noted at 100 mg/kg by different fractions was not due to central analgesic acting activities of the extract. This meant there was no opioid like receptor mediation involved. The different fractions at a dose 20 mg/kg shows greater effect than indomethacin 10 mg/kg. The results were shown in Table 10.5.

Discussion

The anti-inflammatory and analgesic activity of different fractions of B. serrata was investigated in the present study. The carrageenan test was selected because of its sensitivity in defecting orally active anti-inflammatory agents particularly in the acute phase of inflammation. The intraplantar infection of carrageenan in rats leads to paw edema. Its first phase (0-2.5 h after injection of carrageenan) results from the concomitant release of mediators: histamine, serotonin and kinins on the vascular permeability. The second phase is correlated with leukotrienes. The oral administration of different fractions of B. serrata suppresses inflammation during the second phase. The oleo-gum-resin (200 mg/kg) shows maximum inhibitory response as compared to other fractions.

The mechanism for testing analgesic was selected such that both centrally and peripherally mediated effects were investigated. The acetic acid induced abdominal constriction and tail immersion methods elucidated peripheral and central activity, respectively, while the formalin test investigated both. The hot plate method elucidates peripheral mediated effects.

The extract (100 and 200 mg/kg), administered orally, significantly inhibit acetic acid induced writhing in rats. There writhing are related to increase in the peritoneal level of prostaglandins and leukotrienes. The result strongly suggests that the mechanism of action of extract may be linked to lipoxygenase and/or cycloxygenase. In the formalin test there is distinctive biphasic nociceptive response termed neurogenic and inflammatory phases. Drugs that primarily act on central nervous system inhibit both phases equally while peripherally acting drugs inhibit the late phase. The neurogenic and inflammatory phase is due to the release of substance P, histamine, serotonin, bradykinin prostaglandins and leukotrienes respectively. This test is very useful for not only assessing analgesic drugs but also helping in the elucidation of mode of action. The extract (100 and 200 mg/kg) was able to block both phases of formalin in the second phase (77.13 for essential oil). The oleo-gum-resin shows more inhibition (97.18) in the first phase than second phase (56.74).

Tail immersion model of analgesic assessment in best reserved for evaluating compounds for centrally acting analgesic activity. The oleo-gum-resin (100 mg/kg) shows best effect after a latency period of 6 hr which is more than other fractions. To corrobate that the extract had no central analgesic acid, hot plate test were conducted, significant effect noted for 200 mg/kg of different fraction in hot plate test were not due to central acting activities of the fraction. This mean there was no opioid receptors involved. The oleo-gum-resin (200 mg/kg) shows best activity after 5 h than other fractions and also indomethacin.

CONCLUSION

In the present study anti-inflammatory and analgesic activity of different fractions of B. serrata was investigated by means of acetic acid induced writhing, formalin test, tail immersion model of analgesic assessment and hot plate method in rats. The oral administration of different fractions of B. serrata showed suppression of inflammation and mechanism of action of extract might be linked to lipoxygenase and/or cycloxygenase. The oleo-gum-resin showed maximum inhibitory response as compared to other fractions. The result strongly suggests that the oleo-gum-resin can be used efficiently as analgesic and anti-inflammatory agent.

Antimicrobial Activity of Silver Nanoparticles

Nanotechnology is now creating a growing sense of excitement in the life sciences especially biomedical devices and Biotechnology. Nanoparticles exhibit completely new or improved properties based on specific characteristics such as size, distribution and morphology. The silver nanoparticles have various and important applications. Historically, silver has been known to have a disinfecting effect and has been found in applications ranging from traditional medicines to culinary items. It has been reported that silver nanoparticles (SNPs) are non-toxic to humans and most effective against bacteria, virus and other eukaryotic micro-organism at low concentrations and without any side effects. Moreover, several salts of silver and their derivatives are commercially manufactured as antimicrobial agents. In small concentrations, silver is safe for human cells, but lethal for microorganisms. Antimicrobial capability of SNPs allows them to be suitably employed in numerous household products such as textiles, food storage containers, home appliances and in medical devices. The most important application of silver and SNPs is in medical industry such as tropical ointments to prevent infection against burn and open wounds6. Biological synthesis of nanoparticles by plant extracts is at present under exploitation as some researchers worked on it and testing for antimicrobial activities.

For the last two decades extensive work has been done to develop new drugs from natural products because of the resistance of micro-organisms to the existing drugs. Nature has been an important source of a products currently being used in medical practice.

Boswellia ovalifoliolata Bal & Henry and Shorea tumbuggaia are narrow endemic, endangered and medicinal tree species belonging to the family *Burseraceae* and Dipterocarpaceae respectively. Seshachalam hill ranges of Eastern Ghats of India harbour these trees. Tribals like Nakkala, Sugali and Chenchu used these plants to treat number of aliments.

Svensonia hyderobednesis is a rare shrub belonging to the family Verbenaceae and used to cure hepatotoxic disease. The present study is an attempt to test the antibacterial and antifungal efficacy of SNPs produced by using the stem barks and leaf extract of medicinal plants, which have been using in traditional medicine without any validation.

EXPERIMENTAL

Plant Material and Synthesis of Silver Nanoparticle

Leaves of Svensonia hyderobadensis and the stem barks of *Boswellia*, Shorea species were collected from the Seshachalam hills of Andhra Pradesh, India. The bark and leaves were air dried for 10 days and kept in the hot air oven at 60°C for 24-48 hours. The dried barks and leaves were ground to a fine powder. 1 mM silver nitrate was added to the plant extracts separately to make up a final solution of 200 ml and centrifuged at 18,000 rpm for 25 min. The supernatants were heated at 50 to 95°C. A change in the colour of the solution was observed during heating of process with in 10-15 minutes. The colour changes indicate the formation of silver nanoparticles (SNPs). The reduction of pure Ag^{2+} ions were monitored by measuring the UV-Vis spectrum of the reduction media at 5 hours after diluting a small aliquot of the sample in distilled water by using systronic 118 UVVis Spectrophotometer.

Microorganisms

Pure culture of Escherichia coli, *Pseudomonas* aeruginosa, Bacillus subtills, Proteus vulgaris and Klebsiella pneumoneae species of bacteria and Fusarium oxysporum, Curvularia lunata, Rhizopus arrhizus, Aspergillus niger and Aspergillus flavus species of fungi were procured from the Department of Microbiology of Sri Venkateswara Institute of Medical Science (SVIMS). The experiments of antimicrobial activity were carried out in the Department of Applied Microbiology, Sri Padmavathi Mahila University (SPMU), Tirupati, Andhra Pradesh, India.

Table 11.1: Antimicrobial Activity of Medicinal Plants

S.No.	Bacterial species	Bosewellia			Shorea			Svensonia		
		Control	SNPs	$Ag(NO_3)$	Control	SNPs	$Ag(NO_3)_2$	Control	SNPs	$Ag(NO_3)_2$
1.	Bacillus	6	8	16	7	9	11	6	8	16
2	E.coli	6	10	11	8	8	10	8	10	11
3.	Klebsiella	8	12	18	7	7	13	6	12	18
4.	Proteus	6	10	18	6	9	11	7	7	18
5.	Pseudomonas	9	9	20	12	6	10	6	15	20
	Fungal species									
6.	Aspergillus flavus	6	12	8	6	10	8	ne	14	8
7.	Aspergillus niger	ne	10	7	6	9	6	6	10	7
8.	Curvularia	6	7	8	ne	9	8	ne	6	8
9.	Fusarium	ne	10	8	ne	12	ne	6	8	8
10.	Rhizopus	ne	7	6	ne	10	ne	6	15	6

Note: 'ne' indicates no effect

Antibacterial Activity

The antibacterial activities of SNPs were carried out by disc diffusion method. Nutrient agar medium plates were prepared, sterilized and solidified. After solidification bacterial cultures were swabbed on these plates. The sterile discs were dipped in silver nanoparticles solution (10 mg/ml) and placed in the nutrient agar plate and kept for incubation at 37°C for 24 hours. Zones of inhibition for control, SNPs and silver nitrate were measured. The experiments were repeated thrice and mean values of zone diameter were presented.

Antifungal Activity

Potato dextrose agar plates were prepared, sterilized and solidified, after solidification fungal cultures were swabbed on these plates. The sterile discs were dipped in silver nanoparticles solution (10 mg/ml) and placed in the agar plate and kept for incubation for 7 days. After 7 days zone of inhibition was measured.

RESULTS AND DISCUSSION

The green synthesis of silver nanoparticles through plant extracts were carried out. It is well known that silver nanoparticles exhibit yellowish - brown colour in aqueous solution due to excitation of surface plasmon vibrations in silver nanoparticles. The appearances of yellowish-brown colour in the reaction vessels suggest the formation of silver nanoparticles (SNPs) (Figure 11.1).

Fig. 11.1: The colour change of plant extracts after addition of silver nitrate (a), (c), (e) Plant extracts; (b), (d), (f) Silver nanoparticles

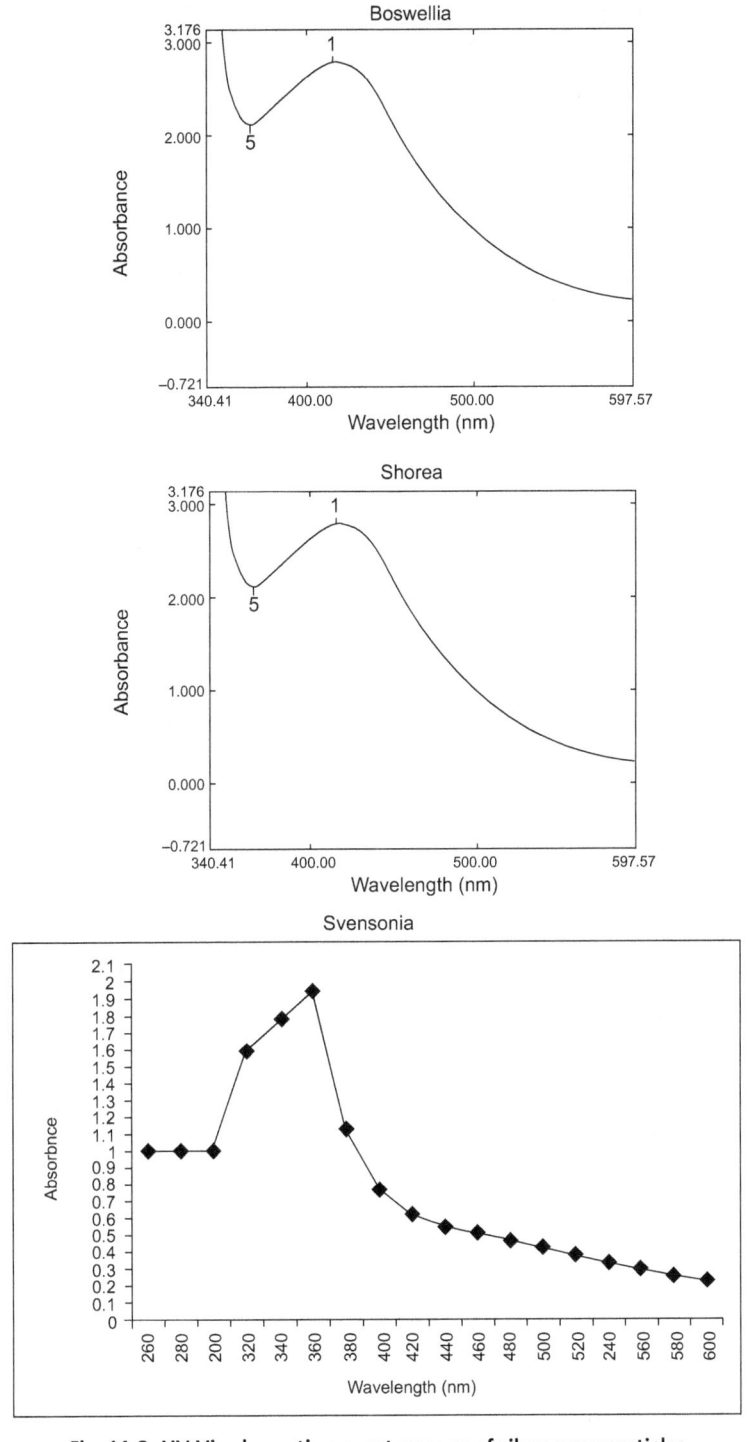

Antimicrobial Activity of Silver Nanoparticles 123

Fig. 11.2: UV-Vis absorption spectroscopy of silver nanoparticles

124 *Salai Gum*

        Boswellia   **Shorea**   **Svensonia**

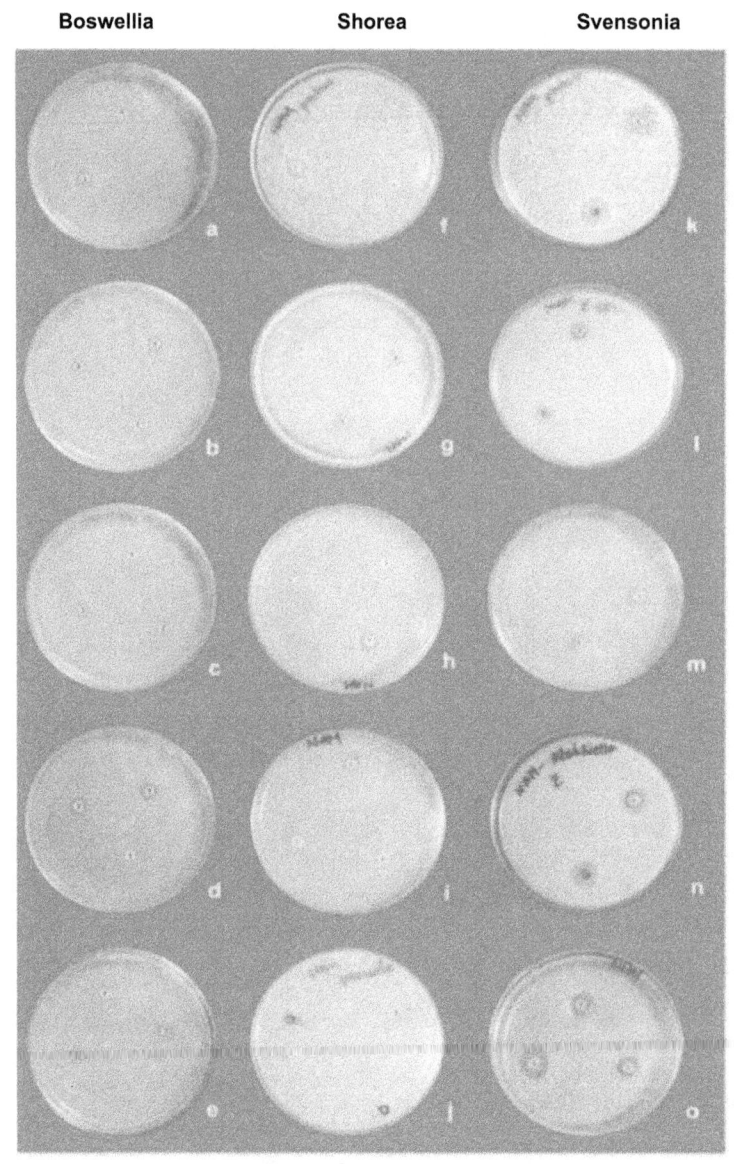

1. Control, 2. Silver nanoparticles, 3. Silver nitrate
a, f, k) *Proteus*; b, g, l) *E. coli*, c, h, m) *Bacillus*; d, i, n) *Klebsiella*; e, j, o) *Pseudomonas*

Fig. 11.3: Antibacterial activity of medicinal plants

    Silver nitrate is used as reducing agent as silver has distinctive properties such as good conductivity, catalytic and chemical stability. The aqueous silver ions when exposed to herbal extracts were reduced in solution, there by leading to the formation of silver hydrosol. The time duration of change in colour varies from plant to plant. *Boswellia* ovalifoliolata synthesized silver nanopartcles within 10 min whereas Shorea tumbuggaia and Svensonia hyderobadensis took 15 min to synthesize nanoparticles. The synthesis of SNPs had been confirmed by measuring the UV-Vis spectrum of the reaction media. The UV-Vis spectrum of colloidal solutions of SNPs synthesized from

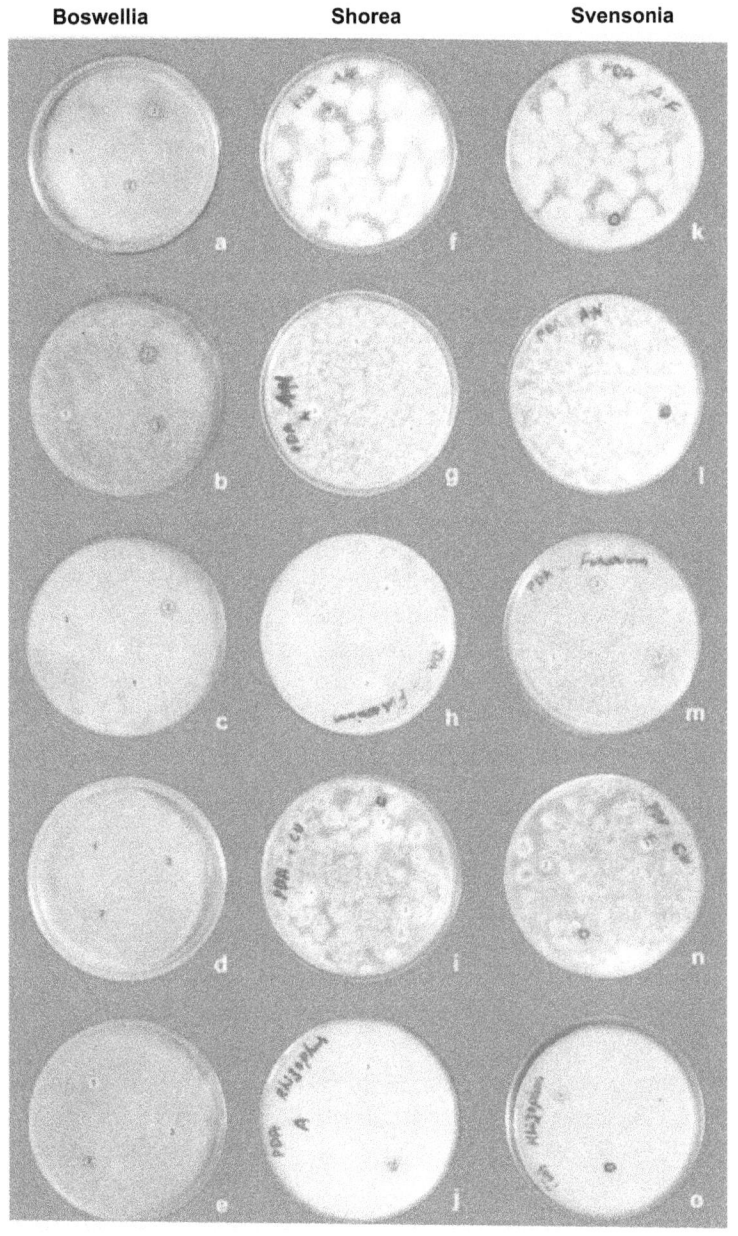

1. Control, 2. Silver nanoparticles, 3. Silver nitrate
a, f, k) *Aspergillus flavus*; b, g, l) *Aspergillus niger*, c, h, m) *Fusarium*; d, i, n) *Curvularia*; e, j, o) *Rhizopus*

Fig. 11.4: Antifungal activity of medicinal plants

Boswellia ovaliofoliolata, Shorea tumbuggaia and Svensonia hyderobadensis have absorbance peaks at 350 nm, 430 and 300 to 400 nm respectively; and the broadening of peak indicated that the particles are poly-dispersed (Figure 11.2).

The weak absorption peak at shorter wave lengths due to the presence of several organic compounds which are known to interact with silver ions. 16Mentioned three different routes for the reduction of silver in plant extracts. The secondary metabolites present in plant systems may be responsible for the reduction of silver and synthesis of nanoparticles. The second biogenic route is the energy (or) electron released during Glycolysis (photosynthesis) for conversion of NAD to NADH led to transformation of $Ag(NO_3)_2$ to form nanoparticles and the another mechanism is releasing of an electron when formation of ascorbate radicals from ascorbate reduces the silver ions. Almost all similar results were observed in Cleodendrum inerme, Euphorbia hirta and Argimone maxicana.

Toxicity studies on pathogen opens a door for nanotechnology applications in medicine. Biological synthesis of metal NPs is a traditional method and the use of plant extracts has a new awareness for the control of disease, besides being safe and no phytotoxic effects. The biologically synthesized silver nanoparticles using medicinal plants were found to be highly toxic against different pathogenic bacteria and fungi of selected species. The SNPs of *Boswellia* ovalifoliolata shows highest antibacterial activity was observed against Klebsiella followed by E. coli and Proteus species; and antifungal activity was observed against Aspergillus and Fusarium. Shorea tumbuggaia shows highest antibacterial activity against *Pseudomonas*, Proteus and Bacillus; and antifungal activity against Fusarium followed by Aspergillus and Rhizopus. Svensonia hyderobadensis shows highest antibacterial activity was observed against *Pseudomonas* followed by Klebsiella, E.coli, Bacillus and Proteus species; and antifungal activity against Rhizopus followed by Aspergillus, Curvularia and Fusarium (Table 11.1). The silver nanoparticles synthesized via green route are highly toxic towards fungal species when compared to bacterial species. Among the three plants tested for antimicrobial effect the silver nanoparticles of Svensonia hyderobadensis have great antifungal efficacy (Figures 11.3 & 11.4). The use of plant extracts is effective against various microorganism including plant pathogens.

Oligodynamic silver antimicrobial efficacy extends well beyond its virotoxicity. The ionic silver strongly interacts with thiol group of vital enzymes and inactivate the enzyme activity. Experimental evidence indicates that DNA loses its replication ability once the bacteria have been treated with silver ions. 16mentioned that the pathogenic effect of nanoparticles can be attributed to their stability in the medium as a colloid, which modulates the phosphotyrosine profile of the pathogen proteins and arrests its growth. The growth of microorganisms was inhibited by the green synthesized SNPs showed variation in the inhibition of growth of microorganisms may be due to the presence of peptidoglycan, which is a complex structure and after contains teichoic acids or lipoteichoic acids which have a strong negative charge. This charge may contribute to the sequestration of free silver ions. Thus gram positive bacteria may allow less silver to reach the cytoplasmic membrane than the gram negative bacteria. The SNPs synthesized from plant species are toxic to multi-drug resistant microorganisms. It shows that they have great potential in biomedical applications. Similar observation was found in Allium cepa, Argimone mexicana Artocarpus heterophyllus. found that silver nanoparticles have an ability to interfere with metabolic pathways. The findings of suggested that the inhibition of oxidation based biological process by penetration of metallic nano sized particles across the microsomal membrane. The use of silver ions as preventing agents in cosmetics was tested by a challenged list in a set of cosmetic dispersions with the addition of known preservative inhibitors or microorganism's growth promoters. Silver has more microbial efficacy and more effective in the presence of proteinaceous material and inorganic binding proteins that associated with inorganic structures in vivo using routine molecular biology techniques. The silver nanoparticles synthesized from leaf extract showed higher toxicity than that of bark extracts. The reason could be that the leaf extract synthesized higher concentration of silver nanoparticles than the bark samples. Moreover green leaves are the site of photosynthesis and availability of more H^+ ions to reduce the silver nitrate into silver nanoparticles. The molecular basis for the biosynthesis of these silver crystals is speculated that the organic matrix contain silver binding proteins that provide amino acid moieties that serve as the nucleation sites. The efficiency of various silver based antimicrobial fillers in polyamide toward their silver ion release characteristics in an aqueous medium was also investigated and discussed in number of plants including algae, yeast and fungi. The selected three plant species have been used in traditional medicine, so for these plants have not been tested to antimicrobial activity. The present work supports the medicinal values of these plants was confirmed and also revealed that a simple, rapid and economical route to synthesis of silver nanoparticles; and their capability of rendering the antimicrobial efficacy. Moreover the synthesized SNPs enhance the therapeutic efficacy and strengthen the medicinal values of these plants.

CONCLUSION

The present study included the bio-reduction of silver ions through medicinal plants extracts and testing for their antimicrobial activity. The aqueous silver ions exposed to the extracts, the synthesis of silver nanoparticles were confirmed by the change of colour of plant extracts. These environmentally benign silver nanoparticles were further confirmed by using UV-V is spectroscopy. The results indicated that silver nanoparticles have good antimicrobial activity against different microorganisms. It is confirmed that silver nanoparticles are capable of rendering high antifungal efficacy and hence has a great potential in the preparation of drugs used against fungal diseases.

12. Antiglycation and Antioxidant Activities and HPTLC Analysis of *Boswellia sacra* Oleogum Resin
The Sacred Frankincense

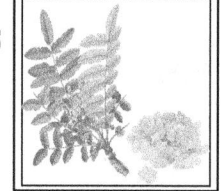

Frankincense from *Boswellia* trees has been used for various therapeutic purposes since the very beginning of the human civilization. It is still used from North Africa to China as a remedy in various formulations for the treatment of inflammation-related disorders, and a multitude of phytochemical and pharmacological properties of the gum resin have been documented. Furthermore, the pharmacological effects of pentacyclic triterpenes, especially those reported from *Boswellia* species (boswellic acid derivatives) are numerous, and these include anti-inflammatory, hepatoprotective, anti-tumour, anti-HIV, anti-microbial, antifungal, anti-ulcer, gastroprotective, hypoglycemic and antihyperlipidemic properties. These boswellic acid derivatives have a similar molecular structure which makes their separation by simple thin-layer chromatography challenging.

High performance thin layer chromatography (HPTLC) is becoming a technique for the routine analysis for the identification of medicinal plants and derived products. The possibility of presenting chromatographic fingerprints as electronic images that can easily be stored, shared and compared for multiple samples in parallel is the principal advantage of the technique over Gas chromatography (GC), highy-performance liquid chromatography (HPLC), and other column chromatography. While simplicity and cost efficiency are preserved, separation power and reproducibility as well as traceability of data are significantly improved over classical thin layer chromatography (TLC).

The present study employs HPTLC identification and biological evaluation of *Boswellia sacra* to explore the antiglycation and antioxidant potentials of the resin derived from *Boswellia* species.

EXPERIMENTAL
Chemicals

Chemicals such as 1,1-diphenyl-2-picrylhydrazyl radical (DPPH), naphthyl-ethylenediamine, sodium nitroprusside, sulfanilic acid, potassium hydrogen phosphate, dipotassium hydrogen phosphate, 3-(2-pyridyl)-5,6-di(p-sulfophenyl)-1,2,4-triazine, disodium salt (ferrozine), reduced β-nicotinamide adenine dinucleotide (NADH), 5-methylphenazium methyl sulfate (PMS), nitro blue tetrazolium salt (NBT), standard radical scavengers: propyl gallate, 3-t-butyl-4-hydroxyanisol, 7,8-dihydroxy flavone; and solvents: dimethylsulfoxide (DMSO), carbon tetrachloride, and ethanol were purchased from Sigma or Fluka and used without further purification. Water used for buffer preparation was deionized using Simplicity water purification system (Millipore).

Plant Materials

The aerial parts of *B. sacra* and the various grades of resin were collected in April and May 2010 from different locations in Dhofar (southern part of Oman) and were supplied by a trusted Dhofari partner (Dr. Saleh Al-Amri). Super hougari green (SHG), hougari regular (HR), royal hougari white (RHW), and hougari yellow (HY) grade resins were collected from Wadi Hougar in Oman, while shabi frankincense (SF) was collected from Wadi Magsyl in Oman. Frankincense Oleogum resins were collected from *Boswellia sacra* tree by making careful incisions into the bark of the tree without harming the tree. A thick milky-white liquid oozed out and then solidified into pea-sized "tears".

These samples were authenticated by Dr Mustafa Mansi (a taxonomist) of the Department of Biological Sciences and Chemistry, University of Nizwa, Sultanate of Oman and voucher specimen (no. BSHR-01/2012) of the plant was deposited in the herbarium of the Department of Biological Sciences and Chemistry.

Extraction and Isolation

The air-dried ground material (500 g) of HR grade resin was exhaustively extracted with 100 % methanol at room temperature. The extract was evaporated to yield the residue (150 g). Subfractionation of the crude methanol extract (150 g) of HR grade resin was carried out by vacuum liquid chromatography. A silica gel column (1000 g, 70-230 mesh, Merck) was used for the fractionation with CH_2Cl_2/n-hexane (50:50) as a mobile phase. Various sub-fractions were obtained from liquid chromatography and compiled on the basis of the similarity observed on TLC plates. The essential oils of all available grades of the resin were extracted by hydrodistillation using 8 Quart Stove Still Home Distillation Unit with Clevenger's apparatus until complete exhaustion.

HPTLC Analysis

Chromatography was performed on pre-coated HPTLC silica gel glass plates 60 F254 (20 × 10 cm; E. Merck, Germany) for the development of characteristic fingerprinting profile of the selected samples of the resin from *B. sacra*. Each sample (0.5 g) was dissolved in HPLC grade methanol (5 mL) and sonicated for 10 min. The solution was then centrifuged at 3000 rpm for 10 min and the upper layer was used for HPTLC analysis after 1:1 dilution with methanol (the standard *Boswellia* extract was diluted 1:20). Thereafter, 0.5 and 2 µL of each sample were applied as bands of 8 mm using Automatic TLC sampler 4 (CAMAG, Switzerland) with a 25 µL syringe.

Linear ascending development was carried out in Automatic Developing Chamber (ADC2, CAMAG, Switzerland) saturated with mobile phase for

20 min at room temperature (24 °C) using a filter paper. For optimum conditions, relative humidity (RH) was controlled at 33% in ADC$_2$ using a saturated solution of MgCl$_2$. Toluene: ethyl acetate: heptane: formic acid (80:20:10:3, v/v/v/v) was used as the mobile phase.

The plates were developed to a distance of 7 cm from the lower edge of the plate. Drying was carried out for 5 min in a stream of cold air. For derivatization, the plate was immersed in anisaldehyde sulphuric acid reagent (170 mL of ice-cooled methanol mixed with 20 mL of acetic acid, 10 mL of sulfuric acid and 1 mL of anisaldehyde) followed by heating at 100 °C for 5 min. Images of the chromatograms were electronically documented with Visualizer (CAMAG Switzerland) under UV 254 nm before derivatization and under UV 366 nm and white light after derivatization. The identity of the zones in the sample corresponding to 3-O-acetyl-11-keto-β-boswellic acid (AKBA) was confirmed by comparing their densitometrically-obtained UV spectra with those of a AKBA reference standard (Phytolab, Vestenbergsgreut, Germany). HPTLC according to PhEur 7 Monograph for Indian Frankincense. Mobile phase: Anhydrous formic acid–heptane–ethyl acetate–toluene (3 + 10 + 20 + 80, v/v/v/v). Detection: UV light at 254 nm.

Reference compound: KBA = 11-keto-β- boswellic acid.

Cytotoxicity and antiradical studies against the 1,1-diphenyl-2-picrylhydrazyl radicals were carried out at 37 °C, while the enzymatic reactions and superoxide scavenging studies were carried out at 28 °C. All studies were performed in 96-well microtitre plates using SpectraMax-340 and SpectraMax-384 spectrophotometers (Molecular Devices, CA, USA).

Antiglycation Assay

Bovine serum albumin (BSA, 10 mg/mL) was dissolved in 67 mM phosphate buffer (20 μL) of pH 7.4 which incorporated 50 mg/mL anhydrous glucose (20 μL). Thereafter, a 3 mM sodium azide (20 μL) was added to inhibit bacterial growth. For assessment of antiglycation activity, each fraction (20 μL; 1 mg/1000 μL) was mixed and the mixture (60 μL in each well of 96-well plate) was incubated for a week at 37 °C. A blank sample containing only BSA dissolved in phosphate buffer and positive control sample containing both BSA and glucose, were prepared and incubated for a week at 37 °C. After incubation in 96-well plate for a week, samples were removed and cooled to room temperature, amd 6 μL of 100% trichloroacetic acid (TCA) was added to each well. The supernatant containing unbound glucose, inhibitor and test sample were removed after centrifugation at 14,000 rpm for 4 min, and 60 ?L of PBS (pH 10) was added to dissolve the pellets left. Comparison of fluorescence intensity at 370 nm excitation and emission at 440 nm was obtained by spectrofluorimetry (RF-1500, Shimadzu, Kyoto, Japan). Rutin was used as standard inhibitor. Inhibition (%) was calculated as in Eq 1

$$\text{Inhibition} = 100 - \{(As/Ab) \times 100\} \quad \ldots(1)$$

where As and Ab are the absorbance of sample and blank, respectively.

Superoxide Anion Scavenging Assay

Superoxide scavenging activities of the samples were determined by the method described by Gaulejac et. al. with some modifications. The reaction was performed in triplicate in a 96-well plate and absorbance was measured on a multiplate reader (SpectraMax 340, Molecular Devices, CA, USA). The reaction mixture contained 40 µL of nicotinamide adenine dinucleotide (NADH), 40 µL of nitroblue tetrazolium (NBT), 90 µL of 0.1M phosphate buffer (pH 7.4) and 10 µL of the test compound pre-read at 560 nm. The reaction was initiated by the addition of 20 µL of phenazine methosulphate (PMS), and incubated at room temperature for 5 min. Formation of blue-colored formazan dye was measured at 560 nm. Control contained 10 µL of dimethyl sul foxide (DMSO), instead of the test samples. The solutions of NBT, NADH and PMS were prepared in phosphate buffer, while the test samples were dissolved in DMSO.

DPPH Free Radical Scavenging Assay

Free radical scavenging activity of the test samples were determined by measuring the change in absorbance of DPPH (l,l-Diphenyl-2-picrylhydrazyl radical) spectrophotometrically at 515 nm. The reaction mixture comprised of 95 µL of ethanol solution of DPPH and 5 µL of the test sample dissolved in DMSO. Total reaction volume was 100 µL, with final concentrations of 300 µM and 1000 µM of DPPH and test compound, respectively. The reaction mixture was then incubated at 37 °C for 30 min. After incubation, decrease in absorption was measured at 515 nm spectrophotometrically (Molecular Devices, CA, USA). The control contained 5 µL of DMSO instead of the test sample and the reactions were performed in triplicates. To avoid solvent evaporation during incubation, the 96-well plate was covered with parafilm immediately after the addition of DPPH solution and the reaction mixtures were thoroughly mixed by shaking the plate for 1 min. The absorbance of the yellow-colored reduced form of DPPH produced after incubation was measured at 562 nm using a multiplate reader (SpectraMax 340), and radical scavenging activity (RSA,%) was determined according to Eq 2.

$$\% \text{ RSA} = 100 - \{At/Ac\} \times 100\} \quad \ldots(2)$$

where, At is the absorbance of radicals and formazan dye in the presence of the test sample and Ac is the absorbance of control, formazan dye without test sample.

Statistical Analysis

The data obtained were analyzed statistically using Statistic Analysis System (SAS, version 9.1). Each experiment was repeated three times and values expressed are means ± standard error. Differences were considered significant at $p < 0.05$.

RESULTS

HPTLC Fingerprinting Profile

Boswellic acids are pharmacologically active compounds isolated from the resins (frankincense) of various species of *Boswellia*. HPTLC allows rapid investigation, identification and comparison of the quality of different kinds of frankincense (Olibanum). In the present study, the HPTLC profile of the crude resin (Figure 12.1; tracks 3 and 4), the crystalline medium polarity fraction (tracks 5 and 6), and the hydrodistillate essential oil (tracks 7 and 8) were analyzed at two quantitative levels (0.5 and 2.0 µL). *Boswellia serrata* extract (track 1) and the gum resin (track 2), and compared with the standard sample, 3-O-acetyl-11-keto-β-boswellic acid (AKBA, track 9). All samples showed the presence of 11-keto-β-boswellic acid (KBA, lower arrow, track 8) and 3-O-acetyl-11-keto-β- boswellic acid (AKBA, upper arrow, track 8) with different concentration (intensity) in all the three test samples (Figure 12.1). The same compounds were identified in approximately the same concentration for the standard *B. serrata* extract and the gum resin (KBA and AKBA, black arrows, tracks 1 and 2). These results were further confirmed by matching the UV spectra of the corresponding bands in the test samples with those of the standard AKBA. These results and comparison with the literature confirm the identity of the investigated samples as *B. sacra* based on various concentrations of KBA and AKBA. The concentrations of the same compounds in *B. serrata* were approximately equal. These observations were further confirmed through derivatization of the HPTLC plate with the anisaldehyde reagent (Figure 12.2).

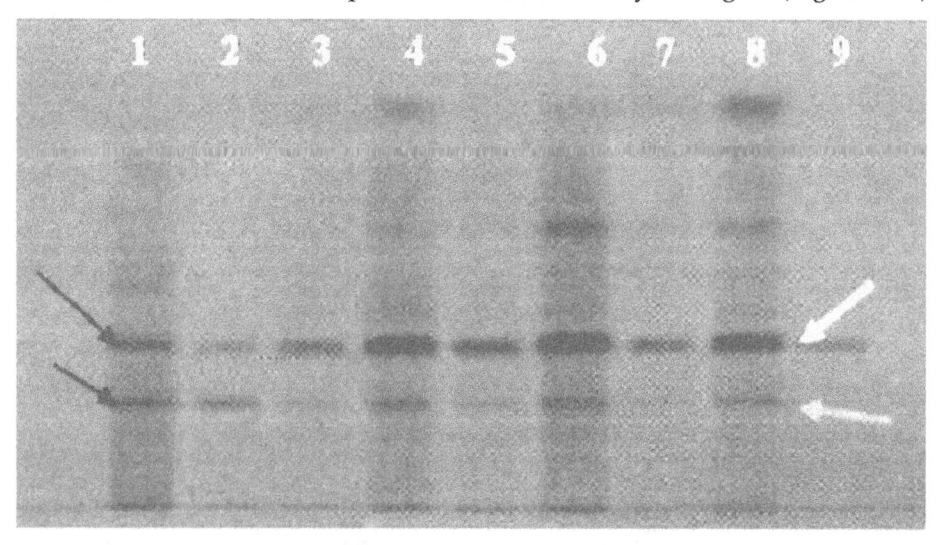

Fig. 12.1: Detection and comparison of boswellic

acids in different samples of *Boswellia sacra*. Track 1 = *Boswellia serrata* extract (CAMAG); Track 2 = *Boswellia serrata* gum (CAMAG); Track 3 & 4 = *Boswellia sacra* resin (test sample, 0.5 and 2.0 µL, respectively); Track 5 & 6 *Boswellia sacra* crystalline fraction (test sample, 0.5 and 2.0 µL respectively); Track 7 & 8 = *Boswellia sacra* resin (test sample, 0.5 and 2.0 µL respectively); Track 9 = standard AKBA.

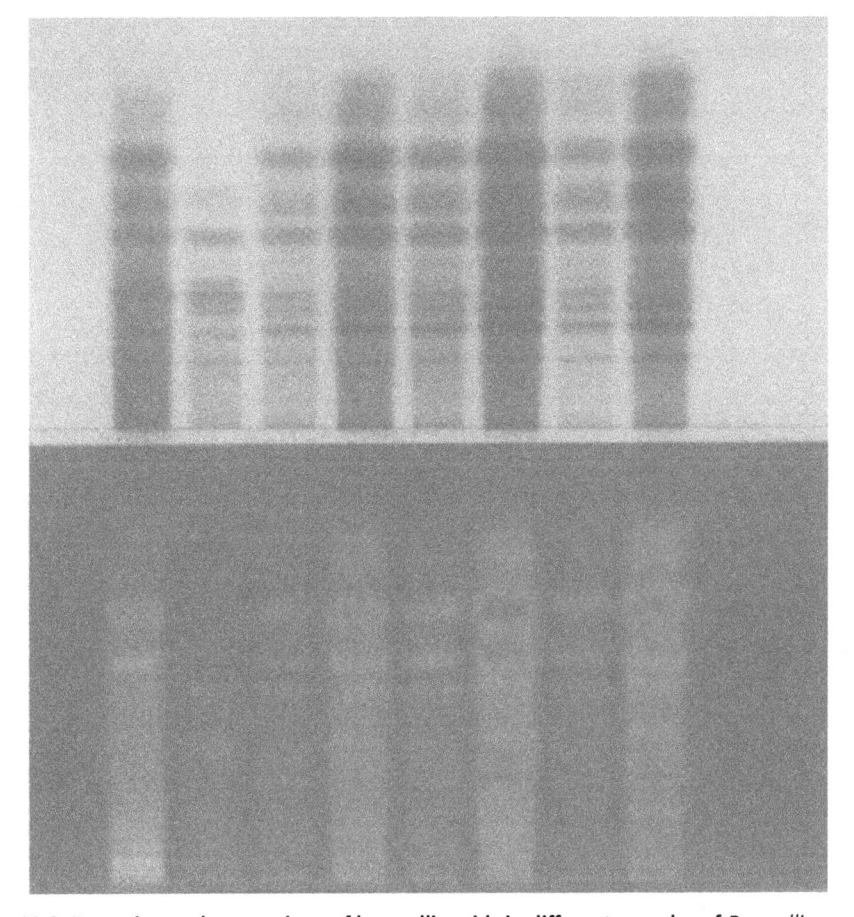

Fig. 12.2: Detection and comparison of boswellic acids in different samples of *Boswellia sacra*.

Track 1 = *Boswellia serrata* extract (CAMAG); Track 2 = *Boswellia serrata* gum (CAMAG); Track 3 & 4 = *Boswellia sacra* resin (test sample, 0.5 and 2.0 µL, respectively); Track 5 & 6 *Boswellia sacra* crystalline fraction (test sample, 0.5 and 2.0 µL respectively); Track 7 & 8 = *Boswellia sacra* resin (test sample, 0.5 and 2.0 µL respectively); Track 9 = standard AKBA.

Antiglycation Activity

All the tested samples showed varied inhibitory potential in vitro at a concentration of 1 mg/1000 µL (Table 12.1). The sub-fraction obtained with 36% CH_2Cl_2/n-hexane showed the highest inhibitory activity (69.5%), followed by 2% methanol/ CH$_2$Cl$_2$ (66.9%) and Royal lower (RL) oil (54.3%). The sub-fraction obtained with 40% methanol/CH$_2$Cl$_2$ and Shabi frankincense (SF) oil showed moderate activity in antiglycation assay whereas the other samples were weakly active or completely inactive (Table 12.1).

Table 12.1: Antiglycation and Antioxidant Activities (mean ± standard error) of Various Fractions of *Boswellia serrata*

Sample	Inhibitory activity (%)		
	Antiglycation	DPPH	Superoxide
HR oil[a]	9.20 ± 0.02	16.30 ± 0.04	56.40 ± 0.01
RL oil	54.30 ± 0.01	5.60 ± 0.02	50.50 ± 0.02
RU oil	5.30 ± 0.06	2.80 ± 0.01	52.80 ± 0.05
SF oil	37.20 ± 0.01	33.40 ± 0.04	33.10 ± 0.08
Crude extract	10.90 ± 0.03	14.30 ± 0.05	49.00 ± 0.02
Pure n-hexane	6.80 ± 0.02	6.60 ± 0.03	50.80 ± 0.14
36% CH$_2$Cl$_2$/n-hexane	69.50 ± 0.06	11.90 ± 0.12	13.40 ± 0.03
40% CH$_2$Cl$_2$/n-hexane	14.40 ± 0.1	31.30 ± 0.03	16.90 ± 0.05
60% CH$_2$Cl$_2$/n-hexane	7.80 ± 0.01	15.60 ± 0.08	23.40 ± 0.01
80% CH$_2$Cl$_2$/n-hexane	10.30 ± 0.03	13.30 ± 0.05	33.50 ± 0.03
Pure CH$_2$Cl$_2$	12.40 ± 0.07	31.80 ± 0.14	49.70 ± 0.04
2% MeOH/CH$_2$Cl$_2$	66.90 ± 0.02	10.90 ± 0.08	6.20 ± 0.01
2% MeOH/CH$_2$Cl$_2$	9.90 ± 0.03	12.10 ± 0.07	11.80 ± 0.02
2% MeOH/CH$_2$Cl$_2$	41.20 ± 0.04	10.00 ± 0.2	50.80 ± 0.04
Standard	Rutin (82.50%)	Propyl gallate (90.30%)	Propyl gallate (92.50%)

[a]HR = Hougari regular; RL = Royal lower; RU = Royal upper; SF = Shabi frankincense

Superoxide Anion Scavenging Activity

The results obtained indicate that the non-polar sub-fractions exhibited > 50% inhibition, except n-hexane fraction, CH$_2$Cl$_2$ fraction and 40% methanol/CH$_2$Cl$_2$ fraction all of which exhibited approximately the level same inhibition which was close to 50%. Other test samples showed < 50% inhibition was close to 50%. Other test samples showed < 50% inhibition.

DPPH Free Radical Scavenging Activity

CH$_2$Cl$_2$ fraction and the sub-fraction of 40% CH$_2$Cl$_2$/n-hexane fraction, as well as SF oil showed moderate activity (Table 12.1), while the other samples were largely inactive. Standard rutin showed 82.5% inhibition of glycation at 3mM concentration with IC50 of 98.01 ± 2.03 μM.

DISCUSSION

Triterpenic acids are an important group of natural compounds with confirmed pharmacological activity. They occur in many medicinal herbs and plants. The similarity of their chemical structures makes their TLC separation very difficult. There are some chromatographic systems described in the literature, but they do not offer better separation, and the result is poor overall yield of the pure natural products. In this regard, our approach using HPTLC offers more effective separation and higher yield. Oxidation process plays an important role in glycation end-products (AGEs) formation and is essential to many living organisms for the production of energy to fuel the biological processes. On the other hand, reactive oxygen species (ROS) can damage DNA and thus cause mutation and chromosomal damage.

Furthermore, production of excessive free radicals stimulates oxidative damage which is responsible for more than one hundred disorders in humans including atherosclerosis, coronary heart disease, neurodegenerative disorders, cancer, and aging process. Therefore, agents with antioxidative or metal-chelating properties may retard the process of AGEs formation by preventing metal-catalyzed glucose oxidation.

Free radicals, such as hydroxyl radical, are generated from sequential reduction of oxygen during the normal course of aerobic metabolism. Overabundant radicals cause oxidative stress which can lead to cell injury and tissue damage. *B. sacra* extract is a potential source of natural antioxidants, and incorporation of these extract into foods could enhance their nutritional and antioxidant potentials.

DPPH radicals are widely used to investigate the scavenging activity of natural compounds. These free radicals are stable in ethanol and show maximum absorbance at 517 nm. When DPPH radicals encounter a proton-donating substance such as an antioxidant, the radicals are scavenged and their absorbance reduced. *B. sacra* extracts and essential oils showed scavenging activities against DPPH radicals.

This is not surprising since they contain a large variety of terpenes, which could be electron donors, and hence can react with free radicals to convert them to more stable products and terminate radical chain reaction. The results gleaned from antioxidant and antiglycation assays indicated that the fractions obtained by the use of a n-hexane or CH_2Cl_2 solvent were comparatively more active in almost all the assays. Furthermore the crystalline subfractions and the more polar fractions (40% methanol/CH_2Cl_2) also showed comparatively higher activity than the other tested samples. These observations indicate that overall activity increases the purer the sample and the higher the polarity of the fraction. The polar subfractions obtained when methanol solvent system was added contain chemical compounds that are believed to be responsible for their higher antiglycation activity. Our assumption is supported by a study on

Plantago asiatica which showed higher antiglycation activity (75%) for polar fractions.

CONCLUSION

An HPTLC method has been applied successfully for the simultaneous fingerprint identification of boswellic acid derivatives in *B. sacra*.

The method was found to be simple and specific and suitable for further qualitative analysis of the plant material. The tested materials possessed high antioxidant and antiglycation activities. Thus the plant may offer additional sources of ingredients that can be formulated into products for health promotion.

13 Formulation and Evaluation of Zidovudine Loaded Olibanum Resin Microcapsules

Drug discovery alone is insufficient in treating diseases; often correct dosing and targeting are equally important for clinical success. Researchers in the area of controlled or sustained drug delivery systems specifically concentrate in to these areas to enhance the efficacy of therapeutics for specific treatment regimens. Controlled drug delivery systems are aimed at controlling the release of the drug at a therapeutically effective rate, prolonging the duration of drug delivery & therapeutic response and targeting the delivery of the drug to a tissue.

One of the very common types of orally administered controlled release system is microparticles which includes microcapsules and microspheres, produced by a process known as microencapsulation. Moreover these are multiunit systems that spread over a large surface area of absorbing mucosa and prevent exposure to a high drug concentration, when compared to single unit dosage form on chronic dosing. They release the drug more uniformly instead of vagaries of gastric emptying and different transit rates through the gastrointestinal tract. Microencapsulation by various polymer and their applications are described in standard text books.

Although a variety of polymeric materials are available to serve as a release retarding microencapsulating agent but use of natural biodegradable polymers to prolong the delivery of the drugs is always an area of active research despite the advent of synthetic biodegradable polymers. Natural biodegradable polymers remains attractive primarily because they are readily available in the nature, relatively inexpensive, products of living organisms, readily undergoes in-vivo degradation, non-toxic and capable of chemical modifications. In the present study olibanum resin was used as a natural biodegradable microencapsulating agent to retard the release of the drug. Olibanum is obtained from the oleo gum resin of incised trunk of the tree *Boswellia serrata* belonging to the family *Burseraceae*, commonly known as Sallaki guggul, Salai gum and *Indian olibanum*. 10 species of *Boswellia* occur in tropical parts of Asia and Africa. In India *B. serrata* species found in dry and hilly area of Bihar, Madhya Pradesh and Gujarat. Olibanum consist of mainly an acid resin (56-60%), gum (30-36%) and volatile oil (3- 8%). Gum is mainly composed of arabinose with small amount of xylose and galactose.

One of the most popular methods for the formulation of biodegradable microparticles is solvent evaporation technique, where the drug is dissolved or dispersed in to an organic polymer solution, which is then emulsified in to a continuous aqueous or oil phase. The microparticles are formed after removing the solvent.

Aquired immunodeficiency syndrome (AIDS), caused by Human Immunodeficiency Virus (HIV) is an immuno suppressive disease results in life-threatening opportunistic infections and malignancies. Since its first identification in California about three decades ago in 1981, more than 25 million people all over the world has been killed by this dreaded killer. UNAIDS 2012 report on global AIDS epidemic showed 34 million people were living with HIV at the end of 2011 and around 1.7 million people died from AIDS related causes worldwide in 2011. To date there are approximately 30 antiretroviral products, formulated singly or in combination to treat patient with HIV.

Zidovudine (3'-azido-3'-deoxythymidine or AZT) originally synthesized in 1964 as a potential anticancer agent, was approved as first antiretroviral agent ever in 1987 for the treatment of AIDS. However along with its therapeutic effectiveness, AZT is also associated with certain limitations like poor-bioavailability, dose-dependent hematological toxicity, short biological half life, low therapeutic index etc. But administration of antiviral agents like AZT is required chronically or possibly for the life time of the patient. In case of oral route the dose of AZT ranges from 3mg/kg to 10mg/kg body weight at every four hours interval to maintain the constant therapeutic blood levels. These frequent dosing intervals are undesirable in terms of patient compliance and generating toxicity (associated with excessive plasma levels) immediately after oral or intravenous administrations. In order to succeed in an effective therapy for AIDS, it is crucial to maintain the systemic drug concentration consistently above their target antiretroviral concentration throughout the course of their treatment without much oscillation in its plasma levels, which can be done by formulating controlled or sustained release dosage forms of AZT. Therefore, AZT is an ideal candidate for sustained release microsphere formulation, resulting in more reproducible drug absorption and reducing the dosing frequency, thereby improving patient compliance as compared to immediate release dosage forms. The objective of the present study was to formulate and evaluate natural biodegradable sustained release microcapsules of AZT using olibanum resin as release retardant.

MATERIALS AND METHODS

Zidovudine was obtained as gift sample from HETERO DRUGS Ltd. (Hyderabad, India). Olibanum resin was obtained as a gift sample from Girijan Corporation, (Viasakhapatnum, India). Acetone (Merck), diethyl ether (Qualigens), Light liquid Paraffin (Qualigens), span 80 (Finnar chemicals) etc. are used. All reagents were of pharmaceutical grade and were used as received.

Preparation of Microcapsules

Zidovudine-loaded microcapsules were prepared by an industrially feasible emulsion solvent evaporation technique. Acetone was used as the polymer solvent, light liquid paraffin as oil phase, Span 80 as emulsifying agent and n-hexane to wash away the paraffin oil. To prepare microcapsules with various drug to polymer ratios (w/w), accurately weighed amount of Zidovudine was dissolved in acetone solution (w/v) of olibanum resin. The drug to polymer ratio was varied keeping the amount of drug and solvent constant in all cases, but changing the amount of polymer. The oil phase was prepared by dispersing Span 80 as the emulsifying agent in liquid paraffin, with a constant composition in all cases. The organic phase was poured into the oil phase under constant stirring rate at 1200 rpm contained in a 500 ml beaker to emulsify the added dispersion as fine droplets. A Remi medium duty stirrer with a digital speed meter (Model RQT 124) was used for stirring. After the emulsion formation, acetone was completely removed by evaporation at room temperature during an approximately 3 h stirring period. The light mineral oil was decanted and the microcapsules were collected, washed three times with 100 ml of n-hexane at room temperature, afterwards the microcapsules were separated by vacuum filtration and air dried for 12 h to obtain discrete microcapsules.

Estimation of Zidovudine

Accurately weighed microcapsules equivalent to 100 mg of drug was crushed and suspended in 100 ml of pH 7.4 phosphate buffer. The resulting mixture was stirred at 1000 rpm for 2 hrs and kept overnight. Then the solution was filtered, diluted suitably and analyzed for drug content at 264.99 nm using UV-visible spectrophotometer (Carry 60, Agilent, Australia).

Production Yield and Microencapsulation Efficiency

The yield of the microcapsules was expressed as percentage of the weight of the dried microcapsules at room temperature compared to the theoretical amount. Production yield or percentage yield is calculated by using the following Equation.

$$\text{Percentage Yield (\%)} = \frac{\text{Weight of microcapsules obtained}}{\text{Weight of raw materials}} \times 100$$

Microencapsulation efficiency was calculated using following formula:

$$\text{Microencapsulation efficiency (\%)} = \frac{\text{Actual drug content}}{\text{Theoretical drug content}} \times 100$$

THEORETICAL DRUG CONTENT

Micromeritic Properties

Micromeritic properties, such as angle of repose, tapped density and bulk density were measured. The angle of repose was calculated by static method using Funnel. The experiments were carried out in triplicate.

Determination of Particle Size Distribution by Sieve Analysis

Separation of the microcapsules into various size fractions was carried out using a mechanical sieve shaker. A series of five standard stainless steel sieves (Geologists Syndicate Pvt. Ltd, India) having mesh size of #10, #20, #30, #50 and #80 were arranged in an order of decreasing aperture size. About 10 g of drug loaded microcapsules were placed on the uppermost sieve. The sieves were shaken for a period of 10 min, and then the particles on each screen were weighed. The procedure was carried out three times for each product.

Characterization of AZT microcapsules

FT-IR Studies

Drug-polymer interactions were studied by FT-IR spectroscopy using the instrument Shimadzu, Japan, FTIR-8400S. The spectra were recorded for pure drug Zidovudine and microcapsules containing drug. Samples were prepared in KBr discs (2 mg sample in 200 mg KBr) with a hydrostatic press at a force of 5.2 N/m^2 for 3 min. The scanning range was 400–4000 cm^{-1} and the resolution was 4 cm^{-1}.

Surface Scanning Electron Microscopy (SEM)

The surface morphology of the microcapsules was observed by using scanning electron microscope (LEO 440i, England). The samples were mounted on an aluminum sample stub using adhesive carbon tape and placed in a low humidity chamber for 12 h prior to analysis. Samples were coated with gold-palladium for 60 sec under an argon atmosphere using ion sputter coater in a high vacuum evaporator equipped with a rotary stage tray. Images were taken at an acceleration voltage of 20 kV.

Differential Scanning Calorimetry

The thermal behavior of the microcapsules was investigated using differential scanning calorimeter (DSC 60, Shimadzu, Japan). Samples of about 5 mg were placed in 50 µm perforated aluminium pans and sealed. All samples were run at a heating rate of 10°/min over a temperature range of 5–300°C in atmosphere of nitrogen as purging gas at a flow rate of 25 ml/min.

X-ray Diffraction Analysis

Microcapsules were subjected to X-ray diffraction analysis, using Philips PW 170 system (Philips USA) with Cu-Kα radiation (400 kV, 30 mA, and scan speed 1°/min) to investigate the physical state of zidovudine entrapped in the microcapsules.

In-vitro Drug Release Studies

The in-vitro release rate study of AZT from resin-coated microcapsules were carried out for 24 hours using paddle type dissolution apparatus (USP-XXIII, ETC-11L, Electrolab, Mumbai) containing 900 ml of dissolution medium maintained at 37 ± 0.5°C and speed of agitation at 100 rpm. An accurately weighed quantity of microcapsules containing around 100mg of drug were suspended in dissolution medium consisting 900 ml of phosphate buffer pH 7.4, and the process was continued up to 24 hours. The system was adjusted to ensure sink conditions. Aliquots (5 ml) of the dissolution medium were withdrawn at predetermined time intervals, filtered by using Whatman No. 42 filter and were replenished immediately with the same volume of fresh medium. Withdrawn samples were assayed spectrophotometrically at 264.99 nm, the detected wavelength of maximum absorbance of zidovudine in pH 7.4 phosphate buffer (Cary 60, Agilent Technologies). Olibanum resin did not interfere with Zidovudine absorption in pH 7.4 phosphate buffer at this wavelength. The analysis was carried out in triplicate.

Kinetic Models and the Analysis of the Release Profiles

The in vitro release profiles were fitted on various kinetic models like Higuchi, first-order, Peppas and zero-order equations in order to find out the mechanism of drug release. The rate constants were calculated from the slope of the respective plots. The data obtained were also put in Korsemeyer-Peppas model in order to find out n value, which describes the drug release mechanism. The mechanism of drug release from spherical polymeric devices may be Fickian diffusion when the value of $n = 0.43$ or less, anomalous (non-Fickian) transport when the value of n lies between 0.43 and 0.85, and case II transport when $n = 0.85$. An exponent value of n greater than 0.85 signifies super case II transport mechanism.

RESULTS AND DISCUSSION

Preparation of Microcapsules, Production Yield (%), Estimation of Drug Content and Microencapsulation Efficiency (%)

In an attempt to modify the release of zidovudine from the microcapsules, different batches of formulations were prepared in which the increasing amounts of olibanum resin were added to the fixed weight of zidovudine. When hydrophilic drugs like AZT are encapsulated using an aqueous phase as the processing medium, preferentially they partition out in to the aqueous medium leading to low encapsulation efficiency. It has been reported that as much as 80% AZT can partition out in to the outer aqueous processing medium depending on the processing conditions. In the present study an attempt was made to encapsulate AZT with sufficiently high encapsulation efficiency employing a natural biodegradable resin like olibanum and using a non-aqueous processing medium (liquid paraffin). Span 80, a non-ionic surface active agent having HLB value 4.3 was used to stabilize the emulsification process by reducing the interfacial tension. The highest product yield and encapsulation efficiency was achieved by increasing the drug-polymer ratio

(Table 13.1). It was observed that the encapsulation efficiencies were within a narrow range suggesting an identical distribution of drug in different batches.

Table 13.1: Data Showing Core: Coat Ratio, Production Yield and Microencapsulation Efficiency

Formulation Codes	Core: Coat ratio	% Yield	Microencapsulation Efficiency
ZO1	1:0.1	46.27	81.615
ZO2	1:0.25	48.59	84.474
ZO3	1:0.5	56.36	85.806
ZO4	1:0.7	58.73	86.616
ZO5	1:0.8	61.98	87.191
ZO6	1:0.9	62.42	88.592

SEM and Micromeritic Studies

The SEM photomicrographs of the optimized formulation of AZT indicated that the microcapsules were discrete, spherical, free flowing, multinucleate, and uniform in shape (Figure 13.1). Surface of the microcapsules appear to be rough, may be due to the presence of drug. The different batches of AZT loaded microcapsules were assessed for parameters like angle of repose, bulk density, tapped density, Carr's index and Hausner's ratio. The results were given in the Table 13.2. The flow properties of different batches of microcapsules were excellent as the angle of repose values were found to be less than 25, compressibility index less than 15% and Hausner's ratio less than 1.25 in case of all the batches. It suggests that microcapsules don't require a glidant.

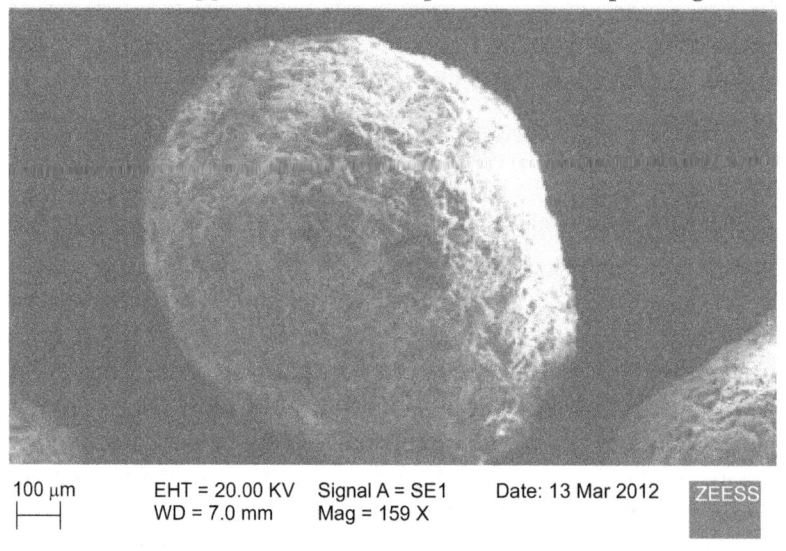

Fig. 13.1: Scanning electron micrographs of AZT loaded microcapsules (ZO4)

Table 13.2: Flow Properties of Microcapsules

Formulation Codes	Angle of Repose ± S.D.	Loose Bulk Density (g/cm³) ± S.D.	Tapped Bulk Density (g/cm³) ± S.D.	Carr's Index (%)	Hausner's Ratio
ZO1	22.4 ± 0.043	0.376 ± 0.004	30.435 ± 0.11	13.56	1.15
ZO2	23.38 ± 0.07	0.402 ± 0.007	0.45 ± 0.017	10.66	1.11
ZO3	21.75 ± 0.117	0.42 ± 0.004	0.476 ± 0.004	11.76	1.13
ZO4	20.36 ± 0.026	0.446 ± 0.006	0.516 ± 0.016	13.97	1.16
ZO5	24.26 ± 0.091	0.463 ± 0.012	0.526 ± 0.014	11.97	1.13
ZO6	22.3 ± 0.062	0.499 ± 0.008	0.553 ± 0.025	9.76	1.1

S.D.: Standard deviation: n = 6

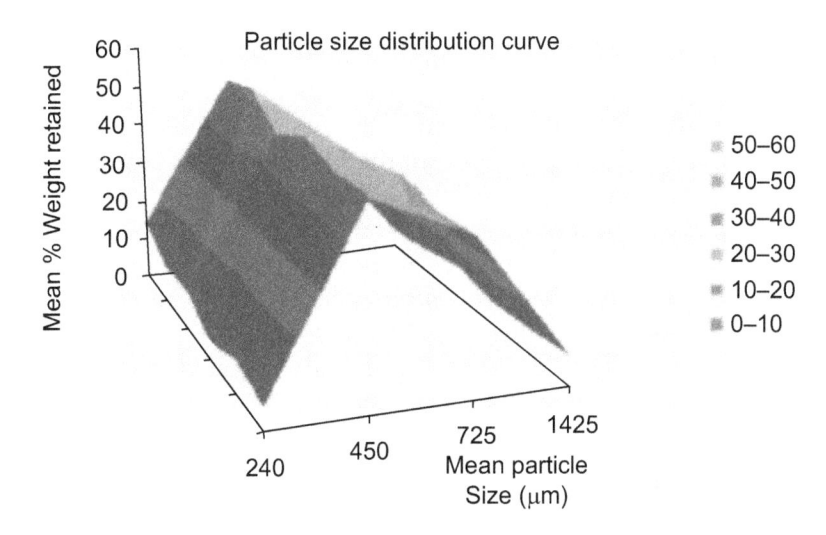

Fig. 13.2: Particle size distribution curve of different batches of microcapsules

FT-IR Studies

The results of FTIR spectral studies showed that there was no significant interaction between the drug and polymer. It was observed that there are no major degenerative interactions and hence the polymers could be used safely to formulate the microcapsules. Pure drug showed sharp characteristic peaks of carbonyl group in 1,678 cm^{-1} and of azide group in 2.085 cm^{-1}. One band in 1378 cm^{-1} is assigned to CH$_2$ and one band in 1285 cm^{-1} is assigned to C-O-C and the C-OH grouping. All the above characteristic peaks appeared in the spectrum of microcapsules too indicating there was no modification or interaction between drug and resin. This is also supported by the fact there was no appearance and disappearance of new or existing peaks.

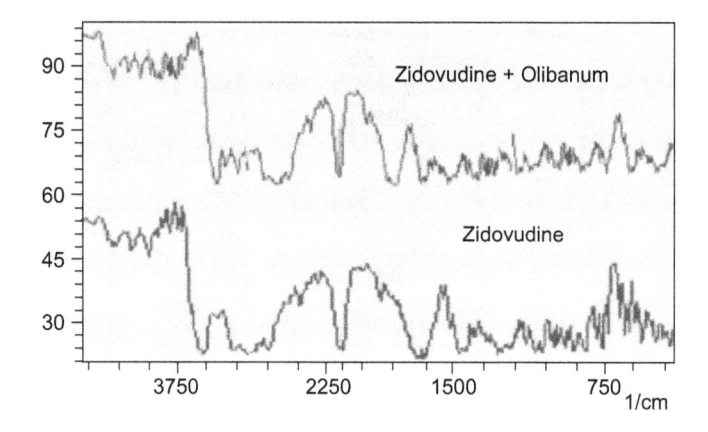

Fig. 13.3: FTIR spectra of pure AZT and AZT loaded microcapsules (ZO4)

Differential Scanning Calorimetry

The compatibility of AZT in olibanum microcapsules was evaluated through DSC analysis. The DSC thermograms of pure AZT and AZT-loaded olibanum microcapsules are presented in Figure 13.4. It was evident from the DSC profile that AZT exhibited a sharp endothermic peak associated with crystal melting at a temperature of 126.79°C, which corresponds to the reported melting temperature of the drug. A similar DSC profile (Figure 13.4) of the drug appeared at the temperature corresponding to its melting point in the AZT-loaded olibanum microcapsules but with a slight change in its sharp appearance. It appears that there is a minor reduction of drug crystallinity in the microcapsules. The DSC study apparently revealed that the drug was compatible with the polymer and neither drug decomposition nor drug-polymer interactions occurred in the freshly prepared microcapsules.

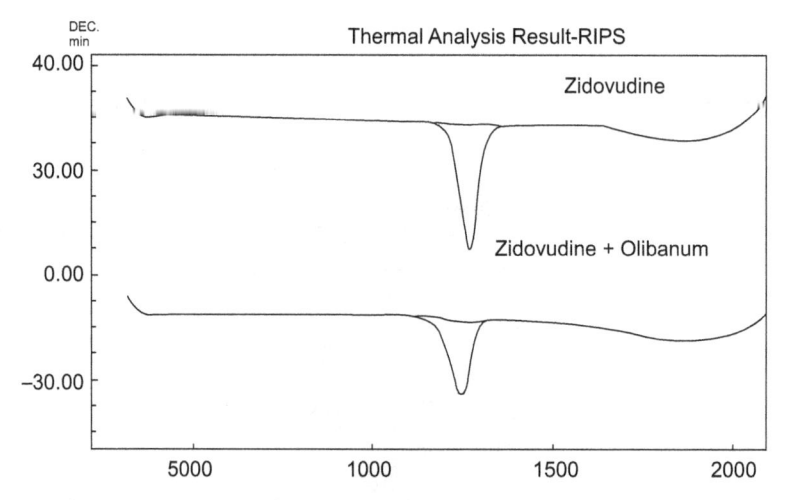

Fig. 13.4: DSC curves of pure AZT and AZT loaded microcapsules (ZO4)

X-ray Diffraction Analysis

The thermal behavior coupled with the X-ray crystallographic data suggested that the diffractogram of pure AZT indicates the crystalline structure of the drug. The diffractogram of AZT-loaded olibanum microcapsules shows a similar pattern with a slight decrease in the intensity of the peaks, which suggests that the drug was able to disperse almost homogenously in the microcapsules. This result confirms a partial change in the solid state of AZT from crystalline to amorphous. Similar results reported for other sustained release microsphere studies had the same interpretation for zidovudine, famotidine etc.

InVitro Drug Release Behavior

The in vitro drug release study of different batches of microcapsules was carried out in pH 7.4 phosphate buffer. In order to keep the total surface area of the microcapsules constant and thus to get comparable results, the release studies were carried out using the same size fractions (450 μm) of microcapsules

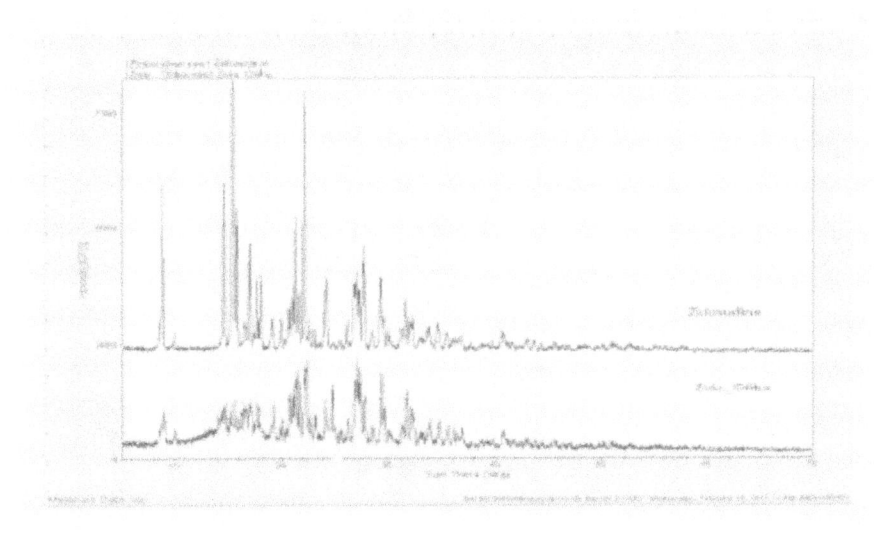

Fig. 13.5: X-ray diffractograms of pure AZT and AZT loaded microcapsules (ZO4)

containing equivalent amount of AZT from different batches of microcapsules. The AZT release from different batches of microcapsules exhibited a biphasic kinetics mechanism; an initial burst release (23-40%), which was due to the presence of drug particles on the surface of the microcapsules followed by a much slower release. The initial burst effect may be attributed as a desired effect to ensure minimum therapeutic plasma drug concentration. The release profiles are illustrated in Figure 13.6. Drug release rates decreased with increasing amounts of resin in the formulation. Lower levels of resin corresponding to the drug in the formulations resulted in an increase in the drug release rate.

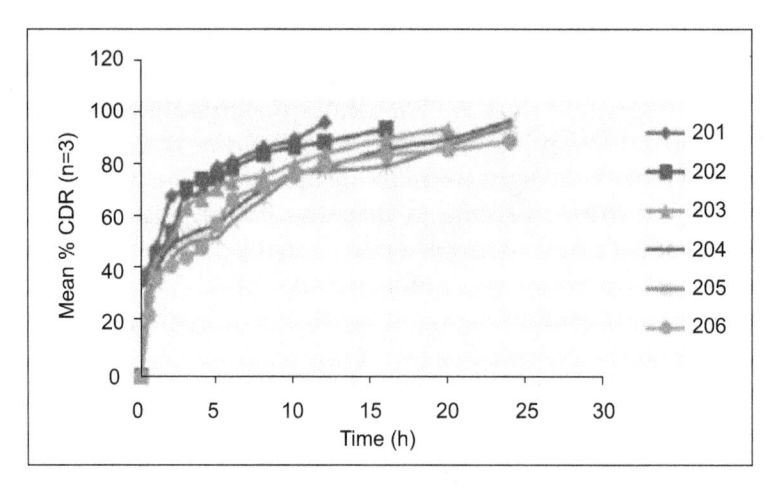

Fig. 13.6: In Vitro release profile (Zero order) of AZT loaded microcapsules from different batches

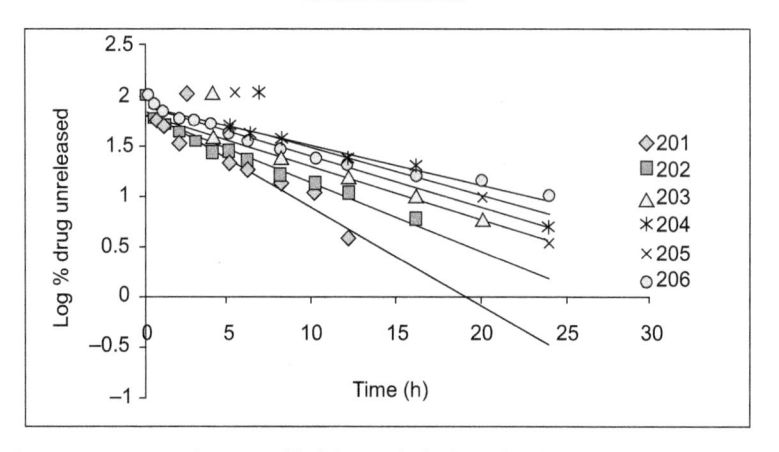

Fig. 13.7: In Vitro release profile (First order) of AZT loaded microcapsules from different batches

Release Kinetics

The in vitro drug release profiles of AZT were applied on various kinetic models in order to evaluate the mechanism of drug release. The different kinetic models evaluated were zero order, first order and Higuchi. After linearization of the results obtained in the dissolution test, the best fit with higher correlation coefficients (R^2) was shown in first order, Higuchi and followed by zero order equations as given in the Table 13.3. High correlation was observed in the first-order rather than Higuchi and zero-order models, indicating that the drug release from resin coated microcapsules was diffusion controlled. The data obtained were also put in Korsemeyer-Peppas model in order to find out n value, which describes the drug release mechanism. The n values of microcapsules of different drug to polymer ratio were ranged between 0.266-0.342 (< 0.43), indicating that the mechanism of the drug release was diffusion controlled based on Fick's law.

Table 13.3: In vitro Release Kinetic Parameters of AZT-loaded Olibanum Microcapsules

Formu-lations	Zero Order		First Order		Higuchi Model		Korsemeyer Peppas Model
	R^2	K_o(%/h)	R^2	$K(h^{-1})$	R^2	K_h(%/h$^{1/2}$)	n
ZO1	0.682	5.752	0.96	0.246	0.894	24.5	0.266
ZO2	0.637	4.34	0.928	0.152	0.874	21.47	0.274
ZO3	0.658	3.406	0.948	0.119	0.885	18.74	0.277
ZO4	0.757	3.037	0.957	0.115	0.937	17.68	0.311
ZO5	0.784	3.024	0.957	0.101	0.95	17.42	0.315
ZO6	0.723	2.984	0.931	0.085	0.926	17.56	0.342

CONCLUSIONS

In conclusion, the attempt to prepare controlled release biodegradable microcapsules of zidovudine using olibanum resin as microencapsulating agent was successful. The method employed was an industrially feasible one, as it involves emulsification and removal of solvent which can be controlled precisely. Since the resin is from natural origin, it is non-toxic, biodegradable and comparatively cheaper than other synthetic biodegradable polymers. Further studies in the area of novel drug delivery systems can be carried out by taking this resin as a natural biodegradable polymer in future.

14 Toxicological Assessments of the Aqueous Extract of *Boswellia dalzielli*

Medicinal plants are various plants thought by some to have medicinal properties, but few plants or their phytochemical constituents have been proven and approved by some regulatory agencies such as National Agency for Food and Drug Administration and Control (NAFDAC) in Nigeria, United State Food and Drug Administration and the European Food Safety Authority to have medicinal effects. For centuries, medicinal plants have been the most important source of life saving drugs for the majority of the world's population. Plants have been an important source of medicine for thousands of years that even currently; the World Health Organization (WHO) estimated that up to 80% of people over the world still rely on traditional remedies such as herbs for their medicines.

Medicinal plants have one or more parts with medicinal properties, and of the pharmacologically active principles found in plant kingdom, higher plants are arguably the most important group. They also cover the wide range of pharmacological effects which remain poorly understood. Out of the estimated 800,000 plant species on earth, about a quarter have been categorized and only a small fraction of these have been examined for pharmalogical efficacy. Toxicity studies which is the study of the symptoms, mechanisms, treatment and detection of poisoning, especially the poisoning of people, is done usually by the assessment of the level of damage done to the liver and the kidneys which are the chief organs responsible for the metabolism of xenobiotics in the body.

The plant D. dalzielli called Frankincense tree in English, 'Ararrhabi' or 'Hano' in Hausa, 'Tiya Shigo' in Dadiya (Gombe), and 'Juguli' in Fulfulde (Adamawa) is a plant (growing up to 13 m high) of the wooded savanna, with characteristically pale papery bark, peeling and ragged, locally abundant in northern Nigeria, Cameroun and Ubangishari. The small white flowers which may appear while the tree is leafless are fragranced.

The tree is sometimes planted in northern parts of Ivory coast and may sometimes be planted as a village stockade on the vocal peak massif of northern Nigeria and often as a live fence to bring prosperity (ba-samu) or to prevent (Hanu) bad luck, hence the Hausa names. The name "hanu" may also have significance to certain prejudices regarding the use of the resin. The bark contains whitish exudates which dries readily and is friable.

It is fragranced and is burnt alone or with other fragrant resin to fumigate clothing and in room to drive out flies, mosquitoes etc.. It is used by catholic mission as a substitute for true incense. It may be added to the juice of acacia berries used in ritual mummification practice by various tribes in northern Nigeria. When mixed with the stem bark extract of Vertex doniana sweet (Verberacea), it forms an important ingredient of malam's ink.

The bark decoction is used as an antiseptic wash for sores in Ivory Coast, and it is an ingredient of a complicated prescription for leprosy. In northern Nigeria, the bark is boiled up in large quantity to make a wash for fever, rheumatism etc and the fluid is taken internally for gastro intestinal troubles. The Fulani tribe of northern Nigeria uses the cold infusion of the stem bark for snake bite treatment. The fresh bark of the root is chewed in Dadiya (Gombe), Nigeria to cause vomiting after a few hours and thus relief symptoms of giddiness and palpation. Both the root and bark are known to be antidotes for arrow poison; for instance the root is combined with that of Daniella oliveri (Rolf) Hutch and Dalzielli (Leguminoidea; caesolpiniodeae) to make a decoction which is drunk by the wounded person, and is said to be effective without causing diarrhea. In northern Ivory Coast, it has been reported to be useful in the treatment of arthritis, rheumatism, asthma and also used in combination with Hibiscus sabdariffa for the treatment of syphilis.

MATERIALS AND METHODS

Plant

The plant sample was collected from Maitunku Hill Bambam, Dadiya District of Gombe State using matchet. The plant was identified by Mr. Daniel M. Mshelbwala, Federal School of Forestry and Horticulture, Department of Forestry, Jos, and was further authenticated by Prof. S. S. Sanusi, Department of Biological Sciences, University of Maiduguri, Borno State. The stem bark of the plant was air dried in the laboratory, Department of Biochemistry, University of Jos. It was then ground into powder using pestle and mortar.

Extraction of the Aqueous Extract of the Plant

Twenty grams (20 g) of the stem bark powder was soaked in 200 mL of distilled water and was allowed to stand for 48 h after which it was filtered using Whatman No. 1 filter paper. The filtrate was concentrated using a rotary evaporator maintained at 40°C.

Experimental Animals

The twenty (20) healthy male mice used for this experiment werepurchased from the animal farm, university of Jos, Plateau State. The mice weighed between 45 to 50 g. They were maintained on commercial preparations of growers' marsh containing 54% carbohydrate, 10% proteins, 19% fat, 20% fibre, 2% minerals and 1% vitamin premix. The mice were divided into four groups, each consisting of four mice, on the basis of their weight. The groups were treated by oral administration of the aqueous extract of the plant as follows:

Group 1-This group was given 200 mg/kg of the plant extract every twelve hours for 14 days;

Group 2-This group was administered 400 mg/kg of the plant extract every twelve hours for 14 days;

Group 3-This group was administered 600 mg/kg of the plant extract every twelve hours for 14 days;

Group 4-The mice in this group were fed normal without being administered with the plant extract for the period of the research, and the parameters from this group served as baseline data.

Phytochemical Screening

Preliminary qualitative phytochemical screening was performed on the aqueous extract of the stem bark of B. dalzielli. The methods of screening used in this study were mainly qualitative analysis and are based on Trease and Evans (1984) and Sofowora (1986).

These methods involved using reagents known to produce a particular color change which is distinct to that particular compound. The test was performed to detect the presence of alkaloids, flavonoid, tannins, saponins, cardiac glycosides, terpenes and steroids, Balsam, phenols, and Resins.

Test for Alkaloids

Dregendorf test was used to detect the presence of alkaloids. To 2 ml of the extract, few drops of Dregendorf reagent were added and observed for orange coloration.

Test for Flavonoids

The general test was used to detect for the presence of flavonoids. To 2 ml of the extract, small quantity of magnesium chips was added followed by the addition of 2 ml of Conc. HCl. The solution formed was observed for reddish coloration which indicated the presence of flavonoids.

Test for Tannins

The ferric chloride test was used to detect the presence of tannins. 2 ml of the extract was diluted with 8 ml of distilled water (in a ratio of 1:4) and few drops of 10% ferric chloride solution was added and it was observed for blue or green precipitate or coloration which showed the presence of tannins.

Test for Saponins

To 2 ml of the extract, 5 ml of distilled water was added and shaken vigorously for 2 min after which few drops of olive oil was added and the formation of an emulsion showed the presence of saponins.

Test for Cardiac Glycoside

Salkowski test was used to detect the presence of cardiac glycoside. 0.5 g of the extract was dissolved in 2.0 ml of chloroform after which sulphuric acid was carefully added to form a lower layer. A reddish brown color at the interphase indicated the presence of cardiac glycoside.

Test for Terpenes and Steroids

Liebermann-Burchard test was employed. To 2.0 ml of the extract, 1 ml of acetic anhydride and Concentrated Tetraoxosulphate (VI) acid (H_2SO_4) was carefully added down the side of the test tube and it was observed for reddish brown coloration at the interphase which indicated the presence of terpenes and steroids.

Test for Balsam

Three (3) drops of alcoholic ferric chloride was added to 2.0 ml of the extract. A dark green coloration showed the presence of balsam.

Test for Phenols

To 2.0 ml of the extract, 2 ml of ferric chloride was added and it was observed for the formation of deep violet coloration, which confirmed the presence of phenols.

Test for Resins

To 2.0 ml of the extract 2 ml of acetic anhydride was added followed by addition of few drops of concentrated sulphuric acid and the solution was observed for the formation of violet coloration which confirmed the presence of resins.

Methodologies for the test of hepatic and renal functions Determination of serum alkaline phosphatase activity by colorimetric method

A reagent kit by Randox was used according to the recommendations of the Dustche Gesselchaft fur Klinische chemie. Goje et al.

Principle: The underlining principle is as follows:

P-nitrophenyl phosphate + H2OALP phosphate + P-nitrophenol

The concentration of P-nitrophenol formed is measured colorimetrically at 405 nm and is proportional to the alkaline phosphatase activity. The buffer (diethalomine buffer) had concentration in the test of 1 mmol/L and pH 9.8, while $MgCl_2$ had concentration of 0.5 mmol/L. The substrate P-nitrophenolphospate had concentration of 10 mmol/L.

Procedure: 0.01 ml of the test sample was added into a clean test tube followed by 0.5 ml of the reagent and mixed, and then the initial reading of the absorbance was taken at 405 nm against air. A timer was started simultaneously and the absorbance was read again after 1, 2 and 3 min at 37°C.

Determination of aspartate amino transaminase (ASAT) by colorimetric method

Reaction principle: The underlining principle is as follows:

L-Oxoglutarate + L-aspartate

aspartate ASAT Glutamate + oxaloacetate.

Glutamate + oxaloacetate.

Aspartate amino transaminase activity is measured by monitoring the concentration of oxaloacetate hydrazone formed with 2,4- dinitrophenyl hydrazine. A reagent kit containing phosphate buffer (10 mmol/L, pH 7.4), L-aspartate (100 mmol/L), L-oxoglutarate (2 mmol/L), 2,4-ditrophenyl hydrazine (2 mmol/L) and sodium hydroxide (NaOH) 0.4 M was used. Sixteen grams (16 g) of NaOH was dissolved and made up to 1 L in distilled water.

Procedure: To each of the two clean test tubes marked 'test' and 'blank', 0.5 ml of substrate buffer solution was placed and incubated at 37°C for 5 min, then 0.2 ml of the test sample was added to the test tube labeled 'test' and further incubated at 37°C for 30 min. To all the test tubes, 0.5 ml of dinitrophenyl hydrazine was added. 0.2 ml aliquot of serum was then added to the test tube labeled 'blank'. The mixture was shaken and allowed to stand at room temperature for 20 min after which 5 ml of 0.5 M NaOH was added to each of the tubes and allowed to stand for 5 min. The absorbance was measured at 540 nm after zeroing the instrument with distilled water.

Determination of serum alanine amino transaminase (ALAT) by colorimetric method

Principle:

L-oxoglutarate + L-alanine

alanine ALT

L-glutamate + pyruvate

Alanine amino transaminase activity is measured by monitoring the concentration of pyruvate hydrazone formed with 2,4-dinitrophenyl hydrazine. Kit used contained Phosphate buffer (10 mmol/L, pH 7.4), L-alanine (200 mmol/L), L-oxoglutarete (2.0 mmol/L), 2,4- dinitrophenyl hydrazine (2 mmol/L) and NaOH (4 M)

Procedure: To 2 test tubes marked 'test' and 'Blank', 0.5 ml of buffer substrate solution was placed and incubated at 37°C for 5To 2 ml of the extract, small quantity of magnesium chips was added followed by the addition of 2 ml of Conc. HCl. The solution formed was observed for reddish coloration which indicated the presence of flavonoids.

Test for Tannins

The ferric chloride test was used to detect the presence of tannins. 2 ml of the extract was diluted with 8 ml of distilled water (in a ratio of 1:4) and few drops of 10% ferric chloride solution was added and it was observed for blue or green precipitate or coloration which showed the presence of tannins.

Test for Saponins
To 2 ml of the extract, 5 ml of distilled water was added and shaken vigorously for 2 min after which few drops of olive oil was added and the formation of an emulsion showed the presence of saponins.

Test for Cardiac Glycoside
Salkowski test was used to detect the presence of cardiac glycoside. 0.5 g of the extract was dissolved in 2.0 ml of chloroform after which sulphuric acid was carefully added to form a lower layer. A reddish brown color at the interphase indicated the presence of cardiac glycoside.

Test for Terpenes and Steroids
Liebermann-Burchard test was employed. To 2.0 ml of the extract, 1 ml of acetic anhydride and Concentrated Tetraoxosulphate (VI) acid (H_2SO_4) was carefully added down the side of the test tube and it was observed for reddish brown coloration at the interphase which indicated the presence of terpenes and steroids.

Test for Balsam
Three (3) drops of alcoholic ferric chloride was added to 2.0 ml of the extract. A dark green coloration showed the presence of balsam.

Test for Phenols
To 2.0 ml of the extract, 2 ml of ferric chloride was added and it was observed for the formation of deep violet coloration, which confirmed the presence of phenols.

Test for Resins
To 2.0 ml of the extract 2 ml of acetic anhydride was added followed by addition of few drops of concentrated sulphuric acid and the solution was observed for the formation of violet coloration which confirmed the presence of resins.

Methodologies for the test of hepatic and renal functions

Determination of serum alkaline phosphatase activity by colorimetric method

A reagent kit by Randox was used according to the recommendations of the Dustche Gesselchaft fur Klinische chemie. Goje et al.

Principle: The underlining principle is as follows:

P-nitrophenyl phosphate + H2OALP phosphate + P-nitrophenol

The concentration of P-nitrophenol formed is measured colorimetrically at 405 nm and is proportional to the alkaline phosphatase activity. The buffer (diethalomine buffer) had

concentration in the test of 1 mmol/L and pH 9.8, while MgCl2 had concentration of 0.5 mmol/L. The substrate P-nitrophenolphospate had concentration of 10 mmol/L.

Procedure: 0.01 ml of the test sample was added into a clean test tube followed by 0.5 ml of the reagent and mixed, and then the initial reading of the absorbance was taken at 405 nm against air. A timer was started simultaneously and the absorbance was read again after 1, 2 and 3 min at 37°C.

Determination of aspartate amino transaminase (ASAT) by colorimetric method

Reaction principle: The underlining principle is as follows:

L-Oxoglutarate + L-aspartate

aspartate ASAT Glutamate + oxaloacetate.

Glutamate + oxaloacetate.

Aspartate amino transaminase activity is measured by monitoring the concentration of oxaloacetate hydrazone formed with 2,4- dinitrophenyl hydrazine. A reagent kit containing phosphate buffer (10 mmol/L, pH 7.4), L-aspartate (100 mmol/L), L-oxoglutarate (2 mmol/L), 2,4-ditrophenyl hydrazine (2 mmol/L) and sodium hydroxide (NaOH) 0.4 M was used. Sixteen grams (16 g) of NaOH was dissolved and made up to 1 L in distilled water.

Procedure: To each of the two clean test tubes marked 'test' and 'blank', 0.5 ml of substrate buffer solution was placed and incubated at 37°C for 5 min, then 0.2 ml of the test sample was added to the test tube labeled 'test' and further incubated at 37°C for 30 min. To all the test tubes, 0.5 ml of dinitrophenyl hydrazine was added. 0.2 ml aliquot of serum was then added to the test tube labeled 'blank'. The mixture was shaken and allowed to stand at room temperature for 20 min after which 5 ml of 0.5 M NaOH was added to each of the tubes and allowed to stand for 5 min. The absorbance was measured at 540 nm after zeroing the instrument with distilled water.

Determination of serum alanine amino transaminase (ALAT) by colorimetric method

Principle:

L-oxoglutarate + L-alanine

alanine ALT

L-glutamate + pyruvate

Alanine amino transaminase activity is measured by monitoring the concentration of pyruvate hydrazone formed with 2,4-dinitrophenyl hydrazine. Kit used contained Phosphate buffer (10 mmol/L, pH 7.4), L-alanine (200 mmol/L), L-oxoglutarete (2.0 mmol/L), 2,4-dinitrophenyl hydrazine (2 mmol/L) and NaOH (4 M).

Procedure: To 2 test tubes marked 'test' and 'Blank', 0.5 ml of buffer substrate solution was placed and incubated at 37°C for 5 min. Then 0.1 ml of the serum was added to the test and incubated for 30 min. To all the test tubes, 0.5 ml of 2,4-dinitrophenyl hydrazine was added. The mixture was shaken and allowed to stand at room temperature for 30 min, and then 5 ml of NaOH was added and allowed to stand for 5 min. The absorbances were measured using a spectrophotometer at 540 nm after zeroing the instrument with distilled water at the same wave length.

Table 14.1: Phytochemical Screening Test for the Stem Bark Extract of *Boswellia* Dalzielli.

Chemical group	Aqueous extract
Alkaloid	+
Flavonoid	+
Tannins	+
Saponins	+
Balsam	+
Cardiac glycoside	+
Terpenes and steroids	+
Resins	+
Phenol	+

+ = present, – = absent.

Determination of Serum Urea Method of Natelson

Principle: Urea reacts with diacetyl monoxime in the presence of strong acids and oxidizing agents to produce a chromogen whose absorbance is directly proportional to the concentration of urea. Procedure: To three clean dried test tubes marked test, blank and standard, 0.02 ml of serum was placed in the tube marked etest f, 0.02 ml of urea standard was placed in a tube marked estandard f and 0.02 ml of distilled water in the tube marked eblank f, then 0.1 ml of diacetyl monoxime solution was added to all test tubes, followed by 5.0 ml of the acid mixture. The tubes were kept in a boiling water bath for 15 min and then cooled in running water. The absorbance of the standard and test were read at 520 nm within the next 15 min against the reagent blank.

Determination of Serum Creatinine Method

Principle: Creatinine reacts with picric acid at an alkaline pH to produce a red colored complex; the absorbance of the complex is directly proportional to the amount of creatinine in the sample.

Procedure: The serum was first deproteinised by adding 1 ml of 5% sodium tungstate, 1 ml of 0.33 M H_2SO_4 and 1 ml of distilled water to 1 ml of the serum. The mixture was centrifuged at 3,000 rpm for 10 min. The clear supernatant was then used for the determination of creatinine. To a clean dried test tubes marked test, standard and blank, 3.5 ml of distilled water was added, then 0.5 ml of creatinine standard was added to tube labeled estandard f and 0.5 ml of protein-free serum was added to tube labeled etest f. Then 1.0 ml of picric acid solution was added to all test tubes, followed by 1.0 ml of NaOH. The tubes were mixed and allowed to stand for 15 min after which the absorbance of the test and standard were measured against reagent blank at 500 nm.

Statistical analysis

Student fs t-test was used to test for significant difference between the groups and the normal control at P. 0.05 using Statistical package for social sciences (SPSS).

RESULTS

The results of the phytochemical screening displayed in Table 14.1 showed the presence of alkaloid, flavonoid, tannins, balsam, cardiac glycoside, terpenes and steroids, resins, and phenol. The results of the toxicity studies of the effect of the oral administration of the aqueous extract of B. dalzielli stem bark on the indices of hepatic and renal functions of male mice at different concentrations of 200, 400 and 600 mg/kg are shown in Tables 14.2, 14.3, 14.4, 14.5 and 6 respectively. The result showed that the serum level of ALT between the group given 200 and 400 mg/kg was not statistically significant ($p > 0.05$). The level of ALT differs between the group given 400 and 600 mg/kg. Also, the level of ALT between the group given 200 and 600 mg/kg was significantly different ($p < 0.05$). There appeared to be no significant difference between the group given 400 mg/kg and the normal control whereas all the other two groups differed significantly from the normal control.

The result in the case of AST showed that the group given 200 mg/kg had a significantly different value for AST from all the other groups, including the normal control. The group given 400 and 600 mg/kg did not differ from each other but all of them differed significantly from the normal control ($p < 0.05$). The result in the case of ALP showed that the group given 200 and 400 mg/kg were not statistically different from each other ($p > 0.05$). Also, there was no significant difference between the group given 200 and 600 mg/kg but there was significant difference between the group given 400 and 600 mg/kg. In general, there was significant difference between all the groups and the normal control ($p < 0.05$).

The result showed that in the case of serum urea, only the two concentrations 200 and 400 mg/kg were not statistically different ($p > 0.05$) but comparison between all the other concentrations with each other and also with the normal control were statistically significant ($p < 0.05$). The result in the case of creatinine showed that comparisons between all the groups with one another and also with the normal control were not significantly different ($p < 0.05$) in each case.

DISCUSSION

The result of the phytochemical screening carried out on the aqueous extract of the stem bark of B. dalzielli showed the presence of alkaloid, flavonoid, tannins, saponins, balsam, cardiac glycoside, terpenes, steroids, resins, and phenols. The organs responsible for the metabolism of xenobiotics, including medicinal plants are the liver and kidney. Therefore, in studying the toxic effects of any xenobiotics involving the dose response relationships, emphasis should be made on the biomarkers of response of these two organs which are necessary for the establishment of the No observed adverse effect level (NOAEL) and/or the toxic level of a xenobiotics.

Table 14.2: Effect of the Oral Administration of Aqueous Extract of *Boswellia Dalzielli* Stem Bark on Serum Urea Level.

Group (mg/kg)	Urea (mmol/L)
1 (200)	5.23 ± 0.16[a]
2 (400)	5.60 ± 0.27[a]
3 (600)	3.53 ± 0.06[b]
4 (normal control)	6.40 ± 0.10[c]

All values are expressed as mean mean ± standard deviation of four replicates. Values with different superscripts down the column for example a, b, c,

Table 14.3: Effect of the Oral Administration of Aqueous Extract of *Boswellia Dalzielli* Stem Bark on Serum Creatine Level.

Group (mg/kg)	Creatine (mmol/L)
1 (200)	62.33 ± 0.58[a]
2 (400)	59.33 ± 1.53[a]
3 (600)	61.00 ± 2.65[a]
4 (normal control)	60.00 ± 1.00a

All values are expressed as mean ± standard deviation of four replicates. Values with different superscripts down the column are statistically different at ($p < 0.05$).

Table 14.4: Effect of the Oral Administration of Aqueous Extract of *Boswellia Dalzielli* Stem Bark on Alanine Amino Transferase (ALT) level.

Group (mg/kg)	ALT (IU/L)
1 (200)	26.00 ± 1.00[a]
2 (400)	28.33 ± 1.53[ac]
3 (600)	49.33 ± 1.53[b]
4 (normal control)	33.00 ± 1.00[c]

All values are expressed as Mean ± standard deviation of four replicates. Values with different superscripts down the column for example a, b, and c, are statistically different at ($p < 0.05$).

The index of liver functions showed a significant decrease in the case of ALT in the groups given 200 and 400 mg/kg compared to the normal control. This is not indicative of liver damage which usually causes an increase in this parameter, but the higher concentration (600 mg/kg) showed a significant increase compared to the normal control which is an indication that there might be some damage to the liver cells. There is an increase in the level of serum AST in all the treatment groups compared to the normal control. This could be as a result of liver damage caused by the administration of this extract as has been confirmed by literatures that there is an increase in the level of AST activities in liver diseases that affect both mitochondrial and cytoplasmic membranes.

Table 14.5: Effect of the Oral Administration of Aqueous Extract of *Boswellia Dalzielli* Stem Bark on Serum Aspartate Amino Transferase (ASAT) Level.

Group (mg/kg)	AST (IU/L)
1 (200)	108.00 ± 1.00[a]
2 (400)	121.33 ± 0.58[b]
3 (600)	122.33 ± 0.58[b]
4 (normal control)	89.00 ± 1.00[c]

All values are expressed as Mean ± standard deviation of four replicates. Values with different superscripts down the column for example a, b, and c, are statistically different at ($p < 0.05$).

Table 14.6: Effect of the Oral Administration of Aqueous Extract of *Boswellia Dalzielli* Stem Bark on Serum Alkaline Phosphatase (ALP) Level.

Group (mg/kg)	ALP (IU/L)
1 (200)	24.61 ± 0.35[a,b]
2 (400)	24.26 ± 0.12[a]
3 (600)	23.52 ± 0.47[b]
4 (normal control)	26.19 ± 0.10[c]

All values are expressed as Mean ± standard deviation of four replicates. Values with different superscripts down the column for example a, b, and c, are statistically different at ($p < 0.05$).

The serum level of ALP showed a significant decrease in all concentrations (200, 400 and 600 mg/kg) compared the normal control. This finding is not clearly indicating liver disease, and hence not in concordance with other findings using ALP which reported an increase in the level of ALP in cholestic liver disease. In general, there is an increased level of AST compared to ALT, which is an indication of damage to both the mitochondrial and cytoplasmic membranes of the liver. Literatures also attested to this fact. The serum urea concentrations between 200 and 400 mg/kg appeared to show no difference but was different from 600 mg/kg and it also decreased significantly ($p < 0.05$) in all the groups compared to the normal control. This could be as a result of increase in the glomerular filtration rate of the kidney, leading to the excretion of more urea in the urine as reported by James *et al.*

The serum level of creatinine appeared to have no significant difference (p<0.05) among all the groups (200, 400 and 600 mg/kg) with the normal control. This is an indication that there is no renal dysfunction with the administration of all the three different concentrations of the extract.

CONCLUSION

There appeared to be a decrease in ALT and ALP in comparison with the normal control. But the level of AST is higher, indicating possible liver damage, and this is also evident by the reduced serum level of urea but the extract in all the three different concentration had no difference with the normal control in the case of AST. Hence, it was concluded that the extract had toxic effect on the liver but had no toxic effect on the kidney of the mice.

15. Synergistic Anti-inflammatory Compositions Comprising *Boswellia serrata* Extract

The gum resin of the plant *Boswellia serrata* (*Burseraceae*) has long been in use for the treatment of rheumatoid arthritis and gout by the practitioners of Ayurvedic medicines in the Indian system of medicine. Various extracts of the gum resin have shown potent anti-inflammatory and anti-atherogenic activity in laboratory animals. Incensole acetate a *Boswellia* compound isolated was proved to be a NFêB inhibitor and useful as anti-inflammatory compound.. It was observed in the past that the ethanolic extract of the gum resin of *B. serrata* inhibits the formation of Leukotriene B4 in rat peritoneal neutrophils. Leukotriene B4 is one of the important mediators of inflammatory reactions. The extract of *Boswellia* was found to be a potent anti-arthritic agent, and immunomodulatory age. The cholesterol lowering action of *Boswellia serrata* was also proved.. In fact, a randomized, double blind, placebo controlled, crossover clinical trial with *Boswellia* extract on a group of patients with osteoarthritis of knee exhibited statistically significant mean improvements with respect to reduction in pain, decreased swelling and increased knee flexion. In an open non-randomized equivalence study, 30 patients with chronic colitis were administered either *Boswellia* gum (300 mg thrice daily) or sulfasalazine (1 g thrice a day) and the therapeutic effects shown by *Boswellia* were comparable to those exhibited by sulfasalazine. In another equivalency study, *Boswellia* standardized extract exhibited therapeutic improvements, comparable to, or better than, mesalazine in a randomized, double-blind study on patients with active Crohn's disease. *Boswellia* gum resin also showed statistically significant improvement in patients with bronchial asthma in a six-week double-blind, placebo controlled study.

The patents also describe various activities of *Boswellia*. Some are quoted below:

PCT Patent publication WO03074063A1 and granted Indian patent #205269 relates to a process for producing a fraction enriched upto 100% of 3-O-acetyl-11-keto-β-boswellic acid. An organic solvent extract of gum resin from *Boswellia* species is first subjected to oxidation and then acetylation or vice versa. This converts the less potent boswellic acids present in the fraction to AKBA. This treated fraction is subjected to further purification and separation by chromatographic separation techniques to enhance its purity and to remove contaminants there from. This process provides an access to a fraction enriched in 10-100% AKBA for therapeutic applications.

The European patent publication EP1637153A1 relates to the association of *Boswellia serrata* extract with plant antifibrotic agent as medicament particularly against inflammatory and fibrotic courses. In such association *Boswellia serrata* is present as dry extract in quantity from 5 to 50% and the plant antifibrotic agent as dry extract in quantity from 50 to 95% by weight.

The U.S. patent U.S. Pat. No. 5,629,351 relates to a novel fraction comprising a mixture of boswellic acids, wherein the fraction exhibits anti-inflammatory and antiulcerogenic activities. Also disclosed is a novel boswellic acid compound exhibiting anti-inflammatory, antiarthritic and antiulcerogenic activities. Also disclosed is a process for isolating a boswellic acid fraction and individual boswellic acids therefrom.

The U.S. patent U.S. Pat. No. 5,720,975 relates to the use of incense (olibanum), incense extracts, substances contained in incense, their physiologically acceptable salts, their derivatives and their physiological salts, pure boswellic acid, of physiologically acceptable salts, of a derivative, of a salt of the derivative, for production of a medicament for the prevention or treatment of Alzheimer's disease.

The U.S. patent U.S. Pat. No. 5,888,514 refers to a composition for treating a mammal having a condition characterized by bone or joint inflammation where extract of *Boswellia serrata* is used as one of the ingredients.

The PCT patent publication WO08036932A2 relates to compositions and methods, for making compositions derived from *Boswellia* species (frankincense or olibanum) having uniquely elevated volatile oil, boswellic acids, and polysaccharide compounds, particularly, human oral delivery formulations, and methods for use of such compositions, useful e.g. for treating/preventing arthritis, inflammatory disorders, osteoarthritis, rheumatoid diseases and low back pain.

There is however no prior art, to the best of inventors knowledge, relating to the compositions comprising *Boswellia* extract especially AKBA enriched extract along with *Boswellia serrata* non-acidic resin extract (BNRE) for the prevention, control and treatment of inflammatory conditions.

FIGURES

Figure 15.1: Figure shows structural formulae 1-9 representing prominent compounds of *Boswellia serrata* non-acidic resin extract (BNRE).

Figure 15.2: Figure shows the HPLC chromatogram depicting the phytochemical profile of the *Boswellia serrata* non-acidic resin extract (BNRE).

Figure 15.3: Figure depicts representative immuno blots showing BE30%-induced inhibition of 5-Lipoxygenase (A) and FLAP (B) expressions in human monocytes THP-1 cells. In each respective panel, bar diagram represent the normalized densitometric values (in arbitrary units). The bars a, b and c represent control, LPS treated and LPS + BE30% treated cells respectively.

Figure 15.4: Figure shows comparative 5-Lipoxygenase inhibitory activity of *Boswellia serrata* extract selectively enriched in 3-O-acetyl-11-keto-β-boswellic acid (AKBA) [BE30%], *Boswellia serrata* non-acidic resin extract (BNRE) and composition-2. The bars represent percentage inhibition of 5-Lipoxygenase enzyme exhibited by BE30%, BNRE and composition-2 at 25 μg/mL concentration.

Figure 15.5: Figure shows inhibition of Matrix Metalloproteinase-3 (MMP-3) production by *Boswellia serrata* extract selectively enriched in 3-O-acetyl-11-keto-β-boswellic acid (AKBA)[BE30%], *Boswellia serrata* non-acidic resin extract (BNRE) and composition-2. Bars represent 50% inhibitory concentrations (IC_{50}) for BE30%, BNRE and Composition-2 in TNα induced SW982 human synovial cells. The values on the bars represent the corresponding IC_{50} values.

Figure 15.6: Figure shows bar diagrammatic representations of percentage inhibition of paw edema volume in Freund's complete adjuvant induced Sprague Dawley rats by *Boswellia serrata* extract selectively enriched in 3-O-acetyl-11-keto-β-boswellic acid to 30% (BE30%, 100 mg/kg) and *Boswellia serrata* min-acidic resin extract (BNRE) (100 mg/kg), Composition-1 (100 mg/kg) and composition-2 (100 mg/kg) comprising BE30% and BNRE in ratio 1:1 and 2:1 respectively, and Prednisolone (10 mg/kg).

Figure 15.7. Figure shows bar diagrammatic representations of serum TNFα (A) and IL-1β (B) concentrations in different groups of animals. After 14 days of FCA challenge, serum TNFα and IL-1β were quantitatively measured by enzyme-immuno assay kit (R&D Systems, USA). The bars a to f represent the levels of the cytokines in groups supplemented with control, prednisolone (10 mg/kg), BE30% (100 mg/kg), BNRE (100 mg/kg), composition-1 (100 mg/kg) and composition-2 (100 mg/kg), respectively. Each bar represents mean±SD. N=6, * $P<0.05$ and ** $P<0.005$ (vs. control).

DESCRIPTION

Inflammation is a response of the vascular tissues to stimuli such as pathogens, damaged cells or allergic agents which enter into the body. It is a protective mechanism by the organism to remove harmful pathogens or agents and protect the tissues. Pro-inflammatory cytokines such as TNFα, IL-1β, IL-6, GM-CSF and CD4+, Th2 subset derived IL-4, IL-5 and IL-13 lymphokines are considered as the key factors of immunopathogenesis of inflammatory diseases. 5-Lipoxygenase is an enzyme critical for leukotriene synthesis from arachidonic acid, a key step in the inflammatory process. Leukotrienes are key mediators of inflammatory disease.

The activation and gene expression of 5-lipoxygenase (5-LOX) is responsible for the disease condition. The 5-Lipoxygenase activating protein (FLAP) is an 18 kDa integral membrane protein which activates 5-Lipoxygenase by specifically binding arachidonic acid and transferring it to the enzyme. FLAP is therefore responsible for the production of leukotrienes. Hence blocking or down regulating the 5-LOX and FLAP is a novel therapeutic approach for the treatment and control of inflammatory condition.

Atherosclerosis is also an inflammatory disease characterized by the formation of arterial lesions over a period of several decades at sites of endothelial cell dysfunction. Inflammation plays important role at many stages of atherosclerotic plaque development.

Matrix Metalloproteinases (MMPs) are zinc dependent endopeptidases, that are capable of breaking down all kinds of extra cellular matrix proteins, such as collagen, that are normally found in the spaces between cells in tissues. MMPs are divided primarily into three principal groups, the fibroblast collagenase-1 (MMP-1) formed of the collagenases, the gelatinases comprising gelatinase A (MMP-2) and the gelatinase B (MMP-9), and the stromelysines comprising stromelysine-1 (MMP-3) and matrilysine (MMP-7). An excess of metalloproteinase leads to degradation of biomolecules such as collagen, proteoglycon and gelatin, which can have fatal consequences on epidermis and can also generate diseases of the cartilages, inflammation etc.

Boswellia serrata Extract Selectively Enriched in AKBA (BE30%):

Boswellia resin and extracts have been in use for the treatment of inflammatory diseases for ages. Boswellic acids were identified as the active compounds responsible for the beneficial effects attributed to *Boswellia serrata*. The minor compound 3-O-acetyl-11-keto-β-boswellic acid (AKBA) was identified as the most potent 5-lipoxygenase inhibitor of all the boswellic acids. As such the extracts or fractions enriched in the AKBA content presumed to show better efficacy compared to the natural extracts. The inventors, in their PCT application #PCT/IN05/000074, dated 7 Mar. 2005 and PCT Patent publication WO03074063A1 and granted Indian patent 205269, have demonstrated a process for producing *Boswellia serrata* extract selectively enriched in 30-100% AKBA from commercial *Boswellia serrata* extracts, which contain around 85% total boswellic acids by titrimetric method of analysis and around 3% AKBA (BE3%) by HPLC method of analysis. The said enriched *Boswellia* extract is a unique composition characterized by the lack of significant quantities of the triterpene components commonly present in regular *Boswellia serrata* extracts, except AKBA, which is a minor component (upto 3%) in regular *Boswellia* extracts, but it is a major component in the enriched extract. The components present in the regular *Boswellia* extracts are 1) β-boswellic acid, 2) 3-O-acetyl-β-boswellic acid, 3) 11-keto-β-boswellic acid, 4) 3-O-acetyl-11-keto-β-boswellic acid, 5) 9-ene-β-boswellic acid, 6) 3α-hydroxyurs-9,11-diene-24-oic acid, 7) 2α,3α-hydroxyurs-12-ene-24-oic acid. The major components of unique *Boswellia serrata* extract enriched in AKBA used in the present inventive composition are 1) 3-O-acetyl-β-boswellic acid, 2) 3-O-acetyl-9(11)-dehydro-β-boswellic acid, 3) 3-O-acetyl-11-keto-β-amirin, 4) 3-O-acetyl-11-keto-α-boswell acid.

The said *Boswellia serrata* extract containing 30% AKBA (BE30%) was tested in several in vitro assays and it was found to be superior to commercial *Boswellia serrata* extract containing 3% AKBA (BE3%). In direct comparison experiments, the said enriched *Boswellia serrata* extract (BE30%) also showed significantly higher inhibition against adjuvant-induced inflammatory response, in Wistar Albino rats, compared to a natural *Boswellia* extract containing 3% AKBA. *Boswellia serrata* extract selectively enriched to 30% AKBA (BE30%) is used to demonstrate the present invention.

Boswellia serrata Non-Acidic Resin Extract (BNRE):

The *Boswellia serrata* resin contains acidic compounds, non-acidic compounds and sugars. During the execution of commercial process for regular *Boswellia serrata* extract (85% total boswellic acids, BE3%), the acidic fraction, which contains predominantly triterpene acids including boswellic acids, is separated from the rest of resin components. The sugars and other polymeric materials also got separated into the aqueous phase during the enrichment of total boswellic acids. The remaining water immiscible non-acidic low polar compounds are separated as *Boswellia* oil fraction/extract. These non-acidic or neutral low polar compounds are either absent or present at very low concentration both in commercial *Boswellia* extracts and AKBA enriched *Boswellia* extracts. The presence of these non-acidic components becomes even lower with the increasing enrichment of AKBA.

The said non-acidic *Boswellia* oil has been a significant component of *Boswellia serrata* gum resin. However, it has very limited commercial utility and it is mostly discarded as a waste material. Potential utilization of this fraction has been long overdue. The inventors have found an unexpectedly utility for *Boswellia serrata* oil for making synergistic compostions. *Boswellia serrata* non-acidic resin extract (BNRE), a fraction obtained after removing the volatile compounds from the *Boswellia serrata* oil, has been used in the present invention. *Boswellia serrata* non-acidic resin extract (BNRE) has been obtained in the following manner, (*a*) the *Boswellia serrata* gum resin was dispersed in methyl isobutyl ketone (MIBK) solvent and the insoluble gum materials were separated by filtration, (*b*) the MIBK solution was extracted repeatedly with 2% KOH solution to remove the acidic compounds, (*c*) the MIBK layer was then washed successively with water and brine, (*d*) the MIBK layer was evaporated under reduced pressure at 60-70° C. and the volatile components are then removed from the oily residue under vacuum at 75-85° C. to obtain a viscous oil, which is herein after referred as *Boswellia serrata* non-acidic resin extract or BNRE. Alternatively, the BNRE can also be prepared by (*a*) preparing the alcohol extract of *Boswellia serrata* resin followed by, (*b*) partitioning the alcohol extract between an aqueous alkali solution and a water immiscible organic solvent, (c) separation of the organic solvent layer, followed by evaporation of the solvent to obtain non-acidic *Boswellia* oil extract, (d) removal of volatile compounds at high temperature and vacuum to obtain *Boswellia serrata* non-acidic resin extract (BNRE).

2 R_1 = OH and R_2 = H
3 R_1 = H and R_2 = OH

Fig. 15.1

The above *Boswellia serrata* non-acidic resin extract (BNRE) was unexpectedly found to have a unique composition. The inventors have carried out extensive separation of BNRE using repeated column chromatography and high performance liquid chromatography and isolated several diterpenoid and triterpenoid compounds. The structures of the compounds were rigorously characterized using ^{1}H NMR, ^{13}C NMR, DEPT, HSQC and HMBC, Mass spectral data. The compounds identified are guiol (1), nephthenol (2), serratol (3), diterpene X (4), lupeol (5), olean-12-ene-3β-ol (6), olean-12-ene-3α-ol (7), lanosta-8,24-diene-3α-ol (8) and urs-12-ene-3α-ol (9) as depicted in Figure 15.1. The pure compounds so obtained were used as phytochemical markers to standardize the *Boswellia serrata* non-acidic resin extract (BNRE). The results of the phytochemical analysis are summarized in the Table 15.1 and the chromatogram depicting the phytochemical profile of BNRE is presented in Figure 15.2.

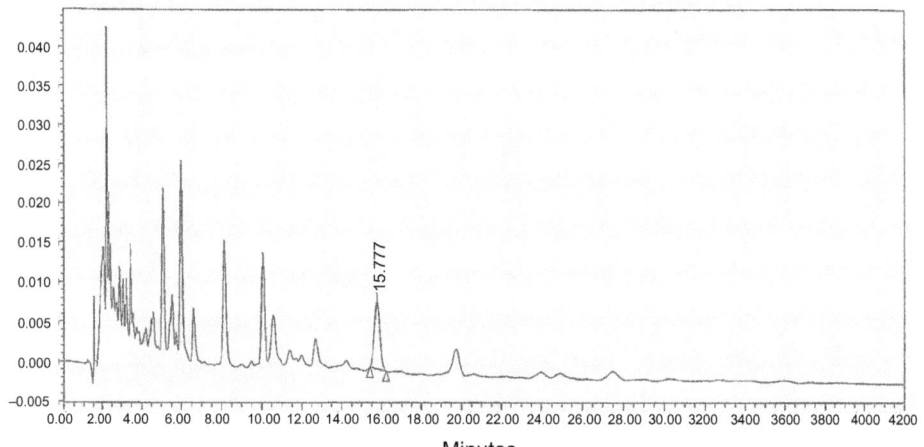

A: chromatogram at 252 nm

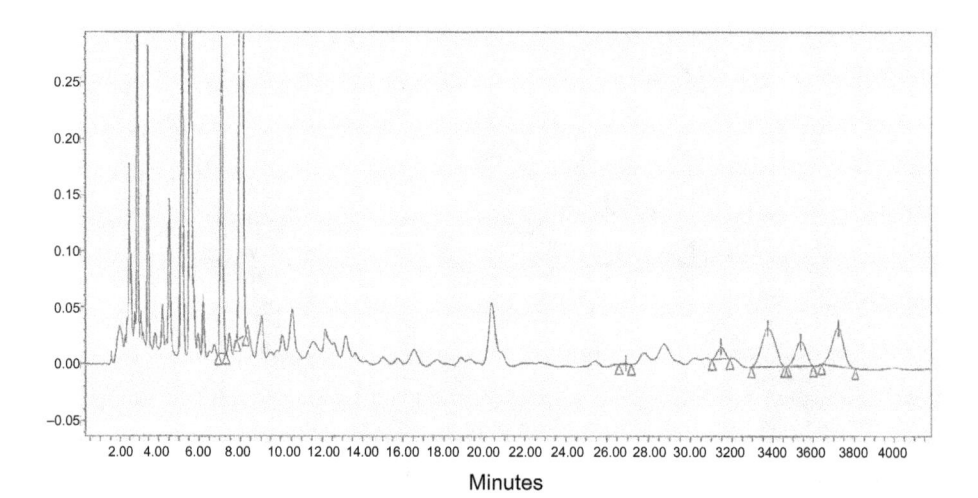

B: chromatogram at 210 nm

Fig. 15.2

Synergistic Compositions Comprising *Boswellia* Extracts:

The inventors have conducted several cell based in vitro anti-inflammatory studies on broad array of *Boswellia* extracts and *Boswellia serrata* extracts selectively enriched in AKBA. These studies have shown unexpectedly that the *Boswellia serrata* extract selectively enriched in 30% 3-O-acetyl-11-keto-β-boswellic acid (AKBA)[BE30%] potently down-regulated the LPS induced expression of 5-LOX and FLAP in THP-1 human-monocyte-macrophage cells in vitro (Figure 15.3).

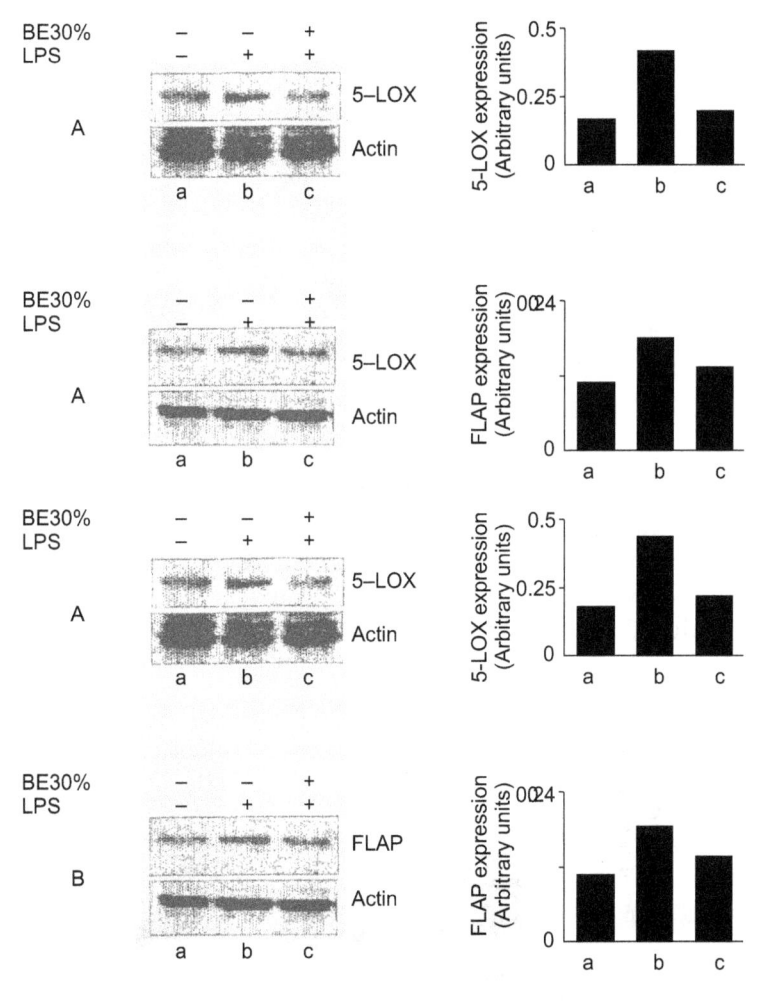

Fig. 15.3

The said *B. serrata* extracts selectively enriched in AKBA were then combined with a few selected ingredients to obtain compositions having better anti-inflammatory activity. The individual extracts and the compositions were tested for their efficacy to inhibit 5-lipoxygenase enzyme (5-LOX). It was found very surprisingly that a composition comprising *Boswellia serrata* gum resin extract selectively enriched in 30% AKBA (BE30%) and *Boswellia serrata* non-acidic resin extract (BNRE), showed synergistic inhibition of 5-LOX. The composition-2 comprising BE30% and BNRE in 2:1 ratio showed 37.7% inhibition at 25 µg/mL compared to 31.8% and 20.6% inhibitions shown by BE30% and BNRE respectively at the same concentrations. The comparative 5-lipoxygenase inhibition shown by composition-2 and its individual ingredients are presented in Figure 15.4.

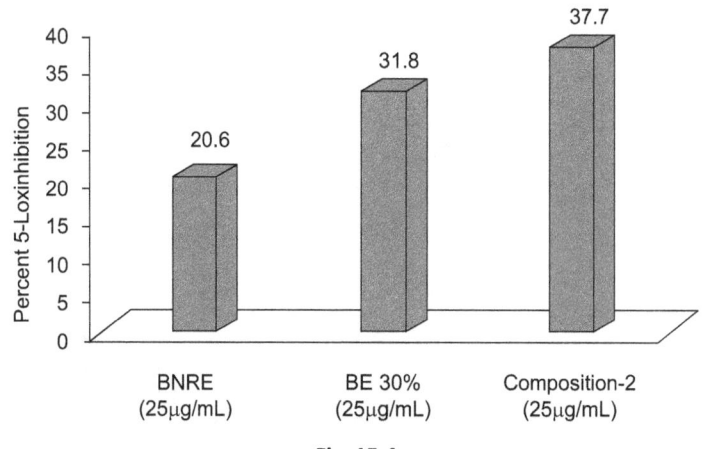

Fig. 15.4

Boswellia serrata extract enriched to 30% AKBA (BE30%), *Boswellia serrata* non-acidic resin extract (BNRE) and Composition-2 were then tested for their efficacy in inhibiting Matrix Metalloproteinase-3 (MMP-3) production in TNFα induced SW982 human synovial cells. The MMP-3 production

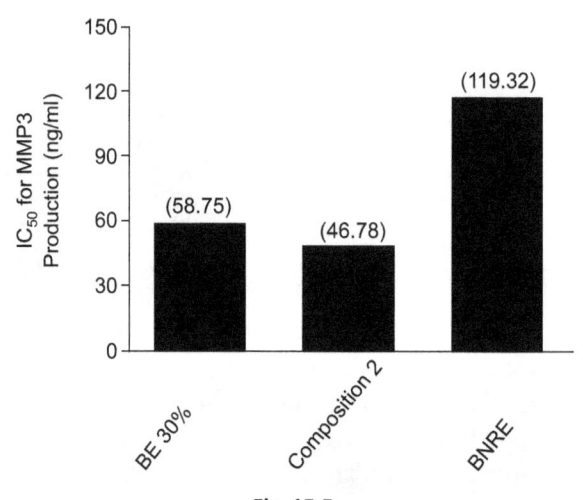

Fig. 15.5

in cell free culture supernatants was estimated by ELISA development kit (R&D System, Minneapolis, Minn., USA). Surprisingly, the composition-2 exhibited better inhibition of MMP-3 production in synovial cells than those shown individually by both BE30% and BNRE, confirming the synergistic effects shown against 5-LOX. Composition-2, BE30% and BNRE showed 50% inhibitory concentrations (IC_{50}) at 46.78, 58.75 and 119.32 µg/mL respectively. The synergistic MMP-3 inhibition shown by composition-2 compared to those shown by its individual ingredients BNRE and BE30% is summarized in Figure 15.5.

The synergistic effects shown by composition-2 in vitro were then put to test in vivo in Freund's Complete Adjuvant induced arthritis model of Sprague Dawley rats. The anti-inflammatory efficacies of composition-1 and composition-2, comprising *Boswellia serrata* extract selectively enriched in 3-O-acetyl-11-keto-β-boswellic acid to 30% (BE30%) and *Boswellia serrata* non-acidic resin extract (BNRE) in the ratio 1:1 and 2:1 respectively, were evaluated by an in vivo study in Freund's Complete Adjuvant induced arthritis model of Sprague Dawley rats and compared their efficacy with the efficacy shown by the individual ingredients, BE30% and BNRE. The treatment group rats were supplemented with 100 mg/kg body weight of *Boswellia* extract selectively enriched to 30% AKBA (BE30%) or *Boswellia serrata* non-acidic resin extract (BNRE) or composition-1 or composition-2 for 14 days. The positive control group was supplemented with Prednisolone at 10 mg/kg body weight. At the 14th day, Freund's Complete Adjuvant (FCA) was injected subcutaneously in the sub-plantar region of the left hind paw of each animal. The experiment was terminated on 28th day. Blood samples were collected from each animal at regular intervals and paw volumes were measured by Plethysmography equipment on the day of FCA injection and after 13 days of FCA inoculation. The difference in volume of paw edema is considered as the inflammatory response. The in vivo anti-inflammatory responses of BE30%, BNRE, composition-1, composition-2 and prednisolone were estimated by calculating the percentage of inhibition of paw edema when compared to the CMC supplemented control.

The treatment groups supplemented with *Boswellia serrata* extract 30% AKBA (BE30%) and *Boswellia serrata* non-acidic resin extract (BNRE) showed 37% and 10% reduction in paw edema respectively. However, the treatment groups supplemented with composition-1 and composition-2 at the same dose level showed better reduction in paw edema and achieved 44% and 54% reductions in paw volumes respectively. The positive control group supplemented with prednisolone exhibited 53% inhibition at 10 mg/kg dose level. The results as summarized in Figure VI confirm the synergistic effects observed in vitro for the inventive compositions-1 & -2.

Further, the levels of biomarkers, tumor necrosis factor-alpha (TNF-α) and Interleukin-1beta, (IL-1β) in the serum of the treatment groups and the control group were evaluated. The treatment groups supplemented with composition-1 and composition-2 showed significantly better reduction in the serum biomarkers, TNF-α and IL-1β compared to the levels exhibited by the treatment groups supplemented with the individual ingredients BE30% and BNRE as shown in Figure 15.7 (A and B).

Therefore, the foregoing data shows that compositions comprising AKBA enriched *Boswellia* extract and *Boswellia serrata* non-acidic resin extract (BNRE) are more potent as anti-inflammatory agents compared to the efficacy obtained with the individual components at the same dose level, manifesting an unexpected synergistic association between these extracts.

Boswellia serrata extract selectively enriched to contain 30% 3-O-acetyl-11-keto-β-boswellic acid (AKBA) is used to demonstrate the present invention. However any other *Boswellia serrata* extract selectively enriched in the AKBA content from 10% to 100% by weight can also be used for making synergistic composition(s) in combination with *Boswellia serrata* non-acidic resin extract (BNRE).

Boswellia serrata extract enriched in the AKBA content from 10% to 100% can be obtained using one or more of the following processes, which include but not limited to (1) conversion of other β-boswellic acids in the commercial *Boswellia serrata* extract to 35-45% AKBA extract using the earlier processes reported by the inventors through their PCT application # PCT/IN05/000074, dated 7th March, 2005 and PCT Patent publication WO03074063A1 and granted Indian patent #205269, (2) followed by diluting the conversion product to 10-45% AKBA extract using pharmaceutically or dietically acceptable carrier or diluent or (3) Purification of the above conversion product to 90-99% AKBA using a combination of the steps which include but not limited to column chromatography, partitions, crystallization and the like and then diluting the pure AKBA to desired AKBA concentration (20-99%) using pharmaceutically or dietically acceptable carrier or diluent or low grade commercial *Boswellia serrata* extract (4) alternately, purification of the naturally existing AKBA in the gum resin to a desired concentration in the range of 10-99% AKBA, using a combination of the steps which include but not limited to extraction, column chromatography, partitions, crystallization and the like, and then diluting the higher percentage fraction to desired concentration using pharmaceutically or dietically acceptable carrier or diluent or low grade commercial *Boswellia serrata* extract.

Different embodiments of the present invention are as outlined below:

In one aspect the present invention provides synergistic anti-inflammatory compositions comprising *Boswellia* extract selectively enriched in 3-O-acetyl-11-keto-β-boswellic acid (AKBA) and *Boswellia serrata* non-acidic resin extract (BNRE). The compositions can be used to prevent or cure or treat inflammation and/or one or more disease conditions related to or associated with inflammation.

In another aspect of the invention it was found that there was a synergistic antiinflammatory effect when therapeutically effective quantities of *Boswellia serrata* extract selectively enriched in AKBA and *Boswellia serrata* non-acidic resin extract (BNRE) were combined at certain specific ratio and the effect is better than that obtained when the components were given individually and also there was a synergistic amelioration of the expression or production of pro-inflammatory biomolecules/protein markers.

In a further aspect, the invention provides synergistic compositions comprising *Boswellia serrata* extracts selectively enriched in AKBA extract and *Boswellia serrata* non-acidic resin extract (BNRE) for the amelioration of the expression or production of the biomolecules/biomarkers/certain redox-sensitive pro-inflammatory genes related to or associated with inflammation which include but not limited to 5-lipoxygenase (5-LOX), 5-Lipoxygenase activating protein (FLAP), macrophage/adipocyte fatty acid-binding protein (aP2/FABP), IFN-γ, IL-4, ICAM, VCAM, Matrix metalloproteinases (MMPs) such MMP-3 and MMP-1, NFκB TNF-α and IL-1β in mammals in need thereof.

In yet another aspect, the invention provides synergistic compositions comprising *Boswellia serrata* extracts selectively enriched in AKBA and *Boswellia serrata* non-acidic resin extract (BNRE) for the prevention, control and treatment of one or more disease conditions related to associated with inflammation which include but not limited to asthma, atherosclerosis, endothelial dysfunction, allergic rhinitis, dermatitis, psoriasis, cystic fibrosis, inflammatory bowel diseases, interstitial cystitis, migraines, angina, chronic prostatitis, sun burn, periodontal disease, multiple sclerosis, uveitis, post-angioplasty restenosis, glomerulonephritis, gastrointestinal allergies, nephritis, conjunctivitis, chronic obstructive pulmonary disease, occupational asthma, eczema, bronchitis, hay fever, hives, allergic disorders and for conditions like wheezing, dyspnea, non productive cough, chest tightness, neck muscle tightness, rapid heart rate, chest pain, joint pain, collagen degradation by UV irradiation, skin-wrinkling and skin-aging and several other conditions associated thereof in mammals.

In still yet another aspect, the invention further provides synergistic compositions comprising *Boswellia serrata* extracts selectively enriched in AKBA extract and. *Boswellia serrata* non-acidic resin extract (BNRE) for the prevention, control and treatment of one or more components of inflammation, arthritis, cognition, neurological disorders, Alzheimer's disease, collagen degradation, aging of skin, cholesterol lowering, metabolic disorders and cancer. Nonlimiting examples of arthritis include rheumatoid (such as soft-tissue rheumatism and non-articular rheumatism, fibromyalgia, fibrositis, muscular rheumatism, myofascil pain, humeral epicondylitis, frozen shoulder, Tietze's syndrome, fascitis, tendinitis, tenosynovitis, bursitis), juvenile chronic, joint disorders, spondyloarthropaties (ankylosing spondylitis), osteoarthritis, hyperuricemia and arthritis associated with acute gout, chronic gout and systemic lupus erythematosus, and degenerative arthritis.

In other preferred embodiment, the invention' further provides a process for producing the *Boswellia serrata* non-acidic resin extract (BNRE), which include extraction of the gum resin of *Boswellia serrata* with a water immiscible organic solvent followed by washing the organic solvent extract with an aqueous alkali solution such as aqueous potassium hydroxide, followed by water and brine, and then finally evaporating the organic layer under vacuum followed by removing the volatile compounds under high vacuum and temperature to obtain BNRE. The water immiscible organic solvent can be selected from hexane, chloroform, dichloromethane, ethyl acetate, methyl isobutyl ketone or any other water immiscible solvent or mixtures thereof.

In a further embodiment, the *Boswellia serrata* intact oil can also be used in place of BNRE for making the synergistic compositions.

In other preferred embodiment, the invention further provides the process for producing compositions comprising the steps including:

(a) extraction of the gum resin of *Boswellia serrata* with a water immiscible organic solvent, filtering the extract carefully to remove the undissolved resin material and then washing the organic solvent extract repeatedly with an aqueous alkali solution such as aqueous potassium hydroxide followed by water and brine, and then finally evaporating the organic layer under vacuum and elevated temperature to remove the solvent, followed by removing the volatile compounds from the oily residue under high vacuum and temperature. to obtain the *Boswellia serrata* non-acidic resin extract (BNRE),

(b) selectively enriching acidic extract of the *Boswellia serrata* gum resin to obtain *Boswellia serrata* extract selectively enriched to 10-100% AKBA (BE),

(c) combining the *Boswellia serrata* non-acidic resin extract (BNRE) and AKBA enriched *Boswellia serrata* extract at desired ratio(s) to obtain present inventive composition(s).

(d) optionally mixing the compositions with one or more ingredients selected from biologically or pharmaceutically acceptable excipients, diluents and additives.

The water immiscible organic solvent in the above process can be selected from hexane, chloroform, dichloromethane, ethyl acetate, methylisobutyl-ketone, tert-butanol or any other water immiscible solvent.

The acidic extract of the *Boswellia serrata* gum resin needed for the enrichment of AKBA can be prepared from the gum resin using a known procedure or selected from a group of commercially available *Boswellia serrata* extracts standardized to boswellic acids, preferably an extract standardized to around 85% total acids by titrimetric method of analysis.

In other embodiment, the invention further provides the method of identifying *Boswellia serrata* non-acidic resin extract (BNRE), which comprises the steps of:

(a) Identifying the prominent compounds of BNRE as markers and isolating the same to >98% purity, followed by characterising them thoroughly using spectral data;

(b) Injecting a known amount each of the marker compounds individually on to a Phenomenex Luna Phenyl-Hexyl analytical column (4.6×250 mm, 5μ), mounted on to an HPLC system with PDA detector, wherein the column is maintained at 30° C. and eluted with a binary solvent mixture, comprising 0.1% v/v Ortho phosphoric acid in water and acetonitrile at 27% and 73% respectively, at a flow-rate of 1.5 mL/min and measuring the retention time and peak area for each marker using the UV detection at 210 nm and 248 nm; and then,

(c) Analyzing a known amount of BNRE sample under similar conditions and identifying the markers in the mixture based on a comparison of retention times of the peaks in the sample with those of the standards and optionally by co-injecting the sample along with each of the marker, and then estimating the percentage of each marker in the sample by comparing its peak area with the peak area corresponding to the standard at a known concentration, and then,

(d) Obtaining the composition of BNRE by expressing the percentages of all the markers together, which include but not limited to nephthenol, serratol, diterpene X, lupeol, olean-12-ene-3β-ol, olean-12-ene-3α-ol, lanosta-8,24-diene-3α-ol, urs-12-ene-3α-ol and guiol, and then using the said composition for comparison with other samples of BNRE.

In yet another aspect of the present invention, the synergistic anti-inflammatory compositions comprising *Boswellia serrata* extracts selectively enriched in AKBA and *Boswellia serrata* non-acidic resin extract (BNRE) contain optionally one or more of pharmaceutically or nutraceutically or dietically acceptable excipient(s) or diluents or salt(s) or additive(s).

The other embodiments of the present invention further provide the usage of the said synergistic compositions as it is or in comminuted form and/or in unmodified form as granules or powder or paste or the active ingredients are formulated into a solid, semi-solid or liquid dosage form by adding a conventional biologically or pharmaceutically acceptable salt(s) or additive(s) or excipient(s).

In a further embodiment, the invention provides that therapeutically effective amount of the novel compositions of the present invention can be administered in a specific dosage form such as orally, topically, transdermally, parenterally or in the form of a kit to a subject or patient in need thereof. Specific dosage form for formulation of the compositions of the present invention includes but not limited to oral agents such as tablets, soft capsules, hard capsules, pills, granules, powders, infusion solution, injection solution, cream, gel, emulsions, ointment, enema, medicinal pack, food supplement, emulsions, suspensions, syrups, pellets, inhalers, mouth sprays and the like; and parenteral agents such as injections, drops, suppositories and the like.

Another embodiment of the invention provides a kit comprising the composition(s) of *Boswellia* extract selectively enriched in 3-O-acetyl-11-keto-β-boswellic acid (AKBA) and *Boswellia serrata* non-acidic resin extract (BNRE). The kit can further comprise instructions for using the composition(s) for control, prevention and treatment of inflammation and inflammatory conditions including but not limited to asthma, arthritis and atherosclerosis.

In a further embodiment of the present invention, the compositions may further comprise effective amounts of one or more pharmaceutical or nutraceutical or dietically acceptable agents including but not limited to antioxidant(s), adaptogen(s), anti-inflammatory agent(s), anti-diabetic agent(s), antiobese agent(s), antiatherosclerotic agent(s), bio-protectants and/or bio-availability enhancer(s) and trace metals or an excipient(s) or pharmaceutically acceptable salt(s) or additive(s) and the compositions or mixtures thereof to form a formulation(s) administered using any of the methods described above.

The examples of pharmaceutically acceptable anti-inflammatory agents employed in the present invention include, but are not limited to prednisolone, hydrocortisone, methotrexate, sulfasalazine, naproxen, diclofenac and ibuprofen.

The examples of the biologically or pharmaceutically acceptable carriers employed in the present invention include, but are not limited to, surfactants, excipients, binders, diluents, disintegrators, lubricants, preservatives, stabilizers, buffers, suspensions and drug delivery systems.

Preferred examples of solid carriers or diluents or excipients include but not limited to glucose, fructose, sucrose, maltose, yellow dextrin, white dextrin, aerosol, microcrystalline cellulose, calcium stearate, magnesium stearate, sorbitol, stevioside, corn syrup, lactose, citric acid, tartaric acid, malic acid, succinic acid, lactic acid, L-ascorbic acid, dl-alpha-tocopherol, glycerin, propylene glycol, glycerin fatty ester, poly glycerin fatty ester, sucrose fatty ester, sorbitan fatty ester, propylene glycol fatty ester, acacia, carrageenan, casein, gelatin, pectin, agar, vitamin B group, nicotinamide, calcium pantothenate, amino acids, calcium salts, pigments, flavors and preservatives.

Preferred examples of liquid carriers (diluents) include, distilled water, saline, aqueous glucose solution, alcohol (e.g. ethanol), propylene glycol and polyethylene glycol; and oily carriers such as various animal and vegetable oils, white soft paraffin, paraffin and wax.

In alternative aspect of the invention, the inventive compositions of the present invention are delivered in the form of controlled release tablets, using controlled release polymer-based coatings by the techniques including nanotechnology, microencapsulation, colloidal carrier systems and other drug delivery systems known in the art. The said formulation can be designed for once a daily administration or multiple administrations per day.

In accordance to the present invention, the compositions of the present invention can also be formulated into or added to existing or new food and beverage form(s) such as solid foods like cereals, baby food(s), chocolate or nutritional bars, semisolid food like cream or jam, or gel, refreshing beverage, coffee, tea, milk-contained beverage, dairy products, lactic acid bacteria beverage, soup, drop, candy, chewing gum, chocolate, gummy candy, yoghurt, ice cream, pudding, soft adzuki-bean jelly, jelly, cookie, bakery products and the like. These various compositions or preparations or foods and drinks are useful as a healthy food for the treatment and/or prevention of inflammation and/or one or more of disease conditions associated with or related to inflammation including but not limited to asthma, arthritis inflammatory bowel disease, rheumatoid arthritis, juvenile rheumatoid arthritis, psoriatic arthritis, osteoarthritis, refractory rheumatoid arthritis, chronic non-rheumatoid arthritis, osteoporosis/bone resorption, coronary heart disease, atherosclerosis, vasculitis, ulcerative colitis, psoriasis, adult respiratory distress syndrome, diabetes, metabolic disorders, delayed-type hypersensitivity in skin disorders and Alzheimer's disease.

Various exemplary embodiments of the invention provides that the amount of present synergistic compositions to be administered or supplemented to humans or mammals may not be uniform and varies depending on the nature of the formulation and suggested human or animal dosage of the extract or the fractions, but preferably, within a range from 0.1 to 750 mg/kg body weight per day, more preferably about 0.5 to 500 mg/kg body weight.

Another embodiment of the invention provides that the quantity of the present inventive compositions in the above-mentioned various formulations, food and beverage compositions may also not be uniform and varies depending on the nature of the formulation and suggested human or animal dosage of the compositions, for example, about 0.001% to 99%, more preferably about 0.001 to 90 wt%.

In one of the important embodiments, the concentration of AKBA in the selectively enriched *Boswellia serrata* extract varies in the range of 10% to 100% by weight.

In another embodiment, the concentration of AKBA in the selectively enriched *Boswellia serrata* extract preferably varies in the range of 25%-95% and more preferably 25%-45%.

In yet another embodiment, the synergistic composition can comprise 10%-90% by the weight of *Boswellia serrata* extract selectively enriched in 3-O-acetyl-11-keto-β-boswellic acid (AKBA) and 90%-10% by weight of *Boswellia serrata* non-acidic resin extract (BNRE).

In still another embodiment, the synergistic composition can comprise 30%-70% by the weight of *Boswellia serrata* extract selectively enriched in 3-O-acetyl-11-keto-β-boswellic acid (AKBA) and 70%-30% by weight of *Boswellia serrata* non-acidic resin extract (BNRE).

Another embodiment of the invention is the health care food or beverage comprising any of the ingredients of the above said synergistic compositions up to 0.001% to 80%, preferably 0.001% to 50% by weight based on the total weight of the food or beverage.

Further embodiment of the invention provides that the amount of the present synergistic composition(s) varies in the range of 1% to 100% by weight based on the total weight of the formulation.

In another embodiment, the invention further comprises; mixing the compositions of the present invention with various components used in the animal feed for the purpose of curing, preventing or treating inflammation and several inflammation associated or related diseases including asthma, atherosclerosis and arthritis and the like.

The form of the composition or formulation to be added to animal feed is not specifically limited and may be added it is, or as a composition(s), to various cooked and processed food products. The quantity may be the same as that used in case of food products. Similarly, the ingredients may also be added during or after preparation of the animal feeds.

The following examples, which include preferred embodiments, will serve to illustrate the practice of this invention, and it being understood that the particulars shown are by way of example and for purpose of illustrative discussion of preferred embodiments of the invention and they are not to limit the scope of the invention.

Example 1. Preparation of *Boswellia serrata* Non-Acidic Resin Extract (BNRE):

The *Boswellia serrata* gum resin (100 g) was dispersed in 600 mL of methyl isobutyl ketone (MIBK) solvent and stirred at room temperature for 6.0 min. The insoluble gum materials were separated by filtration. The MIBK solution was extracted repeatedly with 2% KOH solution (3×200 mL) to remove the acidic compounds. The MIBK layer was then washed successively with water (400 mL) and brine (200 mL). The MIBK layer was evaporated under reduced pressure at 60-70° C. and the volatile components are removed from the oily residue under vacuum at 75-85° C. to obtain *Boswellia serrata* non-acidic resin extract or BNRE as a viscous oil (12 g).

Alternatively, the gum resin (250 g) collected from *Boswellia serrata* was extracted with methanol (300 mL×3) and the combined methanol extract was concentrated. The residue (50 g) was dissolved in ethyl acetate (400 mL) and extracted thrice with 2N KOH (3×100 mL). The organic layer was washed with water (2×200 mL) and brine (200 mL) and evaporated to obtain *Boswellia* oil. The volatile compounds were evaporated from the oil under vacuum at 75-85° C. to obtain 22 g of *Boswellia serrata* non-acidic resin extract (BNRE).

The BNRE was subjected to column chromatography over normal silica gel. The identical fractions were combined based on TLC and combined fractions were subjected individually to repeated column over silica gel using mixtures of hexane/ethyl acetate or hexane/acetone as eluants to obtain pure compounds. Some of the impure fractions were further subjected to preparative HPLC using a reversed phase C18 silica column to obtain pure compounds. The structures were established by analyzing the ^{1}H NMR, ^{13}C NMR, DEPT, HSQC and HMBC and mass spectral data and then comparing the data with that of known compounds. Nine of the prominent compounds are identified as guiol (1), nephthenol (2), serratol (3), diterpene X (4), lupeol (5), olean-12-ene-3β-ol (6), olean-12-ene-3α-ol (7), lanosta-8,24-diene-3α-ol (8) and urs-12-ene-3α-ol (9) as depicted in Figure I. The pure compounds were then utilized to standardize the *Boswellia serrata* non-acidic extract (BNRE) using HPLC method. The novel composition of BNRE evaluated based on analytical HPLC method and the retention times (R_t) is summarized in Table 1 and the HPLC chromatogram was depicted in Figure 15.2.

HPLC Method for the analysis of *Boswellia serrata* non-acidic resin extract (BNRE)

Table 15.1: Composition of *Bosewellia serrata* Non-acidic Resin Extract (BNRE)

Sl. No.	Test substance	R_t in min	Percentage
1	Guiol (1)	4.5	0.96
2	Nephthenol (2)	7.087	2.01
3	Serratol (3)	8.027	13.32
4	Diterpene X (4)	15.777	0.12
5	Lupeol (5)	26.901	0.06
6	Olean-12-ene-3β-ol (6)	31.460	1.29
7	Olean-12-ene-3α=ol (7)	33.718	5.36
8	Lanosta-8, 24-diene -3α-ol (8)	35.371	1.34
9	Urs-12-ene-3α-ol (9)	37.207	4.55

Example 2. Method of identification of *Boswellia serrata* non-acidic resin extract (BNRE): The method of identification of BNRE involves the estimation of its composition, which comprises the prominent compounds of BNRE, using

the following HPLC method. The solvent gradient is summarized in Table 15.2. A known amount of each of the marker compounds were analyzed individually, and the retention times and peak areas for each standard compound are noted. A known quantity of BNRE sample was then analyzed under similar conditions and each marker was identified based on a comparison of retention times of the peaks in the sample with those of the standards, and further by co-injecting the sample along with each of the markers. The percentage of each marker in the sample was estimated by comparing its peak area with the peak area corresponding to the standard compound at known concentration as shown below. The composition of BNRE is summarized in Table 15.3.

HPLC conditions:

Column: Phenomenex Luna Phenyl-Hexyl, (4.6×250 mm) 5μ

Wave length: 248 & 210 nm.

Flow rate: 1.50 mL/min

Volume of Injection: 20 μl

Temperature: 30° C.

System : Gradient

Mobile phase : Pump A: 0.1% v/v Ortho phosphoric acid in water

Pump B: Acetonitrile

Wherein, 0.1% v/v Ortho phosphoric acid is prepared by diluting 1 mL of ortho phosphoric acid to 1000 ml with water.

Standards: The prominent compounds of BNRE were selected as markers and isolated the same to >98% purity using a combination of isolation techniques. These pure standards so obtained were thoroughly characterized as guiol (1), nephthenol (2), serratol (3), diterpene X (4), lupeol (5), olean-12-ene-3β-ol (6), olean-12-ene-3α-ol (7), lanosta-8,24-diene-3α-ol (8) and urs-12-ene-3α-ol (9) using a combination of spectral data.

Table 15.2: Gradient Program

Time (in min)	Pump-A (%)	Pump-B (%)	Flow rate (ml/min)
0.01	27.0	73.0	1.50
40.0	27.0	73.0	1.50
45.0	0.0	100.0	1.50
50.0	0.0	100.0	1.50
52.0	27.0	73.0	1.50
Time (in min)	Pump-A (%)	Pump-B (%)	Flow rate (ml/min)
60.0	27.0	73.0	1.50

Table 15.3: Composition of BNRE

Sl.No.	Name	Retention time (in min)	Wave length (nm)	Composition (%)
1	Guiol	4.5	210	0.96
2	Nephthenol	7.0	210	2.01
3	Serratol	8.0	210	13.32
4	Diterpine X	15.8	252	0.12
5	Lupeol	26.9	210	0.06
6	Olean-12-ene-3β-ol	31.6	210	1.29
7	Olean-12-ene-3α=ol	33.9	210	5.36
8	Lanosta-8, 24-diene -3α-ol	35.5	210	1.34
9	Urs-12-ene-3α-ol	37.5	210	4.55

Standard Preparation

Weigh accurately about 10.0 mg of In house reference sample in to a 50 ml volumetric flask, dissolve and make up to volume with Methanol.

Sample Preparation

Weigh accurately about 250.0 mg of sample into a 50 ml volumetric flask, dissolve and make up to volume with Methanol.

Procedure

Filter both standard and sample solutions through 0.45μ membrane filter and inject.

Calculation

$$= \frac{\text{Peak area of sample} \times \text{conc. of standard} \times \text{purity of STD}}{\text{Peak area of STD} \times \text{conc. of sample}} = \%$$

Example 3. Preparation of *Boswellia serrata* Extract Enriched to 10-100% AKBA:

Commercially available *Boswellia serrata* extract standardized to 85% total boswellic acids by titrimetric method and comprises 3% 3-O-acetyl-11-keto-β-boswellic acid (AKBA) was used in the process for the selective enrichment of AKBA to 10-100%. The mixture contains total β-boswellic acids [3-O-acetyl-11-keto-β-boswellic acid, β-boswellic acid, 3-O-acetyl-β-boswellic acid, 11-keto-β-boswellic acid, 3-O-acetyl-11-keto-β-boswellic acid] in the range of 45-50% by HPLC method of analysis. The mixture was selectively enriched to contain 35-45% AKBA using one of the procedures described in the PCT application #s PCT/IN02/00034, filed Mar. 5, 2002 and PCT/IN05/000074, filed Mar. 7, 2005. It was further enriched to 45-100% AKBA by adding a chromatography step or crystallization or both to the enrichment process. An enriched extract containing 10-35% 3-O-acetyl-11-keto-β-boswellic acid (AKBA) was prepared by diluting an enriched extract having AKBA in the range of 35-100% with an excipient, preferably white dextrin. The *Boswellia serrata* extract enriched to 30% AKBA (BE30%) is used in the present invention.

Example 4. Composition-1: Composition-1 was prepared by mixing unit doses of the following components: One part of *Boswellia serrata* extract enriched to 30% AKBA (BE30%) (1 g) and one part of *Boswellia serrata* non-acidic resin extract (BNRE) (1 g).

Example 5. Composition-2: Composition-2 was prepared by mixing unit doses of the following components: Two parts of *Boswellia serrata* extract enriched to 30% AKBA (BE30%) (2 g) and one part of *Boswellia serrata* non-acidic resin extract (BNRE) (1 g).

Example 6. Composition-3: Composition-3 was prepared by mixing unit doses of the following components: One part of *Boswellia serrata* extract enriched to 30% AKBA (BE30%) (1 g) and two parts of *Boswellia serrata* non-acidic resin extract (BNRE) (2 g).

Example 7. Composition-4: Composition-4 was prepared by mixing unit doses of the following components: 3 parts of *Boswellia serrata* extract enriched to 40% AKBA (BE40%) (3 g) and two parts of *Boswellia serrata* non-acidic resin extract (BNRE) (2 g) and one part of white dextrin (1 g).

Example 8. Inhibition of 5-LOX and FLAP by *Boswellia serrata* extract enriched to 30% AKBA (BE30%): The effect of BE30% on the key intermediary proteins of arachidonic acid mediated inflammatory pathway was assessed in LPS induced-THP-1 human-monocyte-macrophage cells in vitro. Briefly, THP-1 human monocyte-macrophage cells were pre-treated with 10 µg/ml of BE30% for 1 h and thereafter, the cells were primed with LPS for 2 h to induce the inflammatory response. The cellular proteins were extracted by cell lysis buffer and subjected to immuno-western blot to detect the modulation of expression of 5-Lipoxygenase (5-LOX) and FLAP. BE30% significantly inhibited 5-LOX & FLAP expression in LPS induced-THP-1 human-monocyte-macrophage cells as summarized in Figure 15.3.

Example 9. 5-Lipoxygenase Inhibitory Activity of *Boswellia* Extract 30% AKBA (BE30%), *Boswellia serrata* Non-Acidic Resin Extract (BNRE) and Composition-2:

5-Lipoxygenase enzyme inhibitory activity was measured using the method of Schewe *et al.* (Adv Enzymol, Vol 58, 191-272, 1986), modified by Reddanna et. al., (Methods of Enzymology, Vol 187, 268-277, 1990). The assay mixture contained 80 µM linoleic acid and sufficient amount of potato 5-lipoxygenase in 50 mM phosphate buffer (pH 6.3). The reaction was initiated by the addition of enzyme buffer mix to linoleic acid and the enzyme activity was monitored as the increase in absorbance at 234 nm. The reaction was monitored for 120 sec and the inhibitory potential of the test substances BE30%, BNRE and Composition-2 was measured by incubating various concentrations of test substances two minutes before the addition of linoleic acid. All assays were performed three times. Percentage inhibition was calculated by comparing slope of the curve obtained for test substances with that of the control. The percentage inhibitions of BE30%, BNRE and Composition-1 are summarized in Table 15.4 and depicted in the Figure 15.4.

Table 15.4: 5-Lipoxygenase Inhibitory Activity

Sl.No.	Test substance	5-LOX inhibition at 25 µg/mL
1.	Boswellia serrata extract 30% AKBA (BE30%)	31.8%
2.	Bosewellia serrata non-acidic resin extract	20.6
3.	Composition-2	37.7

Example 10. Inhibition of Matrix Metalloproteinase-3 (MMP-3) Production by *Boswellia serrata* Extract 30% AKBA (BE30%), *Boswellia serrata* Non-Acidic Resin Extract (BNRE) and Composition-2:

MMP-3 was evaluated in TNFα induced SW982 human synovial cells. Briefly, the SW982 cells were cultured in DMEM with 2 mM Glutamine, 100 U/mL penicillin, 100 mg/mL streptomycin and 10% fetal bovine serum (Hyclone, Logan, Utah). Five thousand cells per well were seeded into a 96-well cell culture plate (Corning, USA) one day before the experiment. The culture media was replaced with fresh DMEM containing 1% fetal bovine serum. *Boswellia* extract 30% AKBA (BE30%), *Boswellia serrata* non-acidic resin extract (BNRE) and Composition-2 were serially diluted in medium, ranging from 5 to 100 ng/ml and were pre-incubated with cells for 2 hour at 5% CO_2 at 37° C., and then stimulated with 10 ng/ml human recombinant TNFα (R&D System, Minneapolis, Minn.) for 24 hours. The culture supernatant was harvested and used to measure MMP-3 production by ELISA development kit (R&D System, Minneapolis, Minn., USA). The MMP-3 concentration in cell free culture supernatant was estimated quantitatively by interpolating the optical densities into the standard curve generated from known concentrations of MMP-3. The inhibitory concentration for 50% inhibition (IC_{50}) of MMP-3 was calculated from the plot constructed by plotting percentage inhibition against concentration. BE30%, BNRE and Composition-2 showed IC_{50} values of 58.75, 119.32, and 46.78 µg/mL respectively. Their comparative inhibitions are depicted in Figure 15.5.

Example 11. A synergistic in vivo anti-inflammatory activity of composition-1 and composition-2, comprising *Boswellia* extract selectively enriched in 3-O-acetyl-11-keto-β-boswellic acid (AKBA) to 30%, namely BE30% and *Boswellia serrata* non-acidic resin extract (BNRE), in the ratio 1:1 and 2:1 respectively: The anti-inflammatory efficacies of composition-1 and composition-2, comprising *Boswellia serrata* extract selectively enriched in

3-O-acetyl-11-keto-β-boswellic acid to 30% (5-Loxin) and *Boswellia serrata* non-acidic resin extract (BNRE) in the ratio 1:1 and 2:1 respectively were evaluated by an in vivo study in Freund's Complete Adjuvant induced arthritis model of Sprague Dawley rats. The rats of either sex were randomly selected and divided into five groups containing five animals in each group. The treatment group rats were supplemented with 100 mg/kg body weight of *Boswellia* extract selectively enriched to 30% AKBA (BE30%) or *Boswellia serrata* non-acidic resin extract (BNRE) or composition-1 or composition-2, which contain BE30% and BNRE in 1:1 and 2:1 respectively, for 14 days. The positive control group was supplemented with Prednisolone at 10 mg/kg body weight. All supplements were diluted in 10 mL of 1% CMC for administration. The animals of control group received same volume of 1% CMC. At the 14th day, Freund's Complete Adjuvant (FCA) was injected subcutaneously in the sub-plantar region of the left hind paw of each animal. At the end of experiment, the animals were sacrificed and liver tissue samples were excised and stored in aliquot at −80° C. Blood samples were collected from each animal at a regular interval and paw volumes were measured by Plethysmography equipment on the day of FCA injection and after 13 days of FCA inoculation. The difference in volume of edema at the day of FCA injection and at 13th day after induction is considered as the inflammatory response. The in vivo anti-inflammatory responses of BE30%, BNRE, composition-1, composition-2 and Prednisolone were estimated by calculating the percentage of inhibition of paw edema when compared to the CMC supplemented control.

The treatment groups supplemented with *Boswellia serrata* extract selectively enriched to 30% AKBA (BE30%) and *Boswellia serrata* non-acidic resin extract (BNRE) achieved 37% and 10% reduction in paw edema respectively compared to 53% inhibition exhibited by the treatment group supplemented with prednisolone as shown in Figure 15.6. However, the treatment groups supplemented with composition-1 and composition-2 at the same dose level showed 44% and 54% reductions in paw volumes respectively as shown in Figure 15.6. The synergistic efficacy was further substantiated by the evaluation of the biomarkers tumor necrosis factor-alpha (TNF-α) and Interleukin-1beta, (IL-1β). The treatment groups supplemented with composition-1 and composition-2 showed significantly better reduction in the serum biomarkers, TNF-α and IL-1β, compared to the levels exhibited by the treatment groups supplemented with the individual ingredients BE30% and BNRE as shown in Figure 15.7.

16. Water Soluble Bioactive Fraction Isolated from Gum Resin Exudate of *Boswellia serrata*

Background of the invention The gum resin exudate of *Boswellia serrata* (Salai guggal) has traditionally been used in the Ayurvedic system of medicine in India for treatment of inflammatory diseases.

An alcoholic extract of the petroleum ether washed gum resin exudate of *Boswellia serrata* (AEPWR), available in the Indian market under the trade name "Sallaki" since 1982, was found to have anti-inflammatory activity.

This is also available in Switzerland as H-15. It has a novel mode of inhibitory action on the formation of the lipoxygenase product, leukotriene B.

Boswellic acid (BA) and its derivatives, 11-keto-B-boswellic acid (KBA) and acetyl-11-keto-B-boswellic acid (AKBA) have been isolated as active constituents from alcoholic extract of petroleum ether washed gum resin (AEPWR) and show prominent anti-inflammatory and anti-arthritic properties

Immunopharmacol., with a selective inhibitory action on the formation of leukotriene B (LTB4). The gum resin exudate of Bserrata (SG) on extraction with organic solvents like methanol or ethanol, or petroleum ether followed by methanol or ethanol yields about 60-65% of extract. The marc weighing about 35-40% of the gum resin (SG) is composed of water-soluble constituents, dust and plant residues. A polysaccharide was isolated from the gum resin exudate of B.

Serrata and characterized as a 4-0-methyl-glucuronoarabinogalactan. This product, a pure polysaccharide, was isolated from the defatted oleogum resin in about 9% yield by extraction with water followed by dialysis and a number of chromatographic separations using DEAE-Sephacel and Sephadex G-100. This implies that the yield of this pure polysaccharide is much less than 9% on the weight of the gum resin.

While focus has been given to extraction of bioactive fractions from the gum resin exudates to obtain sallaki or H-15, no attention has been given to the waste fraction obtained in such processes. It is also believed that the polysaccharide fraction is less than 9% by weight of the total gum resin. It is therefore important to attempt to obtain useful bioactive fractions from the waste obtained after the production of Sallaki or H-15.

Objects of the invention The main object of the present invention is to provide a process of preparation of a novel water soluble bioactive fraction from *Boswellia serrata*.

Another object of the present invention is to provide a novel water soluble bioactive fraction containing water soluble compounds having marked anti-inflammatory and anti-arthritic activities.

Summary of the invention Accordingly the present invention provides a novel bioactive fraction obtained from the gum resin exudate of *Boswellia serrata* comprising polysaccharides with at least 50 per cent neutral sugars (taken as galactose) consisting of galactose and arabinose and D-glucuronic acid.

In another embodiment of the invention, the fraction prepared comprises a mixture of salts of calcium 1.4 to 2.1% and potassium 0.12 to 0.20%.

The present invention also relates to a process for the preparation of a water soluble novel bioactive fraction from gum resin exudate of *Boswellia serrata* comprising extracting the gum resin exudate or defatted gum resin exudate with an alkanol to produce marc, extracting the marc with water and precipitating the polysaccharide fraction from the aqueous extract by addition of alcohol and purifying the bioactive fraction.

In another embodiment of the invention, the alkanol is selected from ethanol and methanol.

In another embodiment of the invention, the marc left after extraction with alcohol is extracted with water at room temperature.

In one embodiment of the invention, the bioactive fraction obtained comprises polysaccharides with at least 50 per cent neutral sugars (taken as galactose) consisting of galactose and arabinose and D-glucuronic acid.

In another embodiment of the invention, the aqueous extract is precipitated with alcohol to get the crude polysaccharide fraction and purified by repeating this step.

In another embodiment of the invention, the bioactive composition is collected by filtration and dried under vacuum at temperatures below 50°C.

In another embodiment of the invention, the fraction prepared comprises a mixture of salts of calcium 1.4 to 2.1% and potassium 0.12 to 0.20%.

The present invention also relates to a composition for the treatment of arthritis comprising a pharmaceutically effective amount of a bioactive fraction obtained from *Boswellia serrata* comprising polysaccharides with at least 50 per cent neutral sugars (taken as galactose) consisting of galactose and arabinose and D-glucuronic acid in a pharmaceutically acceptable carrier.

In another embodiment of the invention, the fraction prepared comprises a mixture of salts of calcium 1.4 to 2.1% and potassium 0.12 to 0.20%.

The present invention also relates to a method for the treatment of arthritis comprising administering a pharmaceutically effective amount of a bioactive fraction obtained from *Boswellia serrata* comprising polysaccharides with at least 50 per cent neutral sugars (taken as galactose) consisting of galactose and arabinose and D-glucuronic acid in a pharmaceutically acceptable carrier.

In another embodiment of the invention, the fraction prepared comprises a mixture of salts of calcium 1.4 to 2.1% and potassium 0.12 to 0.20%.

The present invention also relates to the use of a bioactive fraction obtained from *Boswellia serrata* comprising comprising polysaccharides with at least 50 per cent neutral sugars (taken as galactose) consisting of galactose and arabinose and D-glucuronic acid to prepare a pharmaceutical composition for the treatment of arthritis.

Detailed description of the invention The bioactive product obtained in this invention is the total polysaccharide fraction and is obtained in about 15% yield on the weight of the oleoresin, the isolation of which has been achieved using a facile process. The fraction is obtained from a waste product viz., the material discarded after production of Sallaki or H-15. In addition the fraction also contains potassium and calcium salts of glucuronoarabino-galactose as ascertained by its hydrolysis and incineration. Hitherto all the pharmaceutical products based on the oleo-gum resin of *B. serrata* are insoluble in water, whereas the fraction of the invention is water soluble and its isolation was the result of an investigation based on activity guided separation of the constituents of the gum resin of *B. serrata*. The marc left after extraction of the gum resin with alcohol (ethanol or methanol) or petroleum ether followed by alcohol, the latter being used for the production of commercial"Sallalci"or H-15 of Switzerland, was processed for isolation of polysaccharide fraction with a view to evaluating it for anti-inflammatory activity. By extracting with water the marc left after extracting the gum resin exudate of *B. serrata* with alcohol (ethanol or methanol) followed by precipitation of the aqueous extract with ethanol it was possible to isolate the crude polysaccharide. The crude polysaccharide was purified by redissolving it in water and reprecipitating with ethanol. This process was repeated once again to give water soluble bioactive composition in 14-16 per cent yields containing polysaccharide with at least 50 per cent neutral sugars (taken as galactose/glucose) as determined by phenol- sulphuric acid method, acid hydrolysis of which yielded galactose, arabinose and D-glucuronic acid. This bioactive polysaccharide composition, has anti-inflammatory activity comparable with that of"boswellic acids" (total acids from SG) or "Sallaki"and anti-arthritic activity stronger than that of boswellic acids or "Sallaki"developed as anti-inflammatory/anti-arthritic agents from the gum resin exudate of *Boswellia serrata*.

The bioactive fraction (composition) prepared by the process of the present invention has the following characteristics: (*i*) it is a white or almost white (pale yellow) solid; (*ii*) it is completely soluble in water; (*iii*) on incineration it gave 4.5 to 6% ash which was found to be a mixture of carbonates of potassium and calcium (corresponding to –0.17% potassium and –1.8% calcium). The ash dissolved partly in water but completely in dilute hydrochloric acid; (*iv*) on hydrolysis with 2N trifluoroacetic acid it gave arabinose, galactose and

D-glucuronic acid. (*v*) the fraction of the invention was found to contain 50 per cent neutral sugars as determined by phenol-H_2SO_4 method.

The detection of potassium and calcium in the ash obtained on incineration of the fraction of the invention indicated that either these metals are present in the fraction as impurities in the form of salts of inorganic acids or as salts of the D-glucuronic acid moiety.

The former, i.e., the presence of potassium and calcium salts of inorganic acids in the fraction of the invention was ruled out as the ash obtained on incineration of the fraction in about 5 per cent yield consisted of potassium carbonate (–0.3 per cent) and calcium carbonate (–4.6 per cent) only and no other anions such as chloride, sulphate or nitrate could be detected in the ash. The composition of the ash obtained on incineration corresponds to –0.17% potassium and 1.8% calcium in the fraction of the invention. Thus the fraction is a mixture of calcium and potassium salts of the polysaccharides, composed of units of galactose, arabinose and D- glucuronic acid, in the ratio of –10 to –1. On comparative evaluation of antiarthritic activities of boswellic acids, the fraction of the invention and 1: 1 mixture of boswellic acids and the fraction of the invention in adjuvant induced developing and developed arthritis in rats based on inhibition (in injected paw) of edema in treated groups as compared to the control groups it was observed that in doses of 200 mg/kg p. o. boswellic acids gave an inhibition of 31.20% whereas the fraction of the invention and the mixture of boswellic acids and the fraction of the invention gave inhibitions of 35.47% and 36.22% respectively on the 13th day. On the 28th day at the same dose levels the percentage inhibitions with boswellic acids, the fraction of the invention and the mixture of boswellic acids and the fraction of the invention were 21.02, 25.15 and 23.72 respectively. Thus, the fraction of the invention and boswellic acids on the combination in equal doses showed additive and not synergistic effect.

A study on the effects of boswellic acids and the fraction of the invention on total leucocytes count and volume of pleural fluid after intrapleural carrageenan injection revealed that percentage inhibitions with boswellic acids and the fraction of the invention in pleural fluid were 6.52 and 7.56 respectively and in TLC 28.08 and 32.28 respectively. The fraction of the invention which like boswellic acids acts as a 5-lipoxygenase inhibitor is free from any ulcerogenic effects, as expected, which makes it a very good therapeutic agent for the treatment of arthritis.

The process of the present invention is illustrated by the following examples, which are, however, not to be construed to limit the scope of the present invention. All the samples of the bioactive composition on analysis were found to conform to the characteristics described above.

Example 1. The finely ground gum resin exudate of *Boswellia serrata* (one year old sample, i.e. one year after collection-20 mesh powder, 1 kg) was charged in a percolator, treated with ethanol (3 litres) and left overnight. The percolate was drained and the marc was extracted twice at room temperature, each time with 3 litres of ethanol. The marc (370g) (the drug left after extraction with ethanol) was air dried and extracted with water (1.85 litres) at room temperature for 8 hours. It was filtered through a cloth and the residue again treated with water (750 ml). After 8 hours it was filtered and combined filtrates on centrifuging gave a clear supernatant liquid (somewhat viscous) (2.25 litres). It was cooled and alcohol (4.5 litres) was added to it with stirring. The mixture was left in a fridge. The precipitate (almost white), which separated out was collected by filtration. It was again dissolved in water (1.5 litres) and the aqueous solution precipitated by adding alcohol (3 litres). It was filtered and one more purification by dissolving it in water (1.4 litres) and reprecipitating with alcohol (2.8 litres) afforded the bioactive composition. It was collected by filtration and dried in a vacuum desiccator at room temperature, yield 159 g (15.9%).

Example 2. The finely ground gum resin exudate of *Boswellia serrata* (one year old sample, 1 kg) was charged in a percolator and extracted thrice with petroleum ether (60-80°C) at room temperature using 2 litres of the solvent each time. The marc was air-dried and extracted thrice with alcohol (3 × 2 litres). The residue (350 g after air-drying) left after extraction with alcohol was extracted with water (1.4 litres) for 8 hours at room temperature and filtered through a muslin cloth. The residue was washed with water (200 ml). The filtrate was combined with the washing and centrifuged. To the clear supernatant (1.1 litres) alcohol (2.2 litres) was added. Precipitate was dissolved in water and reprecipitated with alcohol. One more purification as described in Example 1 gave the bioactive composition, yield 142 g.

Example 3. Powdered gum resin exudate of *Boswellia serrata* (a three-year-old sample, 1 kg) was extracted in a percolator with petroleum ether (3 × 2 litres). The defatted gum thus obtained (715 g) was extracted thrice with alcohol in the percolator (3 × 2 litres). The marc was first extracted with water (1.4 litres) at room temperature and subsequently with 700 ml and then with 450 ml of water. The combined aqueous extracts (expressed through muslin cloth) (1.8 litres) were centrifuged to get a clear supernatant (1.7 litres) which on dilution with alcohol (3.4 litres) deposited pale brown solid. The mixture was left overnight in a fridge and the solid collected by filtration. It was dissolved in water (1.4 litres) and precipitated by adding alcohol (2.8 litres) to the aqueous solution. This process was repeated again when the bioactive composition was obtained as a very light brown (almost white) solid, yield 149 g.

Example 4. Powdered gum resin exudate of *Boswellia serrata* (one year old resin, 0.5 kg) was thrice extracted with methanol (3 × 1.5 litres) at room temperature in a percolator. The marc 175 g was air-dried and extracted twice at room temperature with water using 700 ml of water for the first extraction and then 200 ml for the subsequent extraction. The combined aqueous extracts were clarified by centrifugation and the clear extract (–600 ml) was precipitated by adding alcohol. The light brown solid which separated out on the leaving the mixture overnight was collected by filtration and purified by dissolving it in water (500 ml) and precipitating with alcohol (1 litre). The process was repeated once more when the bioactive composition separated out as a light yellow (off white) solid. It was collected by filtration and dried in vacuum; yield 73 g.

Advantages:

1. The bioactive fraction prepared in the present invention has immense potential in therapeutic use from a waste product viz., discarded material left after production of
 Sallaki or H-15.
2. Its anti-arthritic activity is more than that of well known anti-arthritic drug viz., Boswellic acids.
3. It does not have any ulcerogenic effects that are commonly associated with anti-inflammatory and anti-arthritic drugs.

17 Boswellia Oil, Its Fractions and Compositions for Enhancing Brain Function

The gum resin of *Boswellia serrata* (*Burseraceae*) plant has long been in use for the treatment of several diseases by the practitioners of Ayurvedic medicines in the Indian system of medicine. The extract of *Boswellia* was found to be a potent anti-inflammatory and anti-arthritic agent. The origin of anti-inflammatory actions of *Boswellia* gum resin and its extracts has been attributed to a group of triterpene acids called boswellic acids that were isolated from the gum resin of *Boswellia serrata*. Boswellic acids exert anti-inflammatory actions by inhibiting 5-lipoxygenase (5-LOX). 5-LOX is a key enzyme for the biosynthesis of leukotrienes from arachidonic acid. 3-O-Acetyl-11-keto-β-boswellic acid (AKBA) is biologically the most active component among its congeners, it being able to inhibit 5-LOX with an IC_{50} of 1.5 µM.

Boswellia gum resin and its extracts also demonstrated significant therapeutic improvements in human clinical trials confirming the anti-inflammatory effects shown in vitro and in vivo.

Worldwide aging of the population has increased the incidents of cognitive deficits, such as age-associated memory impairment and senile dementias, and this causes great disruptive impact on the life of the affected individuals. The "cholinergic hypothesis of learning" played a pivotal role in the development of drugs for degenerative diseases.

A disturbance of the cortical cholinergic system accompanied by a reduction of choline acetylase (reduced acetylcholine synthesis) is inter alia detectable biochemically in case of neurological diseases. Hence, there is a demand for a medicament whose active substance can ameliorate this disturbance and highly available at the target organ (brain) and which is well tolerated, particularly in long-term therapy.

Acetylcholinesterase (AChE) is an important enzyme to hydrolyze acetylcholine, a neurotransmitter mediating the activity of parasympathetic nerve, into choline and acetate. AChE is formed in the endoplasmic reticulum, and moves and functions in the cell membrane. AChE is distributed around cholinergic nerve, particularly much at the myoneural junction, and is found in the serum, liver and other tissues.

A wide range of evidence shows that acetylcholinesterase (AChE) inhibition can improve cognitive and mental functions through enhancing cortical cholinergic neurotransmission. The acetylcholinesterase (AChE) inhibitors increase the concentration of acetylcholine and help nerve cells to communicate better. The longer acetylcholine remains in the brain, the longer those cells can call up memories. The earliest known AChE inhibitors are physostigmine and tacrine.

However, clinical studies show that physostigmine has poor oral activity, brain penetration and pharmacokinetic parameters while tacrine has hepatotoxic side effects. Studies were thus focused on finding new types of acetylcholinesterase inhibitors that would overcome the disadvantages of these two compounds.

Donepezil and Rivastigmin inaugurate a new class of AChE inhibitors with longer and more selective action with manageable adverse effects but still small improvement of cognitive impairment. Galanthamine (Reminyl), an alkaloid isolated from Galanthus nivalis, is another recently approved AChE inhibitor for the treatment of Alzheimer's. It is selective, long acting, and reversible. Galanthamine produces beneficial effects in patients. Similarly, huperzine A, a novel Lycopodium alkaloid discovered from the Chinese medicinal plant Huperzia serrata is a potent, reversible and selective inhibitor of AChE with a rapid absorption and penetration into the brain in animal tests. It exhibits memory-enhancing activities in animal and also in clinical trials.

Dementia with Lewy bodies (DLB) is a common cause of dementia. Changes in the acetylcholine system have been reported in brains of patients with DLB, which provides a rational basis for trials of acetylcholinesterase inhibitors in DLB.

Current treatment of dementia in Parkinson's disease (PD) is based on the compensation of profound cholinergic deficiency, as in recent studies with the cholinesterase inhibitors galantamine, donepezil and rivastigmine. It has also been shown that cholinesterase inhibitors can improve motor function in PD. The beneficial effect of cholinesterase inhibitors has been studied on patients suffering from Parkinson's disease and dementia.

Studies show that Wernicke-Korsakoff syndrome is associated with a persisting severe anterograde amnesia in which memory is not transferred from short-to long-term storage. It is believed to be a consequence of a thiamine-deficient state often found in alcohol abusers. The memory deficit has been attributed to a number of brain lesions (corpus mamillare and dorsomedial nucleus of the thalamus), loss of cholinergic forebrain neurons and serotonin-containing neurons. Many studies and case-reports suggest efficacy of acetylcholinesterase inhibitors in the Wemicke-Korsakoff-associated memory deficit. Studies also suggest that neurons in the nucleus basalis are at risk in thiamine deficient alcoholic.

The U.S. Pat. relates to the use of incense (olibanum), incense extracts, substances contained in incense, their physiologically acceptable salts, their derivatives and their physiological salts, pure boswellic acid, of physiologically acceptable salts, of a derivative, of a salt of the derivative, for production of a medicament for the prevention or treatment of Alzheimer's disease.

US publication relates to the use of the hydrogenation products of frankincense (olibanum), its hydrogenated ingredients as well as physiologically acceptable salts and derivatives thereof and hydrogenated frankincense extracts for the production of a medicament for the prophylactic and/or therapeutic treatment of cerebral ischemia, cranial/brain trauma and/ or Alzheimer's disease.

There is currently no prior art, to the best of the Applicants' knowledge, relating to the use of *Boswellia* non-acidic oil fractions and their compositions for the prevention, control and treatment of Memory and Cognition related diseases and enhancing brain functions.

Additionally, there are numerous pharmaceutical ingredients, herbal ingredients and biologically active molecules that are effective in vitro against a disease condition or disorder. However, several of these ingredients are not effective or not bioavailable in vivo, i.e., after administration to warm blooded animals. It is thus important to explore and identify safe and effective agents that help to increase the bioavailability of such ingredients. As set forth in the present disclosure, *Boswellia* non-acidic oil fractions have been found to increase bioavailability of a number of extracts, fractions, phytochemicals and compounds originating from plant, animal or microorganism sources.

There is currently no prior art, to the best of the Applicants' knowledge, relating to the use of *Boswellia* non-acidic oil fractions and their compositions for increasing the bioavailability of biological agents in warm blooded animals.

SUMMARY OF THE DISCLOSURE

Various embodiments of the present disclosure provide use of compositions comprising *Boswellia* non-acidic fraction(s) selected from *Boswellia* low polar gum resin extract fraction (BLPRE) having a novel phytochemical composition, *Boswellia* volatile oil fraction (BVOIL), and a *Boswellia* oil fraction (BOIL) comprising BLPRE and BVOIL fractions, either individually or in combination. These compositions are useful for improving brain health and brain functions, which include but are not limited to cognition, memory, intelligence, motivation, attention, concentration, learning power and better communication. These compositions are also useful to alleviate disease conditions related to cognition and memory deficits and the like.

Various embodiments disclosed herein provide use of *Boswellia* non-acidic fraction(s) selected from *Boswellia* low polar gum resin extract fraction (BLPRE), *Boswellia* volatile oil fraction (BVOIL), and a *Boswellia* oil fraction (BOIL) comprising BLPRE and BVOIL, either individually or as compositions, to prevent, control and treat brain related diseases/disorders which include but not limited to senile dementia, multi-infarct dementia, dyslexia, aphasia, organic brain syndrome, myasthenia gravis, vascular dementia, mild cognitive impairment (MCI), Lewy body dementia, Wemicke-Korsakoff-syndrome, Alzheimer's, Parkinson's disease, Attention-deficit Hyperactivity Disorder (ADHD), hypoxia, anoxia, cerebrovascular insufficiency, epilepsy, myoclonus and hypocholinergic dysfunctions, to slowdown memory deterioration, functional loss and to treat memory impairment disorders, neurodegenerative disorders, and for controlling blood pressure and blood circulation in the brain.

Various embodiments disclosed herein relate to compositions comprising at least one component selected from *Boswellia* low polar gum resin extract fraction (BLPRE), *Boswellia* volatile oil fraction (BVOIL) and non-acidic *Boswellia* oil fraction consisting of BLPRE and BVOIL in combination with at least one component selected from biological agent(s), Nootropic agent(s).

In another aspect, the disclosure provides compositions comprising at least one component selected from *Boswellia* low polar gum resin extract fraction (BLPRE), *Boswellia* volatile oil fraction (BVOIL) and non-acidic *Boswellia* oil fraction (BOIL) consisting of BLPRE and BVOIL in combination with at least one component selected from *Boswellia* extract(s), fraction(s), extracts/fractions enriched in one or more boswellic acids, their salts or derivatives thereof.

In another aspect, the disclosure provides compositions comprising at least one component selected from *Boswellia* low polar gum resin extract fraction (BLPRE), *Boswellia* volatile oil fraction (BVOIL) and non-acidic *Boswellia* oil fraction (BOIL) in combination with one or more agents selected from natural antioxidants, anti-inflammatory agents and immune modulators.

In another embodiment, the disclosure provides *Boswellia* low polar gum resin extract fraction (BLPRE) for increasing the bioavailability of biological agents.

In further embodiments, the disclosure provides compositions comprising at least one component selected from *Boswellia* oil (BOIL), *Boswellia* volatile oil (BVOIL) and *Boswellia* low polar gum resin extract (BLPRE) obtained from *Boswellia* gum resin in combination with a biological agent, for increasing the bioavailability of biological agents in warm blooded animals in need thereof.

In various embodiments, the disclosure provides *Boswellia* derived bioenhancing agents for increasing the bioavailability of one or more biological ingredients or functional ingredients.

In certain embodiments, the disclosure provides *Boswellia* derived bioenhancing agents for increasing the bioavailability of one or more pharmaceutical drugs/synthetic drugs.

In various embodiments, the disclosure provides *Boswellia* derived bioenhancing agents for increasing the bioavailability of one or more *Boswellia* derived components.

In various embodiments, the disclosure provides non-acidic *Boswellia* derived bioenhancing agents for increasing the bioavailability of one or more acidic *Boswellia* derived components.

In certain embodiments, the disclosure provides *Boswellia* derived bioenhancing agents for increasing the bioavailability of one or more Curcuma derived components.

In various embodiments disclosed herein, a non-acidic *Boswellia* oil fraction selected from the group consisting of an intact *Boswellia* oil (BOIL) and a *Boswellia* volatile oil (BVOIL) may be produced by:

(a) procuring the gum resin of a plant of the genus *Boswellia*;

(b) extracting said gum resin with a non-polar organic solvent to produce a non-polar solvent extract solution;

(c) washing the non-polar solvent extract solution with an alkali solution to remove acidic compounds from the non-polar solvent extract solution;

(d) washing the non-polar solvent extract solution successively with water and brine;

(e) evaporating non-polar solvent from the non-polar solvent extract solution to obtain BOIL as an oily residue; and optionally

(f) isolating volatile components from BOIL as BVOIL.

BRIEF DESCRIPTION OF FIGURES

Figures 17.1 and 17.2 show processes for obtaining BLPRE, BOIL, and BVOIL.

Figure 17.3 shows structural formulae I-9 representing prominent compounds of *Boswellia serrata* low polar gum resin extract (BsLPRE).

Figure 17.4 shows the HPLC chromatogram depicting the phytochemical profile of the *Boswellia serrata* low polar gum resin extract (BsLPRE).

Figures 17.5A, 17.5B, and 17.5C show bar diagrammatic representation of number of days required for learning, latency in finding feed and number of wrong entries respectively obtained during learning phase. The bars 1 to 3 represents vehicle treated control, BsLPRE (250 mg/kg) and piracetam (150 mg/kg) respectively. Each bar represent mean±SE, n=8, *$p<0.05$ and **$p<0.01$.

Figures 17.6A and 17.6B show bar diagrammatic representation of latency in finding feed and number of wrong entries respectively obtained during memory retention phase. The bars 1 to 3 represents vehicle treated control, BsLPRE (250 mg/kg) and piracetam (150 mg/kg) respectively. Each bar represent mean ± SE, $n = 8$.

Figures 17.7 shows a plot of serum concentration of AKBA after oral administration of the composition LI13108F containing *Boswellia serrata* low polar gum resin extract (BsLPRE) and *Boswellia serrata* extract selectively enriched to 30% 3-O-acetyl-11-keto-β-boswellic acid (AKBA) and composition LI13119F containing *Boswellia serrata* volatile oil fraction (BsVOIL) and *Boswellia serrata* extract selectively enriched to 30% 3-O-acetyl-11-keto-β-boswellic acid (AKBA) to albino rats at doses equivalent to 30 mg/kg of AKBA.

Figure 17.8 represents a plot of serum concentration of Bisdemethylcurcumin (LI01008) after oral administration of composition (LI13124F1) containing Bisdemethylcurcumin and *Boswellia serrata* low polar gum resin extract (BsLPRE) in 2:1 ratio at concentration of 450 mg/kg or Bisdemethylcurcumin (LI01008) alone at 300 mg/kg body weight.

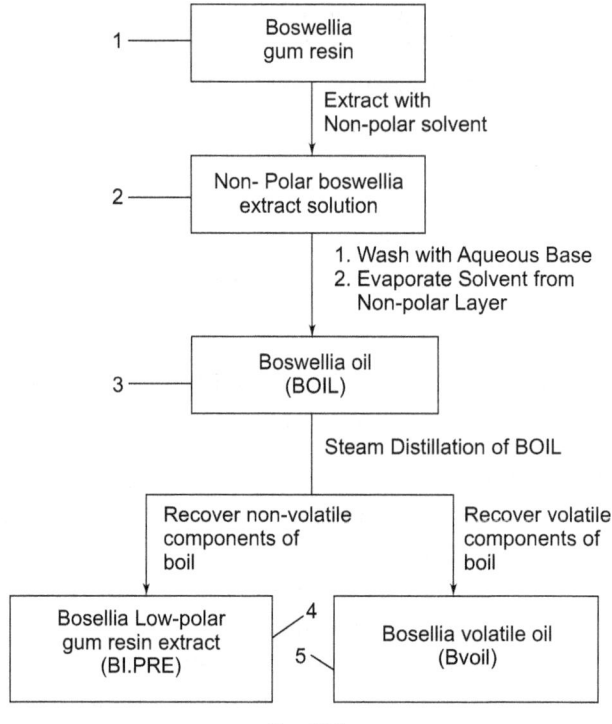

Fig. 17.1

DESCRIPTION

A. Definitions

1. '*Boswellia* oil' or 'non-acidic *Boswellia* extract' or 'BOIL' used herein refers to non-acidic *Boswellia* gum resin extract containing non-acidic *Boswellia* low polar gum resin extract fraction (BLPRE) and *Boswellia* volatile oil fraction (BVOIL) obtained from gum resin of any of the *Boswellia* species. BOIL encompasses 'BsOIL' and 'BcOIL,' as defined below.

2. '*Boswellia serrata* oil' or 'non-acidic *Boswellia serrata* extract' or 'BsOIL' used herein refers to non-acidic *Boswellia serrata* gum resin extract containing non-acidic *Boswellia serrata* low polar gum resin extract fraction (BsLPRE) and *Boswellia serrata* volatile oil fraction (BsVOIL) obtained from gum resin of the *Boswellia serrata* species.

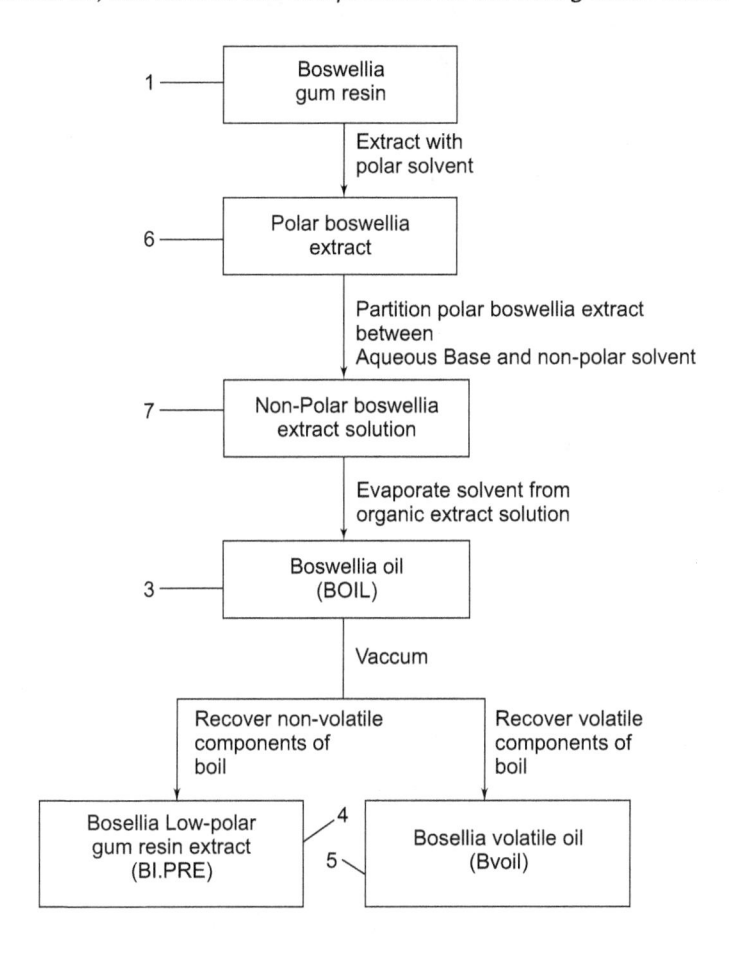

Boswellia Oil, Its Fractions and Compositions for Enhancing Brain Function 195

Fig. 17.2

2 R_1 = OH and R_2 = H
3 R_1 = H and R_2 = OH

Fig. 17.3

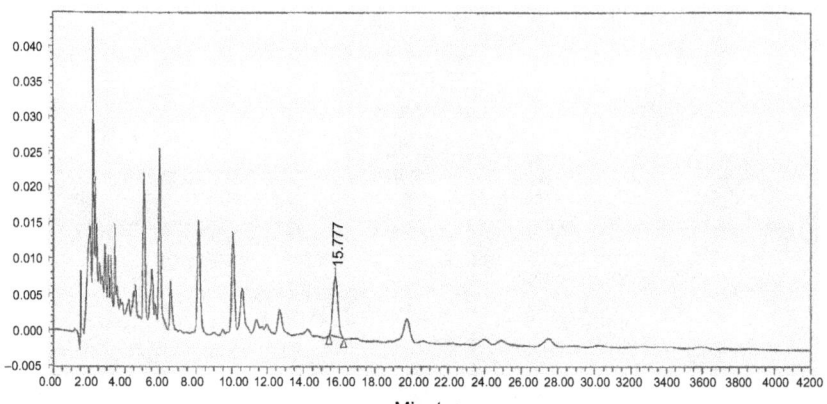

Fig. 17.4

A: chromatogram at 252 nm

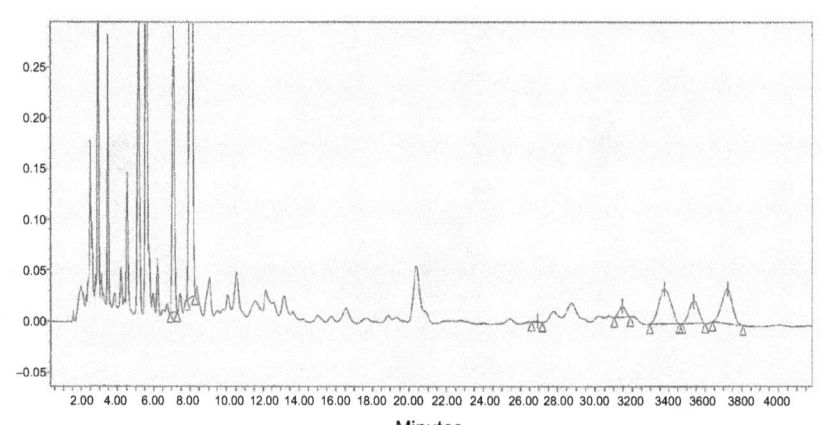

B: chromatogram at 210 nm

Fig. 17.5

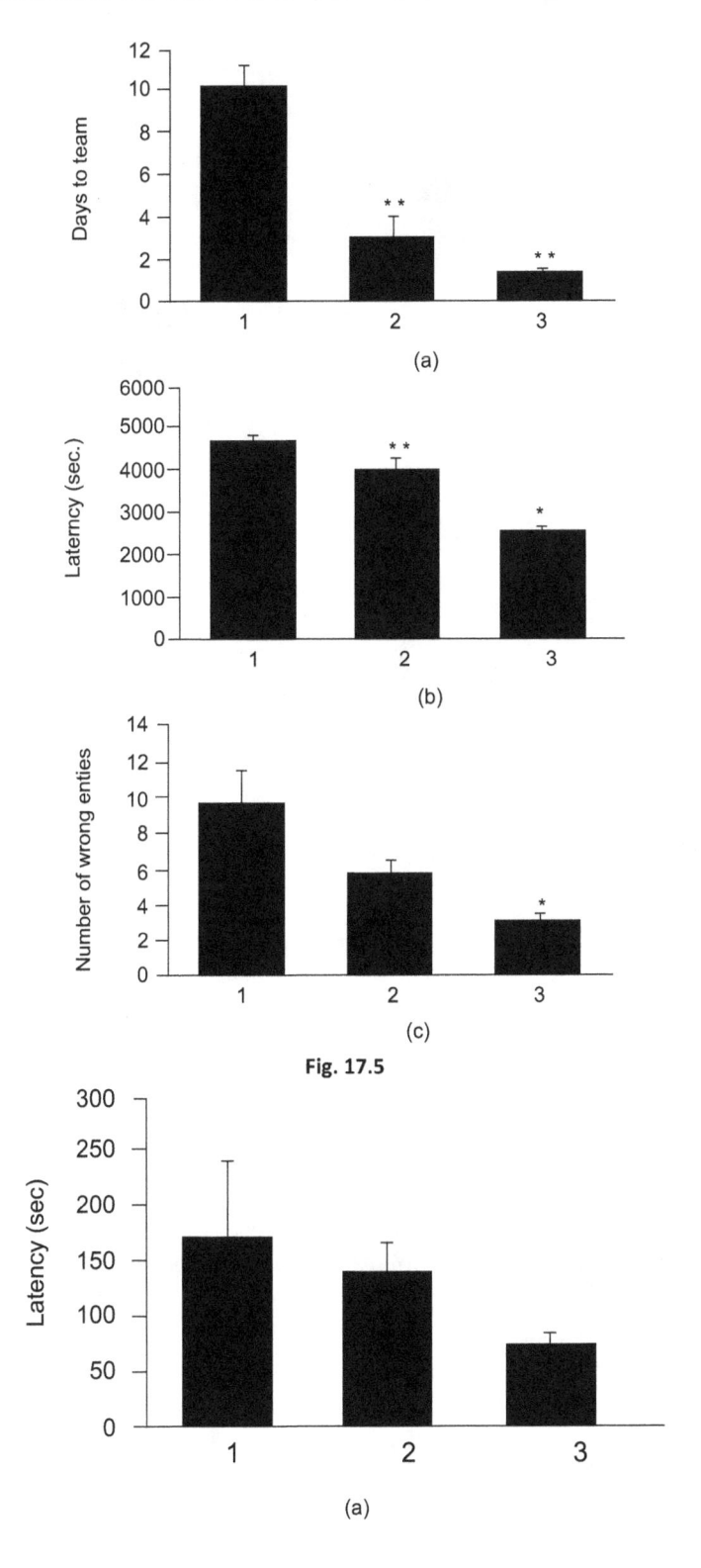

(b)

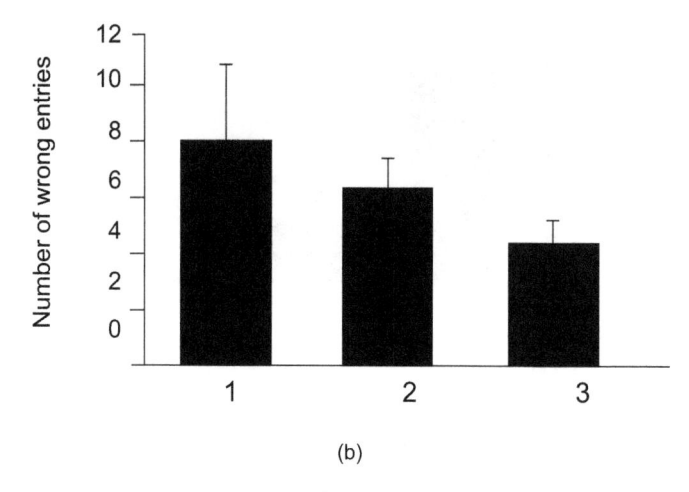

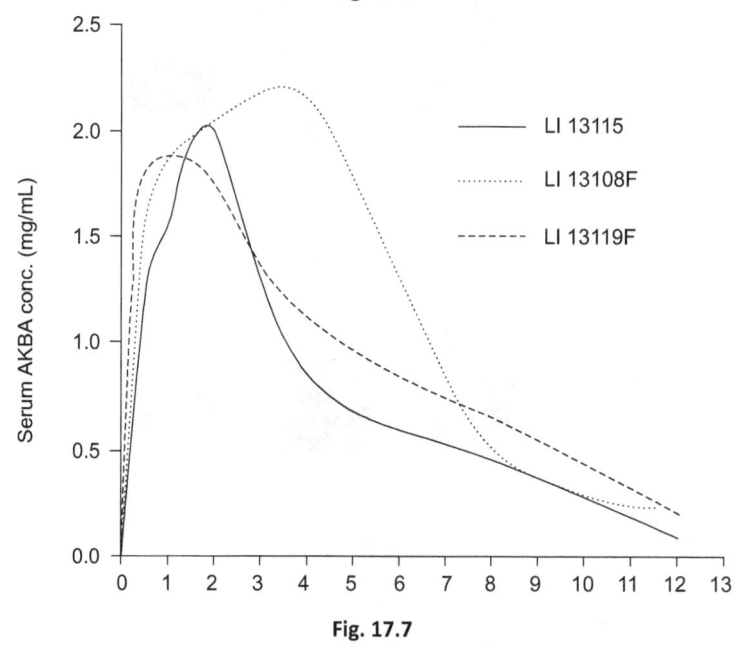

Fig. 17.6

Fig. 17.7

3. '*Boswellia carterii* oil' or 'non-acidic *Boswellia carterii* extract' or 'BcOIL' used herein refers to non-acidic *Boswellia carterii* gum resin extract containing non-acidic *Boswellia carterii* low polar gum resin extract fraction (BcLPRE) and *Boswellia carterii* volatile oil fraction (BcVOIL) obtained from gum resin of the *Boswellia carterii* species.

4. '*Boswellia* low polar gum resin extract fraction' or '*Boswellia* low polar gum resin extract' or 'BLPRE' used herein refers to non-acidic *Boswellia* gum resin extract oil fraction comprising sesquiterpenes, diterpenes, triterpenes and other oily phytochemicals obtained after removing the volatile components

from *Boswellia* oil obtained from gum resin of any of the *Boswellia* species by any of the processes described. BLPRE encompasses 'BsLPRE' and 'BcLPRE,' as defined below.

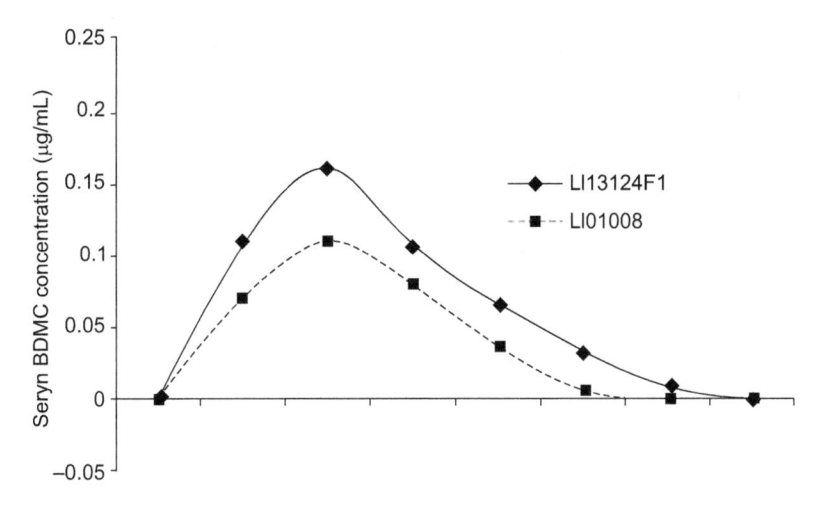

Fig. 17.8

5. '*Boswellia serrata* low polar gum resin extract fraction' or '*Boswellia serrata* low polar gum resin extract' or 'BcLPRE' used herein refers to non-acidic *Boswellia serrata* gum resin extract oil fraction comprising sesquiterpenes, diterpenes, triterpenes and other oily phytochemicals obtained after removing the volatile components from *Boswellia* oil obtained from gum resin of *Boswellia serrata* species by any of the processes described.

6. '*Boswellia carterii* low polar gum resin extract fraction' or '*Boswellia carterii* low polar gum resin extract' or 'BcLPRE' used herein refers to non-acidic *Boswellia carterii* gum resin extract oil fraction comprising sesquiterpenes, diterpenes, triterpenes and other oily phytochemicals obtained after removing the volatile components from *Boswellia carterii* oil obtained from gum resin of *Boswellia carterii* species by any of the processes described.

7. '*Boswellia* volatile oil fraction' or '*Boswellia* volatile oil' or 'volatile oil' or 'volatile fraction' or 'BVOIL' used herein refers to the volatile fraction/extract comprising monoterpenes, sesquiterpenes, volatile oils and other oily phytochemicals obtained from gum resin of any of the *Boswellia* species by any of the processes described. BVOIL encompasses 'BsVOIL' and 'BcVOIL,' as defined below.

8. '*Boswellia serrata* volatile oil fraction' or '*Boswellia serrata* volatile oil' or 'serrata volatile oil' or 'serrata volatile fraction' or 'BsVOIL' used herein refers to the volatile fraction/extract comprising monoterpenes, sesquiterpenes, volatile oils and other oily phytochemicals obtained from gum resin of the *Boswellia serrata* species by any of the processes described.

9. '*Boswellia carterii* volatile oil fraction' or '*Boswellia carterii* volatile oil' or 'carterii volatile oil' or 'carterii volatile fraction' or 'BcVOIL' used herein refers to the volatile fraction/extract comprising monoterpenes, sesquiterpenes, diterpenes, volatile oils and other oily phytochemicals obtained from gum resin of the *Boswellia carterii* species by any of the processes described.

10. 'Gum' or 'Gum resin' or 'resin' used herein refers to an exudate of *Boswellia* plant species.

11. 'Phytochemical' refers to a pure or semi-pure compound or compounds isolated from plants.

12. Cognition refers to acquisition, processing and retention of information.

13. Cognition enhancer(s) refers to substance(s) that enhances concentration and memory.

14. Nootropic agent(s) refers to smart drugs, memory enhancers and cognitive enhancers, dietary supplements, nutraceuticals, functional ingredients and functional foods that are purported to improve mental functions such as cognition, memory, intelligence, motivation, attention and concentration.

15. Biological agent(s) refer to one or more agents selected from biologically active ingredient(s), anti-oxidant(s), dietary supplements, herbal ingredients, nutraceuticals, functional ingredients, functional foods and nootropic agents and oil(s) their mixtures obtained from plant(s)/animal(s)/microorganism(s)/synthesis or semi synthesis.

16. 'Biologically active ingredient(s)' refers to any pharmaceutically or dietetically acceptable active ingredient(s); compound(s), extract(s), fraction(s), phytochemical(s), synthetic drug(s) or their salts or mixtures thereof derived from plants, animals or microorganisms or obtained by chemical synthesis/semi-synthesis.

17. 'Functional ingredient(s)' refers to any herbal ingredients, dietary supplements, antioxidants, vitamins, minerals, amino acids, fatty acids, essential oils, fish oils, enzymes, glucosamine, Chondroitin and probiotics or their salts or mixtures thereof derived from plants or animals or microorganisms or chemical synthesis or semi-synthesis.

18. 'Bioenhancer(s)' refers to agents that enhance the availability of biological agent(s) through one or more mechanism(s) in warm blooded animals comprising increasing the bioavailability, enhancing the serum concentration, improving gastrointestinal absorption, improving systemic utilization, improving cross over through certain biological barriers such as respiratory lining, urinary lining, blood brain barrier and skin.

19. 'Bioenhancing composition(s)' refer to compositions comprising *Boswellia* derived oil fraction as a Bioenhancer in combination with one or more biological agent(s).

20. 'BSE 85%' used herein refers to *Boswellia serrata* extract standardized to 85% Boswellic acids.

21. 'BCE 85%' used herein refers to *Boswellia carterii* extract standardized to 85% Boswellic acids.

22. 'CLE 95%' refers to Curcuma longa extract standardized to 95% Curcuminoids.

23. 'CAE 20%' refers to Curcuma aromatica extract standardized to 20% Curcuminoids.

B. Use of *Boswellia* Non-Acidic Extracts in Enhancing Memory and Brain Function

The gum resin of *Boswellia* has been very widely used since ancient times. The gum resin of various species of *Boswellia* such as *Boswellia serrata*, *Boswellia carterii* or *Boswellia papyrifera* is a complex mixture comprising *Boswellia* oil fraction (BOIL) containing essential oil/*Boswellia* volatile oil fraction (BVOIL) and non-acidic *Boswellia* low polar gum resin extract fraction (BLPRE); boswellic acids, sugars and polysaccharide fraction. The *Boswellia serrata*/*Boswellia carterii*/ *Boswellia papyrifera* extracts widely available in the international markets are acidic fractions separated from the gum resin which are standardized to contain 65% or 85% total Boswellic acids by titrimetric method of analysis. During the execution of commercial process for regular *Boswellia* extracts derived from *Boswellia serrata*/*Boswellia carterii*/*Boswellia papyrifera* (85% total Boswellic acids), the acidic fraction, which contains predominantly triterpene acids including Boswellic acids is separated from the rest of gum resin components. The sugars and other polymeric materials get separated out into the aqueous phase during the enrichment process for total Boswellic acids. The remaining water immiscible low polar compounds are separated as *Boswellia* oil fraction/extract. These low polar compounds are either absent or present at very low concentration in both, commercial *Boswellia* extracts standardized to boswellic acids and *Boswellia* extracts selectively enriched in 3-O-acetyl-11-keto-β-Boswellic acid (AKBA).

The *Boswellia* non-acidic oil fractions BOIL, BVOIL, and BLPRE may be obtained in a number of ways. One method of obtaining the *Boswellia* non-acidic oil fractions BOIL, BVOIL, and BLPRE is outlined in Figure 1. According to this method, *Boswellia* gum resin 1 is extracted with a non-polar or water-immiscible solvent to produce a solution of an extract of *Boswellia* gum resin 2 in a non-polar solvent. The non-polar solvent may be a non-polar organic solvent, such as 1,2-dichloroethane, hexane, dichloromethane, chloroform, ethyl acetate, n-butanol, or methyl iso-butyl ketone (MIBK). Alternatively, the non-polar solvent may be a non-polar inorganic solvent. The non-polar extract solution 2 is then washed with an aqueous base to extract boswellic acids and other acidic components into an aqueous layer, leaving a non-polar solvent layer containing non-acidic components of the extract of *Boswellia* gum resin. The non-polar solvent is then evaporated to produce a *Boswellia* oil (BOIL) 3, which contains volatile components and non-volatile components. BOIL 3 is subjected to steam distillation to volatilize the volatile components of BOIL 3. After removal of the volatile components from BOIL 3, the remaining non-volatile oil, here referred to as *Boswellia* low-polar gum resin extract (BLPRE) 4, may be recovered. Similarly, after steam distillation, the volatile components from BOIL 3 may be condensed or otherwise recovered as a *Boswellia* volatile oil (BVOIL) 5. Thus, BOIL 3 contains both volatile and non-volatile compounds. BLPRE 4 contains non-volatile compounds. BVOIL 5 contains only volatile compounds.

An alternative method of obtaining the *Boswellia* non-acidic oil fractions BOIL, BVOIL, and BLPRE is outlined in Figure 17.2. According to this method, *Boswellia* gum resin 1 is extracted with a polar solvent, which may be alcohol or aqueous alcohol. The resulting polar *Boswellia* extract 6 is portioned between an aqueous base solution and a non-polar solvent to produce an aqueous layer and a non-polar solvent layer of a solution of an extract of *Boswellia* gum resin 7 in a non-polar solvent. The aqueous layer may be discarded. The non-polar solvent may be a non-polar organic solvent, such as 1,2-dichloroethane, hexane, dichloromethane, chloroform, ethyl acetate, n-butanol, or methyl iso-butyl ketone (MIBK). Alternatively, the non-polar solvent may be a non-polar inorganic solvent. The non-polar solvent is then evaporated from non-polar extract solution 7, leaving a *Boswellia* oil (BOIL) 3, which contains volatile components and non-volatile components. BOIL 3 is subjected to vacuum to volatilize the volatile components of BOIL 3. After removal of the volatile components from BOIL 3, the remaining non-volatile oil, here referred to as *Boswellia* low-polar gum resin extract (BLPRE) 4, may be recovered. Similarly, after steam distillation, the volatile components from BOIL 3 may be condensed or otherwise recovered as a *Boswellia* volatile oil (BVOIL) 5.

Process for Obtaining Non-acidic *Boswellia* Oil (BOIL) Fraction:

A representative process for obtaining *Boswellia* oil comprises:

(a) procuring the gum resin of one or more of the plant(s) selected from but not limited to *Boswellia serrata* or *Boswellia carterii* or *Boswellia papyrifera* or mixtures thereof,

(b) extraction of the gum resin with a water immiscible organic solvent,

(c) filtering the extract carefully to remove the insoluble resin material,

(d) washing the organic solvent extract repeatedly with an aqueous alkali solution such as aqueous potassium hydroxide,

(e) washing the organic layer with water and brine,

(f) evaporating the organic layer under vacuum and high temperature to obtain the oily residue (BOIL).

Processes for Obtaining *Boswellia* Volatile Oil (BVOIL) Fraction

The process for obtaining *Boswellia* volatile oil (BVOIL) is through steam distillation or using high vacuum from *Boswellia* gum resin.

A representative process for obtaining *Boswellia* volatile oil comprises:

(a) procuring the gum resin of *Boswellia* and

(b) separating the Volatile oil component by either steam distillation or distillation under high vacuum, low temperature from the said gum resin to obtain BVOIL.

In an alternative process,

(a) BOIL is prepared according to the process described above,

(b) BOIL is then subjected to steam distillation or vacuum distillation to collect *Boswellia* volatile oil (BVOIL).

Processes for Obtaining *Boswellia* Low Polar Gum Resin Extract (BLPRE) Fraction

A representative procedure for obtaining *Boswellia* low polar gum resin extract (BLPRE) comprises:

(a) extraction of the gum resin of *Boswellia* species with a water immiscible organic solvent and filtering the extract carefully to remove the insoluble resin material,

(b) washing the organic solvent extract repeatedly with an aqueous alkali solution such as aqueous potassium hydroxide,

(c) washing the organic layer obtained after the alkali wash, with water and brine,

(d) evaporating the said organic layer under vacuum and high temperature to obtain the oily residue,

(e) removing the volatile compounds from the said oily residue under high vacuum and very high temperature to obtain BLPRE.

Another representative procedure for obtaining *Boswellia* low polar gum resin extract (BLPRE) comprises:

(a) preparing the alcohol or hydroalcohol extract of *Boswellia* gum resin,

(b) partitioning the alcohol extract between an aqueous alkali solution and a water immiscible organic solvent,

(c) separation of the organic solvent layer, followed by evaporation of the solvent to obtain oily residue,

(d) removal of volatile compounds from the said oily residue under high temperature and high vacuum to obtain BLPRE.

Yet another representative procedure for obtaining *Boswellia* low polar gum resin extract (BLPRE) comprises:

(a) extracting the gum resin of *Boswellia* species with alcohol or hydro alcohol,
(b) evaporating the organic solvent to an optimum level of total solids and then
(c) adjusting the pH to the alkaline side, preferably pH 9-12,
(d) repeatedly extracting the solution with an organic solvent,
(e) evaporating the organic solvent under vacuum and high temperature to obtain the oily residue,
(f) evaporating the volatiles from the said oily residue under high vacuum and high temperature to obtain BLPRE as a non-volatile residue.

A representative procedure for obtaining *Boswellia serrata* volatile oil (BsVOIL) comprises:

(a) procuring the gum resin of *Boswellia serrata*.
(b) separating the Volatile oil component by either steam distillation or distillation under high vacuum, low temperature from the said gum resin to obtain BsVOIL.

Yet another representative procedure for obtaining *Boswellia carterii* volatile oil (BcVOIL) comprises:

(a) procuring the gum resin of *Boswellia carterii*.
(b) separating the Volatile oil component by either steam distillation or distillation under high vacuum, low temperature from the said gum resin to obtain BcVOIL.

The representative processes for obtaining *Boswellia* volatile oil (BVOIL) from *Boswellia serrata, Boswellia carterii* are described above. However, a similar process or processes can be applied to any of the gum resin obtained from *Boswellia* species for producing *Boswellia* volatile oil (BVOIL).

A representative procedure for obtaining *Boswellia serrata* low polar gum resin extract (BsLPRE) comprises:

(a) Procuring the gum resin of *Boswellia serrata*.
(b) extraction with an water immiscible organic solvent and the insoluble gum materials were separated by filtration and discarded,
(c) washing the organic solvent extract repeatedly with dilute aqueous alkali solution to remove the acidic compounds,
(d) washing the organic layer successively with water and brine,
(e) evaporating the organic layer under vacuum at 60-70° C. to obtain an oily residue,
(f) the volatile components are then removed from the said oily residue under high vacuum and very high temperature to obtain a viscous oil, which is referred herein after as *Boswellia serrata* low polar gum resin extract (BsLPRE).

Alternatively, the BsLPRE can also be prepared by a process comprising:

(a) preparing the alcohol or hydroalcohol extract of *Boswellia serrata* gum resin,

(b) partitioning the alcohol extract between an aqueous alkali solution and a water immiscible organic solvent,

(c) separation of the organic solvent layer, followed by evaporating the organic layer under vacuum at 60-70° C. to obtain an oily residue,

(d) the volatile components are then removed from the said oily residue under high vacuum and high temperature to obtain a viscous oil, which is referred herein after as *Boswellia serrata* low polar gum resin extract (BsLPRE).

A representative procedure for obtaining *Boswellia carterii* low polar gum resin extract (BcLPRE) comprises:

(a) procuring the gum resin of *Boswellia carterii*,

(b) extracting the gum resin with an water immiscible organic solvent and the insoluble gum materials were separated by filtration and discarded,

(c) washing the organic solvent extract repeatedly with dilute aqueous alkali solution to remove the acidic compounds,

(d) washing the organic layer successively with water and brine,

(e) evaporating the organic layer under vacuum at 60-70° C. to obtain an oily residue.

(f) the volatile components are then removed from the said oily residue under high vacuum and high temperature to obtain a viscous oil, which is referred herein after as *Boswellia carterii* low polar gum resin extract (BcLPRE).

Alternatively, the BcLPRE can also be prepared by process comprising:

(a) preparing the alcohol or hydroalcohol extract of *Boswellia carterii* gum resin,

(b) partitioning the alcohol extract between an aqueous alkali solution and a water immiscible organic solvent,

(c) separation of the organic solvent layer, followed by evaporating the organic layer under vacuum at 60-70° C. to obtain an oily residue,

(d) the volatile components are then removed from the said oily residue under high vacuum and high temperature to obtain a viscous oil, which is referred herein after as *Boswellia carterii* low polar gum resin extract (BcLPRE).

The representative processes for obtaining *Boswellia* low polar gum resin extract (BLPRE) from *Boswellia serrata* and *Boswellia carterii* are described above. However, a similar process or processes can be applied to any of the gum resin obtained from *Boswellia* species for producing the low polar gum resin extract.

In the above processes for obtaining BLPRE, BOIL, and/or BVOIL, the water immiscible organic solvent used for extraction of a *Boswellia* gum resin or for partitioning an alcohol extract may be, but is not limited to, 1,2-dichloroethane, hexane, dichloromethane, chloroform, ethyl acetate, n-butanol, methyl isobutyl ketone (MIBK) or a suitable combination thereof. The alkali solution used for washing the organic solvent extract, or partitioning the alcohol extract, can be selected from Group-I or Group-II metal hydroxides, which include, but are not limited to, Sodium hydroxide, Potassium hydroxide, Calcium hydroxide, Magnesium hydroxide and mixtures thereof.

The said intact *Boswellia* oil (BOIL) or *Boswellia* volatile oil (BVOIL) or *Boswellia* low polar gum resin extract (BLPRE) constitute significant components in *Boswellia* gum resin. However, it has very limited commercial utility and it is mostly discarded as a waste material. Potential utilization of these fractions have been long overdue. It was found unexpectedly that *Boswellia serrata* low polar gum resin extract (BsLPRE), a fraction obtained after removing the volatile compounds from the *Boswellia serrata* oil, has several beneficial properties.

In our earlier Indian patent application 2229/CHE/2008 filed 15 Sep., 2008 and PCT application # PCT/IN2009/000505 filed 14 Sep., 2009 we disclosed synergistic compositions comprising AKBA enriched fraction and *Boswellia serrata* non-acidic extract (BNRE). BNRE composition and method of identification are also disclosed.

In our recent Indian patent application 394/CHE/2010 filed 15 Feb., 2010 we disclosed non Boswellic acid fraction and its synergistic compositions.

As a part of developing new agents for improving brain/mental function and alleviating disease conditions related to cognition and memory deficits, a large number of plant extracts have been screened for their inhibitory property on Acetylcholinesterase enzyme activity. The assay was performed in vitro by the method of Ellman *et al.*, with minor modifications, using acetylthiocholine iodide as a substrate (Lee J. H., et. al. Arch Pharm Res 2004, 27(1): 53-56). It was found very unexpectedly that the non-acidic extract, *Boswellia serrata* oil (BsOIL), *Boswellia serrata* low polar gum resin extract (BsLPRE) fraction and *Boswellia serrata* volatile oil (BsVOIL) fractions, were potent inhibitors of acetylcholinesterase in vitro. BsLPRE for example potently inhibited acetylcholinesterase enzyme activity in vitro as shown in Table 2. BLPRE's in vitro efficacy against acetylcholinesterase enzyme is comparable to commercial drug Neostigmin. BsLPRE exhibited an IC50 value of 37.01 ng/mL compared to 43.29 ng/mL shown by neostigmin. Its acetylcholinesterase inhibitory activity was also evaluated by a cell based in vitro assay in Rat pheochromocytoma PC 12 cells. The inhibitory property of BsLPRE on the enzyme activity was assessed in β-amyloid peptide induced-rat pheochromocytoma PC 12 cells. Rat pheochromocytoma PC 12 cells were equally distributed with phenol red free Dulbecco's modified Eagle's red medium (DMEM) (Sigma Life Science, USA) containing 10% fetal bovine serum (FBS) in 24-well plate. Cells were pretreated separately with BLPRE and positive control Neostigmin for 1 h. Thereafter, cells were induced with 1 µg/mL of β-amyloid peptide (Calbiochem, USA) for 24 h at 37° C. After 24 h, cells were collected and washed twice with 1×PBS by centrifugation at 1200 rpm for 5 min at 4° C. The cell extracts were prepared in solubilization buffer and the cell lysates were analyzed for acetylcholine esterase (AChE) activity. The BsLPRE showed 25.3% inhibition at 100 ng/mL concentration, where as Neostigmin showed 49.1% inhibition at 20 ng/mL as summarized in Table 17.4.

In order to understand the chemical composition of BsLPRE, separation of BsLPRE was carried out using column chromatography and high performance liquid chromatography (HPLC), and several diterpenoid and triterpenoid compounds were isolated. The structures of the compounds were rigorously characterized using ^{1}H NMR, ^{13}C NMR, DEPT, HSQC and HMBC, Mass spectral data. The compounds so obtained and identified are guiol (1), nephthenol (2), serratol (3), diterpene X (4), lupeol (5), olean-12-ene-3β-ol (6), olean-12-ene-3α-ol (7), lanosta-8, 24-diene-3α-ol (8) and urs-12-ene-3α-ol (9) as depicted in Figure 17.3. The fraction, *Boswellia serrata* low polar gum resin extract (BsLPRE) was then standardized to three or more of the phytochemical marker compounds selected from 1 to 9. The typical results obtained are summarized in the Table 1 and a typical chromatogram depicting the profile of BsLPRE is presented in Figure 4. However, compositions of BsLPRE or any other *Boswellia* low polar gum resin extract composition (BLPRE) obtained from any other species may vary based on several factors such as *Boswellia* species used, age of the plant, season of collection of gum resin, geographic location and manufacturing process employed.

The foregoing results manifest that BsLPRE is a novel composition comprising unique combination of sesquiterpenoids, diterpenoids and triterpenoids and other phytochemical(s). A compound tentatively identified as diterpene X (4) and compounds guiol (1), nepthenol (2) and Lanosta-8,24-diene-3α-ol (8) are not known to be metabolites of *Boswellia serrata* gum resin.

The low polar gum resin extract of these as well as other *Boswellia* species comprise a composition having some similarity to that of *Boswellia serrata*. However, the low polar gum resin extract of *Boswellia carterii* (BcLPRE) has shown biological activity and synergistic effect very similar to that exhibited by BsLPRE as summarized in the following in vitro and in vivo studies. The experimental studies are discussed in the examples.

The acetylcholinesterase inhibitory of different boswellic acids was also evaluated in both enzyme based assay and cell based assay and the inhibitory activities are summarized in Tables 17.3 and 17.5.

Oxidative stress induced increased ROS is critical for neuronal damage, which is a serious complication with regard to brain health. Interestingly, the low polar gum resin extract of *Boswellia serrata* (BsLPRE) showed potent inhibition of reactive oxygen species (ROS) generation in RAW 264.7 mouse macrophages (Table 17.6). In addition, BsLPRE also showed protection from oxidative stress induced cytotoxic damage of human neuroblastoma cells. In a cell based assay, oxidative stress induced by H_2O_2 showed potent cytotoxic effect on the proliferation of IMR32 human neuroblastoma cells. However, the treatment with BsLPRE significantly attenuates the proliferation index of IMR32 human neuroblastoma cells back to the normal level (Table 17.7). Hence the observations confirm that the low polar gum resin extract (BLPRE) offers protection from neuronal damage and support improving brain health.

The in vivo efficacy of BsLPRE on learning and memory improvement was proven in rats using elevated radial arm maze (RAM) method. Oral administration of BsLPRE (250 mg/kg) significantly ($P<0.01$) decreased the number of days required to make the rats learned as per set criteria and significantly ($P<0.05$) decreased the time taken to find the food by the learned rats in the elevated RAM model. The positive control Piracetin (150 mg/kg) also showed significant improvement in spatial learning like reduction in latency and Number of wrong entries, when compared with the control group and the results are as stated below (Figure 17.5A to 17.5C). The test product BsLPRE also significantly improves cognition and memory retention (Figures 17.6A and 17.6B). These results confirm the efficacy shown by BsLPRE in vitro and suggest that the use of BsLPRE improves spatial learning and memory retention. According to these findings, BsLPRE is a promising candidate for facilitation of learning and memory.

Synergistic Compositions Comprising *Boswellia* Extracts

Cell based and enzyme based in vitro anti-acetylcholinesterase studies were conducted on a broad array of *Boswellia* extracts standardized to boswellic acids and *Boswellia serrata* low polar gum resin extract (BsLPRE), in addition to other herbal extracts. The individual extracts and different combination of these extracts were tested for their efficacy to inhibit acetylcholinesterase enzyme. It was found surprisingly that a composition (composition-1) comprising a combination of (1) a *Boswellia serrata* extract containing 85% total boswellic acids (BSE85%) and (2) a *Boswellia serrata* low polar gum resin extract (BsLPRE) showed potent inhibition of acetylcholinesterase (AChE).

Hence, the foregoing shows that BOIL, BVOIL and BLPRE alone as well as in combination with Boswellic acid(s)/*Boswellia* extract(s) or fractions(s) containing boswellic acid(s)/extracts standardized to boswellic acids/one or more Nootropic agents are potent inhibitors of acetylcholinesterase and as such can be used for the prevention, control and treatment of cognitive disorders and improving memory and alleviating disease conditions related to cognition and memory deficits.

Pure boswellic acids and commercially available *Boswellia serrata* extract standardized to 85% boswellic acids have been used to demonstrate the subject matter disclosed herein. However, any *Boswellia serrata* standardized to 40%-100% total boswellic acids by titrimetric method of analysis or standardized to 30%-100% total boswellic acids by HPLC method of analysis can also be used.

Similarly, a composition (composition-34) containing low polar gum resin extract (BLPRE) in combination with α-mangostin offers better protection from neuronal damage (Table 17.6) and hence can improve brain health. In addition, composition-34 also showed better protection from oxidative stress induced cytotoxic damage of human neuroblastoma cells in a cell based assay (Table 17.7). This result further confirms the potential role of the composition containing BsLPRE in the improvement of brain health.

Different Embodiments Disclosed Herein are as Outlined Below:

In the primary aspect, the disclosure provides non-acidic *Boswellia* low polar gum resin extract (BLPRE) fraction, *Boswellia* volatile oil (BVOIL) fraction and *Boswellia* oil fraction (BOIL) comprising BLPRE and BVOIL for improving mental condition/brain health, treating impaired memory and alleviating memory and cognition related disorders and other associated diseases in warm blooded animals.

In the other primary aspect the disclosure provides compositions comprising at least one fraction selected from *Boswellia* oil (BOIL), *Boswellia* volatile oil (BVOIL) and *Boswellia* low polar gum resin extract (BLPRE) in combination with one or more biological agents or Nootropic agents for improving mental condition/brain health, treating impaired memory and alleviating memory and cognition related disorders and other associated diseases in warm blooded animal.

In another embodiment the disclosure provides, composition comprising at least one *Boswellia* derived non-acidic extract/fraction selected from *Boswellia* low polar gum resin extract fraction (BLPRE), *Boswellia* volatile oil fraction (BVOIL) and non-acidic *Boswellia* oil fraction (BOIL) in combination with at least one component selected from biological agents, phytochemicals, vitamins, amino acids, minerals; pharmaceutically or dietetically acceptable excipients, vehicles, carriers and diluents or mixtures thereof for improving mental condition/brain health; enhancing brain functions such as cognition, memory, learning, communication; for treating impaired memory, and for preventing, control or treating memory and cognition related disorders/diseases.

In another embodiment the disclosure provides methods for improving brain health and brain functions such as cognition, memory, learning, communication or treating impaired memory in a subject or warm blooded animal in need thereof, wherein the method comprises supplementing the said subject or warm blooded animal with an effective dose of *Boswellia* derived non-acidic extract/fraction or their composition(s).

In another embodiment the disclosure provides methods for preventing, control or treating memory and cognition related disorders/diseases in a subject or warm blooded animal in need thereof, wherein the method comprises supplementing the said subject or warm blooded animal with an effective dose of *Boswellia* derived non-acidic extract/fraction or their composition(s).

In another embodiment the disclosure provides methods of preventing, control or treating memory and cognition related disorders/diseases, wherein memory and cognition related disorders/diseases include but not limited to senile dementia, multi-infarct dementia, dyslexia, aphasia, organic brain syndrome, myasthenia gravis, vascular dementia, mild cognitive impairment (MCI), Attention-deficient Hyperactivity Disorder (ADHD), Lewy body dementia, Wernicke-Korsakoff-syndrome, Alzheimer's, Parkinson's disease, hypoxia, anoxia, cerebrovascular insufficiency, epilepsy, myoclonus and hypocholinergic dysfunctions, memory impairment disorders and neurodegenerative disorders.

In another aspect, the disclosure provides *Boswellia* low polar gum resin extract (BLPRE) fraction, *Boswellia* volatile oil (BVOIL) fraction and *Boswellia* oil (BOIL) fraction comprising BLPRE and BVOIL individually or their composition(s) comprising useful for the prevention, control and treatment of brain related diseases comprising Attention-deficit Hyperactivity Disorder (ADHD) and memory deficits or to enhance brain functions such as cognition, memory, learning and communication Importantly, the said fractions and compositions of the present disclosure help in making the brain healthy.

In another aspect, the disclosure provides compositions comprising at least one component selected from *Boswellia* low polar gum resin extract fraction (BLPRE), *Boswellia* volatile oil fraction (BVOIL) and non-acidic *Boswellia* oil fraction (BOIL) in combination with at least one pharmaceutically/dietetically acceptable excipients/diluents, further optionally comprising one or more agents selected from natural antioxidants, anti-inflammatory agents and immune modulators.

In another embodiment the disclosure provides the composition comprising at least one *Boswellia* derived non-acidic extract/fraction in combination with at least one pharmaceutically/dietetically acceptable excipients/diluents, wherein said pharmaceutically or dietetically acceptable excipients, carriers, vehicles and diluents include but not limited to glucose, fructose, sucrose, maltose, lactose, yellow dextrin, white dextrin, silicon dioxide, microcrystalline cellulose powder, calcium stearate, magnesium stearate, sorbitol, stevioside, corn syrup, citric acid, tartaric acid, malic acid, succinic acid, lactic acid, L-ascorbic acid, dl-alpha-tocopherol, glycerin, propylene glycol, glycerin fatty ester, poly glycerin fatty ester, sucrose fatty ester, sorbitan fatty ester, propylene glycol fatty ester, acacia, carrageenan, casein, gelatin, pectin, agar, nicotinamide, calcium pantothenate, calcium salts, pigments, flavors, preservatives, distilled water, saline, aqueous glucose solution, alcohol, propylene glycol and polyethylene glycol, various animal and vegetable oils, white soft paraffin, paraffin and wax.

In another aspect, the disclosure provides *Boswellia* non acidic extracts/fractions selected from *Boswellia* low polar gum resin extract fraction (BLPRE), *Boswellia* volatile oil fraction (BVOIL) and non-acidic *Boswellia* oil fraction (BOIL) and their compositions to prevent, control and treat brain related diseases/disorders which include but not limited to senile dementia, multi-infarct dementia, dyslexia, aphasia, organic brain syndrome, myasthenia gravis, vascular dementia, mild cognitive impairment (MCI), Lewy body dementia, Wemicke-Korsakoff-syndrome, Alzheimer's, Parkinson's disease, Attention-deficit Hyperactivity Disorder (ADHD), hypoxia, anoxia, cerebrovascular insufficiency, epilepsy, myoclonus and hypocholinergic dysfunctions, memory impairment disorders and neurodegenerative disorders

In another aspect, the disclosure provides *Boswellia* derived non-acidic extract/fraction or their composition(s) for improving mental condition/brain health by slowing down memory deterioration, functional loss, by inhibiting beta-amyloid plaque deposition, by controlling blood pressure and blood circulation in the brain.

In another aspect, the Nootropic agent(s) used for making the composition comprise one or more agent(s) selected from smart drugs, memory enhancers and cognitive enhancers; dietary supplements, herbal ingredients, nutraceuticals, functional ingredients and functional foods that improve mental functions such as cognition, memory, intelligence, motivation, attention and concentration.

In another aspect, the Nootropic agents can be selected from one or more components selected from the extract(s)/fraction(s)/phytochemicals derived from herbs including but not limited to Bacopa species, Curcuma species or Rosmarinus species.

In another aspect, the herbal ingredients that can be used for preparing compositions are selected from including but not limited to *Boswellia serrata*, *Boswellia carterii*, Bacopa monniera, Curcuma longa, Withania somnifera, Rosmarinus officinalis, Garcinia mangostana, α-mangostin, Annona squamosa and Sphaeranthus indicus.

In another aspect of the disclosure, the Nootropic agents can be selected from extract(s)/fraction(s)/phytochemicals, extracts/fractions enriched in one or more phytochemicals selected from including but not limited to Bacopa monnieri, Withania somnifera, Emblica officinalis, Centella asiatica; extract or fraction enriched in one or more phytochemicals selected from including but not limited to Bacoside A3, Bacopaside II, Jujubogenin isomer of bacopasaponin C, Bacopasaponin C, Bacopaside I, Bacosine, Apigenin, Luteolin and Sitosterol-D-glucoside, curcumin, demethoxycurcumin, bisdemethoxycurcumin, monodemethylcurcumin, bisdemethylcurcumin, tetrahydrocurcumin, tetrahydrodemethoxycurcumin, tetrahydrobisdemethoxycurcumin and ar-turmerone, carnosic acid, rosmarinic acid, camphor, caffeic acid, ursolic acid, betulinic acid, rosmaridiphenol, rosmanol and their salts thereof.

In yet another aspect, the disclosure provides compositions comprising therapeutically effective combination of *Boswellia* oil (BOIL/*Boswellia* volatile oil BVOIL)/*Boswellia* low polar gum resin extract (BLPRE) in combination with at least one *Boswellia* derived component selected from the extract(s), fraction(s) enriched with one or more boswellic acids/pure boswellic acid compounds or Nootropic agents for improving memory, impaired memory and alleviating memory and cognition related disorders and other associated diseases.

In another aspect, the disclosure provides compositions for the cognition enhancement achieved through one or more biological actions comprising inhibition of Acetylcholinesterase, increase in Butyrylcholinesterase and inhibition of (3-amyloid aggregation.

In yet another aspect, the disclosure further provides compositions comprising *Boswellia* oil (BOIL)/*Boswellia* volatile oil (BVOIL)/*Boswellia* low polar gum resin extract (BLPRE) and at least one component, derived from gum resin of *Boswellia* species, which include but not limited to α-boswellic acid, 3-boswellic acid, 3-O-acetyl-α-boswellic acid, 3-O-acetyl-β-boswellic acid, 3-O-acetyl-11-keto-α-boswellic acid and 3-O-acetyl-11-keto-β-boswellic acid or mixtures thereof for improving memory, impaired memory and alleviating memory and cognition related disorders and other associated diseases.

In yet another important aspect, the disclosure further provides compositions comprising *Boswellia serrata* low polar gum resin extract (BsLPRE) or BsVOIL or BsOIL and at least one *Boswellia* derived component selected from the extracts or fractions enriched in or standardized to one or more compounds derived from the gum resin of *Boswellia* which include but not limited to α-boswellic acid, β-boswellic acid, 3-acetyl-α-boswellic acid, 3-acetyl-β-boswellic acid, 3-acetyl-11-keto-α-boswellic acid and 3-acetyl-11-keto-β-boswellic acid or mixtures thereof for improving memory, improving impaired memory and alleviating memory and cognition related disorders and other associated diseases.

In another aspect, the disclosure further provides compositions comprising *Boswellia serrata* low polar gum resin extract (BsLPRE) or BsVOIL or BsOIL and a *Boswellia serrata* extract standardized to 30-100% total boswellic acids by titrimetric method of analysis or 20-100% total boswellic acids by HPLC method of analysis.

In preferred aspect, the disclosure further provides compositions comprising *Boswellia serrata* low polar gum resin extract (BsLPRE) or BsVOIL or BsOIL and *Boswellia serrata* extract standardized to 85% total boswellic acids by titrimetric method of analysis or 65% total boswellic acids by titrimetric method of analysis.

In another preferred aspect, the disclosure provides compositions comprising *Boswellia serrata* low polar gum resin extract (BsLPRE) or BsVOIL or BsOIL and *Boswellia serrata* extract selectively enriched in AKBA concentration varying from 3-99% by HPLC method of analysis.

In other preferred embodiment, the disclosure further provides a process for producing the *Boswellia* low polar gum resin extract (BLPRE), which include extraction of the gum resin of *Boswellia* species with a water immiscible organic solvent followed by washing the organic solvent extract with an aqueous alkali solution such as aqueous potassium hydroxide, followed by water and brine, and then finally evaporating the organic layer under vacuum to obtain an oil, followed by removing the volatile compounds under high vacuum and temperature to obtain BLPRE. The water immiscible organic solvent can be selected from hexane, chloroform, dichloromethane, ethyl acetate, methyl isobutyl ketone or any other water immiscible solvent or mixtures thereof.

The process for producing the *Boswellia serrata* low polar gum resin extract (BsLPRE) is variable and the alternative process for example comprise, extracting the gum resin with alcohol or hydroalcohol, and then evaporating the organic solvent to optimum concentration of total solids and then adjusting the solution to pH to 9-11, followed by repeatedly extracting the solution with a low polar organic solvent and then evaporating the organic solvent followed by removing the volatiles under vacuum at high temperature to obtain BsLPRE.

In a further embodiment, the *Boswellia serrata* intact oil can also be used in place of BsLPRE for improving memory, impaired memory and alleviating memory and cognition related disorders and for making the compositions of the present disclosure.

The water immiscible organic solvent in the above process can be selected from the solvents but not limited hexane, chloroform, dichloromethane, ethyl acetate, methylisobutylketone, tert-butanol or any other water immiscible solvent.

The *Boswellia* serrate extract standardized to 30-100% total boswellic acids by a titrimetric method of analysis or 20-100% total boswellic acids by HPLC method of analysis can be prepared from the gum resin using a known procedure or obtained from a group of commercially available *Boswellia serrata* extracts standardized to boswellic acids.

In another aspect of the disclosure, the non acidic extracts *Boswellia* oil (BOIL), *Boswellia* volatile oil (BVOIL), *Boswellia* low polar gum resin extract (BLPRE) used for the demonstration of the disclosure can be obtained from the *Boswellia* species selected from *Boswellia serrata*, *Boswellia carterii*, *Boswellia papyrifera*, *Boswellia* ameero, *Boswellia* bullata, *Boswellia* dalzielii, *Boswellia* dioscorides, *Boswellia* elongata, *Boswellia* frereana, *Boswellia* nana, *Boswellia* neglecta, *Boswellia* ogadensis, *Boswellia* pirottae, *Boswellia* popoviana, *Boswellia* rivae, *Boswellia sacra* and *Boswellia* socotrana.

In another aspect of the disclosure one or more of the Curcuma species that can be used for making the compositions of the present disclosure can be selected from Curcuma longa, Curcuma aromatica, Curcuma domestica, Curcuma aeruginosa, Curcuma albicoma, Curcuma albiflora, Curcuma alismatifolia, Curcuma angustifolia, Curcuma elata, Curcuma ferruginea, Curcuma flaviflora, Curcuma yunnanensis and Curcuma zedoaria.

In yet another aspect of the present disclosure, BOIL, BVOIL or BLPRE alone or in combination with one or more *Boswellia* derived extracts selectively enriched in boswellic acids/commercially available boswellic extract(s) standardized to 50-100% total boswellic acids/*Boswellia serrata* extracts wherein AKBA concentration varies from 3-99% HPLC method of analysis and optionally contains one or more of pharmaceutically/nutraceutically/dietically acceptable excipient(s), diluents, salt(s), additive(s), natural antioxidants or natural anti-inflammatory agents.

In another aspect, the disclosure provides the usage of BOIL, BVOIL or BLPRE alone or their compositions as it is or in comminuted form and/or in unmodified form as granules or powder or paste or the active ingredients are formulated into a solid, semi-solid or liquid dosage form by adding a conventional biologically or pharmaceutically acceptable salt(s) or additive(s) or excipient(s).

In yet another aspect, the disclosure provides use of therapeutically effective amount of BOIL, BVOIL or BLPRE alone or their compositions with one or more biological agents or Nootropic agents for administration in a specific dosage form such as orally, topically, transdermally, parenterally or in the form of a kit to a subject or patient in need thereof. Specific dosage form for formulation of the compositions of the present disclosure include but not limited to oral agents such as tablets, soft capsule, hard capsule, soft gel capsules, pills, granules, powders, emulsions, suspensions, syrups, pellets, food, beverages, concentrated shots, drops and the like; parenteral agents such as injections, intravenous drip and the like; suppositories; transdermal agents such as patches, topical creams and gel; ophthalmic agents and nasal agents.

In another aspect, the present disclosure provides compositions containing at least one extract/fraction selected from BOIL, BVOIL or BLPRE in combination with one or more functional ingredient(s) comprising herbal ingredients, dietary supplements, antioxidants, vitamins, minerals, amino acids, fatty acids, essential oils, fish oils, enzymes, glucosamine, Chondroitin and probiotics or their salts or mixtures thereof derived from plants or animals or microorganisms or chemical synthesis or semi-synthesis.

In a further aspect, the present disclosure provides BOIL, BVOIL or BLPRE alone or their compositions further optionally combined with effective amounts of one or more pharmaceutical/nutraceutical/dietically acceptable agents including but not limited to antioxidant(s), adaptogen(s), anti-acetylcholinesterase agent(s), anti-inflammatory agent(s), anti-diabetic agent(s), antiobese agent(s), antiatherosclerotic agent(s), bio-protectants and/or bio-availability enhancer(s) and trace metals.

The examples of the biologically/pharmaceutically acceptable carriers employed in the present disclosure include, but are not limited to, surfactants, excipients, binders, diluents, disintegrators, lubricants, preservatives, stabilizers, buffers and suspensions.

In alternative aspect of the disclosure, the BOIL, BVOIL or BLPRE alone or their compositions can be optionally delivered in the form of controlled release dosage forms; and by using techniques including nanotechnology, microencapsulation, colloidal carrier systems and other drug delivery systems. The said formulation can be designed for once a daily administration or multiple administrations per day.

In accordance to the present disclosure, the BOIL, BVOIL or BLPRE alone or their compositions can also be formulated into or added to existing or new food and beverage form(s) and animal feeds as a healthy food or beverage or feed.

In accordance to the present disclosure, the BOIL, BVOIL or BLPRE alone or their compositions can also be formulated into or added to existing or new food and beverage form(s) and animal feeds as a healthy food or beverage or feed for prevention, control and treatment of brain related diseases/disorders.

In yet another embodiment, the composition can comprise 10%-99% by the weight of *Boswellia serrata* derived component selected from the extract(s) and fraction(s) enriched with one or more boswellic acids, pure boswellic acid compounds and mixtures thereof and 90%-10% by weight of *Boswellia serrata* low polar gum resin extract BsLPRE or BsVOIL or BsOIL.

C. Use of *Boswellia* Non-Acidic Extracts as Bio-Enhancing Agents

During the search for bioenhancing agents, it was found that non-acidic *Boswellia* low polar gum resin extract fraction (BLPRE), *Boswellia* volatile oil fraction (BVOIL) or *Boswellia* oil fraction (BOIL) comprising BLPRE and BVOIL enhance the bioavailability of bioactive agents. The compositions LI13108F containing *Boswellia serrata* low polar gum resin extract (BsLPRE; LI13115) and *Boswellia serrata* extract selectively enriched to 30% 3-O acetyl-11-keto-β-boswellic acid (AKBA) and LI13119F containing *Boswellia serrata* volatile oil fraction (BsVOIL) and *Boswellia serrata* extract selectively enriched to 30% 3-O acetyl-11-keto-β-boswellic acid (AKBA) were supplemented to Albino Wistar rats. The control group of animals was supplemented with *Boswellia serrata* extract selectively enriched to 30% AKBA. Blood samples were collected from all animals prior to oral administration of test products and at 0.5, 1, 2, 4, 8 and 12 hrs after oral administration. The comparative oral bioavailability of AKBA from these *Boswellia* products was evaluated by measuring the serum AKBA concentration for each test animal using LC-MS.

Surprisingly, both the compositions LI 13108F and LI 13119F showed better oral bioavailability with AUCs 14.08 and 11.23 respectively compared to AUC 9.825 shown by individual ingredient *Boswellia serrata* extract containing 30% AKBA (LI 13115). The bioavailability (in terms of AUC) of LI 13108F is 43.33% more than LI 13115. The bioavailability of LI 13119F is 14.33% more than that of LI 13115. The study details are summarized in example-5 and depicted in Figure 17.7.

To exert optimal therapeutic efficacy, an active substance should reach systemic circulation and site of its action in an effective concentration during the desired period. Improving bioavailability and reducing dosage frequency without losing therapeutic benefit is crucial in achieving therapeutic efficacy and patient compliance in chronic treatment regimes. The compositions disclosed herein achieve this objective by enhancing the oral bioavailability of AKBA in compositions containing BsLPRE.

The bioavailability enhancing effect of BsLPRE was further confirmed by evaluating the composition LI13124F1 containing BsLPRE and a novel curcumin compound called bisdemethylcurcumin (LI01008) in comparison with LI01008 alone in Alibino Wistar rats. Bisdemethylcurcumin is a potent curcuminoid, far superior to other naturally occurring curcuminoids with respect to antioxidant and other biological activities commonly exhibited curcumins. The composition LI13124F1 showed better bioavailability of LI01008 in serum samples compared to the animals supplemented with LI01008 alone. The serum samples of animals supplemented with LI13124F1 showed 75% better bioavailability compared to the serum samples of the animals supplemented with LI01008 alone. The experimental studies are discussed in example-6 and depicted in Figure 17.8.

The foregoing thus suggest that the non-acidic *Boswellia* low polar gum resin extract fraction (BLPRE), *Boswellia* volatile oil fraction (BVOIL) or *Boswellia* oil fraction (BOIL) comprising BLPRE and BVOIL enhance the bioavailability of bioactive agents. These bio-enhancing agents thus can be useful to improve the efficacy and reduce the dose of bioactive agents.

In an important aspect, the current disclosure provides bioenhancing agents selected from intact *Boswellia* oil (BOIL), *Boswellia* volatile oil (BVOIL) and *Boswellia* low polar gum resin extract (BLPRE) obtained from *Boswellia* gum resin of *Boswellia* species for increasing the bioavailability of biological agents.

In an important aspect, the current disclosure provides compositions comprising one or more ingredients selected from intact *Boswellia* oil (BOIL), *Boswellia* volatile oil (BVOIL) and *Boswellia* low polar gum resin extract (BLPRE) obtained from *Boswellia* gum resin of *Boswellia* species in combination with a biological agent for increasing the bioavailability of biological agent.

In another aspect, the current disclosure provides *Boswellia* derived bioenhancing agents for improving the bioavailability and/or bio-efficacy of nutraceuticals or dietary supplements is also relevant to animal health besides being important for humans.

In another aspect the current disclosure provides *Boswellia* derived bioenhancing agents for increasing the bioavailability of one or more biological ingredient(s) or functional ingredient(s).

In another aspect the current disclosure provides *Boswellia* derived bioenhancing agents for increasing the bioavailability of one or more *Boswellia* derived components.

In another aspect the current disclosure provides *Boswellia* derived bioenhancing agents for increasing the bioavailability of one or more Curcuma longa derived components.

In another aspect the current disclosure provides the method of using *Boswellia* derived bioenhancing agents for enhancing the bioavailability of biological agents.

In another aspect, the current disclosure provides bioenhancing agents, which function through one or more of the mechanisms comprising increasing the bioavailability, enhancing the serum concentration, improving gastrointestinal absorption, improving systemic utilization and improving cross over through certain biological barriers like respiratory lining, urinary lining, blood brain barrier and skin.

In another aspect, the current disclosure provides bio-enhancing agents *Boswellia* oil (BOIL), *Boswellia* volatile oil (BVOIL) and *Boswellia* low polar gum resin extract (BLPRE) derived from the gum resin of *Boswellia* where in the gum resin can be obtained from one or more of the *Boswellia* species selected from *Boswellia serrata*, *Boswellia carterii* and *Boswellia papyrifera*.

In another aspect the current disclosure provides compositions for bioenhancing the activity of biological agents in warm blooded animals in need thereof.

In another aspect the current disclosure provides compositions comprising *Boswellia* oil (BOIL), *Boswellia* volatile oil (BVOIL) and *Boswellia* low polar gum resin extract (BLPRE) for enhancing the bioavailability of nutraceutical or dietary ingredients in warm blooded animals in need thereof.

The nutraceutically/dietetically acceptable agents comprise one or more ingredients selected from phytochemicals, Nootropic agents, anti obese agents, anti-inflammatory agents, anti cholesterol agents, anti arthritic agents, anti diabetic agents, antimicrobial agents, anti fungal agents, anti cancer agents, anti hypertensive agents, analgesic agents, anti platelet aggregation agents, anti atherosclerotic agents, antioxidants, anti thrombotic agents, antibiotic agents, anti malarial agents, anti osteoporotic agents, probiotics agents, anti fungal agents, immune potentiating agents, anti viral agents, anti histamines, muscle relaxants, anti depressants, hypnotic agents and their salts thereof.

In another aspect the current disclosure provides composition(s) for increasing the bioavailability of one or more biological ingredient(s) selected from biologically active ingredient(s), functional ingredient(s), herbal ingredient(s), dietary supplement(s), nutrient(s), anti-oxidant(s), vitamin(s), mineral(s), amino acid(s), and oil(s) their mixtures obtained from plant(s)/animal(s)/microorganism(s)/synthesis/semi-synthesis.

The functional ingredient(s) comprise one or more ingredients selected from nutrients, dietary supplements, nutritional ingredients, herbal ingredients, phytochemicals, animal proteins, glucosamine, chondroitin, plant proteins, fruit extracts, animal extracts, algae extracts, probiotics and their salts thereof.

The herbal ingredient(s) comprise one or more ingredients selected from extracts/fractions/phytochemicals and their salts derived from Withania somnifera, Bacopa monniera, *Boswellia* species, Curcuma species, Centella asiatica, Sphaeranthus indicus, Annona squamosa, Holoptelia integrifolia, Piper betel, Dolichos biflorus, Moringa oleifera and Murraya koenigii.

The anti-oxidant(s) comprise one or more ingredients selected from vitamin A, vitamin C, vitamin E, alpha-carotene, trans-beta-carotene, betacryptoxanthin, lycopene, lutein/zeaxanthin, pine bark bioflavonals complex, germanium, selenium and zinc. The vitamin(s) comprise one or more water soluble vitamins selected from vitamin B1 vitamin B2, niacinamide, vitamin B6, vitamin B12, folic acid and vitamin C; fat-soluble vitamins selected from vitamin A, vitamin D, vitamin E and vitamin K.

The mineral(s) comprise one or more minerals selected from calcium, iron, zinc, vanadium, selenium, chromium, iodine, potassium, manganese, copper and magnesium. The amino acid(s) comprise one or more amino acids selected from lysine, isoleucine, leucine, threonine, valine, tryptophan, phenylalanine, methionine, L-selenomethionine and their mixtures thereof.

The oil(s) comprise one or more oils selected from omega-3 fatty acid, flaxseed oil, fish oils, krill oil, essential oils and volatile oils.

The biological activity of *Boswellia* derived compounds/phytochemicals that can be enhanced by bioenhancing agents include extracts of fractions standardized to one or more boswellic acids selected from α-Boswellic acid, β-Boswellic acid, 3-O-acetyl-α-Boswellic acid, 3-O-acetyl-β-Boswellic acid, 3-O-acetyl-11-keto-α-Boswellic acid, 11-keto-β-Boswellic acid and 3-O-acetyl-11-keto-β-Boswellic acid.

In another aspect, the current disclosure provides bio-enhancing agents selected from *Boswellia* oil (BOIL), *Boswellia* volatile oil (BVOIL) and *Boswellia* low polar gum resin extract (BLPRE) derived from the gum resin of *Boswellia* for enhancing the bioavailability of extracts/fractions particularly standardized to 3-O-acetyl-11-keto-β-Boswellic acid (AKBA).

In another aspect, the current disclosure provides *Boswellia* derived agents and compositions for enhancing the bioavailability of the phytochemicals derived from *Boswellia* species including but not limited to boswellic acids selected from α-boswellic acid, β-boswellic acid, 3-acetyl-α-boswellic acid, 3-acetyl-β-boswellic acid, 3-acetyl-11-keto-α-boswellic acid and 3-acetyl-11-keto-β-boswellic acid or mixtures thereof.

The *Boswellia* species that can be used for producing the oil (BOIL) or volatile oil (BVOIL) or low polar gum resin extract (BLPRE) from the gum resin comprise one or more species selected from *Boswellia serrata*, *Boswellia carterii*, *Boswellia* payrifera. *Boswellia* ameero, *Boswellia* bullata, *Boswellia* dalzielii, *Boswellia* dioscorides, *Boswellia* elongata, *Boswellia* frereana, *Boswellia* nana, *Boswellia* neglecta, *Boswellia* ogadensis, *Boswellia* pirottae, *Boswellia* popoviana, *Boswellia rivae*, *Boswellia sacra* and *Boswellia* socotrana.

In another aspect, the current disclosure provides *Boswellia* oil or *Boswellia* volatile oil or *Boswellia* low polar gum resin extract for enhancing the bioavailability of one or more Curcuma derived extracts/fractions/components/phytochemicals that can be enhanced by bioenhancing agents include extracts of fractions standardized to selected from curcumin, demethoxycurcumin, bisdemethoxycurcumin, monodemethylcurcumin, bisdemethylcurcumin, tetrahydrocurcumin, tetrahydrodemethoxycurcumin, tetrahydro bisdemethoxycurcumin and ar-turmerone or mixtures thereof.

In another aspect, the current disclosure provides bio-enhancing agents *Boswellia* oil (BOIL), *Boswellia* volatile oil (BVOIL) and *Boswellia* low polar gum resin extract (BLPRE) derived from the gum resin of *Boswellia* for enhancing the bioavailability of extracts/fractions particularly standardized to curcumin or demethoxycurcumin or bisdemethoxycurcumin or mixtures thereof.

In another aspect, the current disclosure provides *Boswellia* derived bioenhancing agents and for enhancing the bioavailability of the one or more phytochemicals derived from Curcuma species selected from curcumin, demethoxycurcumin, bisdemethoxycurcumin, monodemethylcurcumin, bisdemethylcurcumin, tetrahydrocurcumin, tetrahydrodemethoxycurcumin, tetrahydro bisdemethoxycurcumin and ar-turmerone or mixtures thereof.

The Curcumin derived components that can be bioenhanced are derived from Curcuma longa, Curcuma aromatica, Curcuma domestica, Curcuma aeruginosa, Curcuma albicoma, Curcuma albiflora, Curcuma alismatifolia, Curcuma angustifolia, Curcumaelata, Curcuma ferruginea, Curcuma flaviflora, Curcuma yunnanensis and Curcuma zedoaria.

D. Examples

The following examples, which include various embodiments, will serve to illustrate the practice of the disclosed subject matter, and it should be understood that the particulars shown are by way of example and for purpose of illustrative discussion of certain embodiments of the invention; the following examples do not limit the scope of the invention.

Example 1. A Process for Preparation of the Non-Acidic *Boswellia* Extract (BOIL) Comprises

(g) Procuring the gum resin of one or more of the plant(s) selected from but not limited to *Boswellia serrata* or *Boswellia carterii* or *Boswellia papyrifera* or mixtures thereof,

(h) Extraction of the gum resin with a water immiscible organic solvent,

(i) Filtering the extract carefully to remove the insoluble resin material,

(j) Washing the organic solvent extract repeatedly with an aqueous alkali solution such as aqueous potassium hydroxide,

(k) Washing the organic layer with water and brine,

(l) Evaporating the organic layer under vacuum and high temperature to obtain the oily residue (BOIL).

Example 2. A Process for Preparation of the Non-Acidic *Boswellia* Volatile Oil Fraction (BVOIL) Comprises

(a) Procuring the gum resin of one or more of the plant(s) selected from but not limited to *Boswellia serrata* or *Boswellia carterii* or *Boswellia papyrifera* or mixtures thereof,

(b) Separating the Volatile oil component by either steam distillation or distillation under high vacuum and temperature from the said gum resin to obtain *Boswellia* volatile oil fraction (BVOIL).

Example 3. A Process for Preparation of the Non-Acidic *Boswellia* Low Polar Gum Resin Extract Fraction (BLPRE) Comprises

(a) Procuring the gum resin of one or more of the plant(s) selected from but not limited to *Boswellia serrata* or *Boswellia carterii* or *Boswellia papyrifera* or mixtures thereof,

(b) Extraction of the gum resin with a water immiscible organic solvent,

(c) Filtering the extract carefully to remove the insoluble resin material,

(d) Washing the organic solvent extract repeatedly with an aqueous alkali solution such as aqueous potassium hydroxide,

(e) Washing the organic layer with water and brine,

(f) Evaporating the organic layer under vacuum and high temperature to obtain the oily residue (*Boswellia* oil).

(g) Taking the said oily residue and removing the volatiles under high vacuum and high temperature to obtain *Boswellia* low polar gum resin extract fraction (BLPRE).

Example 4. Representative Procedure for the Preparation of *Boswellia serrata* Low Polar Gum Resin Extract Fraction (BsLPRE)

The *Boswellia serrata* gum resin (100 g) was dispersed in 600 mL of methyl isobutyl ketone (MIBK) solvent and stirred at room temperature for 60 min. The insoluble gum materials were separated by filtration. The MIBK solution was extracted repeatedly with 2% KOH solution (3 × 200 mL) to remove the acidic compounds. The MIBK layer was then washed successively with water (400 mL) and brine (200 mL). The MIBK layer was evaporated under reduced pressure at 60-70° C. and the volatile components are removed from the oily residue under high vacuum at 75-110° C. to obtain BsLPRE as a viscous oil (12 g).

Alternatively, the gum resin (250 g) collected from *Boswellia serrata* was extracted with methanol (300 mL × 3) and the combined methanol extract was concentrated. The residue (50 g) was dissolved in ethyl acetate (400 mL) and extracted thrice with 1N KOH (3 × 100 mL). The organic layer was washed with water (2 × 200 mL) and brine (200 mL) and evaporated to obtain *Boswellia* oil. The volatile compounds were evaporated from the oil under vacuum at high temperature (75-110° C.) to obtain 22 g of BsLPRE.

The BsLPRE was subjected to column chromatography over normal silica gel using solvents of increasing polarity starting from hexane to hexane/ethyl acetate mixtures to ethyl acetate. The identical fractions were combined based on TLC and combined fractions were subjected individually to column chromatography over silica gel using mixtures of hexane/ethyl acetate or hexane/acetone as eluents to obtain pure compounds. Some of the impure fractions were further subjected to preparative HPLC using a reversed phase C18 silica column to obtain pure compounds. The structures were established by analyzing the ^{1}H NMR, ^{13}C NMR, DEPT, HSQC and HMBC and mass spectral data and then comparing the data with that of known compounds. Nine of the prominent compounds are identified as guiol (1), nephthenol (2), serratol (3), diterpene X (4), lupeol (5), olean-12-ene-3β-ol (6), olean-12-ene-3α-ol (7), lanosta-8,24-diene-3α-ol (8) and urs-12-ene-3α-ol (9) as depicted in Figure 17.3. The pure compounds were then utilized to standardize the *Boswellia serrata* low polar gum resin extract (BsLPRE) using HPLC method. The novel composition of BsLPRE evaluated based on analytical HPLC method along with the retention times (R_t) is summarized in Table 17.1. The HPLC chromatogram for BsLPRE is depicted in Figure 17.4.

Table 17.1: Composition of *Boswellia serrata* Low Polar Gum Resin Extract Fraction (BsL PRE)

Sl.No.	Test substance	R_t in min	Percentage
1.	Guiol (1)	4.5	0.96
2.	Nephthenol (2)	7.087	2.01
3.	Serratol (3)	8.027	13.32
4.	Diterpene X (4)	15.777	0.12
5.	Lupeol (5)	26.901	0.06
6.	Olean-12-ene-3β-ol (6)	31.460	1.29
7.	Olean-12-ene-3α-ol (7)	33.718	5.36
8.	Lanosta-8, 24-diene -3α-ol (8)	35.371	1.34
9.	Urs-12-ene-3α-ol (9)	37.207	4.5Ace5

Example 5. *Boswellia serrata* Extract Standardized to 50-100% Total Boswellic Acids (Titrimetric Method).

Boswellia serrata extracts standardized to 85% or 65% total boswellic acids are commercially available. These extracts are standardized using titrimetric method of analysis. These extracts can be prepared using a known procedure. For example, by extracting the gum resin of *Boswellia serrata* using a water immiscible solvent and then selectively extracting the acidic compounds from the organic solvent extract using aqueous alkali solution through phase separation. Finally acidification of the alkali solution to precipitate the boswellic acids followed by vacuum drying to yield *Boswellia serrata* extract enriched to 85% boswellic acids (BE85%). *Boswellia serrata* extracts standardized to a selected concentration of total boswellic acids in the range of 40-100% by titrimetric method of analysis or 30-100% by HPLC method of analysis can be obtained by purification of the gum resin or the extracts or by dilution of higher grade material.

Example 6. Determination of Acetylcholinesterase Inhibitory Activity of BsOIL, BsLPRE, BcLPRE, BsVOIL and Different Boswellic Acid Compound in an In Vitro Enzymatic Assay.

Acetylcholinesterase activity is measured using the substrate acetylthiocholine iodide, which is converted to thiocholine. The reaction of thiocholine with the chromogenic substrate Dithionitrobenzoic acid (DTNB) leads to the formation of a yellow anion, Nitrobenzoic acid, which absorbs strongly at 412 nm Incubation was done for 10 min.

The AChE assay was performed by the method of Ellman *et al.*, with minor modifications, using acetylthiocholine iodide as a substrate (Lee J. H., et. al. Arch Pharm Res 2004, 27(1): 53-56). Ellmans reaction mixture contains 0.5 mM acetylthiocholine iodide and 1 mM 5,52 -dithio-bis-(2-nitrobenzoic acid) in a 50 mM sodium phosphate buffer (pH 8.0). The assay mixture contained 50 µl of 50 mM phosphate buffer at pH–8.0, 30 µl of test substance (BsOIL or

BsLPRE or BcLPRE or BsVOIL, different boswellic acids and positive control Neostigmin) at various concentrations and 20 μl of (100 mU/mL) enzyme. For blanks, enzyme was replaced with phosphate buffer. The reaction mixture was mixed thoroughly, 100 μl of Ellman's reagent was added and incubated at room temperature for 10 min. The absorbance was measured at 412 nm using microplate reader. The percentage inhibition of enzyme activity was calculated by comparing OD's of tests wells with that of control wells using the following formula. Calculations: % inhibition = [(control − sample) / control] × 100. The results of Acetylcholinesterase inhibitory activity of BsOIL, BsLPRE, BcLPRE, BsVOIL and boswellic acids are summarized in Table 17.2 and 17.3.

Table 17.2: Acetylcholinesterase Inhibitory Activity of BsOIL, BsL PRE, BcL PRE, BsVOIL

Name of the compound	% Inhibition at concentration of			IC50
	10 ng	25 ng	50 ng	ng/mL
BsOIL	10.65	17.09	32.69	>50
BsLPRE	31.5	43.7	57.87	37.01
BcLPRE	15.6	23.18	42.56	>50
BsVOIL	16.5	25.49	33.01	>50
BSE-85	—	4.22	6.27	—
Composition-1	—	—	—	42.7
Neostigmin	25.17	37.19	54.69	43.29

Table 17.3: Acetylcholinesterase Inhibitory Activity of Pure *Boswellic* Acids

Name of the Product	% Inhibition at concentration of				IC50
	10 ng	25 ng	50 ng	100 ng	ng/mL
11-Keto-β-boswellic acid	—	11.82	16.36	24.55	>100
3-O-acetyl-11-keto-β-boswellic acid	—	9.64	16.07	27.5	>100
α-boswellic acid	—	13.85	21.92	39.23	>100
β-boswellic acid	—	16.75	21.23	31.37	>100
3-O-acetyl-α-boswellic acid	—	14.86	21.28	33.11	>100
3-O-acetyl-β-boswellic acid	—	36.29	40.23	52.02	91.77
Neostigmin	25.17	37.19	54.69	—	43.29

Example 7. Acetylcholine Esterase Inhibitory Activity of BsOIL, BsLPRE, BcLPRE, BsVOIL and Boswellic Acids in PC 12 Cells.

The inhibitory property on the enzyme activity was assessed in (3-amyloid peptide induced-rat pheochromocytoma PC 12 cells. Rat pheochromocytoma PC 12 cells were equally distributed with phenol red free Dulbecco's modified Eagle's red medium (DMEM) (Sigma Life Science, USA) containing 10% fetal bovine serum (FBS) in 24-well plate. Cells were pretreated with test agents (BsOIL, BsLPRE, BcLPRE, BsVOIL and different boswellic acids and positive control Neostigmin) for 1 h. Thereafter, cells were induced with 1 μg/mL of β-amyloid peptide (Calbiochem, USA) for 24 h at 37° C. After 24 h, cells were collected and washed twice with 1×PBS by centrifugation at 1200 rpm for 5 min at 4° C. Cell extracts were prepared in solubilization buffer (10 mM Tris, pH 7.2; 100 mM NaCl, 50 mM MgCl2, 1% Triton X-100). The cell extracts were used as samples for measuring the acetylcholine esterase (AChE) activity.

Cell extract samples (100 μl) were dispensed into each well of 96-well microtitre plate. Fifty micro litres of DTNB (Dithiobisnitro benzoate) solution was added to each well and incubated for 5 min at room temperature. After incubation, 50 μl of acetyl choline iodide solution was added to each well and absorbance was read immediately at 405 nm for 12 min at 2 min intervals. A standard curve was constructed by using serial concentrations of acetyl cholinesterase (0-100 mU). Total protein present in 100 μl aliquot of cell extract was calculated by Bradford method and the enzyme activity was normalized and expressed as unit activity per milligram of protein. Efficacy of test samples was expressed in terms of percent inhibition of AChE activity and compared with a standard drug, Neostigmin as the positive control.

Results: Table 17.4 and Table 17.5 are summary of the acetyl cholinesterase inhibitory activities exhibited by various non acidic extracts from *Boswellia serrata* and *Boswellia carterii* (BsOIL, BsLPRE, BcLPRE and BsVOIL) and different boswellic acids. A standard drug, Neostigmin was used as the positive control for comparing the AChE inhibitory efficacies of the *Boswellia* products.

Table 17.4: Acetyl Cholinesterase Inhibitory Property of BsOIL, BsLPRE, BcLPRE and BsVOIL

Test samples	Treatment Conc.	% inhibition in AChE activity
BsOIL	100 ng/ml	19.92
BsLPRE	100 ng/mL	25.31
BcLPRE	100 ng/mL	18.67
BsVOIL	100 ng/mL	16.46
Neostigmin	20 ng/ml	49.09

Table 17.5: Comparative Efficacy of Different Boswellic Acids in Inhibiting Acetyl Cholinesterase Activity

Test samples	Treatment Conc.	% inhibition in AChE activity
11-Keto-β-boswellic acid	100 ng/ml	31.39
3-O-acetyl-11-keto-β-boswellic acid	100 ng/ml	41.67
α-boswellic acid	100 ng/ml	38.42
β-boswellic acid	100 ng/ml	46.54
3-O-acetyl-α-boswellic acid	100 ng/ml	29.22
3-O-acetyl-β-boswellic acid	100 ng/ml	37.34
Neostigmin	20 ng/ml	54.65

Example 8. Preparation of Composition-1.

Composition-1 was prepared by mixing unit doses of the following components; four parts of *Boswellia serrata* low polar gum resin extract (BsLPRE) (4 g) and one part of *Boswellia serrata* extract standardized to 85% total Boswellic acids (BSE 85%) (1 g).

Example 9. Composition-2.

Composition-2 was prepared by mixing unit doses of the following components; one part of *Boswellia serrata* volatile oil (BsVOIL) (1 g) and four parts of *Boswellia serrata* extract standardized to 85% total Boswellic acids (BSE 85%) (4 g).

Example 10. Composition-3.

Composition-3 was prepared by mixing unit doses of the following components; one part of *Boswellia serrata* non acidic oil (BsOIL) (1 g) and four parts of *Boswellia serrata* extract standardized to 85% total Boswellic acids (BSE 85%) (4 g).

Example 11. Composition-4.

Composition-4 was prepared by mixing unit doses of the following components; one part of *Boswellia carterii* low polar gum resin extract (BcLPRE) (1 g) and four parts of *Boswellia serrata* extract standardized to 85% total Boswellic acids (BSE 85%) (4 g).

Example 12. Composition-5.

Composition-5 was prepared by mixing unit doses of the following components; one part of *Boswellia carterii* volatile oil (BcVOIL) (1 g) and three parts of *Boswellia carterii* extract standardized to 85% total Boswellic acids (BCE 85%) (3 g).

Example 13. Composition-6.

Composition-6 was prepared by mixing unit doses of the following components; one part of *Boswellia serrata* low polar gum resin extract (BsLPRE) (1 g), four parts of *Boswellia serrata* extract enriched with 20% of 3-O-acetyl-11-keto-13-Boswellic acid (AKBA) (4 g).

Example 14. Composition-7.

Composition-7 was prepared by mixing unit doses of the following components; one part of *Boswellia carterii* low polar gum resin extract (BcLPRE) (1 g), four parts of *Boswellia carterii* extract enriched with 20% of 3-O-acetyl-11-keto-13-Boswellic acid (AKBA) (4 g).

Example 15. Composition-8.

Composition-8 was prepared by mixing unit doses of the following components; one part of *Boswellia serrata* low polar gum resin extract (BcLPRE) (1 g), four parts of *Boswellia serrata* extract enriched with 40% of 3-O-acetyl-11-keto-13-Boswellic acid (AKBA) (4 g).

Example 16. Composition-9.

Composition-9 was prepared by mixing unit doses of the following components; one part of *Boswellia carterii* low polar gum resin extract (BcLPRE) (1 g), three parts of *Boswellia carterii* extract enriched with 40% of 3-O-acetyl-11-keto-13-Boswellic acid (AKBA) (3 g).

Example 17. Composition-10.

Composition-10 was prepared by mixing unit doses of the following components; one part of *Boswellia serrata* low polar gum resin extract (BsLPRE) (1 g) and three parts of Bacopa monniera standardized extract (3 g).

Example 18. Composition-11.

Composition-10 was prepared by mixing unit doses of the following components; one part of *Boswellia serrata* volatile oil fraction (BsVOIL) (1 g) and three parts of Bacopa monniera standardized extract (3 g).

Example 19. Composition-12.

Composition-12 was prepared by mixing unit doses of the following components; one part of non-acidic *Boswellia serrata* oil fraction (BsOIL) (1 g) and three parts of Bacopa monniera standardized extract (3 g).

Example 20. Composition-13.

Composition-13 was prepared by mixing unit doses of the following components; one part of *Boswellia serrata* low polar gum resin extract (BsLPRE) (1 g) and four parts of Bacopa monniera water extract (4 g).

Example 21. Composition-14.

Composition-14 was prepared by mixing unit doses of the following components; one part of *Boswellia serrata* low polar gum resin extract (BsLPRE) (1 g) and four parts of Bacopa monniera 90% methanol extract (4 g).

Example 22. Composition-15.

Composition-15 was prepared by mixing unit doses of the following components; one part of *Boswellia serrata* low polar gum resin extract (BsLPRE) (1 g) and three parts of Bacopa monniera standardized extract (3 g).

Example 23. Composition-16.

Composition-16 was prepared by mixing unit doses of the following components; one part of *Boswellia serrata* low polar gum resin extract (BsLPRE) (1 g) and four parts of Bacopa monniera extract standardized to 25% bacopasaponins (4 g).

Example 24. Composition-17.

Composition-17 was prepared by mixing unit doses of the following components; one part of *Boswellia carterii* low polar gum resin extract (BcLPRE) (1 g) and four parts of Bacopa monniera extract standardized to 25% bacopasaponins (4 g).

Example 25. Composition-18.

Composition-18 was prepared by mixing unit doses of the following components; one part of *Boswellia papyrifera* low polar gum resin extract (BpLPRE) (1 g) and four parts of Bacopa monniera extract standardized to 25% bacopasaponins (4 g).

Example 26. Composition-19.

Composition-19 was prepared by mixing unit doses of the following components; one part of *Boswellia serrata* low polar gum resin extract (BsLPRE) (1 g) and four parts of Curcuma longa extract standardized to 95% total Curcuminoids (CLE 95%) (1 g).

Example 27. Composition-20.

Composition-20 was prepared by mixing unit doses of the following components; one part of *Boswellia serrata* volatile oil fraction (BsVOIL) (1 g) and four parts of Curcuma longa extract standardized to 95% total Curcuminoids (CLE 95%) (4 g).

Example 28. Composition-21.

Composition-21 was prepared by mixing unit doses of the following components; one part of non-acidic *Boswellia serrata* oil fraction (BsOIL) (1 g) and four parts of Curcuma longa extract standardized to 95% total Curcuminoids (CLE 95%) (4 g).

Example 29. Composition-22.

Composition-22 was prepared by mixing unit doses of the following components; one part of *Boswellia serrata* low polar gum resin extract (BsLPRE) (1 g) and three parts of curcumin (3 g).

Example 30. Composition-23.

Composition-23 was prepared by mixing unit doses of the following components; one part of *Boswellia serrata* low polar gum resin extract (BsLPRE) (1 g) and three parts of bisdemethylcurcumin (BDMC) (3 g).

Example 31. Composition-24.

Composition-24 was prepared by mixing unit doses of the following components; one part of *Boswellia serrata* low polar gum resin extract (BsLPRE) (1 g) and four parts of Withania somnifera methanol extract (4 g).

Example 32. Composition-25.

Composition-25 was prepared by mixing unit doses of the following components; one part of *Boswellia carterii* low polar gum resin extract (BcLPRE) (1 g) and four parts of standardized Withania somnifera extract (4 g).

Example 33. Composition-26.

Composition-26 was prepared by mixing unit doses of the following components; one part of *Boswellia* low polar gum resin extract (BLPRE) (1 g) and four parts of standardized Rosmarinus officinalis extract (4 g).

Example 34. Composition-27.

Composition-27 was prepared by mixing unit doses of the following components; one part of *Boswellia serrata* low polar gum resin extract (BsLPRE) (1 g) and four parts of standardized Rosmarinus officinalis extract (4 g).

Example 35. Composition-28.

Composition-28 was prepared by mixing unit doses of the following components; one part of *Boswellia carterii* low polar gum resin extract (BcLPRE) (1 g) and four parts of standardized Rosmarinus officinalis extract (4 g).

Example 36. Composition-29.

Composition-29 was prepared by mixing unit doses of the following components; one part of *Boswellia serrata* low polar gum resin extract (BsLPRE) (1 g) and four parts of Rosmarinus officinalis extract standardized to 30% Rosmarinic acid (RA 30%) (4 g).

Example 37. Composition-30.

Composition-30 was prepared by mixing unit doses of the following components; one part of *Boswellia carterii* low polar gum resin extract (BcLPRE) (1 g) and three parts of Rosmarinus officinalis extract standardized to 30% Rosmarinic acid (RA 30%) (3 g).

Example 38. Composition-31.

Composition-31 was prepared by mixing unit doses of the following components; one part of *Boswellia* non acidic oil (BOIL) (1 g) and three parts of Garcinia mangostana methanol extract (3 g).

Example 39. Composition-32.

Composition-32 was prepared by mixing unit doses of the following components; one part of non-acidic *Boswellia serrata* oil (BsOIL) (1 g) and three parts of Garcinia mangostana methanol extract (3 g).

Example 40. Composition-33.

Composition-33 was prepared by mixing unit doses of the following components; one part of *Boswellia serrata* low polar gum resin extract (BsLPRE) (1 g) and three parts of Garcinia mangostana methanol extract (3 g).

Example 41. Composition-34.

Composition-34 was prepared by mixing unit doses of the following components; two parts of *Boswellia serrata* low polar gum resin extract (BsLPRE) (2 g) and one part of α-mangostin (1 g).

Example 42. Composition-35.

Composition-35 was prepared by mixing unit doses of the following components; four parts of *Boswellia serrata* low polar gum resin extract (BsLPRE) (4 g) and one part of α-mangostin (1 g).

Example 43. Composition-36.

Composition-40 was prepared by mixing unit doses of the following components; one part of *Boswellia* low polar gum resin extract fraction (BLPRE) (1 g) and three parts of Sphaeranthus indicus ethyl acetate extract (3 g).

Example 44. Composition-37.

Composition-40 was prepared by mixing unit doses of the following components; one part of non acidic *Boswellia* oil fraction (BOIL) (1 g) and four parts of Sphaeranthus indicus ethyl acetate extract (4 g).

Example 45. Composition-38.

Composition-40 was prepared by mixing unit doses of the following components; one part of *Boswellia* volatile oil fraction (BVOIL) (1 g) and four parts of Sphaeranthus indicus ethyl acetate extract (4 g).

Example 46. Assay for Measuring Reactive Oxygen Species (ROS).

Formation of ROS was measured using of the fluorescent probe DCFH-DA. The method is based on the incubation of the RAW 264.7 mouse macrophages with DCFH-DA, which diffuses passively through the cellular membrane. Intracellular esterase activity results in the formation of DCFH, which emits fluorescence when oxidized to 20, 70-dichlorofluorescein (DCF). Briefly, the cells (final concentration 2×10^6/ml suspension) were incubated with DCFH-DA (5 mM) in HEPES-buffered (20 mM) HBSS ($CaCl_2$ 1.26 mM, KCL 5.37 mM, KH_2PO_4 0.44 mM; $MgCl_2$ 0.49 mM, MgSO4 0.41 mM, NaCl 140 mM, $NaHCO_3$ 4.17 mM, Na_2HPO_4 0.34 mM) with glucose (5 mM) at 37° C. for 15 mM Following centrifugation, the extracellular buffer with DCFH-DA was exchanged with fresh buffer and the suspension was mixed gently. The cells (2×10^6/ml, 125 ml) were transferred to 250 ml wells (microtiter plate reader, 96 wells) containing 125 ml buffer with the different concentrations of test samples (α-mangostin, BsLPRE, Composition-34 and Composition-35) in presence or absence of 100 mM H_2O_2. Fluorescence was recorded using excitation wavelength 485 nm, emission wavelength 530 nm in a Modulus luminescence spectrometer (Turner Biosystems, USA) for 120 mM Results are calculated as area under the curve (AUC) and the percentage of inhibition of intracellular ROS generation was calculated from the cultures treated with H_2O_2. The results are summarized in Table 17.6.

Table 17.6: Anti-oxidant Properties of Herbal Products and their Combinations

Sl.No.	Treatments	Inhibition of Reactive Oxygen Species (ROS) generation (IC50)
1.	α-mangostin	49.817 ug/ml
2.	BsLPRE	53.879 ug/ml
3.	Composition-34	33.342 ug/ml
4.	Composition-35	50.776 ug/ml

Example 47. Cell Proliferation Assay.

Effect of BsLPRE or α-mangostin or their combination (Composition-34) on cell growth was tested in oxidative stress induced IMR32 human neuroblastoma cells SW 982 human synovial cells by using MTT based cell proliferation assay. Briefly, IMR32 human neuroblastoma cells were cultivated in Dulbecco's modified Eagle's red medium (DMEM) (Sigma Life Science, USA) containing 10% fetal bovine serum (FBS). Equal number of IMR32 cells was seeded in to each well of 96 well microplate and incubated at 37° C. with 5% CO_2. The cells were treated with 250 μM H_2O_2 in presence or absence of different concentrations of BsLPRE or α-mangostin or their combination (Composition-34) for 72 h. Control wells were supplemented with 0.05% DMSO. After 72 h of treatment, equal volume of MTT reagent (R&D Systems, USA) was added to each well and incubated for 4 h. Thereafter, 50 μl of solublization buffer (R&D Systems, USA) was added to each well to solubilize the colored formazan crystals produced by the reduction of MTT. After 24 h, the optical density was measured at 550 nm using microplate reader (Bio-Rad, USA). In each assay, the vehicle control and the treatments were done in quadruplicates. The average OD obtained in the vehicle control wells is considered as the cell proliferation index of 100. The results are summarized in Table 17.7 below.

Table 17.7: Protection from Oxidant Stress Induced Cytotoxic Damage of Human Neuroblastoma Cells

S. No.	Treatments	Treatment conc.	Cell proliferation Index
1	Vehicle Control	100.00	
2	H_2O_2	250 uM	78.71
3	α-mangostin	10 ng/ml	80.32
		25 ng/ml	86.78
		50 ng/ml	87.21
		100 ng/ml	91.78
4	BsLPRE	10 ng/ml	87.81
		25 ng/ml	92.24
		50 ng/ml	95.19
		100 ng/ml	97.30
5	Composition-34	10 ng/ml	92.81
		25 ng/ml	95.82
		50 ng/ml	99.05
		100 ng/ml	101.33

Example 48. Inhibition of acetylcholinesterase activity by herbal products and their combinations in Beta Amyloid protein induced PC12 cells: The

acetylcholinesterase inhibitory activity of α-mangostin, BsLPRE and Composition-34, recorded in Table 17.8, was measured using the procedure described in example 7.

Table 17.8: Inhibition of Acetylcholinesterase Activity by Herbal Products

Sl.No.	Treatments	Treatment conc.	% inhibition in Acetylcholinesterase (AChE) activity
1	α-mangostin	100 ng/ml	26.83
		250 ng/ml	29.48
2	BsLPRE	100 ng/ml	30.99
		250 ng/ml	35.15
3	Composition-34	100 ng/ml	37.97
		250 ng/ml	40.57

Example 49. Determination of Spatial Learning and Memory Improvement Efficacy of BsLPRE in Rats Using Elevated Radial Arm Maze Method.

The animal study protocol was approved by institutional animal ethics committee. Sprague Dawley rats were acclimatized for one week and healthy rats were selected for the study. The selected rats were pre-trained in elevated radial arm maze (RAM) adapted rats were allocated to various treatment groups each containing eight rats. After completion of pre-training, the oral treatment was initiated to the animals and continued daily up to two weeks. During this treatment phase the rats were placed on the RAM for 10 min each to recognize the food pellets present in the three different colored arms. During training the spatial learning was estimated by measuring various parameters like number of days required to learn the task, latency in finding food and number of wrong entries/attempts. After this treatment and training the animals were given rest without treatment or training for one week (3rd week). On 4th week, the animals were treated with allocated doses of test products and memory retention test was assessed using the same animals by measuring latency and number of wrong entries. The data was analyzed using ANOVA followed by a suitable post-hoc test.

Result (Spatial Learning)

Oral administration of BsLPRE (250 mg/kg) significantly ($P<0.01$) decreased the number of days required to make the rats learned as per set criteria and significantly ($P<0.05$) decreased the time taken to find the food by the learned rats in the elevated RAM model. Piracetam showed significant improvement in spatial learning represented by reduction in latency and Number of wrong entries, when compared with the control group and the results are as stated below (Figure 17.5A to 17.5C). The test product BsLPRE also significantly improves cognition and memory retention (Figures 17.6A and 17.6B). These results suggest that the use of BsLPRE improves spatial learning and memory retention. According to these findings, BsLPRE is a promising candidate for facilitation of learning and memory.

Example 50. Preparation of *Boswellia carterii* Low Polar Gum Resin Extract (BcLPRE).

The *Boswellia carterii* gum resin (100 g) was dispersed in 600 mL of methyl iso butyl ketone (MIBK) solvent and stirred at room temperature for 60 min The insoluble gum materials were separated by filtration. The MIBK solution was extracted repeatedly with 2% KOH solution (3 × 200 mL) to remove the acidic compounds. The MIBK layer was then washed successively with water (400 mL) and brine (200 mL). The MIBK layer was evaporated under reduced pressure at 60-70° C. and the volatile components are then removed from the oily residue under vacuum at 75-85° C. to obtain *Boswellia carterii* low polar gum resin extract or BcLPRE as a viscous oil (9.5 g).

Alternatively, the gum resin (250 g) collected from *Boswellia carterii* was extracted with methanol (300 mL × 3) and the combined methanol extract was concentrated. The residue (50 g) was dissolved in ethyl acetate (400 mL) and extracted thrice with 1N KOH (3 × 100 mL). The organic layer was washed with water (2 × 200 mL) and brine (200 mL) and evaporated to obtain *Boswellia* oil. The volatile compounds were evaporated from the oil under vacuum at 75-85° C. to obtain 17.75 g of BcLPRE.

Example 51. Comparative Bioavailability of 3-O-acetyl-11-keto-²-boswellic Acid (AKBA) from Different *Boswellia* Products.

Albino Wistar rats were quarantined and healthy rats were selected for the study. The selected animals were acclimatized for 7 days prior to the study initiation in the allocated room Animals employed for the study were randomized into various treatment groups, fasted overnight at free access to water, body weights were noted and individual doses were calculated based on the body weights. Blood samples were collected from all animals prior to oral administration of test products and at 0.5, 1, 2, 4, 8 and 12 hrs after oral administration. Collected blood samples were allowed to clot for 10 min and centrifuged at 4° C. at 1800 g for 10 min The serum samples were deproteinized with 100 µL TCA (20%) and 1.8 mL of HPLC grade methanol, centrifuged at 4° C. at 1800 g for 10 min and supernatants were subjected to LCMS analysis for total AKBA. The Composition LI 13108F comprising *Boswellia serrata* extract selectively enriched to 30% 3-O-acetyl-11-keto-β-boswellic acid (AKBA) (LI 13115) and *Boswellia serrata* non-volatile oil (BsLPRE) in the ratio 2:1; and composition LI13119F comprising *Boswellia serrata* extract standardized to 30% AKBA and *Boswellia serrata* steam distilled oil (BVOIL) in the ratio 2:1 showed better oral bioavailability with Area under the curve (AUC) 14.08 and 11.23 respectively compared to individual *Boswellia serrata* extract standardized to 30% AKBA (LI 13115) (AUC: 9.825). The bioavailability [in terms of [AUC] of LI 13108F is 43.33% more than LI 13115. The bioavailability of LI 13119F is 14.33% more than that of LI 13115. The serum concentration of AKBA in animals of various treatment groups at various time points was summarized in Table 17.9. The serum concentration against time was plotted and the details are summarized in Figure 17.7.

Table 17.9: Serum Concentration of AKBA Mean Serum AKBA Concentration µg/mL

Time (h)	LI 13115 (Mean ± SE)	LI 13108F (Mean ± SE)	LI 13119F (Mean ± SE)
0	0.000 ± 0.00	0.000 ± 0.00	0.000 ± 0.00
0.5	1.200 ± 0.19	1.533 ± 0.06	1.805 ± 0.21
1	1.545 ± 0.28	1.853 ± 0.11	1.865 ± 0.32
2	1.980 ± 0.45	2.000 ± 0.16	1.750 ± 0.26
4	0.850 ± 0.32	2.147 ± 0.41	1.100 ± 0.07
8	0.452 ± 0.22	0.520 ± 0.16	0.645 ± 0.13
12	0.095 ± 0.10	0.199 ± 0.14	0.20 ± 0.20
AUC	9.825	14.0825 (43.33%)	11.2325 (14.33%)

Example 52. Comparative Bioavailability of LI01008 and its Composition

LI13124F1 Animals (Wistar Rats) were acclimatized for 7 days prior to study initiation. Six animals were divided randomly into 2 groups, each comprised of 3 animals. The body weights were noted and doses were calculated based on initial body weights. Animals were treated orally with 450 mg dose of a composition (LI13124F1) containing bisdemethylcurcumin (LI01008) and BsLPRE (LI13115) in 2:1 ratio or 300 mg/kg LI01008 as suspension in 0.5% CMC. Blood samples were collected before treatment and several time intervals after treatment at 0.5, 1, 2, 4, 6, 8 and 12 hours, as plotted in Figure 8. Collected blood samples were processed in a refrigerated centrifuge and serum samples were deproteinized using HPLC grade methanol, mixed thoroughly and centrifuged to remove precipitated proteins clear supernatants were subjected for LI01008 estimation by HPLC. The data is summarized in Table 17.10 below.

Table 17.10: Serum Concentration of Bisdemethylcurcumin

S. No.	Time after Admn.	LI131124F1 suspension in 0.5% CMC	LI01008 suspension in 0.5% CMC
1	0	0	0
2	0.5	0.1075	0.07
3	1	0.16	0.1085
4	2	0.105	0.078
5	4	0.065	0.035
6	6	0.032	0.00535
7	8	0.0085	0
8	12	0	0

As per the data, the bioavailability of LI01008 in the composition LI13124F1 is 75% better compared to that when LI01008 is administered alone.

It will be appreciated to those of ordinary skill in the art that changes could be made to the embodiments described above without departing from the broad inventive concept thereof. It is understood, therefore, that this invention is not limited to the particular embodiments or examples disclosed, but is intended to cover modifications within the objectives and scope of the present invention.

18 Herbal Pain Killer Compositions

People of all ages, genders and races suffer at some point from various types of pain. This ranges from general muscle aches and headaches, to significant pain from arthritis, acute injuries, surgery related pain as well as pain from chronic conditions. Chronic pain is the leading cause of adult disability in the United States and is one of the most common reasons for patient visits to primary care clinicians.

Conventional treatment with prescribed and over the counter (OTC) drugs such as acetaminophen (Tylenol) or non-steroidal anti-inflammatory drugs (NSAIDs, such as ibuprofen (e.g., Motrin and Advil) and naproxen (e.g., Aleve and Naprosyn)), COX-2 inhibitor's (e.g., Celebrex), and narcotics have remained the mainstay of current treatments. However, these treatments are typically associated with significant adverse side effects (e.g., gastrointestinal, cardiovascular, and addiction).

NSAIDs are among the most frequently used class of drugs worldwide, with yearly over-the-counter sales amounting to $30 billion. Gastrointestinal safety continues to be a high priority for patients and clinicians when choosing an NSAID treatment for pain. In fact, the gastrointestinal harm induced by NSAIDs may be the most prevalent adverse event associated with any drug class. Clinical manifestations of adverse gastrointestinal events include gastric and duodenal mucosal erosions, ulcers and ulcer complications, dyspepsia, abdominal pain and nausea. Dyspeptic symptoms include epigastric pain, bloating, nausea and heartburn, which account for the most common reason for discontinuation of NSAID therapy. Gastric or duodenal ulceration occurs in about 20% of NSAID users, and 40% of these individuals develop a serious complication. Other problems in the lower gut linked to the use of NSAIDs are gut inflammation, increase in gut permeability, stricture, protein malabsorption, bleeding, and perforation. Therefore, as a result of the widespread use of these agents, the potential for a significant number of adverse events, particularly gastrointestinal related, is high. Gastrointestinal adverse events associated with NSAID use are reported to account for more than 100,000 hospitalizations and more than 15,000 deaths annually. Noteworthy are the numbers of hospitalizations for patients taking long-term, low-dose aspirin who are admitted with upper gastrointestinal bleeding. This accounts for about 10-15% of the hospital admissions for upper gastrointestinal bleeding. The resulting economic costs incurred in managing NSAID related gastrointestinal adverse events are significant; where it is estimated that $0.66-1.25 of every dollar spent on the cost of the NSAID is associated with treating adverse events.

Selective (COX-2) inhibitors have demonstrated improved gastrointestinal tract safety over traditional NSAIDs drugs. There is important evidence from clinical trials showing that compared with traditional NSAIDs, COX-2 inhibitors are associated with a reduced rate of serious GI events such as bleeding, perforation and obstruction, and other symptoms such as dyspepsia, as well as a reduced requirement for concomitant gastroprotective therapies such as proton pump inhibitors. This relative benefit may be related to a lack of COX-1-mediated inhibition of gastric mucous production and a lack of effect on platelet thromboxane production. However, the differential effects of COX-2 inhibitors compared with traditional NSAIDs on platelet aggregation, prostacyclin/thromboxane balance, and inflammatory mediators involved in the development of atherosclerosis have also led to concerns that there is a physiological basis for COX-2 inhibitors to increase the risk for thrombotic events. These negative cardiotoxic effects (myocardial infarctions) of the COX-2 inhibitors were first documented in the Vioxx Gastrointestinal Outcomes Research (VIGOR) trial and the Celecoxib Long-term Arthritis Safety Study (CLASS). Although the cardiotoxic effects were thought to be limited to myocardial infarctions, a subsequent meta analysis showed an increase in the occurrence of arrhythmias in COX-2 treated patients as well. The ensuing body of evidence relating to adverse cardiovascular outcomes prompted the FDA to remove rofecoxib (Vioxx®) from the market and led to modified warnings and use of Celecoxib (Celebrex®). Additionally, resulting changes to pain treatment recommendations have led to a significant decline in the use of the COX-2 inhibitors.

Because of the widespread use of NSAIDs and COX-2 inhibitors, the risks associated with their use are of increasing concern. In the recently concluded 2009 American Geriatrics Society (AGS) annual meeting; as a result of their troubling side effect profiles, the revised AGS guidelines on the management of persistent pain to be published in the August issue of the Journal of the American Geriatrics Society adopted the position and will advise physicians to have their elderly patients avoid the use of NSAIDs and COX-2 inhibitors and consider the use of low-dose opioid therapy instead. This position reflects general safety concerns with the use of these agents.

As the population ages, more patients will experience osteoarthritis, rheumatoid arthritis, chronic back pain, chronic musculoskeletal injuries, and migraines. Other ailments such as pain from overexertion, perimensual pain, etc, will also necessitate treatment. It is therefore very likely that gastrointestinal problems will continue to increase as the use of the traditional nonselective NSAIDs in the United States increases because of the concern for cardiovascular complications associated with the COX-2 inhibitors. The elderly are especially at risk for gastrointestinal events, including serious complications.

There therefore remains a need for just as effective, but safer alternatives for the treatment of pain.

Many anecdotal as well as recent studies support the use of natural remedies (herbal) for relief of pain. Historically herbal remedies have not only been reported as effective, but they have been used to treat various ailments and conditions and generally have had very low risk profiles. But such remedies are not typically as effective as pharmaceutical pain relief products that are currently available OTC or by prescription.

THE FIGURES

Embodiments of the invention are herein described, by way of non-limiting example, with reference to the following accompanying Figures:

Figure 18.1 is a graph showing patient response to treatment with the composition of Example 1;

Figure 18.2 is a graph showing the onset of action of the composition of Example 1; and

Figure 18.3 is a graph summarizing the duration of pain relief achieved with use of the composition of Example 1.

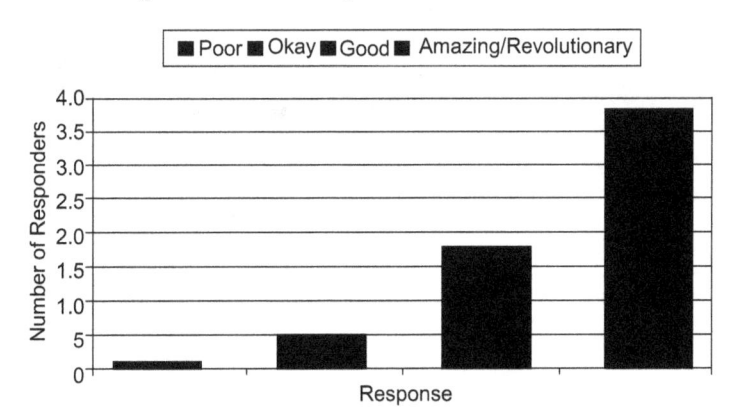

Fig. 18.1: Responder Response to Symptoms Across Pain Scales

DETAILED DESCRIPTION

Generally provided herein are various compositions and methods that provide general analgesic relief of pain for the treatment of pain in mammals. Present embodiments include methods of treating or preventing pain caused e.g., by headaches, including migraines, arthritis, toothaches, menstrual cramps, muscle aches, post operative surgical pain, strains, sprains, inflammation, including acute and chronic pain. Also included are methods of making the compositions herein.

Fig. 18.2: Onset of Analgesic Effect

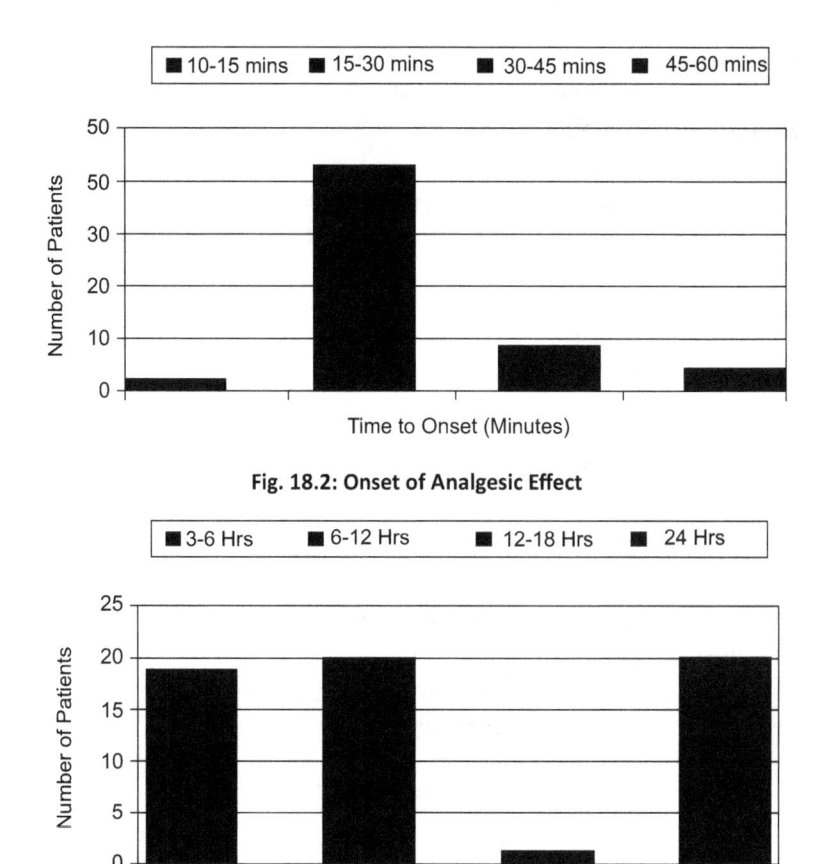

Fig. 18.3: Duration of Pain Relief

Various combinations of natural products have been tried in the past, but the potency and effect of such products was not sufficient to replace prescription or over-the-counter ("OTC") pain reliever products that are synthetically derived in a laboratory. The present inventors discovered that particular combinations of ingredients have unexpectedly superior synergistic pain relieving effects. The potency of the present compositions is much higher for the general analgesic relief of pain than of prior natural products. Therefore, the present compositions can be used as a substitute for synthetic pain relievers, while retaining the safety of a natural product.

The aspects, advantages and/or other features of example embodiments of the invention will become apparent in view of the following detailed description, taken in conjunction with the accompanying drawings. It should be apparent to those skilled in the art that the described embodiments of the present invention provided herein are merely exemplary and illustrative and not limiting. Numerous embodiments of modifications thereof are contemplated as falling within the scope of the present invention and equivalents thereto. All publications, patent applications, patents, and other references mentioned herein are incorporated by reference in their entirety.

In describing example embodiments, specific terminology is employed for the sake of clarity. However, the embodiments are not intended to be limited to this specific terminology.

As used herein, "a" or "an" may mean one or more. As used herein, "another" may mean at least a second or more. Furthermore, unless otherwise required by context, singular terms include pluralities and plural terms include the singular.

As used herein, "composition", "therapeutic composition" and "formulation" may be used interchangeably and refer to a combination of elements that is presented together for a given purpose. Such terms are well known to those of ordinary skill in the art.

As used herein, the term "core ingredient" is intended to encompass those ingredients of the present composition that are the most important in the present compositions and methods. According to non-limiting example embodiments, compositions provided herein include at least the following five core ingredients, *Boswellia serrata*, harpagophytum procumbens (devil's claw), turmeric, white willow and phellodendron amurense. According to other example embodiments, "core ingredients" may include one or more additional or different ingredients than those listed above, such as one or more synergistic ingredients or other natural ingredients that may be used to treat a mammal in need of treatment.

As used herein, the term "synergistic ingredient" is intended to encompass natural ingredients that are not necessarily "core ingredients" in the present compositions, but may be added to the present compositions for example to add to the pain relief that may be achieved by the compositions, or to add to the synergistic effects to be achieved by the present compositions, or to improve efficacy, etc. Non-limiting example embodiments of possible synergistic ingredients include one or more ingredients selected from Chiococca Alba, Dihydroxybergamottin, Lactuca Virosa, Mimosa Pudica, Naringen, Paullinia Tomentosa, and Yerba Mate. According to non-limiting example embodiments, Ulmus Glabra may be a synergistic ingredient, for example as a substitute for Paullinia Tomentosa.

The terms "drug" and "active ingredients" are used herein to include any drug or other active ingredient that may be added to the present compositions in addition to the core and synergistic ingredients for treating mammals for a variety of different conditions.

By way of non-limiting example embodiment, additional core ingredients or other drugs or active ingredients that may be added to the present compositions may include the addition of Bromelian, Green Tea (for example, replacing Yerba mate), and possibly Fish Oil, Lecithin, Essential Fatty acids, Magnesium and/or other minerals. These terms are not meant to be limiting and may include any "active ingredient" and "drug" known to those skilled in the art, which may be incorporated in the formulations herein.

The terms "core ingredients," "synergistic ingredients," and "active ingredients" and "drugs" are intended to encompass such ingredients in all forms including, but not limited to extracts, powders, analogs, prodrugs, salts, esters, polymorphs and/or crystalline forms thereof as would be apparent to those skilled in the art.

The term "excipient" is used herein to include pharmaceutically acceptable inert substances added to a drug formulation to give e.g., a desired consistency or form, or used as a carrier. Non-limiting examples of excipients that may be included in the present compositions and/or formulations herein may include, but are not limited to binders, fillers, diluents, lubricants, disintegrants, super-disintegrants, and other excipients known to those skilled in the art, depending e.g., on the composition being formed, method of formation, active ingredient(s) being used, etc.

As used herein, the term "binder" is intended to encompass binders known to those skilled in the art. The following is a list of non-limiting example embodiments of binders that may be used in accordance with various embodiments herein: acacia, alginic acid, carbomer (e.g., carbopol), carboxymethylcellulose sodium (CMC), dextrin, ethyl cellulose, gelatin, guar gum, hydroxyethyl cellulose (HEC), hydroxypropyl cellulose (e.g., Klucel) (HPC), hydroxypropyl methyl cellulose (e.g., Methoce HPMC), magnesium aluminum silicate, maltodextrin, methylcellulose, polymethacrylates, povidone (e.g., Kollidon, Plasdone PVP K29/32), pregelatinized starch, sodium alginate, starch and zein. As with other excipients herein, the amount of the binder may vary depending on various factors as would be known or can be determined by those skilled in the art.

As used herein, the terms "filler" and "diluent" are intended to encompass fillers known to those skilled in the art. The following is a list of non-limiting example fillers that may be used in accordance with various embodiments herein: microcrystalline cellulose, dextrose, calcium phosphate anhydrous, calcium carbonate, calcium sulfate, compressible sugars, dextrates, dextrin, dibasic calcium phosphate dihydrate, glyceryl palmitostearate, hydrogenated vegetable oil (type I), kaolin, lactose, magnesium carbonate, magnesium oxide, maltodextrin, mannitol, polymethacrylates, potassium chloride, powdered cellulose, pregelatinized starch, sodium chloride, sorbitol, starch, sucrose, sugar spheres, talc and tribasic calcium phosphate. The amount of the filler or diluent may vary depending on various factors as would be known or can be determined by those skilled in the art.

Other "fillers" may act for example, more as compression aids. The following is an additional list of such non-limiting example fillers that may be used in accordance with various embodiments herein: lactose, calcium carbonate, calcium sulfate, compressible sugars, dextrates, dextrin, dextrose, calcium phosphate, kaolin, magnesium carbonate, magnesium oxide, maltodextrin mannitol, powdered cellulose, pregelatinized starch, and sucrose. The amount of such fillers may vary depending on various factors as would be known or can be determined by those skilled in the art.

As used herein, the term "lubricant" is intended to encompass lubricants known to those skilled in the art. The following is a list of non-limiting example embodiments of lubricants that may be used in accordance with various embodiments herein: magnesium stearate, stearic acid, calcium stearate, glyceryl monostearate, glyceryl palmitostearate, hydrogenated castor oil, hydrogenated vegetable oil, light mineral oil, mineral oil, polyethylene glycol, sodium benzoate, sodium lauryl sulfate, sodium stearyl fumarate, talc and zinc stearate. The amount of the lubricant may vary depending on various factors as would be known or can be determined by those skilled in the art.

As used herein, the term "disintegrant" is intended to encompass disintegrants known to those skilled in the art. The following is a list of non-limiting example embodiments of disintegrants that may be used in accordance with various embodiments herein: microcrystalline cellulose, sodium starch glycolate (e.g., Explotab®), croscarmellose sodium (e.g., Ac-Di-Sol®, Primellose®), crospovidone (e.g., Kollidon®, Polyplasdone®), magnesium aluminum silicate, polacrilin potassium, pregelatinized starch, sodium alginate, and starch. The amount of the disintegrant may vary depending on various factors as would be known or can be determined by those skilled in the art.

As used herein, the term "super-disintegrant" is intended to encompass super-disintegrants known to those skilled in the art. The following is a list of non-limiting example embodiments of super-disintegrants that may be used in accordance with various embodiments herein: croscarmellose sodium, crospovidone, and sodium starch glycolate. The amount of the super-disintegrant may vary depending on various factors as would be known or can be determined by those skilled in the art.

As used herein, "extract" or "herbal extract" refers to an extract from a plant, tree, bush, shrub, or other botanical organism, which may be used to impart a positive health benefit when administered to a subject. Extracts may be formed using any suitable technique known to those skilled in the art. By way of non-limiting example, extracts of Harpagophytum procumbens (Devil's claw), may be formed according to the methods set forth in U.S. Pat. No. 6,280,737 or 6,197,307.

As used herein, "an effective amount" refers to an amount of the specified constituent or of an overall composition (such as a tablet, granule, powder, etc.) that is effective in attaining the purpose for which the constituent or composition is provided. Therefore, an effective amount of a composition would be an amount suitable for relieving pain in the mammal to which the composition is administered.

Concentrations, amounts, and other numerical data may be presented herein in a range format. It is to be understood that such range format is used merely for convenience and brevity and should be interpreted flexibly to include not only the numerical values explicitly recited as the limits of the range, but also to include all the individual numerical values or sub-ranges encompassed within that range as if each numerical value and sub-range is explicitly recited.

Depending on the composition or formulation, other excipients may be used as would be apparent to those skilled in the art. For example, as discussed further below, example compositions may include tablets, which may be coated on the outside for easier swallowing by a mammal. If tablets or other formulations are produced without a coating, it may be desirable to add one or more flavoring agents for example, as would be apparent to those skilled in the art. By way of further example, liquid compositions for example, may require one or more carriers.

Example embodiments are directed to therapeutic compositions or formulations that include natural ingredients for the treatment of pain in mammals. In particular, according to non-limiting example embodiments, compositions provided herein may include one or more core ingredients, and optionally one or more synergistic ingredients.

As discussed above, example core ingredients may include one or more (or all) of the following core ingredients, *Boswellia serrata*, harpagophytum procumbens (devil's claw), turmeric, white willow and phellodendron amurense. Thus, non-limiting example embodiments are directed to therapeutic compositions that include *Boswellia serrata*, harpagophytum procumbens, turmeric, white willow and phellodendron amurense.

Also encompassed by the term "core ingredients" are ingredients that provide the same or similar active components as the indicated core ingredients. By way of non-limiting example, *Boswellia serrata* is a source of boswellic acid, which may provide relief from pain and inflammation. Other sources of boswellic acid may include for example, extracts of: *Boswellia* bhau-dajiana, *Boswellia frereana*, *Boswellia papyrifera*, Sudanese *Boswellia sacra*, and *Boswellia carterii*, Commiphora incisa, Commiphora myrrha, Commiphora abyssinica, Commiphora erthraea, Commiphora molmol, and Bursera microphylla, may be used as a substitute for or in conjunction with *Boswellia serrata*, and are also encompassed by the term "core ingredients". An extract providing the boswellic acid preferably comprises in the range from about 20% to about 40% (could be up to 65%) by weight of the dose.

According to other example embodiments, "core ingredients" may include one or more additional or different ingredients than those listed above, such as one or more synergistic ingredients or other natural ingredients. Thus, additional compositions encompassed hereby may include *Boswellia serrata*, harpagophytum procumbens, turmeric, white willow, phellodendron amurense, and at least one additional core ingredient.

According to example embodiments, the present compositions may additionally include one or more synergistic ingredients. As indicated above, the term "synergistic ingredient" is intended to encompass natural ingredients that are not necessarily "core ingredients" in the present compositions. Non-limiting example embodiments of possible synergistic ingredients include one or more (or all) ingredients selected from Chiococca Alba, Dihydroxybergamottin, Lactuca Virosa, Mimosa Pudica, Naringen, Paullinia Tomentosa, and Yerba Mate. Further example compositions include all of the following synergistic ingredients Chiococca Alba, Dihydroxybergamottin, Lactuca Virosa, Mimosa Pudica, Naringen, Paullinia Tomentosa, and Yerba Mate. According to non-limiting example embodiments, Ulmus Glabra may be a synergistic ingredient, for example as a substitute for Paullinia Tomentosa.

According to non-limiting example embodiments, the "core" ingredients may be added to the composition in approximately equal weight amounts. By way of example, the core ingredients may be present in the composition generally in an amount of about 25 to about 100 mg, or in an amount of about 30 to about 70 mg each or about 50 mg each. This amount may vary however, depending for example on the particular ingredient. For example, white willow may be present in an amount up to 240 mg per pill, or 5-17 weight% but this may also vary depending on the composition of the blend, adding or subtracting ingredients, which may increase or decrease the total mg dose and weight of the tablet. According to further embodiments, the synergistic ingredients may also be added in approximately equal weight amounts, which may be for example about 25 to about 100 mg, or about 30 to about 70 mg each, or about 50 mg each. But each ingredient may vary in amount such that it is present for example, in an amount of about 5-40 weight percent of the tablet.

According to example embodiments, the dose of core ingredients, synergistic ingredients, and active ingredient in the present formulations may vary up to about 200, 100 or 50 mg. Dosages may be determined by those skilled in the art.

Non-limiting example embodiments are directed to tablet compositions that include approximately 50 mg each of the following core and synergistic ingredients formed into an approximately 600 mg tablet for oral administration to a mammal.

- *Boswellia serrata*;
- Turmeric;
- White willow;
- Phellodendron Amurense;
- Devil's claw (Harpagophytum Procumbens);
- Paullinia Tomentosa (or optionally Ulmus Glabra);
- Milkberry;
- Mimosa Pudica;
- Lactuca Virosa;
- Naringen;
- 6-7 Dihydroxybergamottin; and
- Yerba mate.

Each ingredient herein may be present in an appropriate extract, powder or other form for adding to the present compositions, as would be apparent to those skilled in the art.

Example compositions may include one or more excipients that may be selected, for example based on the type of composition being formed. Such excipient(s) may include for example, at least one excipient comprises at least one excipient selected from the group consisting of binders, fillers, diluents, lubricants, disintegrants, and super-disintegrants. By way of non-limiting example embodiment, the present compositions may include at least one excipient selected from the group consisting of microcrystalline cellulose, dextrose sodium starch glycolate, magnesium stearate, stearic acid, silica, and carnauba wax.

According to non-limiting example embodiments, mammals or patients may be directed to take for example two tablets (or other formulation) up to three times daily, depending for example on the weight of the mammal, symptom being treated, etc. Appropriate dosages may be determined by those skilled in the art.

According to non-limiting example embodiments, the present compositions help provide general analgesic relief of the pain associated with headaches, migraines, arthritis, toothaches, menstrual cramps, muscle aches, post operative surgical pain, strains, sprains, inflammation, chronic pain and other sources of pain.

Example compositions may include at least one additional drug or active ingredient that may be added to any of the present compositions, for example, to improve the ability of the present compositions to provide such pain relief. By way of non-limiting example embodiments, compositions herein may include one or more known natural or synthetic pain relievers or other drugs, such as NSAIDs, synthetic COX-2 inhibitors, etc.... By way of further example, such a pain reliever or other drug may include such drug in a smaller dosage than a typical formulation of such drug, to add some of the synergistic effect of the composition, while lessening potential side effects.

According to non-limiting example embodiments the compositions or formulations may be in the form of a tablet (which may be coated or uncoated). Other possible formulations may include capsules (hard or soft), liquid, powders, granules, suspensions, sachets, or additives to food substances or beverages, or even may be made into a tea, etc.

In embodiments in which the compositions are formed into tablets, the tablets formed herein can be at least partially or fully coated with a tablet coating composition known to those skilled in the art. An example coating may include one or more coating known to those skilled in the art, including, but not limited to, one or more of the following:

e.g., Surelease® (ethylcellulose), carnauba wax, cellulose acetate phthalate (CAP), cetyl alcohol, ethyl cellulose, gelatin, hydroxyethyl cellulose, hydroxypropyl cellulose, hydroxypropyl methylcellulose, microcrystalline wax, Opadry and Opadry II, polymethacrylates, polyvinyl alcohol, shellac, zein, Eudragit NE30D, Eudragit RS 30D, Eudragit RL30D, Methylcellulose, Cellulose Acetate Pthalate CAP), HPMCAS, Opadry, and Opadry II. According to non-limiting examples, a coating may be present in an amount of about 10% to about 20% by weight or in a thickness of about 10 to about 15 μm. The coating method may be performed by methods available to those skilled in the art.

Formulations, such as tablets, may be formulated into controlled release, immediate release, sustained release or extended release formulations.

Tablets in accordance herewith may weigh approximately 400 mg to about 800 mg or about 600 mg. Other tablet weights can also be used depending on ingredients and dosages desired, and depending on the mammal to whom the tablet is to be administered.

Example embodiments are also directed to methods of making the compositions or formulations herein. Such methods may include known tableting methods. A tablet may be made by compression or moulding, optionally with one or more accessory ingredients. Compressed tablets may be prepared by compressing in a suitable machine the active ingredient in a free-flowing form such as a powder or granules, optionally mixed with a binder (e.g. inert diluent, preservative disintegrant, sodium starch glycollate, cross-linked povidone, cross-linked sodium carboxymethyl cellulose) surface-active or dispersing agent. Moulded tablets may be made my moulding in a suitable machine a mixture of the powdered compound moistened with an inert liquid diluent.

By way of non-limiting example embodiment, tableting methods may include combining all or many of the ingredients (such as core, and/or synergistic ingredients and/or excipients) to form a mixture and compressing or compacting the mixture to form a tablet.

The present methods may further include adding a coating over the tablet according to techniques known to those skilled in the art. Tablets may optionally be coated or scored and may be formulated so as to provide slow or controlled release of the active ingredient therein using, for example, hydroxypropylmethyl cellulose in varying proportions to provide the desired release profile. Tablets may optionally be provided with an enteric coating, to provide release in parts of the gut other than the stomach.

For preparing solid orally administered compositions such as capsules or tablets, the principal active ingredients may be mixed with at least one pharmaceutical carrier (e.g., conventional tableting ingredients such as cellulose, corn starch, lactose, sucrose, sorbitol, talc, stearic acid, magnesium stearate, dicalcium phosphate or gums) and other pharmaceutical diluents (e.g., water) to form a solid preformulation composition containing a substantially homogenous mixture of the composition of this invention, or a non-toxic pharmaceutically acceptable salt thereof. When referring to the preformulation compositions as substantially homogenous, it is meant that the active ingredients are dispersed reasonably evenly throughout the composition so that the composition may be readily subdivided into equally effective unit dosage forms such as capsules, pills and tablets. This solid preformulation composition can then be subdivided into unit dosage forms containing, for example, of the active-ingredient composition (which may include for example, the core ingredients or the core and synergistic ingredients).

Liquid preparations for oral administration may take the form of, for example, solutions, syrups or suspensions, or they may be presented as a dry product for reconstitution with water or other suitable vehicles before use. Such liquid preparations may be prepared by conventional means with pharmaceutically acceptable additives such as suspending agents (e.g., sorbitol syrup, methyl cellulose, or hydrogenated edible fats); emulsifying agents (e.g., lecithin or acacia); non-aqueous vehicles (e.g., almond oil, oily esters or ethyl alcohol); preservatives (e.g., methyl or propyl p-hydroxybenzoates or sorbic acid); and artificial or natural colors and/or sweeteners.

Also encompassed herein are methods of treating a mammal (including, but not limited to humans). Example methods include administering to a mammal in need thereof, an effective amount of a composition or formulation provided herein.

Such administration, for example in the case of tablets, is typically by oral administration to a mammal. Other forms of administration known to those skilled in the art are contemplated, depending on the formulation. By way of non-limiting example embodiment, other potential methods of administration may include methods known to those skilled in the art including, but not limited to, intraperitoneally, intravenously, orally, subcutaneously, intradermally, transdermally (e.g. pain patch), intramuscularly, intravascularly, endotracheally, intraosseously, intra-arterially, intravesicularly, intrapleurally, topically, intraventricularly, or through a lumbar puncture (intrathecally).

Formulations, such as tablets, may be used for treating mammals for a variety of different conditions. The present embodiments are generally to be used for the symptomatic relief of pain, such as minor to moderate acute pain (such as headaches, toothaches, menstrual cramps, muscle strains/sprains, inflammation etc). Thus, the compositions herein should be taken as directed until the pain is relieved. In a case of chronic pain (such as pain caused by osteoarthritis and rheumatoid arthritis, degenerative joint and disc disease), the present compositions may need to be taken for longer periods of time, but one must follow up with a physician for such uses, in order to minimize the potential for adverse events and to make sure that no other intervention is needed.

A recommended dosage for non-limiting example embodiments may include two tablets every 6-8 hours, or 3 times a day. Dosage may be adjusted however, (e.g., 3 at a time) to achieve desired affects; however, it is recommended that one should not exceed 6 tables in any given 24 hour period.

The herbal composition of this invention may be combined with a physiologically acceptable oral vehicle into unit dosages. A unit dosage may comprise a therapeutically effective amount of each herbal extract for a single daily administration (e.g., orally), or it can be formulated into smaller quantities of each ingredient to provide for multiple doses in a day. A unit dosage will depend upon many factors including age, size, and condition of the individual being treated and the number of times the unit will be taken in a single day. In any event, the entire daily dosage will be that which is physiologically acceptable to an individual and may be administered daily over a prolonged period of time.

The present compositions are unlike any other pain management product on the market. They combine the analgesic effect of natural opioid agonists with natural anti-inflammatories and also support gastro-intestinal health. Example compositions according to the present application are believed to be safer, more potent, and provide effective, lasting relief of pain from many conditions including for example, headaches, migraines, arthritis, toothaches, menstrual cramps, muscle aches, post operative surgical pain, strains, sprains, inflammation, chronic pain, etc.

The present compositions are presently believed to work by inhibiting damaged tissue from making prostaglandins. Prostaglandins are chemicals that allow one to feel pain. They are produced by the breakdown of arachidonic acid. By inhibiting prostaglandin production, the present compositions effectively decrease pain and inflammation.

As discussed further in the examples, below, to Applicants' knowledge, the present compositions are not associated with the adverse side effects of synthetic over-the-counter NSAID's and prescription pain relievers, such as COX-2 inhibitors.

The following examples are provided to further illustrate various non-limiting embodiments and techniques. It should be understood, however, that these examples are meant to be illustrative and do not limit the scope of the claims. As would be apparent to skilled artisans, many variations and modifications are intended to be encompassed within the spirit and scope of the invention.

EXPERIMENTAL EXAMPLES

Example 1. Example Composition

In this example, an herbal pain killer was formulated in accordance with example embodiments. This example provides an example of a blend of twelve specific medicinal herbs (five (5) core ingredients and seven (7) synergistic ingredients), in accordance with non-limiting example embodiments provided herein. Extensive research was performed by the present inventors on medicinal herbs and herbs with antioxidant qualities and those that may inhibit certain cytokines/mediators of pain and inflammation e.g. PGE2, COX-2, TNF, IL-1, etc. Twelve specific medicinal herbs were chosen and then processed utilizing specific manufacturing techniques. Typically the ingredients are purchased by the manufacturer from the raw materials distributor who has already performed any extracting and puts the ingredient in a form amenable to further processing, e.g. powder etc. to obtain a tablet of specific dosage.

According to examples herein the following twelve ingredients are combined in approximately 50 mg increments into an approximately 600 mg tablet:

- Paullinia Tomentosa Extract (leaves); Milkberry Extract (leaves);
- Mimosa Pudica Extract (whole plant);
- Phellodendron Amurense Extract (bark);
- Lactuca Virosa Extract (leaves);
- White willow bark extract, 25% Salicin;
- Turmeric Extract (rhizome);
- Devil's claw (Harpagophytum Procubens);
- *Boswellia serrata* extract (resin/gum) (e.g., 65% total acids);
- Naringen (fruit);
- 6-7 Dihydroxybergamottin; and

- Yerba mate extract 8%.

Additionally, the following excipients were included in the composition of this example:
- Microcrystalline cellulose;
- Dextrose;
- Sodium starch glycolate;
- Magnesium stearate;
- Stearic acid;
- Silica; and
- Carnauba wax.

Example 2. Tablet Formulation of Herbal Pain Killer

In this example, the herbal pain killer of Example 1 was formulated into a tablet composition, which included approximately 50 mg each of the following ingredients formed into an approximately 600 mg tablet:
- Paullinia Tomentosa Extract;
- Milkberry Extract;
- Mimosa Pudica Extract;
- Phellodendron Amurense Extract;
- Lactuca Virosa Extract;
- White willow bark 25% extract;
- Turmeric Extract;
- Devil's claw;
- *Boswellia serrata* extract;
- Naringen;
- 6-7 Dihydroxybergamottin; and
- Yerba mate extract 8%.

Also included in the present tablet formulation were the following excipients Microcrystalline cellulose; Dextrose; Sodium starch glycolate; Magnesium stearate; Stearic acid; Silica; and Carnauba wax.

The tablets were formed using common compression tableting techniques. The tablets were thereafter coated using well known coating techniques using a coating of Carnauba wax.

Example 3. Non-Randomized, Open Label, Efficacy Study.

This example provides observational results of administering the composition of Examples 1 and 2, of twelve specific medicinal herbs, in a non-randomized, open-label study to evaluate the efficacy for the general relief of pain in healthy volunteers. The objectives of this phase II study were to determine if the composition of Examples 1 and 2 is effective at providing general relief of various types of pain and compare the subjective results participants obtained with this composition to other OTC or prescription pain relief products they commonly use, as well as describe any adverse events the participants experienced.

In this study various parameters were specifically evaluated. The present inventors found that the composition of Example 1 was just as effective if not better than the synthetic pain relievers typically utilized by the participants in most cases, was well tolerated and that most of the participants would not only recommend it to others but would utilize it as their primary pain reliever in the future. The inventors ultimately concluded that the composition of Example 1 is a safe and effective pain reliever and will become a very popular alternative to typical OTC and prescription pain relief products.

Extensive research was preliminarily done by the present inventors on medicinal herbs that may be utilized to treat conditions such as arthritis, menstrual cramps, headaches etc., as well as on herbs that had been known for their anti-oxidant qualities and for those known to inhibit certain cytokines/mediators of pain and inflammation e.g. PGE2, COX-2, TNF, IL-1 etc. The twelve specific medicinal herbs were chosen and then processed utilizing specific manufacturing techniques to obtain a tablet of specific dosage.

Study Population

Patients selected for inclusion in the trial were:
- generally otherwise healthy and experiencing pain; acute or chronic;
- *at least 16 years of age and able to complete a questionnaire capturing self-reported use of OTC/prescription analgesics for pain relief; and
- able to comprehend and comply with requirements of the study. (*Participants who were currently utilizing pain medication were advised to discontinue it during the study, unless medically contraindicated. Potential risks associated with concomitant use of multiple pain products were also explained in detail to participants prior to their inclusion.)

Patients were excluded from the trial if:
- they had a participated in a study involving OTC/prescription pain relief products within the past 12 months;
- they had a known allergy to any of the ingredients in the composition of Example 1;
- if they were pregnant, trying to become pregnant, or breastfeeding;
- they had previous treatment with herbal pain relief remedies with similar ingredients;
- they had a medical condition, in the judgment of the examiner and/or study investigators, that may preclude the safe participation in the

protocol or prevent completion of the study, such as: uncontrolled angina and/or congestive heart failure, severe chronic obstructive pulmonary disease, active treatment for cancer, major psychiatric disease, other systemic disease, or significant abnormalities of hematological, cardiac, pulmonary, metabolic, renal, hepatic, gastrointestinal or other systems;
- they were currently using anti-coagulants (Coumadin, heparin, aspirin >325 mg day); or
- they had a history of drug and/or alcohol abuse sufficient to hinder compliance with treatment or follow up procedures.

A total of 62 healthy volunteers completed the study. Patients in this trial had an age range of 16-77 years. There were 38 females, and 24 males. One group of 32 was required to take the composition of example 1 for at least 4 weeks for various pain related conditions e.g. degenerative arthritis, post-surgical etc. The remaining 30 were asked to take the composition of example 1 on an as needed basis for acute pain relief e.g. headaches, menstrual cramps, toothaches etc. Questionnaires were designed to assess how effective the composition of example 1 was at relieving their pain, and to compare it with other pain relievers they've taken in the past and also assess any adverse events. The following parameters were also assessed: pain severity (mild, moderate, severe), relief after using the composition of example 1 (poor, okay, good, amazing, revolutionary), onset of action (e.g. 20 min, 1 hr etc.), duration of relief, # of pills needed to achieve desired effect, adverse events/side effects, and if they would continue to utilize it and possibly recommend it to others.

RESULTS

Table 18.1: Baseline Characteristics of Subjects

	Characteristic	Treatment Group
Age-yr		
	Range	16 77
Sex-number (%)		
	Female	38 (61.3)
	Male	24 (38.7)
Pain Severity-number		
	Mild	5
	Moderate	38
	Severe	19
Past Pain Reliever Use		
	Advil	10
	Aleve	8
	Aspirin	7

	Diclofenac	1
	Ibuprofen	28
	Imitrex	1
	Methadone	1
	Mobic	1
	Nubaine	1
	Naproxen	2
	Oxycodone	1
	Tylenol	12
	Tylenol, Extra Strength	4
	Ultram	1
	Vicodin	2

Cause of Painful Condition

Osteoarthritis of the spine, hip, knee, hands and shoulder

Rheumatoid arthritis

Chronic rotator cuff tears

Tendonitis

Menstrual cramps

Headaches (tension, migraine)

Muscle strains (cervical, lumbar)

General aches

Motor vehicle accident

High level sports related muscle soreness

Post Surgical

A significant proportion of patients rated their pain as either moderate or severe, 61% and 31% respectively. Prior to entry in the trial patients consumed a wide variety of medications for their pain. Ibuprofen, Tylenol, including the extra strength variety, and Advil were the most widely used analgesics. On entering the trial, patients listed an assortment of reasons as the causative nature of their pain; these are listed in Table 18.1.

Relief Experienced w/ the composition of Example 1 by subjective pain scale

- Mild Group:
- Okay (2)
- Good (2)
- Amazing/Revolutionary (1)

- Moderate Group:
- Okay (3)
- Good (10)
- Amazing (20)
- Amazing/Revolutionary (1)
- Revolutionary (4)
- Moderate/Severe Group:
- Amazing (3)
- Revolutionary (1)
- Severe Group:
- Poor (1)
- Good (5)
- Good/Amazing (1) Amazing (5)
- Revolutionary (3)

Figure 18.1 shows patient response to treatment with the composition of Example 1. Responders were asked to rate their level of pain relief after using the composition of Example 1 as either poor, okay, good, amazing or revolutionary. 56 (90.4%) of patients rated their response as good, amazing or revolutionary. Significantly, 45% of patients rated their response as either amazing or revolutionary. Overall response to treatment was similar when patients were assessed based on their initial assessment of pain rated as mild, moderate, or severe. Of all the patients followed only 1 patient (in the severe pain group) rated their response as poor. However, even in this group of patients with severe pain, 8 of 15 patients rated their pain relief as amazing or revolutionary while the remaining 6 patients rated their relief as good or amazing.

Onset of Action ranged from 10 minutes to 1 hour with 76% experiencing relief within 30 minutes and the remaining 24% within the first hour. Figure 2 is a graph showing the onset of action of the composition of Example 1. Most patients (76%) achieved pain relief within 30 minutes after dosing. Ninety four (94%) percent of patients achieved relief within 45 minutes and after 1 hour all patients reported having relief of pain.

- 10-15 min (3)
- 15 min (1)
- 15-30 min (1)
- 20 min (6)
- 20-30 min (7)
- 25 min (4)
- 25-30 min (4)

- 30 min (21)
- 30-45 min (2)
- 35 min (4)
- 40-45 min (1)
- 45 min (4)
- 45 min-1 hr (4)

Figure 3 summarizes the duration of pain relief achieved with the use of the composition of Example 1. Duration of relief ranged from 3 hours to all day, with one even reporting relief of osteoarthritis pain for 4 days. Thirty-four percent experienced at least 6-16 hours of relief and thirty-three percent reported all day relief of symptoms.

- 3 hrs (2)
- 4 hrs (8)
- 4-5 hrs (2)
- 5 hrs (6)
- 5-6 hrs (1)
- 6 hrs (6)
- 6-8 hrs (3)
- 7 hrs (4)
- 8 hrs (5)
- 10 hrs (1)
- 12 hrs (1)
- 16 hrs (1)
- All day (20)
- 4 days (1)
- Discontinued (1)

Number of pills utilized to achieve desired effects ranged from 1 to 4 per dose.

Patients	# of pills per does
3	1
23	2
14	3
22	4

Reported adverse events/Side effects
- Constipation (1)**

- Heartburn (1)
- Sedation (1)
- Abdominal cramping (1)*** *

In the patients reporting adverse events all except the patient who experienced abdominal cramping still reported achieving amazing, okay, and okay relief of their pain complaints, respectively. Furthermore, 2 of the 3 would also consider taking the compositions of example 1 in the future and recommend it to others.**This patient had a history of gastritis and was concomitantly taking ibuprofen despite our specifically advising her to discontinue it.***This patient had a history of significant gastroesophageal reflux disease.

The composition of Example 1 was generally well tolerated with the only adverse events reported being single reports of constipation, heartburn, sedation and abdominal cramping, respectively.

The number of patients that indicated they would make the composition of Example 1 their primary pain relief choice and recommend to others was as follows:
- Yes (58)
- No (2)
- Will use in combination with other meds (1)
- Maybe (1)

Overall results were good to excellent in both treatment groups, e.g. 94% in the 4 week group and 90% in the acute pain group for subjective pain relief, average onset of action duration of relief and # of pills utilized.

Based on the results obtained from this study, the present example composition is surprisingly as effective if not more effective than the reported OTC and prescription NSAIDs and COX-2 inhibitors typically utilized by the consumers who participated in this study. Furthermore, the very low incidence of reported adverse events supports the historically excellent safety profiles of these particular ingredients. Overall the composition of Example 1 was shown to be both effective and safe.

The inventors acknowledge that this was not a randomized blinded study. However, as the information provided was given subjectively from volunteer participants who received no compensation, except free product during the study, potential bias is mitigated. The inventors are confident that based on its efficacy and safety, the composition of Example 1 will become a very attractive OTC natural pain relief alternative for consumers.

Example 4. Formation of Extracts

Some of the core and synergistic ingredients of the present application, may initially require being formed into an extract. An extract of certain ingredients is formed prior to mixing the ingredients to form a composition for administration to a mammal. This example provides a non-limiting example of how an extract may be formed from leaves.

Once leaves of a specific ingredient have been harvested, it may be desirable to reduce the leaves in size, for example leaf fragments, rather than adding to water (and/or other aqueous substances such as ethanol or methanol) as whole leaves. Those of ordinary skill in the art will recognize a variety of mechanisms for reducing the leaves to leaf fragments or bits, such as by chopping, cutting, crushing, tearing, slicing, etc., any of which may be suitably used. While the temperature of the cold water may vary, in some aspects, it may be less than about 25° C. Additionally, the amount of water (and/or other ingredient such as methanol or ethanol as would be apparent to those skilled in the art) with which the quantity of leaves is mixed may also vary.

Once the appropriate mixture ratio of leaves to water is obtained, the leaves of the mixture are then pulverized, in order to ruptured the cells of the tea leaves, and the mixture is maintained for an amount of time sufficient to release intracellular material from the leaves into the water and create an aqueous extract component and a leaf residue component. It should be understood that any method of pulverizing which physically ruptures the leaf cells, such as homogenizing, milling, grinding, chopping, blending, cutting, tearing, etc., may be used. A number of specific devices that may be suitably used to pulverized the tea leaves in the leaf and water mixture will be recognized by those of ordinary skill in the art, such as homogenizer, colloidal mills, stone mills, ball mills or tangential fluid energy mills. In accordance with the present method, the leaves in the leaf and water mixture may be subjected to various degrees of pulverization. However, in one aspect, at least about 75% of all leaf cells may be ruptured. In another aspect, at least about 80% to about 99% of all leaf cells may be ruptured.

The specific degree of pulverization, as well as other factors such as the exact type of plant used, the time of year at which the leaves were harvested, and the amount of time that the leaf and water mixture is maintained following pulverization, will determine the efficiency of the overall extract process.

Once the aqueous extract component has received a desired amount of intracellular material, the leaf residue component may be removed or separated from the aqueous extract component, and the aqueous extract component may then be collected. Those of ordinary skill in the art will recognize a number of ways in which the leaf residue component may be physically separated from the aqueous extract component, such as by centrifugation, super centrifugation, filtration, ultra filtration, etc., which do not require elevated temperatures, or any chemicals, such as solvents, etc.

After the aqueous extract component has been collected it may be used in the formation of compositions herein, or it may, optionally be further processed in order to create an extract formulation having desired characteristics. For example, in one aspect, after collection, the aqueous extract may be dried into a solid or a semi-solid state, such as a powdered form. Any of the various well known drying techniques, such as freeze-drying, or spray drying may be used. Additionally, various excipients may be added to the extract, either before or after drying, which may be required in order to provide a formulation with desired properties or forms, such as a powder, granule, tablet, capsule, etc. Those of ordinary skill in the art will recognize a number of excipients that may be suitably added, such as fillers, binders, sweeteners, flavors and other ingredients. Nearly any excipients that are known for use in the preparation of oral dosage pharmaceutical products, or natural supplement products, can be used. Examples of such excipients include without limitation, carbomer, carboxymethylcellulose sodium, cellulose, dextrin, dextrose, ethylcellulose, fructose, gelatin, guar gum, hydroxyethyl cellulose, hydroxypropyl cellulose, hydroxypropyl methylcellulose, glucose, maltodextrin, mannitol, methylcellulose, microcrystalline cellulose, polymethacrylates, povidone, sorbitol, starches, sucrose, sugar, sucralose, stevia, and flavor agents.

A number of agents may be included in the extraction process and the formulation of the present invention in order to improve the stability thereof by decreasing degradation of polyphenols, chlorophyll, or other beneficial ingredients, provided by the plant, such as L-theanine, tannins, vitamins, amino acids, minerals, proteins, and soluble fiber. Non-limiting examples of such agents which may be used include without limitation, may include vitamin C, or its derivatives, vitamin E or its derivatives, grape seed and its extract, wine and fruit polyphenols, beta-carotene, co-enzyme Q-10, alpha lipoic acid, N-acetyl cysteine, ascorbyl palmitate, butylhydroxinon, butylated hydroxyanisole (BHA), butylated hydroxytoluene (BHT), citric acid, calcium lactate, dodecyl gallate, erythorbic acid, fumaric acid, gallic acid, lactic acid, malic acid, magnesium lactate, octyl gallate, phosphoric acid, potassium citrate, potassium lactate, potassium tartrate, sodium ascorbate, sodium citrate, sodium erythobate, sodium lactate, sodium metabisulfite, sodium phosphate, sodium tartrate. In a detailed aspect, the antioxidant may be vitamin C or a vitamin C derivative, vitamin E or a vitamin E derivative, citric acid or its derivative, gallic acid or its derivative, and malic acid.

Although the invention has been described in example embodiments, additional modifications and variations would be apparent to those skilled in the art. It is therefore to be understood that the inventions herein may be practiced other than as specifically described, for example with respect to the formulation type, tablet size, coating, excipients, etc.... Thus, the present embodiments should be considered in all respects as illustrative and not restrictive. Accordingly, it is intended that such changes and modifications fall within the present invention as defined by the claims appended hereto.

19 Preparation for Weight Loss Management

A relatively high percentage of U.S. population is overweight, that is, exhibiting a basic metabolic index or body mass index (BMI) greater than 25, and one quarter of the U.S. population is obese, exhibiting a BMI greater than 30. Annually, a large number of deaths can be attributed to obesity. Therefore, a healthy weight maintenance requires a balance between energy intake and energy output for an individual.

Adipose derived hormones such as adiponectin and leptin are secreted by adipose tissue and control various physiological systems in a mammalian body. Low leptin levels, for example, stimulate food intake, reduce energy expenditure, and modulate neuroendocrine and immune functions to conserve energy stores. While normally leptin is a signal that reduces appetite, it is known that obese persons have an unusually high circulating concentration of leptin and may be resistant to the usual effects of leptin in a manner similar to patients suffering from Type 2 diabetes that are resistant to the effects of insulin. High sustained concentrations of leptin may result in undesirable leptin desensitization or leptin resistance.

Adiponectin is produced by adipocytes in adipose tissue and is secreted into the bloodstream. Levels of adiponectin in the bloodstream are inversely correlated with body fat percentage in adults. It is believed that adiponectin plays a role in the suppression of metabolic events that may result in Type 2 diabetes and obesity.

DESCRIPTION

The present compositions include an ethanolic extract from Gymnema sylvestre leaves in powder form. This ethanolic extract is constituted by about 25 to about 55 weight percent of gymnemic acids, but may also contain gymnemasaponins. There are 18 known gymnemic acids, i.e., gymnemic acids I-XVIII, and the term "gymnemic acid" as used herein includes one or more of the aforementioned gymnemic acids which may or may not be acylated. Particularly desirable for the present compositions are gymnemic acids III, IV, V and VII.

A preferred solid, ethanolic extract from Gymnema sylvestre is prepared as set forth below.

1. Gymnema sylvestre leaves are sourced and checked for their botanical purity. The leaves are then disintegrated (powdering the leaves into

smaller size using a pulveriser) to a size passing through a 20 Mesh sieve, U.S. Standard Sieve Series.
2. Obtained powder is then extracted with 50% v/v ethanol and demineralized water (solvent). 40 grams of powdered leaves are held in 1 liter of solvent at room temperature overnight-up to 12 hours in a shaker, distributed in four Erlenmeyer flasks. The contents are then pooled and filtered.
3. The obtained micelle is concentrated under reduced pressure (650-700 mm) to 30% solids at pH of less than or equal to 2.
4. The concentrate from above is dissolved in 1 liter of demineralized water at room temperature, in a shaker for 4 hours while adjusting the final pH to about 4.5 to about 5, and filtered to remove any precipitate and sludge.
5. The obtained filtrate is adjusted to a pH of about 2 and filtered to remove any precipitate and sludge.
6. The new filtrate is concentrated under reduced pressure (650-700 mm) to 30% solids, and sterilized (Heat Sterilization) at about 80° C. for 2 hours.
7. The product is adjusted for at least 25 but no more than 55% by weight gymnemic acid, preferably about 35 to about 45 weight percent gymnemic acid.
8. The product is then dried in spray dryer at inlet temp of 160° C. and outlet temp of 85° C.
9. The dried product is checked for gymnemic acid content.
10. The powder is homogenized and sifted to 80-100 Mesh, U.S. Standard Sieve Series.

The solid, ethanolic extract from *Boswellia serrata* gum is rich in boswellic acids, particularly the alpha, beta, and gamma boswellic acids. These acids comprise a pentacyclic triterpene, a carboxyl group, and at least one other functional group which can be a hydroxyl group, an acetyl group or a keto group.

A preferred solid, ethanolic extract from *Boswellia serrata* gum is prepared as set forth below.

1. The *Boswellia* gum exudate is cleaned by removing bark and foreign organic matter adhering to the exudate.
2. The exudate is then extracted with ethanol.
3. The ethanol is then partially distilled from the obtained micella which is adjusted to a slightly alkaline pH.
4. The obtained gum product is then extracted with petroleum ether and ethanol in a liquid—liquid extractor at ambient temperature.

5. The obtained liquid phases are separated and processed separately.
6. The petroleum ether fraction affords an aromatic fraction mainly composed of essential oil and resinous matter. The recovery is done by distillation. This matter is removed.
7. The ethanolic fraction is further processed by heating under vacuum to remove residual petroleum ether.
8. The processed ethanolic fraction is concentrated to 30-35% solids and poured under vigorous stirring into demineralized water to produce a boswellic acid precipitate which is recovered.
9. The precipitate is washed with 80/20 v/v ethanol and ethyl acetate mixture to remove any unwanted fractions of boswellic acid until 70% boswellic acid by weight is achieved with only an alpha, beta, and gamma boswellic acid present.
10. The aqueous phase is decanted off. Precipitate is washed further with demineralized water, and dried under vacuum at a temperature of about 60° C.
11. The dried flakes obtained are pulverized, and contain at least 70% by weight of boswellic acids.

The solid, ethanolic extract from the stems of Tinospora cordifolia contains diterpenes such as tinosporaside, cordiofolide, cordifol, heptacosanol, clerodane furano diterpene, diterpenoid furanolactone tinosporidine, columbin and beta-sitosterol.

A preferred solid, ethanolic extract can be prepared as shown below.
1. Well matured Tinospora cordifolia stems, \!3 to ⅓ diameter and 33 to 53 in length, with the outside bark color of dark brown having irregular thin red lines, are washed with water and dried in cool shade, and then crushed in a disintegrator into coarse chunks, from which the bark pieces are removed.
2. The coarse chunks of the stems are pulverized and the remainder of the bark is separated therefrom. The inner body of the stems, having light beige to light brown color, constitute the starting powder material ("core") which is then treated further.
3. 200 Grams of the "core" powder material are then extracted with two liters of 50% v/v ethanol followed by demineralized water.
4. The extracted solutions received from the foregoing hydro-alcoholic and aqueous extractions are concentrated separately, and then mixed in a homogenizer to make a homogenous solution before final concentration.
5. The concentration is done under controlled temperature at pH of less than about 4 for about two hours.

6. When a concentration of 30-35% solids is achieved, the material can be spray dried, or it can be further concentrated to a thick paste of 65-70% solids.
7. The concentrate or the thick paste are then dried in vacuum tray dryer or rotary vacuum dryer at a temperature not to exceed about 65° C.
8. The obtained dried flakes are pulverized to 80-100 Mesh, U.S. Sieve Series, and packed under hygienic conditions.
9. Before packing the powder can be sterilized, if desired, by passing through a hot duct maintained at a temperature of 120° C.

The solid, ethanolic extract from Commiphora mukul gum contains guggalsterone, also known as guggal lipid.

A preferred extract can be prepared as shown below.

1. The Commiphora mukul gum is first checked for purity by TLC, and subjected to a four step grading process.
2. 200 Grams of selected, crushed gum is then loaded into an extractor and ethanol, about five times the weight of gum with water (50/50) is charged through the extractor.
3. In the extractor the temperature is kept between 65-70° C. and the ethanol-water is circulated under turbulence conditions for through mixing and efficient extraction.
4. Extracted mucilage is then taken to a falling film evaporator for solvent recovery.
5. The obtained guggal paste is then enriched in guggalsterones by solvent fractionation.
6. The enriched paste obtained in this manner is then kept under vacuum for solvent removal.
7. The product is then dried in a fluid bed dryer.
8. The dried product is sieved and again tested for guggalsterone content.

The present invention is illustrated by the following examples.

Example 1. Weight Reduction Using Enhanced G. sylvestre Extract

Obese volunteers (n=10; 6 male, 4 female), marginally diabetic and about 20 percent overweight patients, were treated with a solid, ethanolic extract of G. sylvestre or a solid, ethanolic extract of G. sylvestre enhanced by the addition of an amount of a solid, steranolic extract of B. serrata in an amount sufficient to provide a boswellic acid content of about 3.5 percent by weight of the total composition.

The patients exhibited a fasting blood sugar level (FBS) of 130-140 milligrams per deciliter (mg/dl). The average age of the patient group was 35-45 years.

The composition was administered orally in a capsule form. Each capsule contained 250 milligrams of the composition. One or more capsules were administered to obtain the desired dosage.

Physical parameters and blood chemistry were monitored. Serum leptin and adiponectin were determined using an ELISA kit (R&D System, Inc., Minneapolis, Minn., U.S.A.).

Table 19.1: Physical Parameters (Average Values)

Dosage			Body wt.	Chest	Waist		Hip	W/H	
		Sex	(Kg)	(cm)	(cm)	(cm)	Ratio	BMI
500	mg	Male	(−) 3.00	No Change	(−) 1.18	(−) 0.35	(−) 3.37	(−) 2.09
60	days	Female	(−) 2.10	(−) 0.125	(−) 1.02	(−) 0.26	(−) 3.92	(−) 1.44
1000	mg	Male	(−) 2.70	(−) 0.80	(−) 2.12	(−) 1.25	(−) 1.94	(−) 2.51
60	days	Female	(−) 4.24	(−) 0.63	(−) 1.25	(−) 0.50	(−) 2.35	(−) 2.35
		W/O Male	(−) 3.10	No Change	(−) 1.19	(−) 0.36	(−) 3.30	(−) 2.08

W/H—waist-to-hip ratio
BMI—basic metabolic index (body mass index)
W/O—G. sylvestre extract without added enhancer

Table 19.2: Blood Chemistry Improvements (Average Values)

Dosage			Sex	FBS	TGL	CHOL	HDL	LDL
500	mg		Male	(−) 11.50	(−) 6.00	(−) 6.00	(+) 6.50	(−) 2.80
60	days		Female	(−) 17.50	(−) 14.50	(−) 6.00	(+) 4.50	(−) 3.50
1000	mg		Male	(−) 14.61	(−) 14.61	(−) 6.50	(+) 18.00	(−) 11.16
60	days		Female	(−) 19.50	(−) 6.25	(−) 14.00	(+) 8.00	(−) 14.50
			W/O Male	(−) 11.62	(−) 6.10	(−) 6.15	(+) 6.60	(−) 2.78

FBS—fasting blood sugar, mg/dl
TGL—triglycerides
CHOL—Cholesterol
HDL—high density lipoprotein
LDL—low density lipoprotein
W/O—G. sylvestre extract without added enhancer

Table 19.3: Leptin and Adiponectin Concentration After 60 Days at 500 mg/day

Sex	Leptin (picogram/ml) Code Name	\multicolumn{3}{c}{Adiponectin (nanogram/ml)}				L/A (BT)	L/A (AT)
		% decrease			% increase				
		BT	AT	(−)	BT	AT	(+)		
Male	DS	4987	4388	−13%	879	975	+11%	5.67	4.50
	TH	4498	3868	−8%	2129	2320	+9%	2.11	1.67
	NB	5237	4294	−18%	3267	3659	+12%	1.60	1.17
	PB	3847	3269	−15%	6981	7609	+9%	0.55	0.42
	SH	4428	3810	−14%	5390	5929	+13%	0.82	0.64
	SM	4611	4252	−8%	1400	1568	+12%	3.29	2.71
Female	GP	3911	3324	−15%	5742	6316	+10%	0.68	0.53
	DH	3787	3181	−17%	1059	1165	+10%	3.57	2.73
	UC	4498	3643	−18%	1456	1630	+12%	3.08	2.23
	TS	3618	3003	−17%	4488	5929	+13	0.81	0.50

BT—before treatment
AT—after treatment
L/A (BT)—leptin-to-adiponectin ratio before treatment
L/A (AT)—leptin-to-adiponectin ratio after treatment

Table 19.4: Leptin and Adiponectin Concentration After 60 Days at 1000 mg/day

Sex	Leptin (picogram/ml) Code Name	% decrease			% increase			L/A (BT)	L/A (AT)
		BT	AT	(−)	BT	AT	(+)		
Male	AG2	4498	3643	−19%	911	1056	+16%	4.94	3.45
	UM	5237	4032	−23%	7313	8409	+15%	0.72	0.48
	GR	4264	3112	−27%	2543	2975	+17%	1.68	1.05
	AG	4264	3411	−20%	5265	5844	+11%	0.81	0.58
	AS	5012	3362	−33%	2666	3441	+29%	1.88	0.98
	DC	4672	3504	−25%	1994	2392	+20%	2.34	1.20
Female	GK	3632	2978	−18%	8923	10439	+17%	0.41	0.29
	SM	3798	2772	−27%	1145	1385	+21%	3.32	2.00
	UH	3911	2463	−37%	1783	2175	+22%	2.19	1.13
	AM	4108	3286	−20%	3612	4478	+24%	1.14	0.73

BT—before treatment
AT—after treatment

The foregoing results indicate the achievement of reduced fasting blood sugar level as well as an improved lipid profile and a decrease in the leptin-to-adiponectin ratio for each patient.

Example 2: Effect of Enhancers on G. sylvestre Efficacy.

Capsules containing solid, ethanolic extract of G. sylvestre were prepared as well as capsules containing solid, ethanolic extracts of Tinospora cordifolia and Commiphora mukul. Predetermined dosages of the G. sylvestre extract alone or together with the extract of T. codifolia or C. mukul were administered to volunteer male patients which were marginally diabetic, exhibiting a fasting blood sugar level of 125-135 mg/dl, and about 20 percent overweight. The average age of the patient group was 30-45 years.

The patient's physical parameters, levels of changes in fasting blood sugar, blood cholesterol, high density lipoprotein, low density lipoprotein, as well as triglyceride were determined. Leptin and adiponectin concentrations were measured. The results are reported below.

Table 19.5: Effects on Obesity Achieved by G. sylvestre Extract with Enhancers

Extract Dosage	% decrease - after 60 days					
	Body wt. (Kg)	(Cm)	Chest (Cm)	Waist (Cm)	Hip ratio	W/H BMI
500 mg G. sylvestre	(–) 3.10	No change	(–) 1.19	(–) 0.36	(–) 3.30	(–) 2.08
250 mg G. sylvestre 250 mg. T. cordifolia	(–) 2.90	No change	(–) 1.28	(–) 0.36	(–) 3.55	(–) 2.10
250 mg G. sylvestre 250 mg G. mukul	(–) 3.10	No change	(–) 2.00	(–) 0.48	(–) 4.16	(–) 2.21

W/H ratio—waist-to-hip ratio
BMI—basic metabolic index (body mass index)

Table 19.6: Effects on Blood Chemistry Achieved by G. sylvestre Extract with Enhancers

Extract Dosage	% decrease - after 60 days				
	FBS	TGL	CHOL	HDL	LDL
500 mg G. sylvestre	(–) 11.62	(–) 6.10	(–) 6.15	(+) 6.60	(–) 2.78
250 mg G. sylvestre 250 mg T. cordifolia	(–) 12.20	(–) 8.00	(–) 4.50	(+) 2.80	(–) 3.00
250 mg G. sylvestre 250 mg C. mukul	(–) 13.00	(–) 7.06	(–) 5.50	(+) 4.80	(–) 2.60

FBS—fasting blood sugar, mg/dl
TGL—triglycerides
CHOL—cholesterol
HDL—high density lipoprotein
LDL—low density lipoprotein

The data shown in Tables 19.5 and 19.6 show a beneficial decrease in the serum levels of fasting blood sugar, triglycerides, cholesterol and low density lipoproteins but a beneficial increase in high density lipoprotein level.

Table 19.7: Decrease in Leptin-to-Adiponectin Ratio in Male Patients

Dosage	Leptin (picogram/ml)				Adiponectin (nanogram/ml)				L/A	L/A
					% decrease			% increase		
	Code	BT	AT	(−)	BT	AT	(+)	(BT)	(AT)
500 mg	SG	3925	3780	−3.69%	1020	1110	+8.82%	3.89	3.41
G. sylvestre	TL	4045	3850	−4.82%	2215	2420	+9.25%	1.83	1.59
	SK	4126	3910	−5.23%	2890	3120	+7.95%	1.43	1.25
	AB	3950	3170	−19.74%	4950	5200	5.05%	0.80	0.61
	SD	4880	4218	−13.56%	4612	4950	+7.32%	1.06	0.85
	BP	4666	4155	−10.95%	1680	1920	+14.28%	2.78	2.16
250 mg	MP	3980	3660	−8.04%	2566	3100	+20.80%	1.55	1.18
G. sylvestre	BG	4610	4120	−10.62%	1880	2106	+12.02%	2.45	1.96
250 mg	PG	4235	3980	−6.02%	1200	1300	+8.33%	3.53	3.06
T. cordifolia	TS	5432	4880	−10.16%	2681	2920	+8.91%	2.03	1.67
	MM	3656	3200	−12.47%	4880	5200	+6.55%	0.73	0.61
	KC	3980	3650	−8.29%	5415	5820	+7.47%	0.73	0.63
250 mg	KM	4220	3660	−13.27%	1120	1310	+16.96%	3.77	2.79
G. sylvestra	BS	3568	2900	−8.72%	6520	6800	+4.27%	0.55	0.43
250 mg	ST	4164	3020	−27.47%	2646	3100	+17.15%	1.57	0.97
C. mukul	SP	5015	3960	−21.03%	5210	5920	+13.62%	0.96	0.67
	NS	4522	3880	−14.19%	2800	3460	+23.57%	1.61	1.12
	PB	3156	2220	−29.65%	2222	2480	+11.61%	1.42	0.90

BT—before treatment
AT—after treatment
L/A (BT)—leptin-to-adiponectin ratio before treatment
L/A (AT)—leptin-to-adiponectin ratio after treatment

Data in Table 19.7 show a consistent decrease in the leptin-to-adiponectin ratio for all patients.

The foregoing discussion and the Examples are intended to be illustrative but are not to be taken as limiting. Still other variants within the spirit and scope of the present invention are possible and will readily present themselves to those skilled in the art.

Polyherbal Preparation for the Prevention of Atherosclerosis and Hyperlipidemia

Atherosclerosis is one of the major problems for young age death. It is an active process of inflammation and cell proliferation. It starts when normal vascular functions go away. Basically, there is blockage in the coronary artery, which leads to the heart attack. This blockage could be due to deposition of lipid, formation of wound or sudden release of lipid from the endothelial wall due to bursting of plaque. Slow and gradual deposition of fat in the intimal layer of artery is called fatty lesion or plaque. Slowly these fatty lesions get fibrosed and calcium is deposited in it. Initially, it is a reversible process but after fibrosis, it becomes irreversible. In fact, fat deposition in the blood vessel is a natural process with aging, but in some individuals, its rate of formation is significantly high and therefore leads to pathological state of coronary artery disease.

There are several reasons for this deposition. However, the basic cause is considered to be the faulty metabolism of lipid in the body. High cholesterol diet or high level of endogenous cholesterol synthesis in the body is the basic cause of arteriosclerosis. Of course, there are several precipitating factors for this pathology, such as stress, smoking, diabetes, hypertension, age, male sex, family history leading to elevated homocystein, high serum lipoprotein-a and infection with cytomegalovirus or chlamydia. More free radical production leading to rapid oxidation of LDL, followed by the excess uptake of oxidized LDL by the macrophages leading to the formation of foam cells is the basic pathology.

PRIOR ART

As this disease is multi-factorial, there are several approaches to manage artherosclerosis. First and foremost, it is to reduce the lipid load in the body to or to increase the HDL content or to reduce the burden of free radicals and oxidized LDL or to remove foam cells and fatty lesions. There are two major steps, (a) Prevention of the formation of fatty plaque; (b) Regression of plaque already formed. At present, there are two main approaches for the management of atherosclerosis (1) Invasive techniques; and (2) Non-invasive techniques. In the non-invasive group of techniques, the most prominent approach is to lower the blood lipid, specially the cholesterol and triglycerides. In this approach, the main pathway is to inhibit the endogenous cholesterol synthesis by blocking the HMG-Co synthase. A drug known is different kind of Statins. In this way, there is reverse cholesterol transport from the tissue to the blood leading to the lowering of the LDL and VLDL. Several medicinal plants products are also available with a hypolipidemic claims, eg. Commiphora mukul, Terminalia arjuna, Acorus calamus, etc. In fact ayurvedic literature discloses such plant names, but not much scientific study has been made with these plants.

Yet another approach is to increase the HDL in the blood. Unfortunately, there is no good medicines which can increase the serum HDL, The exercise is the only way to achieve this goal. Use of cow butter/milk has also shown the property of raising serum HDL upto some extent, but it can not be used as a medicine in the patients of hyperlipidemia and artherosclerosis.

Third approach is to prevent the oxidation of LDL in the blood, because ox LDL is the basic cause of foam cell formation and thereafter its deposition in the arterial wall, forming arteriosclerotic plaque. To achieve this goal, antioxidants are being recommended as the diet supplements. Although the use of antioxidants has increased significantly as a diet supplement in the management of artherosclerosis and other coronary artery diseases, but does not fall in the group of therapeutic medicine, because of its non-specific role. Metal chelaters are also used to prevent the formation of free radicals, because iron mediated Fenton's reaction is one the basic cause of hydroxyl radical production.

After knowing the molecular pathway of atheroma formation, gene therapy is being tried in the management of this disease. It is reported that stable atheroma is not as dangerous as the unstable one. For this unstability, a group of proteases known as MMPs (Matrix Metallo proteinases) are responsible. In fact, they digest the fibrous cap of the plaque and allow the lipid to come out of the plaque and block the arterial blood flow.

Attempts are now being made to introduce the genes to inhibit these MMPs. Similarly, the most recent approach of gene therapy is to inhibit a growth factor M-CSF (Macrophage colony stimulating factor), which is responsible for the proliferation of smooth muscle cells and rapid formation of foam cell leading to their deposition.

One more approach to manage artherosclerosis is to regulate the inflammatory cytokines and various enzymes like lipoxygenase and cyclooxygenase, because inflammation is one of the basic factors, responsible for plaque formation.

Since artherosclerosis is a multiethiological factor disease, so doctors recommend a series of medicine to manage this disease and still the disease is not manageable because of uncoordinated approach. However, there is no medicine which can target several etiological factors simultaneously by giving one tablet. The patient is supposed to take several medicines in a day, which gives him a kind of psychological depression. These medicines, when given in isolation does not give significant impact on the prevention of atheromaformation, because other factors become more prominent. The genetherapy, which is being developed is at the infancy stage and if at all, it comes to the public use, it will be very expensive and also with several side effects, only the time will tell for its success.

There are many claims to prevent the formation of plaque, by reducing the risk factors, by taking more antioxidants or by lowering the cholesterol by the use of several hypolipidemic drugs like Statins, etc. Once atheroma is detected, the coronary bypass, etc. are the only remedies. In fact, no good drug is available to regress the plaque, already formed.

OBJECTS OF THE INVENTION

An object of this invention is to propose a novel polyherbal preparation which has the capacity to target several etiological pathways, and finally lead to atherosclerosis.

Another object of this invention is to propose a novel polyherbal preparation which is anti-inflammatory anti oxidant and increases serum HDL, and more specifically, it inhibits Lox-15, Cox-2 and Ca-deposition in the plaque, increases Collagen in the chronic plaques, increases serum HDL and decreases serum TG.

Still another object of this invention is to propose a novel polyherbal preparation which enhances serum HDL and prevents plaque formation even in the presence of high-serum lipid.

Yet another object of this invention is to propose a novel polyherbal preparation which enhances the collagen tissue in the old plaque indicating towards the stabilization of the plaque.

A further object of this invention is to propose a novel polyherbal preparation which inhibits the Cyclooxygenase-2 and lipoxygenase-15, which are responsible for atherosclerosis.

A still further object of this invention is to propose a novel polyherbal preparation which is cost-effective, more effective than its component medicinal plant and does not have any toxic or side effect with high therapeutic safety margin.

DESCRIPTION OF INVENTION

According to this invention, there is provided a polyherbal preparation for the prevention of atherosclerosis and hyperlipidemia comprising a mixture of Commiphora mukul, Bosewellia serrata, Semecarpus anacardium Strychnos nux vomica, Terminalia arjuna and Shankha Bhasma.

The polyherbal composition may further include Rubia cordifolia, Bacopa monnieri, Triphala and Trikatu.

In accordance with this invention, the constituents are present in the following ratio:

Purified Commiphora mukul	1 to 4
Pure *Boswellia serrata*	0.5 to 4
Purified Semecarpus anacardium	0.1 to 0.4

Purified powder Strychnos nux vomica 0.4 to 2
Pure powder of water extract Termenalia arjuna 0.3 to 2
Shankha Bhusma 0.5 to 2

Further, any one or more of the following constituents are added in the following ratio:

Rubia cordifolia 0.05 to 1
or Bacopa monnieri 0.5 to 3
or Triphala 0.5 to 3
and Trikatu 0.5 to 3

Specifically, an advantageous ratio is:

Purified Commiphora mukul 3.7
Pure *Boswellia serrata* 3.0
Purified Semecarpus anacardium 0.1
Purified powder Strychnos nux vomica 1.0
Pure powder-water extract Termenalia arjuna bark 0.7
Shankha Bhusma 1.5

Example: Composition of Atherogenic Diet.

Antherogenic diet consists of cholesterol rich-rabbit chow, cabbage and gram in the same amount as in control rabbits. Atherogenic diet is made as follows:

The chow is powdered and mixed with the following items in a specific ratio as given below and again pellet is made. It is dried in oven and kept in refrigerator. At one time, diet was prepared only for 4 days.

Composition of Diet:

Rabbit chow 57%
Milk powder 14%
Yeast powder 04%
Salt 01%
Multivitamin 0.1%
Cholesterol 05%
Hydrogenated fat 17%
Cholic acid 01%

Experimental Details

Male rabbits were randomly divided into 3 groups, having 12 animals in each. They were kept for 15 days for acclimatization in the laboratory condition. During this period, de-worming was done to each animal and Hostacycline and Vimeral was given in drinking water. The animals were divided into the following groups;

Control diet (CD)

Atherogenic diet (AD)

Atherogenic diet—BHUx 60 mg/100 g body weight (AD$_{40}$)

Control diet consists of rabbit chow, cabbage and gram 400 g/day and water ad libitum.

Atherogenic diet was given to the rabbits in the control group, 3 months later, BHUx was given in the experimental group along with the atherogenic diet for another 3 months. Therefore, total duration of the experiment was of 6 months. After every one month, lipid profile was carried out in blood and at the end of experiment, animal was sacrificed and heart, liver, kidney, dorsal aorta were saved. These tissues were processed for histological studies. Sections of 5 micron thickness were cut and stained with different stains. In the AD groups (Experimental control) only 2 ml of gum acacia suspension in distilled water (5%) was given in the similar way. Lipip profile was carried out by using Zydus Pathline kits (a croup and Cadila Healthcare Ltd.) in terms of cholesterol, TG, LDL and HDL. After 3 months, animals were sacrificed to collect heart and dorsal aorta.

(A) Histology:

(1) Study with Dorsal Aorta—It was separated from the heart at the point of aortic arch origin and longitudinally cut open. It was stained in Sudan IV stain. After making a tracing of the atherogenic patches, the tissue was fixed and processed for block preparation and section cutting.

(2) Study with aortic arch and coronary artery—Whole heart was divided into 2 parts, named H$_1$ and H$_2$. The upper H$_1$ part was cut at 6 u thickness and stained with Hematoxylin and Eosin (H&E). Microscopic study was made in the region of aortic arch and coronary artery with reference to intimal thickening. These sections were separately stained with specific stains for the vistalization of collagen tissue and calcium deposition.

(3) Study with kidney and liver—Sections were stained with H & E and with AgNO3 separately to evaluate the degree of fibrosis to and necrosis.

(B) Biochemical tests—Blood of each animal was selected and plasma/serum was isolated as per need to assay SGOT, SGPT, Alkaline phosphatase and complete lipid profile.

(C) In vitor assay—To study the effect of the preparation of the present invention on cyclooxygenase and lipoxygenase, in vitro enzyme assay was carried out by using standard oxygraph technique. The results show that the preparation of the present invention is more sensitive to Cox-2 inhibition than the Cox-1. Similarly, on Lipoxygenase assay, it showed high sensitivity to the 15-Lipoxygenase than the other isoenzymes.

BRIEF DESCRIPTION OF THE ACCOMPANYING DRAWINGS AND TABLES RELATED TO RESULT

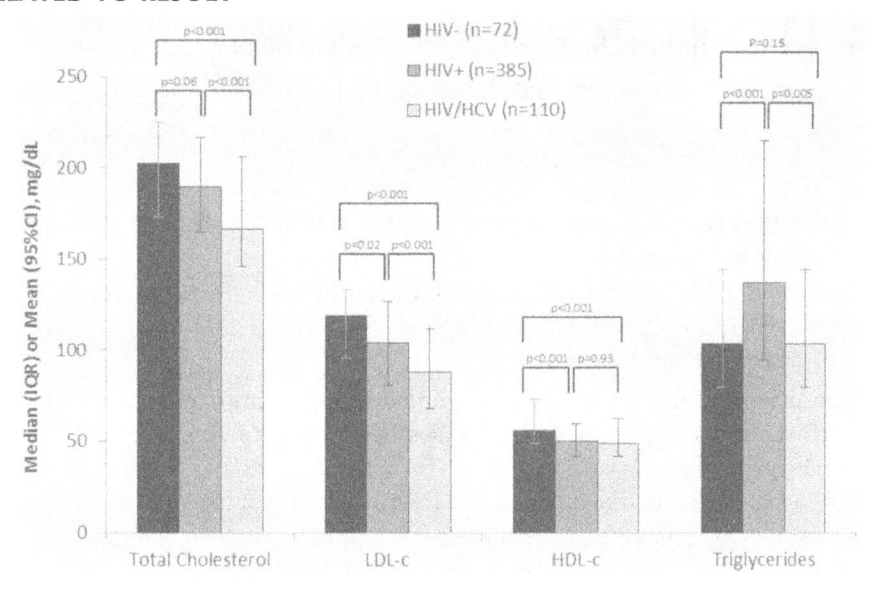

Fig. 19.1: Bar diagram showing lipid profile with raised HDL.

20. Natural Composition for Treating Bone or Joint Inflammation

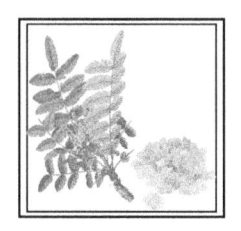

This invention relates to a mixture of natural ingredients for the treatment of bone or joint inflammation.

Bone and joint inflammation is a scourge of both animals and humans. Examples of this debilitating condition include arthritis, including rheumatoid arthritis, rheumatism, tendonitis, etc.

Those who suffer from bone or joint inflammation experience pain and discomfort, and may, in advanced cases, lose the effective use of inflamed joints. The goal of therapeutic methods for treating bone or joint inflammation is the relief of pain and discomfort, and the restoration of use of inflamed joints.

Most western countries have adopted traditional western medicine to treat bone and joint inflammation. The treatments usually involve synthetic drugs, such as Motrin, Fildene, Indocin, Clinoril, Naprosyn, Vicoden, and Meclomen. These drugs do not always alleviate pain and discomfort, or restore significant use of inflamed joints. Moreover, such drugs may lead to undesirable side effects.

Natural ingredients, including Ayurvedic formulations, have also been used to treat bone and joint inflammation, especially in eastern countries, and, increasingly, in western countries. Such natural ingredients include cartilage, glucosamine sulfate, proteolytic and other enzymes, and herbs, such as the gummy extract of *Boswellia serrata*, Ashwagandha, and ginseng. While not leading to the kinds of side effects observed with western drugs, the eastern formulations do not always provide sufficient relief of pain and discomfort, or restore significant use of inflamed joints.

There is, therefore, a need for new treatments of conditions characterized by inflamed bone or joints that avoid the disadvantages of known treatments, including the disadvantages described above. It is an objective of the present invention to provide such new treatments. More specifically, it is an objective of the present invention to provide new treatments for bone or joint inflammation that are able to relieve pain and discomfort, and to restore significant use of inflamed joints, better than known methods, while at the same time avoiding the side effects observed with traditional drugs.

DESCRIPTION

It has now surprisingly been discovered that compositions formed by preparing mixtures of known components are able to act efficiently in the treatment of

Natural Composition for Treating Bone or Joint Inflammation 273

conditions characterized by bone or joint inflammation. The mixture consists of mostly natural components, and preferably consists of all natural components. A "natural component" is component that is found in nature.

The components may be mixed in any order to prepare the composition. The composition may comprise the same components that were added to the mixture, or any components that result from an interaction between two or more of the components after mixing.

All conditions characterized by bone or joint inflammation are able to benefit from the composition of the invention. These conditions include, for example, all forms of arthritis, rheumatism, including rheumatoid arthritis, bursitis, tendonitis, gout, etc. The composition is effective for all mammals, including farm animals, laboratory animals, pet animals, and humans.

The components of the composition are in a form that are systemically absorbable in a mammal. The components are preferably soluble. After being absorbed, the cartilage and other components of the composition, or their metabolic products, are delivered to the inflamed bone or joints.

The compositions are formulated for systemic administration to mammals. Any mode of systemic administration is suitable. Some examples include intravenous, intramuscular, and oral administration. The preferred mode of administration is oral administration.

The quantities of the various doses are described below in terms of unit doses. Mammals receive unit doses of the composition on the basis of various parameters, as is well known in the medical and veterinary arts. The parameters include, for example, size, sensitivity to the components, severity of the condition being treated, etc. One to three unit doses are normally administered one to four times a day.

The composition may be formulated, along with customary pharmaceutically acceptable excipients, in any form suitable for systemic administration. Some suitable forms include capsules, powders, liquids, and suspensions.

Each capsule contains a unit dose of each component. In the case of a powder, liquid, or suspension, a unit dose is considered, roughly, to be contained in a teaspoonful or a tablespoonful.

For the purpose of the present specification, an effective amount of a component is considered to be a unit dose in the case of a capsule. In the case of a powder, solution, or suspension, an effective amount is considered to be a multiple of the unit dose, calculated by multiplying the unit dose by the number of unit doses in a container. Of course, those having ordinary skill in the art could formulate comparable effective amounts based on a unit dose being contained in a volume other than that of a standard teaspoonful or a tablespoonful.

The components may be formulated for administration into one composition containing all the components. Alternatively, the components may be formulated into more than one composition, each of which contains one or more components. In addition, each component may constitute a separate composition, and be administered separately. It is preferable to administer the smallest number of separate compositions.

In the discussion below, all numbers are approximate, unless otherwise stated. The weights of extracts and concentrates do not include the weights of the solvents. Unless otherwise specified, extracts and concentrates are substantially saturated in the component or components being extracted.

The mixture contains systemically absorbable, preferably soluble, cartilage. The cartilage may be derived from any source, such as from mammals or fish. The preferred mammalian cartilage is bovine cartilage. A suitable source of soluble bovine cartilage is Enzymatic Therapy, Green Bay, Wis.

The preferred fish cartilage is selachian fish cartilage. The preferred selachian fish cartilage is shark cartilage, preferably soluble shark cartilage.

A particularly effective form of cartilage is a mixture of mammalian cartilage and fish cartilage. The mammalian cartilage is preferably bovine cartilage. The fish cartilage is preferably selachian fish cartilage, and more preferably shark cartilage. The fish cartilage preferably constitutes up to about 25%, more preferably up to about 20%, and most preferably about 10 to about 20% of the total cartilage.

The minimum unit dose of cartilage is about 1,500, preferably about 1800, and more preferably about 2000 mg. The maximum unit dose of cartilage is about 3,500, preferably about 3,000, and more preferably about 2,500 mg.

The cartilage is mixed with an aminosaccharide. Any aminosaccharide that is effective in combination with the cartilage is suitable. The aminosaccharide is preferably an aminomonosaccharide, more preferably a glucosamine, and more preferably glucosamine sulfate. A suitable source of aminosaccharide is GS-500 sold by Enzymatic Therapy, Green Bay, Wis.

The minimum unit dose of aminosaccharide is about 500, preferably about 700, and more preferably about 900 mg. The maximum unit dose of aminosaccharide is about 3,500, preferably about 3,000, and more preferably about 1,500 mg.

A preferred composition is formed by preparing a mixture comprising effective amounts of cartilage and aminosaccharide, as described above, and an effective amount of a mucopolysaccharide. The mucopolysaccharide is preferably a concentrate derived from connective tissue, preferably bovine connective tissue, more preferably tracheal connective tissue, and most preferably bovine tracheal connective tissue. A suitable source of mucopolysaccharide concentrate is Cardiovascular Research Ltd., Concord,

Calif. The mucopolysaccharide may also be prepared by hydrolyzing beef tracheas with papain.

The minimum unit dose of mucopolysaccharide is about 100, preferably about 200, and more preferably about 300 mg. The maximum unit dose of mucopolysaccharide is about 1000, preferably about 500, and more preferably about 400 mg.

Another preferred composition is formed by preparing either of the mixtures described above, and an effective amount of one or more proteolytic enzymes. A suitable source of proteolytic enzymes is pancreatic extract (pancreatin), preferably hog pancreatic extract. It is desirable to use a full-strength, undiluted pancreatic extract (10X U.S.P.), preferably hog pancreatic extract. It is desirable for the units of activity of proteolytic enzymes to be about 50,000-200,000, preferably about 100,000.

It is also desirable for the extract to contain additional enzymes, such as amylase and lipase. It is desirable for the units of activities to be: amylase, 50,000-200,000, preferably about 100,000; and lipase 12,500-50,000, preferably about 25,000. Preferably, the ratio of units of activity of proteolytic enzymes, amylase, and lipase should be about 2-6:2-6:1.

It is also desirable to include other enzymes, such as papain, bromelain, trypsin, chymotrypsin, and lysozyme. A suitable source of proteolytic enzymes is sold in the form of tablets under the name Mega-Zyme from Enzymatic Therapy, Green Bay, Wis. Each tablet of Mega-Zyme contains the following enzymes: pancreatic enzymes (10X), 325 mg; trypsin, 75 mg; papain, 50 mg; bromelain, 50 mg; amylase, 10 mg; lipase, 10 mg; lysozyme, 10 mg; and chymotrypsin, 2 mg.

The minimum unit dose of proteolytic enzymes is about 100, preferably about 150, and more preferably about 200 mg. The maximum unit dose of proteolytic enzymes is about 400, preferably about 300, and more preferably about 250 mg.

Another preferred composition is formed by preparing any of the mixtures described above, and an effective amount of one or more extracts, preferably standardized extracts, of an herb of the genus Withenia, of the bark of an herb of the genus Salix, or of a root of an herb of the genus Panax. The herb of the genus Withenia is preferably derived from the species somnifera (ashwagandha). The bark of an herb of the genus Salix is preferably willow bark. The root of an herb of the genus Panax is preferably gensing..

The minimum unit dose of the extracts of an herb of the genus Withenia, of the bark of an herb of the genus Salix, or of a root of an herb of the genus Panax is about 150, preferably about 250, more preferably about 350 mg. The maximum unit dose of the extracts is about 2,000, preferably about 1,200, and more preferably about 800 mg. The bark of an herb of the genus Salix and the root of an herb of the genus Panax may also be cut into pieces or ground into a powder. Grinding into a powder is preferred.

Another preferred composition is formed by preparing any of the mixtures described above, and an effective amount of one or more isomers of boswellic acid or its derivatives. The isomers include alpha, beta, and 11-keto-beta boswellic acid. Derivatives include the acetyl derivatives.

The isomers of boswellic acid and its derivatives are preferably naturally occuring, and may be derived from sources known in the art. They may, for example, be synthesized, or obtained from aqueous or ethanolic extracts of an herb of the genus *Boswellia*, preferably from the gum resin of the species serrata..

A suitable source of boswellic acids is an extract of *Boswellia serrata* resin standardized to 60% boswellic acids. Such an extract is available from Ayush Herbs, Inc., Bellevue, Wash. under the name Boswelya Plus. Each unit dose of Boswelya Plus contains boswellic acid (150 mg), ginger (100 mg), tumeric (50 mg), and winter cherry (ashwagandha) (100 mg).

The minimum unit dose of boswellic acids is about 50, preferably about 75, and more preferably about 100 mg. The maximum unit dose of boswellic acids is about 1,000, preferably about 500, and more preferably about 200 mg.

Another preferred composition is formed by preparing any of the mixtures described above, and an effective amount of chondroitin, preferably chondroitin polysulfate. The minimum unit dose of chondroitin is about 500, preferably about 700, and more preferably about 900 mg. The maximum unit dose of chondroitin is about 3,500, preferably about 3,000, and more preferably about 1,500 mg.

Another preferred composition is formed by preparing any of the mixtures described above, and an effective amount of an extract of sea cucumber preferably from the Australian coast. The minimum unit dose of sea cucumber is about 30, preferably about 60, and more preferably about 90 mg. The maximum unit dose of sea cucumber is about 400, preferably about 300, and more preferably about 150 mg.

Another preferred composition is formed by preparing any of the mixtures described above, and an effective amount of black currant oil, preferably black currant seed oil. The minimum unit dose of black currant oil is about 80, preferably about 150, and more preferably about 250 mg. The maximum unit dose of black currant oil is about 1,000, preferably about 500, and more preferably about 400 mg.

A suitable unit dose of black currant oil contains: GLA (about 45 mg), linoleic acid (about 95 mg), alpha-linolenic acid (about 34 mg), and stearidonic acid (about 9 mg).

A suitable source of black currant oil is Eclectic Institute, Inc. of Sandy, Oreg.

Another preferred composition is formed by preparing any of the mixtures described above, and an effective amount of ascorbic acid (vitamin C). The minimum unit dose of ascorbic acid is about 1,000, preferably about 2,000, and more preferably about 3,000 mg. The maximum unit dose of ascorbic acid is about 6,000, preferably about 5,000, and more preferably about 4,000 mg.

Another preferred composition is formed by preparing any of the mixtures described above, and an effective amount of pyridoxine HCl (vitamin B6). The minimum unit dose of pyridoxine HCl is about 30, preferably about 75, and more preferably about 125 mg. The maximum unit dose of pyridoxine HCl is about 700, preferably about 400, and more preferably about 200 mg.

Another preferred composition is formed by preparing any of the mixtures described above, and an effective amount of a secondary root (tuber) of a plant of the genus Harpagophytum. The plant is preferably from the species procumbens (devil's claw, also known as grapple plant). The secondary root may be extracted, cut into pieces, or ground into a powder. Grinding into a powder is preferred.

The minimum unit dose of the secondary root is about 70, preferably about 400, and more preferably about 800 mg of the secondary root. The maximum unit dose of the secondary root is about 3,500, preferably about 2,500, and more preferably about 1,500 mg of the secondary root.

Another preferred composition is formed by preparing any of the mixtures described above, and an effective amount of L-proline. The minimum unit dose of L-proline is about 80, preferably about 400, and more preferably about 600 mg. The maximum unit dose of L-proline is about 1,000, preferably about 900, and more preferably about 800 mg.

EXAMPLES

Example 1. A composition is prepared by mixing unit doses of the following components:

2,250 mg soluble bovine cartilage,

250 mg soluble shark cartilage,

1,000 mg glucosamine sulfate.

Example 2. A composition is prepared by mixing unit doses of the following components:

2,250 mg soluble bovine cartilage,

250 mg soluble shark cartilage,

1,000 mg glucosamine sulfate,

350 mg mucopolysaccharide concentrate.

Example 3. A composition is prepared by mixing unit doses of the following components:

2,250 mg soluble bovine cartilage,

250 mg soluble shark cartilage,

1,000 mg glucosamine sulfate,

350 mg mucopolysaccharide concentrate,

225 mg proteolytic enzymes from hog pancreatic extract.

Example 4. A composition is prepared by mixing unit doses of the following components:

2,250 mg soluble bovine cartilage,

250 mg soluble shark cartilage,

1,000 mg glucosamine sulfate,

350 mg mucopolysaccharide concentrate,

225 mg proteolytic enzymes from hog pancreatic extract,

500 mg standardized extract of ashwagandha.

Example 5. A composition is prepared by mixing unit doses of the following components:

2,250 mg soluble bovine cartilage,

250 mg soluble shark cartilage,

1,000 mg glucosamine sulfate,

350 mg mucopolysaccharide concentrate,

225 mg proteolytic enzymes from hog pancreatic extract,

500 mg standardized extract of ashwagandha,

470 mg extract of *Boswellia serrata* comprising 150 mg boswellic acids.

Example 6. A composition is prepared by mixing unit doses of the following components:

2,250 mg soluble bovine cartilage,

250 mg soluble shark cartilage,

1,000 mg glucosamine sulfate,

350 mg mucopolysaccharide concentrate,

225 mg proteolytic enzymes from hog pancreatic extract,

500 mg standardized extract of ashwagandha,

470 mg extract of *Boswellia serrata* comprising 150 mg boswellic acids,

1,000 mg chondroitin polysulfate.

Example 7. A composition is prepared by mixing unit doses of the following components:

2,250 mg soluble bovine cartilage,

250 mg soluble shark cartilage,
1,000 mg glucosamine sulfate,
350 mg mucopolysaccharide concentrate,
225 mg proteolytic enzymes from hog pancreatic extract,
500 mg standardized extract of ashwagandha,
470 mg extract of *Boswellia serrata* comprising 150 mg boswellic acids,
1,000 mg chondroitin polysulfate,
100 mg extract of sea cucumber.

Example 8. A composition is prepared by mixing unit doses of the following components:
2,250 mg soluble bovine cartilage,
250 mg soluble shark cartilage,
1,000 mg glucosamine sulfate,
350 mg mucopolysaccharide concentrate,
225 mg proteolytic enzymes from hog pancreatic extract,
500 mg standardized extract of ashwagandha,
470 mg extract of *Boswellia serrata* comprising 150 mg boswellic acids,
1,000 mg chondroitin polysulfate,
100 mg extract of sea cucumber,
300 mg black currant seed oil.

Example 9. A composition is prepared by mixing unit doses of the following components:
2,250 mg soluble bovine cartilage,
250 mg soluble shark cartilage,
1,000 mg glucosamine sulfate,
350 mg mucopolysaccharide concentrate,
225 mg proteolytic enzymes from hog pancreatic extract,
500 mg standardized extract of ashwagandha,
470 mg extract of *Boswellia serrata* comprising 150 mg boswellic acids,
1,000 mg chondroitin polysulfate,
100 mg extract of sea cucumber,
300 mg black currant seed oil,
3,500 mg ascorbic acid.

Example 10. A composition is prepared by mixing unit doses of the following components:
2,250 mg soluble bovine cartilage,
250 mg soluble shark cartilage,

1,000 mg glucosamine sulfate,

350 mg mucopolysaccharide concentrate,

225 mg proteolytic enzymes from hog pancreatic extract,

500 mg standardized extract of ashwagandha,

470 mg extract of *Boswellia serrata* comprising 150 mg boswellic acids,

1,000 mg chondroitin polysulfate,

100 mg extract of sea cucumber,

300 mg black currant seed oil,

3,500 mg ascorbic acid (vitamin C),

150 mg pyridoxine HCl (vitamin B6).

Example 11. A composition is prepared by mixing unit doses of the following components:

2,250 mg soluble bovine cartilage,

250 mg soluble shark cartilage,

1,000 mg glucosamine sulfate,

350 mg mucopolysaccbaride concentrate,

225 mg proteolytic enzymes from hog pancreatic extract,

500 mg standardized extract of ashwagandha,

470 mg extract of *Boswellia serrata* comprising 150 mg boswellic acids,

1,000 mg chondroitin polysulfate,

100 mg extract of sea cucumber,

300 mg black currant seed oil,

3,500 mg ascorbic acid (vitamin C),

150 mg pyridoxine HCl (vitamin B6),

1,000 mg devil's claw powder.

Example 12. A composition is prepared by mixing unit doses of the following components:

3,000 mg soluble shark cartilage, and

1,000 mg glucosamine sulfate.

Example 13. A composition is prepared by mixing unit doses of the following components:

2,500 mg soluble bovine cartilage,

3,000 mg glucosamine sulfate, and

200 mg mucopolysaccharide concentrate.

Example 14. A composition is prepared by mixing unit doses of the following components:

2,250 mg soluble bovine cartilage,

500 mg soluble shark cartilage,
2,000 mg glucosamine sulfate,
250 mg mucopolysaccharide concentrate,
500 mg proteolytic enzymes from hog pancreatic extract.

Example 15. A composition is prepared by mixing unit doses of the following components:
4,000 mg soluble bovine cartilage,
300 mg soluble shark cartilage,
1,000 mg glucosamine sulfate,
700 mg mucopolysaccharide concentrate,
400 mg proteolytic enzymes from hog pancreatic extract,
1,000 mg standardized extract of ashwagandha.

Example 16. A composition is prepared by mixing unit doses of the following components:
1,750 mg soluble bovine cartilage,
200 mg soluble shark cartilage,
3,000 mg glucosamine sulfate,
600 mg mucopolysaccharide concentrate,
500 mg proteolytic enzymes from hog pancreatic extract,
800 mg standardized extract of powdered willow bark.
670 mg extract of *Boswellia serrata* comprising 150 mg acetyl derivative of boswellic acids.

Example 17. A composition is prepared by mixing unit doses of the following components:
1,850 mg soluble bovine cartilage,
600 mg soluble shark cartilage,
2,000 mg glucosamine sulfate,
500 mg mucopolysaccharide concentrate,
100 mg proteolytic enzymes from hog pancreatic extract,
700 mg standardized extract of gensing,
900 mg extract of *Boswellia serrata* comprising 150 mg boswellic acids,
5,000 mg chondroitin polysulfate.

Example 18. A composition is prepared by mixing unit doses of the following components:
1,650 mg soluble bovine cartilage,
350 mg soluble shark cartilage,
4,000 mg glucosamine sulfate,

150 mg mucopolysaccharide concentrate,

400 mg proteolytic enzymes from hog pancreatic extract,

400 mg standardized extract of ashwagandha,

670 mg extract of *Boswellia serrata* comprising 150 mg Boswelya Plus

2,000 mg chondroitin polysulfate,

600 mg extract of sea cucumber.

Example 19. A composition is prepared by mixing unit doses of the following components:

5,250 mg soluble bovine cartilage,

250 mg soluble shark cartilage,

500 mg glucosamine sulfate,

450 mg mucopolysaccharide concentrate,

300 mg MegaZyme,

750 mg standardized extract of ashwagandha,

350 mg extract of *Boswellia serrata* comprising 150 mg boswellic acids,

3,000 mg chondroitin polysulfate,

200 mg extract of sea cucumber,

100 mg black currant seed oil.

Example 20. A composition is prepared by mixing unit doses of the following components:

1,900 mg soluble bovine cartilage,

500 mg soluble shark cartilage,

750 mg GS-500,

850 mg mucopolysaccharide concentrate,

150 mg proteolytic enzymes from hog pancreatic extract,

500 mg standardized extract of ashwagandha,

300 mg extract of *Boswellia serrata* comprising 150 mg boswellic acids,

3,000 mg chondroitin polysulfate,

200 mg extract of sea cucumber,

500 mg black currant seed oil,

1,500 mg ascorbic acid.

Example 21. A composition is prepared by mixing unit doses of the following components:

8,000 mg soluble bovine cartilage,

500 mg soluble shark cartilage,

3,000 mg glucosamine sulfate,

700 mg mucopolysaccharide concentrate,

125 mg proteolytic enzymes from hog pancreatic extract,

400 mg standardized extract of ashwagandha,

370 mg extract of *Boswellia serrata* comprising 150 mg boswellic acids,

2,000 mg chondroitin polysulfate,

50 mg extract of sea cucumber,

600 mg black currant seed oil,

8,500 mg ascorbic acid (vitamin C),

450 mg pyridoxine HCl (vitamin B6).

Example 22. A composition is prepared by mixing unit doses of the following components:

1,500 mg soluble hog cartilage,

500 mg soluble shark cartilage,

500 mg glucosamine sulfate,

500 mg mucopolysaccharide concentrate,

550 mg proteolytic enzymes from bovine pancreatic extract,

700 mg standardized extract of ashwagandha,

800 mg extract of *Boswellia serrata* comprising 150 mg boswellic acids,

3,000 mg chondroitin polysulfate,

100 mg extract of sea cucumber,

400 mg black currant seed oil,

6,500 mg ascorbic acid (vitamin C),

450 mg pyridoxine HCl (vitamin B6),

3,000 mg devil's claw powder.

21 Topical Formulations for the Symptomatic Treatment of Musculoskeletal Disorders

The present invention relates to topical compositions or extracts containing capsaicin, boswellic acids or *Boswellia serrata* extracts, and escin or Aesculus hippocastanum extracts.

Prior Art

Musculoskeletal disorders are always associated with joint damage and pain. They are consequently defined as painful musculoskeletal disorders. They include a large number of disorders, ranging from peripheral joint diseases (such as rheumatic disease, rheumatoid arthritis, connective tissue disease, osteoarthritis, gout, sarcoidosis and infectious arthritis) to myalgia (such as polymyalgia rheumatica, ankylosing spondylitis and psychogenic rheumatism), or joint, neurological, degenerative, autoimmune, vascular and traumatic disorders which can involve the joints, limbs, ankles and lumbosacral region, causing pain and functional impairment.

The most common degenerative inflammatory disease of the musculoskeletal apparatus is osteoarthritis (OA), also known as degenerative joint disease.

This disease affects women more than men up to the age of 50 years. After that age the percentages are equivalent, but complications are more frequent in men. Alterations may also occur in healthy young people in their twenties (rare), whereas more than 60% of the population aged over 60 present joint alterations of varying extents. Over 20 million people in the USA suffer from this disease, and at least 200,000 hip and knee replacement operations are caused by osteoarthritis every year.

The etiology of the disease has not yet been identified, but it has strong links with genetic factors, obesity and mechanical stress on the joint. In particular, trauma affecting the cartilage surface of the joint or trauma of the subchondral bone can create cartilage microfractures and give rise to the disease. Occupational fatigue or microtraumas caused by sport can also operate with the same mechanism. An altered immune response can also damage the cartilage surface, causing the chondrocytes to release proteolytic and collagenolytic enzymes which degrade collagen and proteoglycans and cause subsequent synthesis of bone repair tissue with the formation of osteophytes. The deposit of calcium pyrophosphate dihydrate (CPPD) microcrystals triggers inflammatory symptoms, with the release of proteolytic enzymes that cause cartilage damage. A number of endocrine disorders can cause the deposit of CPPD crystals: hyperparathyroidism, Wilson's disease, haemochromatosis and hypothyroidism. The anatomopathological damage is represented by cracking with erosion of the cartilage, and formation of areas wholly devoid of cartilage. The proliferative response of the bone tissue is once again sclerosis, thickening of the subchondral bone, and production of osteophytes.

In the case of OA, the joints most affected are the small joints of the hands (first carpometacarpal joints, proximal and distal interphalangeal joints) and feet (metatarsophalangeal joints), and the hip, knee and spine joints. The main symptoms are progressive pain, which is initially mild, but later becomes constant and disabling, crepitation of the affected joints, joint deformity due to increased bone tissue in the synovial fluid and synovitis, limited joint movements with spasms, and joint instability. Valgus deformity of the knee may also be present. The disease has a chronic-degenerative trend. The painkilling drugs most commonly used are paracetamol, acetylsalicylic acid, NSAIDs, indometacin, methotrexate and cyclosporin A, which present serious side effects such as liver disease, kidney disease, gastroenteric ulcers, and immunosuppression. The same drugs are used for nearly all painful rheumatic syndromes, especially in rheumatoid arthritis, where the anatomopathological damage leads to clinical symptoms substantially similar to those of osteoarthritis.

The transcutaneous approach, using topical preparations or medical devices that release the drug, involves a lower incidence of side effects and also allows a lower dose of the drugs to be used than with the oral route.

Particularly favourable results have been reported with capsaicin-based preparations.

Capsaicin is present, at different concentrations, in plants of the genus Capsicum. Capsaicin and capsaicinoids are very stable alkaloids: they remain unchanged for a long time, even after cooking and freezing. Like all capsaicinoids, capsaicin is an irritant, and produces a stinging sensation in the mucous membranes, where it passes into solution and stimulates the VR1 receptors (vanilloid receptor type 1), which in turn activate the protein VRL-1 (vanilloid receptor-like 1), which under "normal" conditions is activated at temperatures of between 43 and 52°C.

Although capsaicin is rather toxic by oral administration, if administered topically at a very low dose it effectively reduces pain symptoms due to its local analgesic activity, but has no effect on the inflammatory component of the disorder.

Description of the Invention

It has now surprisingly been found that the topical activity of capsaicin in reducing the symptoms of osteoarthritis and similar chronic osteoarticular symptoms can be improved by combining it with escin and boswellic acids or extracts containing them.

The invention therefore provides topical compositions containing:

(a) capsaicin or extracts containing it,

(b) boswellic acids or *Boswellia serrata* resin extracts containing them (preferably a 60% *Boswellia* extract in boswellic acids),

(c) escin in free form or complexed with beta-sitosterol and/or with phospholipids or Aesculus hippocastanumseed extracts.

Boswellia serrata Roxb., also known as Indian frankincense, is a tree belonging to the *Burseraceae* family which is native to the forests of some parts of India, North Africa and the Orient. The constituent most widely used for medicinal purposes is a yellow-brown rubbery oleoresin also called gum resin or "guggal", obtained by incision of the bark or extraction from the leaves. *Boswellia serrata* gum resin and alcoholic extracts thereof are used as anti-inflammatory remedies in the treatment of disorders such as ulcerating colitis, bronchial asthma and pulmonary emphysema. *Boswellia* contains numerous terpenoid substances, polysaccharides, uronic acids, β-sitosterol and phlobaphenes, which are used to treat various disorders. The terpenoid fraction consists of pentacyclic triterpenic acids called boswellic acids, which are the main active constituents. The acids are classified as α-, β- and γ-boswellic acids. The β form is the predominant one. The extracts available on the market are standardised in boswellic acids with percentages of between 37 and 65%. The dried extract content, titrated in acetyl-11-keto-β-boswellic acid (AKBA), the most active constituent, is 30%. Boswellic acids, the active constituents of *Boswellia serrata*, perform a strong anti-inflammatory action and act similarly to a non-steroidal anti-inflammatory drug. In vivo studies conducted on rats have demonstrated their ability to reduce oedema caused by local inoculation of carrageenan. Experiments conducted in vitro demonstrate that *Boswellia* extracts inhibit, to a dose-dependent extent, synthesis of products of the enzyme 5-lipoxygenase, such as 5-hydroxyeicosatetraenoic acid (5-HETE) and leukotriene B4 (LTB4), which are responsible for bronchoconstriction, stimulating chemotaxis and increasing vascular permeability, with consequent oedema formation. In particular, AKBA is a powerful inhibitor of leukotriene synthesis, acting on 5-lipoxygenase with a direct, non-redox and non-competitive mechanism: it is the only compound currently known which acts as allosteric regulator of the enzyme. *Boswellia* derivatives are consequently considered to be specific inhibitors of 5-lipoxygenase. It has also been observed that boswellic acids perform an inhibitory action towards human leucocyte elastase (HLE), an enzyme that stimulates mucus production in the respiratory apparatus. Said enzyme, which seems to play an important part in diseases such as pulmonary cystic fibrosis, chronic bronchitis and acute respiratory distress syndrome, also appears to contribute to the inflammatory symptoms typical of osteoarthritis.

Inflammatory processes are characterised by multiple symptoms, such as loss of functionality of the tissue involved, oedema formation, swelling and pain, and are at least partly attributable to the presence of leukotrienes, known inflammation mediators with chemotactic activity, which cause spasms of the smooth muscles and increase vascular permeability. Moreover, the ability of boswellic acids to prevent the migration of polymorphonucleated leucocytes by inhibiting the release or production of some chemotactic factors has recently been demonstrated in vitro. Said cells appear to act locally by releasing elastase, a proteolytic enzyme jointly responsible for the destruction of tissues inflamed by chronic degenerative syndromes.

Although oedema has no relevance to the symptoms of the disorder in question, a surprising further synergy of action has been observed in local treatment if preparations with an anti-oedema action are combined with the preparation based on capsaicin and *Boswellia* derivatives. The tissue oedema typical of traumatic events can be treated either with drugs that reactivate the lymphatic circulation, resorb liquids and redirect them to the venous region, or drugs that physically reduce the endothelial slit through which the liquids exit. An example of the second type of drug is escin, a mixture of saponins contained in Aesculus hippocastanum seeds; said saponins consist of a mixture of aglycons known as desglucoescin to which one molecule of glucuronic acid and two monosaccharide residues are connected, together with tiglic acid or angelic acid in position 21. Escin possesses excellent anti-oedema properties which make it particularly useful for treating post-traumatic intra-cranial effusions and, in the cosmetic field, for resorbing the tissue oedema typical of cellulitis. The action mechanism of escin is based on its ability to reduce the number and diameter of the endothelial pores responsible for the physiological exchange of liquids between the blood vessels and the surrounding connective tissue. Action at this level, by reducing the exit of interstitial liquids, generates tissue resorption of the oedema. However, after topical administration, in a very small percentage of cases, escin can cause mild irritation due to its ability to sequester cholesterol (which it takes from the cell membranes, causing cytolysis). It is therefore preferable to use escin in the form complexed with beta-sitosterol and/or with distearoyl phosphatidylcholine. Said complexing saturates the cholesterol-binding site and eliminates the risk of irritation without altering the pharmacological properties of pure escin.

The formulation to which this patent relates contains between 0.0001 and 1% by weight of capsaicin, between 0.001 and 5% of 60% *Boswellia* extract in boswellic acids, and between 0.01 and 5% of escin/beta-sitosterol/distearoylphosphatidylcholine complex.

A particularly preferred composition contains 0.075% by weight of capsaicin, 1% by weight of *Boswellia* extract, and 1.5% by weight of escin/beta-sitosterol/distearoyl phosphatidylcholine complex.

The compositions according to the invention may also contain antioxidants such as curcumin, OPC from Vitus vinifera, vitamins C and E, lipoic acid and/or preparations which act on the lymphatic system (e.g. melilotus, coumarin, esculoside, fraxetine, etc.) and/or preparations which implement the anti-inflammatory action by acting on endogenous cortisol (18-beta glycyrrhetinic acid, liquorice root extract). The compositions can take the form of creams, gels, hydrocreams, ointments and emulsions. If osteoarticular pain occurs in elderly patients with ulcers and sores close to the inflamed, painful joint, a spray formulation could be used, as its application does not require manual contact with the ulcerated/painful area. As the formulations according to the invention are designed for chronic use, the active constituents may also be applied to devices which effect programmed, long-term release, such as patches, bandages, applicators or simply sterile gauze, which is useful for outdoor use, for example.

The following examples illustrate the invention in greater detail.

EXAMPLES

Example 1: Cream (for joints)

Ingredient	Percentage by weight
Capsaicin	0.075%
Boswellic acids	1.0%
Escin/beta-sitosterol/phytosome	1.5%

Example 2: Gel (for hands)

Ingredient	Percentage by weight
Capsaicin	0.025%
Boswellic acids	0.5%
Escin/beta-sitosterol/phytosome	0.5%

Example 3: W/O emulsion (lumbar area and back)

Ingredient	Percentage by weight
Capsaicin	0.075%
Boswellic acids	1.0%
Escin/beta-sitosterol/phytosome	1.5%
OPC from Vitis vinifera	1.0%
18-beta glycyrrhetinic acid phytosome	1.5%

Example 4: Spray

Ingredient	Percentage by weight
Capsaicin	0.075%
Boswellic acids	0.5%
Escin/beta-sitosterol/phytosome	0.5%
Lipoic acid	0.5%

Example 5: Medicated gauze

Ingredient	Percentage by weight
Capsaicin	0.075%
Boswellic acids	1.5%
Escin/beta-sitosterol/phytosome	1.5%

Example 6: Controlled-release patches

Ingredient	Percentage by weight
Capsaicin	0.075%
Boswellic acids	0.5%
Escin/beta-sitosterol/phytosome	0.5%
Curcumin	0.5%

22. Amazing Benefits of Frankincense for Skin, Hair and Health

In no way related to Frankenstein – frankincense oil is one of the essential oils used in aromatherapy. This fragrant oil is extracted from *Boswellia sacra* tree or *Boswellia carterii* . It is also known as Shallaki or Salai Guggulu in Ayurveda. Possessing a number of health benefits, frankincense oil is also used to make several perfumes, skin-care products and incense sticks. According to the Bible, frankincense was one of the three gifts brought by the three wise men for baby Jesus. Mainly found in countries like Oman, Somalia and Yemen, this aromatic oil has a history that dates back to centuries. The lemony musky smell of frankincense is refreshing, to say the least. No wonder that this oil is a favorite when it comes to aromatherapy!

Benefits of Frankincense Oil

Frankincense and frankincense oil are known to have several medicinal properties. In ancient times, people used it widely to treat a number of health conditions. In fact, at one point in history, frankincense trade became the most lucrative trade in the world! Fortunately, modern scientists are slowly waking up to the benefits offered by this amazing resin-like natural wonder. Apart from playing a key role in aromatherapy, frankincense oil is also known for its anti-inflammatory and anti-cancer properties.

Skin Benefits of Frankincense

Our skin is the most visible organ of our body. Frankincense for skin can do amazing wonders. Here's how:

1. *Skin conditioner:* Usage of Frankincense floral water can act as skin conditioner if used externally. Regular use of this natural conditioner can leave your skin soft and smooth.
2. *Scar reduction:* A blemish free skin is a dream for many. Frankincense can help in fading away acne, surgery marks, stretch marks and other type of scars from the skin, making your dream a reality.
3. *Regeneration of skin:* Frankincense can reduce wrinkles and fine lines by regenerating healthy skin cells. The use of this sap can keep you looking as young as feel in your heart! This is considered to be the best Frankincense skin care benefit.
4. *Strengthen finger nails:* Application of frankincense on finger nails can strengthen weak or brittle and delicate finger nails.

5. *Anti-infection:* Frankincense, being a disinfectant, can be used to clean wounds or cuts, making way for quicker healing without leaving scars behind.
6. *Cure warts:* Application of frankincense to warts twice a day for couple of weeks can show gradual cure.
7. *Insect bites:* A drop of frankincense oil has the ability to reduce the swelling caused due to insect bites. It also helps in quicker healing.

Hair Benefits of Frankincense

If you are unhappy with your hair, frankincense can be the answer to your prayers!

8. *Cures dandruff:* Almost all essential oils, including frankincense, can provide relief from dandruff if used regularly.
9. *Gives shiny hair:* You can use only frankincense oil or mix it with some myrrh to get hair that shines with health. You can use these two as a styling gel and get amazing results.
10. *Stops hair fall and gives healthy hair:* Frankincense oil is known to make the hair roots stronger, putting a stop to hair fall and giving way to healthier hair.

Health Benefits of Frankincense

Frankincense health benefits are innumerable so it is also known for its myriad of health benefits, some of which are:

11. *Relieves pain:* Joint pains and other pains caused due to inflammation can be relieved using frankincense oil.
12. *Stress relief:* Stress has a part and parcel of modern living. But you can use frankincense oil as perfume or apply it to the temple, whichever is convenient, to get relief from stress.
13. *Muscular pain:* Frankincense helps in circulating blood to the affected area and helps in relieving muscular pains. It is mainly helpful for people suffering from rheumatism.
14. *Relieves itching:* Direct application of frankincense on the affected area results in gradual relief from itching.
15. *Back pain relief:* Lifting heavy weights, pregnancy, bad posture—al these can cause severe back pain. If you are suffering from back pain, you can get relief with the application of frankincense oil on the affected area.
16. *Inflammation relief:* Application of frankincense directly or intake of it in the form of a capsule can help in providing relief from inflammation.
17. *Improves immunity:* A weak immune system equals falling sick frequently. Intake of frankincense capsules and application of frankincense oil at the bottom of the feet can strengthen one's immune system, enabling one to live a healthier life.

18. *Visual problems:* Though it makes the eyes to water, but the application of frankincense around the eyes, cheek bones and brow bones for couple of months can help in enhancing your vision. Rubbing the palms together with one drop of frankincense and by placing these palms over opened eyes for less than 5 min every day can provide relief from several visual problems.

19. *Improves concentration:* Regular application of 1 to 2 drops of frankincense oil on the temple and back of neck can improve one's concentration.

20. *Anti-carcinogenic:* With many documented cases, frankincense has proved itself as an anti-carcinogenic and can be used to fight cancer. This is considered to be one of the best frankincense benefits for health.

21. *Natural cure for rheumatoid arthritis:* The gum resin extract of this herb is rich in anti-inflammatory properties. Boswellic acid present in *Boswellia* prevents healthy tissues from breaking down. Thus, it harnesses the inflammation and pain experienced due to rheumatoid arthritis. Studies suggest that this is one of the most sought after rheumatoid arthritis drug, next to the NSAID – ketoprofen. This herb also strengthens the connective tissues, thereby improving the supply and flow of blood to the affected region. This, in turn, helps in easing down the inflammation and pain experienced at the site. You can either use this in the form of tablets or powder or just apply as a poultice on the affected region for the benefits.

22. *Treats osteoarthritis:* This herb is an effective cure for osteoarthritis. Various studies have been conducted on the efficiency of shallaki and Cox-2 inhibitors. And, as per the study, it was revealed that even though it required a longer duration for the herb to work effectively, the results lasted even after the herb was discontinued. The case of Cox-2 inhibitors is different. The results are visible faster, but it was noticed that the effect lasted only till the moment the drug was in use. Plus, there were no side effects found when shallaki was used while the latter gave rise to constipation, upset stomach, diarrhea, and even gastric bleeding.

23. *Treats chronic asthma:* Frankincense is known to offer relief to those who are victims of chronic asthma. Studies conducted on the effectiveness of this drug to cure asthma suggest that regular use is known to ease the symptoms of asthma and lower the rate of attacks. However, more studies are required to assess whether this drug can be used for a longer duration.

24. *Cures irritable bowel syndrome:* Research prove that Sallai Guggulu contain certain elements that possess the ability to obstruct the functioning of leukotrienes. Leukotrines are produced by the immune system of your body in events where the body comes under the provocation of a negative reaction within the body. These, in turn, cause irritable bowel syndrome and inflammation associated with it. Studies suggest that regular use of *Boswellia* can help in lowering such inflammations, offering relief from IBS. It is also known to have a positive impact on Crohn's disease as well as ulcerative colitis.

25. *Aids in shedding excess weight:* Shallaki is a rich source of gugglesterones. These elements are known to aid in weight loss. It stimulates the thyroid, normalizing its functioning. This, in turn, aids in losing weight. Studies conducted on mice under lab conditions suggest that regular ingestion of this herb aids in fat loss. However, more research needs to be conducted and that too on humans to ascertain its power. Nevertheless, it is quite a safe weight loss supplement when compared to the other over the counter weight loss drugs.

26. *Good for heart:* Frankinsense is known to lower the cholesterol level and triglyceride levels and keep them under control. This, in turn, safeguards the heart from various medical conditions inflicted by high cholesterol levels including atherosclerosis.

27. *Eases fever and headaches:* This herb is known to possess aspirin like properties. This, in turn, enables it to be used as an analgesic and antipyretic agent when you have high fever.

28. *Helps in curing bronchial conditions:* Various studies conducted on the benefits of frankincense suggest that the anti-inflammatory nature of this herb along with the antibacterial properties enable it to ease bronchial infections. It eases the contraction experienced by the blood vessels by lowering the inflammation. Thus, it improves the flow of blood to the bronchial region, offering immense relief from pain experienced due to the condition.

29. *Effective antidote for bad breath:* The antibacterial properties of Salai guggulu enable it to be used as a natural cure for bad breath triggered by gum diseases. Gum disorders cause inflammations, which in turn triggers bad breath. Once the inflammation is eased and the bacteria are eliminated, the bad breath automatically ceases. Add 2 to 3 drops of the oil of *Boswellia* to lukewarm water and gargle twice a day for faster relief.

30. *Works as a natural diuretic:* Certain studies point out that this herb has diuretic properties also. This, along with its anti-inflammatory and anti-bacterial nature, treats urinary tract infections.
31. *Natural tonic for the brain:* Studies suggest that this herb can be used to pep up the concentration and intelligence levels. Thus, it acts as a tonic for the brain.
32. *Helps in improving male fertility:* Shallaki is known to possess aphrodisiac properties. Ayurveda suggests that regular ingestion of this herb helps in improving the fertility levels in male by enhancing the quality and count of sperm. Not for nothing is frankincense oil known as the king of all essential oils! With such amazing benefits, frankincense truly deserves all the kudos it gets.

References

1. European Scientific Cooperative on Phytotherapy (2009). E/S/C/O/P Monographs: The Scientific Foundation for Herbal Medicinal Products. Second Edition, Supplement 2009. European Scientific Cooperative on Phytotherapy. p. 184. ISBN 9781901964080.
2. "USDA GRIN Taxonomy". Retrieved 15 October 2014.
3. "Joint Relief". www.herbcompanion.com. Retrieved 2009-01-12.
4. Cameron, M; Chrubasik, S (May 22, 2014). "Oral Herbal Therapies for Treating Osteoarthritis". Cochrane Summaries. Retrieved June 6, 2014.
5. Ammon HP."Modulation of the Immune System by *Boswellia serrata* Extracts and Boswellic Acids. [Review]" Phytomedicine. 17(11):862-7, 2010 Sep.
6. Open, Randomized, Controlled Clinical Trial of *Boswellia serrata* Extract as Compared to Valdecoxib in Osteoarthritis of Knee. Indian Journal of Pharmacology. 2007; 39(1) 27-29
7. Efficacy and Tolerability of *Boswellia serrata* Extract in Treatment of Osteoarthritis of Knee—A Randomized Double Blind Placebo Controlled Trial. Phytomedicine. 2003 Jan;10(1):3-7.
8. Pharmacokinetic Study of 11-Keto beta-Boswellic acid. Phytomedicine. 2004 Feb;11(2-3):255-60.
9. Abdel-Tawab M, Werz O, Schubert-Zsilavecz M., "*Boswellia serrata*: an Overall Assessment of in vitro, Preclinical, Pharmacokinetic and Clinical Data." Clin Pharmacokinet. 2011 Jun 1;50(6):349-69
10. Wrinkle Breakthrough Claim from L'Oreal
11. L'Oreal Slammed Over Cream Claims
12. Sharma ML, Khajuria A, 1. Kaul A, *et al*. Effects of Salai Guggal ex-*Boswellia serrata* on Cellular and Humoral Immune Responses and Leukocyte Migration. Agents Actions 1988; 24:161-164.
13. Sharma ML, Bani S, Singh GB. Anti-arthriticactivity of Boswellic Acids in Bovine Serum Albumin (BSA)-induced Arthritis. Int J Immunopharmacol 1989;11:647-652.
14. (Planta Med. 1971 Apr; 19(4): 333-41 for Analgesic and Psychopharma-Cological Effects of Gum Resin of Boswalia Serrata by Memon MK)
15. Abdel-Tawab M, Werz O, Schubert-Zsilavecz M. "*Boswellia serrata*: An Overall Assessment of in vitro, Preclinical, Pharmacokinetic and Clinical Data." Clin Pharmacokinet. 2011 Jun 1;50(6):349-69

Index

A

A. tschirch, 18
AIDS, 54, 138
AKBA, 174, 175, 176
ALT, 158
Antiglycation and antioxidant activity and HPTLC analysis of *Boswellia sacra* oleogum resin, 128-136
    anti-glycation assay, 130-131
    chemicals, 128-129
    discussion, 135-136
    DPPH free radical scavenging assay, 131
    extraction and isolation, 129
    HPTLC analysis, 129-130
    plant materials, 129
    results, 132
        anti-glycation activity, 133-134
        DPPH free radical scavenging activity, 134
        HPTLC fingerprinting profile, 132-133
        superoxide anion scavenging activity, 134
    statistical analysis, 131-132
    superoxide anion scavenging assay, 131
Anti-inflammatory and analgesic activity of different fractions of boswellia serrata, 114-119
    plant material, 114
        analgesic activity, 115
            acetic acid induced writhing response, 115
            formalin induced pain in rats, 115
            hot plate method, 116
            statistical analysis, 116
            tail flick method, 116
        animals, 114
        anti-inflammatory activity, 115
        extraction and isolation of gum essential oil and resin, 114
        materials, 114
        preparation of suspension of different fractions, 115
    results, 116
        analgesic activity, 117
        anti-inflammatory acidity, 116-117
        discussion, 118-119
        formalin induced pain, 117
        hot plate method, 118
        tail flick method, 117-118
Anti-microbial activity of silver nanoparticles, 120-127
Anti-microbial activity of silver nanoparticles, 121
    antibacterial activity, 122
    antifungal activity, 122
    microorganisms, 121
    plant material and synthesis of silver nanoparticles, 121
    results and discussion, 122-127
APT, 109
Aspergillus, 126
AST, 158

B

B. ameero, 5
Bacillus, 126
Benefits of frankincense for skin, hair and health, 290-294

298 Salai Gum

benefits of frankincense oil, 290
hair benefits of frankincense, 291
health benefits of frankincense, 291-294
skin benefits of frankincense, 290-291
BHA, 257
BHT, 257
Boswellia, 1, 2, 3, 5-17, 137
  boswellic acids, 5-10
Boswellia carterii, 16, 100-113, 148-159
Boswellia oil, 189-234
  brief description of figures, 193-194
  description, 194-202
  examples, 220-231
  for enhancing brain function, 189-234
  process for obtaining non-acidic boswellia oil (BOIL) fraction, 202
  processes for obtaining boswellia low polar gum resin extract (BLPRE) fraction, 203-208
  processes for obtaining boswellia volatile oil (BVOIL) fraction, 203
  result (Spatial learning), 231-234
  summary of the disclosure, 191-193
  synergistic compositions comprising boswellia extracts, 208-215
Boswellia papyrifera, 16
Boswellia sacra oleogum resin, 128-136
Boswellia serrata, 16, 52-87, 88-99, 114-119, 183-188
  extract, 160-182
Burseracea family, 1

C

Chemical history of olibanum, 18-21
Chiococca alba, 239
CMC, 49, 169
Commiphora mukul, 268
COSY, 109
CPPD, 284
Curcuma albiflora, 219
Curcuma angustifolia, 219
Curcuma aromatic, 219

D

DEPT, 109
DMSO, 113
DNA, 113

E

E. coli, 126
Effect of oleo-gum-resin of *Boswellia serrata* on renal functions, 48-51
  results, 50-51
  discussion, 51
Essential oil of olibanum, 22-37
  identification of m-camphorene (4), 28-32
  identification of p-camphorene (5), 33-37
  isolation and identification of 5,5-dimethyl-1-vinylbicyclo-[2,1.1] hexane (3), 25-27
  isolation of m-Camphorene (4) and p-camphorene (5), 27-28

F

FCA, 169
FCS, 112
Formulation of zidovudine loaded olibanum resin microcapsules, 137-147
  estimation of zidovudine, 139
  preparation of microcapsules, 139
  production yield and microencapsulation efficiency, 139
  results and discussion, 141
    differential scanning calorimetry, 144
    FT-IR studies, 143-144
    in vitro drug release behavior, 145-146
    preparation of microcapsules, production yield (%), estimation of drug content and microencapsulation efficiency (%), 141-142
    release kinetics, 146-147
    SEM and micromeritic studies, 142-143
    x-ray diffraction analysis, 145
  theoretical drug content, 139
    characterization of AZT microcapsules, 140

determination fo particle size distribution by sieve analysis, 140
differential scanning calorimetry, 140
in-vitro drug release studies, 140-141
kinetic models and the analysis of the release profiles, 141
micromeritic properties, 139
surface scanning electrol microscopy, 140
x-ray diffraction analysis, 140

G
Gymnema sylvestre, 258

H
Habbe Suzak, 48
HDL, 266
Herbal pain killer compositions, 235-257
cause of painful condition, 252
detailed description, 237-248
figures, 237
post surgical, 252-257
results, 251-252
study population, 250-251
tendonitis, 252
HMBC, 177
HMQC, 109
HPTLC, 128

I
Immunomodulatory triterpenoids from the oleogum resin of boswellia carterii, 100-113
assessment of the immunomodulatory activity: lymphocyte blast transformation assay, 112
compound 1: hexadecanoic acid; palmitic acid, 110
compounds, 110-112
extraction, 109
general instrumentation, 109
isolation and identification, 109-110
lymphocyte transformation assay, 112-113
materials for chromatographic study, 107
plant material, 109
reagents for lymphocyte transformation assay, 107-108
results and discussion, 100-107
separation of peripheral blood lymphocytes, 112
Indian olibanum, 137
Introduction, 1-4
Isolation of compounds from boswellia, 5-17
boswellic acids, 5-10
lupeolic acids, 10-11
neutral terpenic compounds, 13-17
roburic acids, 12-13
tirucallic acids, 11-12

K
Kundur, 51, 88

L
LDL, 266

M
Madhya Pradesh, 137
Maharashtra, 88
Majoon Kundur, 48
Majoon Murawwah-ul-Arwah, 48
Mimosa pudica, 239

N
NAFDAC, 148
National Meteorological Agency, 40
Natural composition for treating bone or joint inflammation, 272-283
description, 272-277
examples, 277-283
NMR, 7, 91
NSAID, 235, 285

O
OECD, 70
Olibanum resin microcapsules, 137-147

P
Parkinsons disease (PD), 190
PDA detector, 173

Phytochemical and pharmacological studies of B. serrata, 88-99
action (Afal), 89-90
analgesic and psychopharmacological effects, 92
anti-artherosclerotic agent, 92-93
anti-complementary activity of boswellic acids (BA), 92
antifungal activity of B. serrata, 92
anti-hyperlipidmic activity, 92
anti-inflammatory and anti-arthritic activities, 93-94
anti-microbial and anti-oxidant effect, 94
anti-tumor and anti-carcinogenic activities, 94
effect of boswellia serrata
in hepatitis C-virus (HCV), 97
on gonads of male dysedercus of boswellia serrata oil, 97
on liver and cardiac function, 97
effects of boswellia serrata gum resin in
bronchial asthma, 95
ulcerative colitis, 96
effects of boswellia serrata in
chronic colitis, 95
polyarthritis, 96-97
effects of boswellic acids extracted on autoimmune encephalomyelitis, 96
immunomodulatory effect of boswellia serrata, 97-98
inhibition of 5-LO by boswellic acids, 98-99
inhibitory activity of human leukemia HL-60 cells in culture, 98
istemal (therapeutic uses), 90
juvenomimetic activity of boswellia serrata, 99
mizaj (temperament), 89
oleo-gum-resin, 88-89
pharmacological studies, 92
phytochemical studies, 90
gum, 91

oil, 90
terpenoids, 90-91
Phytochemical investigation and biological activity of leaves extract of plant boswellia serrata, 52-87
acute (oral) toxicity studies, 70
animals, 65-66
anthelmintic activity, 70
antiulcer activity by pylorus ligation method, 70-71
chemicals, 65
collection of plant material, 65
determination of free acidity and total acidity, 71-72
dose response relationship, 64
extraction of plant material, 66
helminth, 65
herbal medicine drug-interactions, 60
herbal side effects, 60
histopathological evaluation, 72
how plant substances can harm, 64-65
medicinal and aromatic plants, 57-59
need and scope of herbal therapy, 59-60
Phytochemical investigation and biological activity of leaves extract of plant boswellia serrata, 65
popularity of herbal medicine, 59
preliminary phytochemical screening, 66
results and discussion, 72
acute toxicity (LD50) studies, 77
anthelmintic activity, 74-75
antiulcer activity, 77-78
aqueous extract, 73-74
effect of B. seratta on
free acidity following pyloric ligation in rats, 79
pH in pyloric ligation in rats, 80
total acidity following pyloric ligation in rats, 79
ulcer index pylorus ligation induced ulcer in rats, 81

Index   301

volume of gastric juice following pyloric ligation in rats, 78
histopathological studies in pylorus ligation induced ulcer in rat, 81-86
isolation and characterization of bioactive constituent, 75
statistical analysis, 72
tests for
  alkaloids, 67
  carbohydrates, 66
  cardiac glycosides, 68-69
  flavonoids, 68
  glycosides, 68
  proteins, 67
  saponins, 69
  steroids, 67
  tannins and phenolic compounds, 68
understanding drug-herb interactions, 60-63
what is a poison, 63-64
what is an herbal medicine, 59
what is toxicology, 63
why herbal remedies, 59
Preparation for weight loss management details, 269-270
Preparation for weight loss management, 258-271
  brief description of the accompanying drawings and tables related to result, 271
  description, 258-265
    of invention, 268-269
  objects of the invention, 268
  polyherbal preparation for the prevention of atherosclerosis and hyperlipidemia, 266
  prior art, 266-268
Pseudomonas, 48, 121

R

RAM, 231
Renal functions, 49-50

Resin secretory structures of boswellia, 38-47
  data analysis, 41-42
  discussion, 44
    implications for tapping, 46-47
    resin secretory structures of B. papyrifera, 44-46
  mateirlas and methods: bark and resin secretory structures, 40-41
  results, 42-43
    distribution, density and size of axial resin canals in the inner bark, 44
    resin secretory structures of B. papyrifera, 43-44
  study site, 40
  study species, 39-40
  study trees, sampling and sample preparation, 40

S

Shankha Bhasma, 268
SNPs, 120
SPSS, 156
Strychnos nux vomica, 268
Synergistic anti-inflammatory compositions comprising *Boswellia serrata* extract, 160-182
  calculation, 179-182
  description, 162-179
  figures, 161-162
  procedure, 179
  sample preparation, 179
  standard preparation, 179

T

Terminalia arjuna, 268
Tiya Shigo, 148
TLC, 75
Topical formulations for the symptomatic treatment of musculoskeletal disorders, 284-289
  description of the invention, 285-288
  examples, 288-289
  prior art, 284-285

Toxicological assessments of the aqueous extract of boswellia daizielli, 148-159
   determination of serum
      creatinine method, 155-156
      urea method of natelson, 155
   discussion, 156-159
   extraction of the aqueous extract of the plant, 149
   phytochemical screnning, 150
   plant, 149
   results, 156
   statistical anlaysis, 156
   test for
      alkaloids, 150
      balsam, 151, 153
      cardiac glycoside, 151, 153
      flavonoids, 150
      phenols, 151, 153
      resins, 151-152, 153-155
      saponins, 150, 153
      tannins, 150, 152
      terpenes and steroids, 151, 153

W

Water soluble bioactive fraction isolated from gum resin exudates of *Boswellia serrata*, 183-188

WHO, 53, 54, 148

Y

Yerba Mate, 239

Z

Zidovudine, 137-147